AN INTRODUCTION TO POLICING AND POLICE POWERS

Second Edition

This book is supported by a Companion Website, created to keep *An Introduction to Policing and Police Powers* up to date and to provide enhanced resources for both students and lecturers.

Key features include:

◆ termly updates
◆ links to useful websites
◆ 'ask the author' – your questions answered

www.cavendishpublishing.com/policing

AN INTRODUCTION TO POLICING AND POLICE POWERS

Second Edition

Leonard Jason-Lloyd
Visiting Lecturer in Criminal Justice,
Department of Criminology,
University of Leicester

Cavendish
Publishing
Limited

London • Sydney • Portland, Oregon

Second edition first published in Great Britain 2005 by
Cavendish Publishing Limited, The Glass House,
Wharton Street, London WC1X 9PX, UK.
Telephone: +44 (0)20 278 8000   Facsimile: +44 (0)20 278 8080
Email: info@cavendishpublishing.com
Website: www.cavendishpublishing.com

Published in the United States by Cavendish Publishing
c/o International Specialized Book Services,
5824 NE Hassalo Street, Portland,
Oregon 97213–3644, USA

Published in Australia by Cavendish Publishing (Australia) Pty Ltd
45 Beach Street, Coogee, NSW 2034, Australia
Telephone: +61 (2)9664 0909   Facsimile: +61 (2)9664 5420

© Jason-Lloyd, L	2005
First edition	2000
Second edition	2005

British Library Cataloguing in Publication Data
Jason-Lloyd, Leonard, 1945–
Introduction to policing and police powers – 2nd ed
1 Police – Great Britain 2 Police power – Great Britain
I Title
345.4'1'052

ISBN 1-85941-705-1
ISBN 978-1-859-41705-8

Printed and bound in Great Britain

PREFACE

In recent years, general interest in the study of policing and the application of police powers has increased substantially. As far as academic activity is concerned, the study of police powers and certain aspects of the nature of policing have formed part of constitutional law courses for many years and, more latterly, as a major component in the study of civil liberties. The most recent development has been their inclusion within criminal justice studies.

This book has been written with the newcomer in mind, including those with little or no legal knowledge who need to understand policing and police powers as part of wider study. It is not intended to provide an exhaustive treatise on this subject since this service is provided for in other works which are cited in the appropriate footnotes and constitute recommended further reading on particular topics. This publication is therefore focused on the key issues affecting the exercise of police powers which are most likely to be of interest to students as well as practitioners.

This publication is therefore designed for complete beginners as well as those with some knowledge of policing and police powers in an endeavour to help bring them as close to degree level on the subject as they are able to reach. It is also intended that this book will be of use to practitioners, whether in the legal profession or otherwise, who need a quick but comprehensive grasp of some of the most important aspects of this subject. The principal aim of this work is to make this study as accessible as possible to a wide range of students and practitioners, and to act as a stepping-stone to further in-depth study, particularly to higher degree level. A further aim is to provide an updated textbook on the most widely used police powers which has become necessary in view of extensive changes in the law since the mid-1990s, as well as those that occurred in this early part of the 21st century.

In order to facilitate a better understanding of the subject and the way that it has evolved, the relevant statutory and other provisions have been reproduced at the appropriate stages where their wording is self-explanatory, as well as case law applicable to the points in question. However, it is not intended to submerge the reader in too many cases, rather than cite the most important and relevant case law applicable to the key areas of the subject. Charts and diagrams have also been included in order to facilitate better understanding of the more complex issues arising from the subject.

My thanks go to Jon Lloyd, Managing Editor at Cavendish Publishing for his help and encouragement. Special thanks are extended to my wife, Usha, for her unfailing patience and support which is always most prominently displayed whenever I embark upon any major project. I have endeavoured to state the law as at 1 February 2005.

Crown copyright is reproduced with the permission of the Controller of Her Majesty's Stationery Office.

Leonard Jason-Lloyd
April 2005

CONTENTS

TABLE OF CASES

TABLE OF LEGISLATION

STATUTES

STATUTORY INSTRUMENTS

EUROPEAN LEGISLATION

INTRODUCTION

One of the main reasons why so much interest has been generated in the study of police powers in modern times is that increasing numbers of the wider populace are beginning to question the exercise of such authority. Indeed, some go further and actually challenge the legitimacy of such powers and the way they are exercised. This was done in a particularly violent manner during the 1980s when it became evident through a spate of serious disorder in this country that certain sections of the public were seriously questioning the manner and form in which some police powers were being employed. But concerns regarding policing in general have not, by any means, been confined to public protest alone. For instance, in 1978, the Royal Commission on Criminal Procedure[1] was convened to examine the exercise of police powers with particular reference to the investigation of crime and the rights of suspects. This body consisted of 15 members, who included its chairman Sir Cyril Philips and also a judge, two police officers, a Queen's Counsel, a stipendiary magistrate, a defence lawyer, several lay magistrates as well as other lay persons.[2] Three years later, the Commission published its findings which not only concerned the subject of police powers but also addressed the issue of an independent system for conducting criminal prosecutions. In short, the former resulted in the passing of the Police and Criminal Evidence Act 1984 and the latter resulted in the Prosecution of Offences Act 1985 being enacted which, *inter alia*, led to the institution of the Crown Prosecution Service.

In response largely to concerns regarding a spate of miscarriage of justice cases in previous years, another Royal Commission was instituted. In 1991, under the leadership of Lord Runciman, the Royal Commission on Criminal Justice[3] began to examine this issue as well as address wider concerns regarding the effectiveness of the criminal justice system in convicting the guilty and acquitting the innocent. Its findings were reported two years later and a number of the Commission's recommendations were later enacted in the Criminal Justice and Public Order Act 1994 and the Criminal Procedure and Investigations Act 1996. However, these are certainly not the only statutes which have affected police powers since then. For example, in 1996, two further Acts were passed which significantly affected the police service. The first was the Prevention of Terrorism (Additional Powers) Act 1996 (see Chapters 2 and 4) and the second was the Offensive Weapons Act 1996 (see Chapter 4). In 1997, the Knives Act was passed, and this was followed later in the same year by the passing of the Confiscation of Alcohol (Young Persons) Act 1997 (see Chapter 4). The powers available to the police have been further augmented by a number of provisions under the Crime and Disorder Act 1998 (see Chapter 3), as well as six statutes passed since the year 2000, namely: the Terrorism Act 2000, the Criminal Justice and Police Act 2001, the Anti-terrorism, Crime and Security Act 2001, the Police Reform Act 2002, certain parts of the Anti-social Behaviour Act 2003 and the Criminal Justice Act 2003. All this is indicative of the rate at which police powers have been amended and increased in recent years. It is partly because of this flood of enactments, together with a build-up of relevant case-law, that the publication of this book has been necessitated. Concurrent with all these legislative changes, the Codes of Practice that accompany the

---

1   Otherwise known as the Philips Royal Commission.
2   Zander, M, *The Police and Criminal Evidence Act 1984* (4th edn, London: Sweet and Maxwell, 2003).
3   Cm 2263 (London: HMSO, 1993).

Police and Criminal Evidence Act 1984 have been revised many times and this trend will undoubtedly continue. However, the effects of the Human Rights Act 1998 on police powers have been very significant. This is likely to continue as the exercise of virtually all police powers may fall potentially within the mechanisms of this statute.

It should be mentioned that whilst the relevant Royal Commissions have endeavoured to address wider and longer-term concerns regarding policing in this country, specific incidents have also been the subject of judicial inquiries into the police such as that conducted by Lord Scarman in the early 1980s in respect of the Brixton disorders. In addition, other enquiries and investigations have been commissioned arising from concerns stemming from a number of other issues, for example, an investigation by the Avon and Somerset Police during the mid-1980s into the conduct of the Greater Manchester Police during a demonstration outside the Manchester University Students Union. Also, in 1979, Sir David McNee, who was then Commissioner of the Metropolitan Police, commissioned a study of his force by the Policy Studies Institute with particular reference to community relations.[4] Whilst many of these inquiries and investigations have impacted mainly on internal rules governing police conduct, some have motivated law reform to a certain extent. A fairly recent example is the Macpherson Report published in 1999 regarding the murder of Stephen Lawrence which, *inter alia*, led to the Law Commission proposing reform of the double jeopardy rule which, under the Criminal Justice Act 2003, enables certain criminal cases to be retried as a result of significant new evidence becoming available.

The most significant law reform as far as substantive police powers are concerned was the Police and Criminal Evidence Act 1984, which accounts for the bulk of this book. As mentioned above, this was primarily the result of recommendations made by the Royal Commission on Criminal Procedure, necessitated by on going concerns regarding certain police powers and the way they were exercised. Much of this criticism ultimately stemmed from the lack of codification of such powers and the generally outdated mode in which they existed:

> Before 1 January 1986, when the Police and Criminal Evidence Act 1984 came into effect, the law governing police powers for the investigation of crime was unclear and antiquated. It had developed piecemeal since the establishment of professional police forces in the 19th century. Parliament had added fitfully to the few common law principles but there was no clear statement of police powers. This varied and scant law was supplemented by:
>
> (a) rules of guidance as to the admissibility of confessions provided by the Lord Chief Justice (the Judges' Rules);
>
> (b) national administrative guidance in the form of Home Office Circulars (notably that attached to the Judges' Rules); and
>
> (c) local administrative guidance in the shape of standing orders issued within each police force.
>
> The result was patchy legal obligations and powers for the police and local variations in powers (eg some police forces had wide stop and search powers whereas others were tied to a few narrow national powers). New and heavier pressures on the police and

---

4   Emsley, C, *The English Police: A Political and Social History* (2nd edn, London: Longman, 1996).

more critical public opinion demanded that the powers of the police be placed on a modern statutory footing.[5]

On analysis perhaps a fundamental cause of this state of affairs was that the modern police service at that time was, to a significant extent, based on certain laws, practices and procedures that were often rooted in the largely Victorian origins of this law enforcement body. During a debate on this issue during the 1980s, one media commentator referred to the police service as 'The Bow Street Runners with cars and radios', which possibly encapsulates this argument in those few words.

How did the modern police service develop? What is the current structure of the police service in modern times? What is the general legal and constitutional status of a police officer? These questions will be addressed in the following chapter.

---

5   Lidstone, K and Palmer, C, *Bevan and Lidstone's The Investigation of Crime: A Guide to Police Powers* (2nd edn, London: Butterworths, 1996).

CHAPTER 1

THE DEVELOPMENT AND FOUNDATIONS OF MODERN POLICING

INTRODUCTION

> I *(name)* ... of *(place)* ... do solemnly and sincerely declare and affirm that I will well and truly serve the Queen in the office of constable, with fairness, integrity, diligence and impartiality, upholding fundamental human rights and according equal respect to all people; and that I will, to the best of my power, cause the peace to be kept and preserved and prevent all offences against people and property; and that while I continue to hold the said office I will, to the best of my skill and knowledge, discharge all the duties thereof faithfully according to law.

The above constitutes the solemn declaration or oath taken by all those newly appointed to the office of constable within England and Wales, in accordance with the wording under Sched 4 to the Police Act 1996.[1] This is declared during a ceremony known as the 'attestation', which takes place before a justice of the peace.[2] On analysis, this oath provides an interesting indication as to the constitutional status of a police officer in modern times and, in essence, describes the manner in which police powers should be exercised.

Compared with many policing systems abroad, the system in England and Wales has a number of similarities and distinctions. Perhaps two of the greatest distinctions are based upon the main principle of policing in this country and the basic structure of our police service. With regard to the former, policing in this country is still fundamentally based upon the principle or concept of 'policing by consent'. This means that the police service functions in society with the consent of the majority. This has great advantages compared with many foreign policing systems, which do not enjoy this concept to the extent that it is still evident here. Among other things, this ensures a greater level of public co-operation with the police and has also enabled our police to avoid being fully and permanently equipped with firearms throughout the 20th century and, so far, into the present millennium. Although in recent years they have been equipped with a greater range of protective weaponry, such as extendable batons and CS gas spray, these are not intended to be lethal in their effects if used correctly and, so far, we have avoided a permanent para-military police force in this country.

---

1   The wording of the original Sched 4 to the Police Act 1996 has been amended by s 83 of the Police Reform Act 2002 in order to make it more compatible with the Human Rights Act 1998.

2   Newly appointed constables in the Metropolitan Police previously took the attestation before either the Commissioner or an Assistant Commissioner who, technically at least, are also justices of the peace. This practice discontinued as a result of Sched 27, para 83 of the Greater London Authority Act 1999, which provides that all constables in England and Wales will be attested before magistrates. It is this statute which contains the measures under which the relatively new Metropolitan Police Authority has been instituted.

A further distinction between foreign policing and our own domestic system is that this function in England and Wales is currently divided between 43 individual police forces, whereas policing abroad, including Europe, is often under more centralised control. In other words, we do not have a national police service, but a network of individual police forces, responsible for policing specified counties, areas or cities. During times of emergency, these forces may be co-ordinated through a centralised mutual aid procedure, but such occasions are infrequent, one of the most well known in recent times being the miners' dispute during the winter of 1984–85, where police officers from many parts of the country were sent to key mining areas to reinforce the local police presence there.

A BRIEF HISTORICAL OVERVIEW

The general concept of policing in this country is certainly not new; in fact, various forms of law enforcement which were in the nature of policing existed since early Saxon times. Even the term 'constable' originated as far back as the Norman era.

Constables were also evident during the reign of the Tudors and Stuarts but, following a period of apparent decline in the role of such constables, growing concerns during the Georgian period regarding increasing crime and disorder led, ultimately, to the formation of the famous Bow Street Runners. A fragmented system of policing gradually evolved in other parts of London but, in 1785, the London and Westminster Police Bill was introduced, designed to form a co-ordinated policing system for the capital. This was defeated due to fierce opposition and poor management of the Bill in its passage through Parliament, although a more limited version was successfully passed seven years later.[3] However, crime and fears of public disorder continued to rise and, eventually, Sir Robert Peel introduced his famous Bill, which was enacted on 19 June 1829 as the Metropolitan Police Act and, subsequently, the Metropolitan Police was born. The preamble to this landmark statute reads as follows:

> Whereas offences against property have, of late, increased in and near the Metropolis, and the local establishments of nightly police have been found inadequate to the prevention and detection of crime, by reason of the frequent unfitness of the individuals employed, the insufficiency of their number, the limited sphere of their authority and their want of connection and co-operation with each other. And, whereas it is expedient to substitute a new and more efficient system of police in lieu of such establishments of nightly watch and nightly police, within the limits hereinafter mentioned, and to constitute an office of police which, acting under the immediate authority of one of His Majesty's Principal Secretaries of State, shall direct and control the whole of such new system of police within those limits. Be it therefore enacted, etc ...

This signalled the formation of the first modern-style professional policing system in this country and, by 1856, all of England and Wales was covered by a network of police forces. It remains a popular belief that the main driving force behind the 1829 Act was the appalling crime rate, particularly in London. Although this was undoubtedly a major factor, there was also another issue which was equal in

---

3   Emsley, C, *The English Police: A Political and Social History* (2nd edn, London: Longman, 1996).

importance, namely the increase in the level of public disorder that had escalated in the 18th and early 19th centuries:

> The prevention of crime was stressed as the first duty of the new Metropolitan Police constables and the whole system of beat patrols … was ostensibly designed with this in mind. But the uniform, the discipline and the organisation of the new force suggest that Peel had imported into London many of the policing practices developed in Ireland to deal with civil disorder.[4]

Whilst the military were used to quell rioting in London and other big cities, there were serious tactical and political disadvantages in using armed troops for this purpose. First, long delays were often experienced in transporting troops from their barracks to the scene of public disorder; subsequently, the situation was well out of hand by the time they arrived. Secondly, the only forms of weaponry available to them were potentially lethal, namely bullets or bayonets, the use of which often had drastic consequences in terms of fatal or serious injuries. In contrast, the new police were frequently able to resolve both problems by mainly using wooden truncheons to control riots and, by being deployed throughout London on regular 24 hour patrols, were able to disperse many unruly gatherings before they escalated into full scale disorder.

Although in their early days the new police were often regarded with disdain and suspicion by both general populace and even some in authority, they quickly gained the respect still found amongst the majority of the public today. Although some assert that this effect is waning, the policing system in this country is still characterised by the concept of policing by consent, which to a certain extent remains the envy of policing systems in many other parts of the world.

THE STRUCTURE OF POLICING IN ENGLAND AND WALES

As mentioned above, there are currently 43 police forces in England and Wales. This excludes those with special jurisdiction, such as the British Transport Police and the Ministry of Defence Police, who operate in various parts of the country. The 43 police areas include the two forces in London, namely the Metropolitan Police and the City of London Police. These two London forces warrant separate coverage as distinct from those outside the capital, and these will be discussed below. At this stage, it should be noted that the chief officers of police for both the London forces are commissioners rather than chief constables; it is the latter who head police forces outside the capital.

Since 1964, the Home Secretary has had the power to amalgamate police forces and this power now exists under s 32 of the Police Act 1996, where such a move can be made on grounds of efficiency and effectiveness. Prior to enacting the 1996 Act, the Conservative Government announced plans to implement such action, although, to date, this has not occurred. Although the fragmentation of police forces throughout this country lends itself to the notion that policing in England and Wales is not under centralised control, recent developments in the structure of our police service indicates an increasing movement towards this end, which will now be discussed.

---

4   *Ibid.*

In 1962, the Report of the Royal Commission on the Police[5] rejected the concept of a national police force under direct central government control and, in response to its report, the Police Act 1964 was passed, which enshrined the principle legal rules governing the organisation of the police service up until the mid-1990s. An important consequence of this legislation is that policing in this country is governed by three points of power, namely: the Home Secretary, who represents central government and is responsible for the overall supervision of the police service, as well as being answerable to Parliament regarding the service's function; local police authorities, responsible for the overall maintenance of police forces within their jurisdiction and ensuring local accountability; and chief officers of police, responsible primarily for making operational decisions, as well as the routine management of their forces. However, it is the subject of debate as to whether there is now an equal balance of power within this tripartite structure.

The police authorities

The balance of power regarding policing in England and Wales was changed controversially through Pt I of the Police and Magistrates' Courts Act 1994, which was later consolidated into the Police Act 1996, and these provisions, among other things, generally endeavour to make the police service function under a more 'business management' regime.[6] They have also created new style police authorities, in contrast to those which existed earlier. Previously, police authorities outside London consisted of two-thirds local councillors and one-third local magistrates. These bodies varied considerably in size – at the extreme ends, from between six to over 40 members in total, although the proportion of magistrates and councillors was always the same. The Government White Paper, entitled *Police Reform – A Police Service for the 21st Century*, contained, *inter alia*, proposals that police authorities should be set to a prescribed number of 16 members. This was not itself a controversial measure, since some authorities were regarded as too small, whereas, in contrast, others had become too large and unwieldy. The main controversy was that these bodies should consist of eight local councillors, three magistrates and five persons appointed by the Home Secretary, who would also appoint the chairperson, who, in turn, would have the casting vote where necessary. These proposals were severely criticised, both within and outside Parliament, on the grounds that this would have given central government a significant increase in power over local police forces.[7] In the end, the Government modified its original proposals, which included allowing each police authority to elect its own chairperson and increasing the size of each authority to 17 members, of which nine are local councillors, three are local magistrates and five are independent members appointed from a shortlist compiled by the Home Secretary.

There is provision under the Police Act 1996 for the Home Secretary to increase the size of police authorities where appropriate, but the outcome must result in such bodies reaching odd numbers and the proportion of councillors, magistrates and

5   Cmnd 1728 (London: HMSO, 1962).
6   Molan, M, *Constitutional Law: The Machinery of Government* (London: Old Bailey, 1997).
7   See Jason-Lloyd, L, 'Who should have power to police the police?' (1993) *The Times*, 24 August; and also 'Changes in the police service' (1994) LXVII(2) Police Journal 105, April–June.

independent members approved by the Home Secretary remaining unchanged. Other aspects of these reforms included the transformation of police authorities into corporate bodies which, in turn, must have regard to any objectives determined by the Home Secretary, as well as to formulate annual local policing plans and comply with these accordingly in order to meet performance targets. Also, they must publish an annual report, which includes the extent to which the local policing plan has been complied with, as well as submit reports on relevant police matters to the Home Secretary as required by him.

Under s 40 of the Police Act 1996, the Home Secretary may direct any police authority to take remedial action if the inspectorate of constabulary report that its police force is not efficient or effective. Sections 4 and 5 of the Police Reform Act 2002 extend these provisions to include situations where the inspectorate of constabulary makes a routine or a special inspection and concludes that all or part of a police force is, or is likely to be, inefficient or ineffective. Remedial action may include the requirement to submit an action plan to the Home Secretary in conjunction with the relevant chief police officer.

Many functions of the police authorities remain as they did prior to the Police Act 1996, which include the overall duty to secure the maintenance of an effective and efficient police force by, among other things, acting as its paymaster in terms of local expenditure and controlling the police budget. Police authorities are also responsible for appointing chief constables, deputy chief constables and assistant chief constables (the latter two in consultation with the chief constable),[8] and may suspend or require any of them to resign or retire, although these decisions can be vetoed by the Home Secretary, who can also require a police authority to suspend, retire or require the resignation of a chief officer of police on his own initiative. The power of the Home Secretary's veto was last used in 1990 and resulted in a dispute with the Derbyshire Police Authority over the appointment of the then-chief constable for Derbyshire, which lasted for several months. However, in 2004, there was a dispute between the Home Secretary and the Humberside Police Authority regarding the Home Secretary's requirement for them to suspend the then-chief constable, which initially they refused to do.

Under the Police Reform Act 2002, police authorities of their own volition may suspend chief constables who are, or are likely to be called upon, to retire or resign on grounds of efficiency. The Home Secretary must approve this decision and may require a police authority to initiate such action. These suspension rules will also apply to the Commissioner and Deputy Commissioner of Police of the Metropolis. Similar provisions exist regarding the other Association of Chief Police Officers (ACPO) ranks, namely assistant commissioners, deputy assistant commissioners and commanders in London, and deputy chief constables and assistant chief constables outside the capital, the difference being that the Home Secretary does not have the power to require a police authority to exercise its power of suspension in such cases.

Police authorities may also employ civilian staff to assist the police force maintained by it and to enable the authority to discharge its functions, although such

---

8   Or the equivalent ranks in London.

employees are under the direction and control of the chief constable. It should be noted that under the new police complaints system, civilian employees within the police service fall within the jurisdiction of the Independent Police Complaints Commission. This will include designated civilians who have been given certain police powers under the concept of the 'extended police family' (see Chapter 7). Section 51 of the Police Reform Act 2002 places a duty on police authorities to make arrangements for the independent inspection of custody suites at police stations as well as reporting on the way that detainees are dealt with. Finally, s 92 of the Police Reform Act 2002 places a duty on police authorities to produce three-year strategy plans in addition to their existing annual plans, in order to formulate medium and long-term strategies.

Other moves towards centralised control

The Police Act 1997 (not to be confused with the Police Act 1996) contains a number of provisions which have implications for the police service as well as the exercise of certain powers regarding surveillance. As far as the structure of the police service is concerned, Pt I of the 1997 Act has placed the National Criminal Intelligence Service (NCIS) on a statutory footing. This organisation is staffed by police and HM Customs and Excise officers, as well as persons from the security services and has, since 1992, been involved with collating and analysing information and other intelligence in respect of matters such as international drug trafficking and money laundering, as well as other specialist crimes, including kidnap, extortion and counterfeit currency. Part II of the Act makes provision for the formation of a National Crime Squad (NCS), designed to deal with serious crime. Both these bodies, under the 1997 Act, will have implications in more than one police area. Sections 88 and 89 of the Police Reform Act 2002 inserted new ss 34A and 79A into the Police Act 1997, regarding the regulation of the NCIS and NCS within the context of their governance and administration as well as conditions of service within these bodies. The Serious Organised Crime and Police Bill 2004 proposes to replace these two bodies with a Serious Organised Crime Agency that many describe as this country's version of the FBI.

Under ss 23 and 24 of the Police Act 1996, chief constables have the power to collaborate with other police forces or provide mutual aid where additional officers or other assistance may be provided. The collaboration under s 23 includes sharing resources such as premises, training facilities, technical support and specialised services. An example of the latter includes the use of police helicopters. With regard to s 24, as mentioned above in the introduction to this chapter, the last time mutual aid was used on any mass scale was during the winter of 1984–85, during the series of strikes by the coal mining industry. As a consequence, police officers from many parts of England and Wales were sent to areas where large scale picketing was taking place. Some observers reported that seeing so many different police forces represented in one place gave the impression of a national police force, although this venture only lasted for the duration of one winter. Parallel provisions also exist under s 98 of the Police Act 1996 (previously enacted under s 141 of the Criminal Justice and Public Order Act 1994), whereby chief officers of police may request assistance from any UK police force, which includes providing additional constables. There is also provision for the Home Secretary to act on his own volition, presumably in times of emergency, where he may direct a police force within another part of the UK to provide such assistance. In other words, police officers from Northern Ireland can be called upon to reinforce the police in any part of England, Wales or Scotland, or police in Scotland can be asked to provide mutual aid to any police force in England and Wales or to Northern Ireland, and the police in England and Wales can be called upon to provide assistance to the police in Northern Ireland or to any force in Scotland. One hopes that such an interchange may never be necessary, in view of the prospective turmoil that would necessitate such action.

Mention should also be made regarding the Association of Chief Police Officers (ACPO), which is the representative body of all police chiefs and has existed since 1948. This organisation constitutes a powerful pressure group, capable of influencing central government to a significant extent on a variety of matters affecting policing in this country. It is this body which, among other things, facilitates co-operation between police forces where necessary. Another organisation in relation to police chiefs is the Chief Police Officers' Staff Association.

Policing in London

It should be noted that the police authority in respect of the City of London Police is the Common Council of the City of London, although separate and quite unique arrangements once existed regarding the Metropolitan Police. In July 2000, the Metropolitan Police Authority was instituted and this was the first time that such an authority existed within the Metropolis of London. For many years, the issue of accountability of the Metropolitan Police had been severely criticised by a number of commentators. The Home Secretary had previously constituted the police authority for the Metropolis, which has the largest police force in the UK (approximately 35,000 police officers). Although there was provision originally under s 106 of the Police and Criminal Evidence Act 1984 and, more recently, under s 96 of the Police Act 1996 for consultations between the police and local consultative groups, there had never been an actual police authority for the Metropolis of London compared with those that exist in other parts of England and Wales. Therefore, under s 106 of the 1984 Act and then s 96 of the 1996 Act, special provision was made whereby the Home Secretary issued guidance to the Metropolitan Police Commissioner in respect of obtaining the views of the community on policing the capital.

Sections 310–325 of the Greater London Authority Act 1999 now institute a police authority for the Metropolis of London. However, in April 1995, a body was formed called the Metropolitan Police *Committee*. This originally consisted of 12 members appointed by the Home Secretary to advise and assist the Metropolitan Police Commissioner in maintaining an efficient and effective police service, and this body was used to prepare for the institution of the Metropolitan Police *Authority* in July 2000. The Committee compiled regular annual reports and was under the chairmanship of Sir John Quinton.

The institution of the Metropolitan Police Authority is inextricably linked with the Greater London Authority, since the relatively new police authority consists of 23 members, 12 of which are selected by the Mayor of London and are members of the Greater London Assembly, including the Deputy Mayor. The Metropolitan Police Authority may select its own chairperson from among its own members and this does not discount the Deputy Mayor of London. Other members of the new police authority include seven independent persons and four magistrates. The independent faction includes one person appointed directly by the Home Secretary and, up until recently, the four magistrates were appointed by the Greater London Magistrates' Courts Authority. This has been changed as a result of s 6 of the Courts Act 2003, which abolished magistrates' courts committees, including the Greater London Magistrates' Courts Authority. This change is due to the Lord Chancellor taking over responsibility for the magistrates' courts.

In effect, the powers and duties of this police authority are almost identical to those which function outside the Metropolitan Police area. These include publishing annual reports, consultations with local communities and setting objectives.

The introduction of the Metropolitan Police Authority has automatically resulted in abolishing the post of the Receiver, whose functions are now, to a large extent, performed by the new police authority, especially matters regarding finance, responsibility for which falls upon the Treasurer. The new body also plays a role in recommending to the Home Secretary the appointment of future commissioners, as well as their deputies, assistant commissioners, deputy assistant commissioners and commanders. However, whilst a similar selection procedure may be used to appoint the Commissioner, as in the police authorities outside London regarding their chief constables, this will be modified to take into account the need to protect the national interest and the international obligations of the Metropolitan Police Service, and not just its local remit. This is a particularly sensitive issue which has constituted one of the primary objections in the past to having a police authority for the Metropolis (see the coverage of the role of the Home Secretary below). The Metropolitan Police Authority is expected to account for its actions when summoned before the Greater London Assembly in much the same way as do representatives of police authorities outside London when under scrutiny by their respective local authorities. See Appendix 1, which depicts the basic structure of the Metropolitan Police Service.

THE CONSTITUTIONAL AND GENERAL LEGAL STATUS OF THE POLICE

Historically, many constitutional lawyers have expressed varying opinions regarding the legal status of police officers. Notwithstanding the recent reforms of the police service mentioned above, there is common agreement that police officers are not servants of central government, but are officers of the Crown or of the State. Interestingly, whilst the police service is part of the executive aspect of our constitutional framework, it also has a significant measure of independence from it. As mentioned in other parts of this chapter, chief officers of police are not subject to direct orders from any person or body in relation to operational matters although, ultimately, they are answerable to their police authorities and the Home Secretary for their actions.

The general legal status of the police which is of prime interest to certain sections of the populace is their liability for wrongful acts in the course of their duty. In view of the wide duties and responsibilities incumbent upon the average police officer, inevitably, things will go wrong from time to time. There is, of course, the complaints procedure in dealing with grievances against police actions (see the end of this chapter) and, also, the police are not immune from criminal prosecutions in extreme circumstances, but to what extent are individual police officers liable for civil wrongs (torts) such as negligence, trespass and false imprisonment? Under the common law, a police officer was personally liable for his or her wrongful or unlawful acts although, prior to the Police Act 1996, it was left to police authorities as to whether they were prepared to pay an officer's damages and legal costs. Under s 88 (as amended) of the 1996 Act, chief constables are now vicariously liable for torts and other unlawful conduct committed by their police officers in the course of their duties. Costs and damages incurred as a result or claims settled out of court are paid from the local police budget, provided the police authority gives its approval in the case of the latter. Whether the chief constable has been sued or not, the police authority may pay damages or costs awarded against a police officer within that force.

It is important to mention that police officers are not essentially employees, but holders of a public office determined principally by statute. They can be dismissed only under regulations which deal with breaches of discipline, such as misuse of authority, neglect of duty, racist behaviour, insubordination and other transgressions which bring the police service into disrepute (see also the end of this chapter). However, police officers are certainly not subject to unlimited privileges and immunities, as illustrated in the following commentary:

> Indeed, legislation restricts the freedom of a police officer in a way in which no employer could by a contract of employment. Thus, police officers are not allowed to be members of a trade union or of any association which seeks to control or influence the pay or conditions of service of any police force; instead, there are Police Federations for England and Wales and for Scotland, which represent police officers in all matters of welfare and efficiency, other than questions of promotion affecting individuals, and with limited powers in relation to discipline. Police regulations impose a great many restrictions upon the private life of serving police officers, including one of constitutional importance, namely that a police officer 'shall, at all times, abstain from any activity which is likely to interfere with the impartial discharge of his duties or which is likely to give rise to the impression amongst members of the public that it may so interfere; and, in particular, [he] shall not take any active part in politics'.[9]

This is reinforced by para 2 of the Police (Amendment) Regulations 2004, which states:

> A member of a police force shall at all times abstain from any activity which is likely to interfere with the impartial discharge of his duties or which is likely to give rise to the impression amongst members of the public that it may so interfere. A member of a police force shall in particular (a) not take any active part in politics; (b) not belong to any organisation specified or described in a determination of the Secretary of State.

Other obligations are incumbent upon police officers apart from the above duties. These include restrictions on where they may live and being obliged to report for duty with little or no prior notice under urgent circumstances. An off-duty police officer may even be expected to place him or herself on duty immediately in the event of being confronted with a particularly serious situation which may demand instant police intervention. In essence, a police officer is always on duty, hence the requirement that they carry their warrant cards at all times. This brings us to the well

---

9   Bradley, A and Ewing, K, *Constitutional and Administrative Law* (12th edn, London: Longman, 1997).

worn definition of a police officer who is described as a citizen in uniform *and/or the holder of a warrant card*, who has been given additional powers in the execution of his or her duty (the words in italics are mine and apply to non-uniformed officers). Is this now an accurate definition, in view of the substantial increases in police powers since it was first formulated? Can the average police officer be regarded as an ordinary citizen, even when off-duty, in view of the observations made above?

Chief constables

With the exception of the two London forces, which were discussed above, chief officers of police in the remaining 41 police areas in England and Wales are known as chief constables. The unique constitutional status of chief constables has been described as follows:

> A chief constable is nobody's servant, but an independent officer, upon whom powers and duties are directly conferred by law for the benefit of the populace. His constitutional status remains anomalous and puzzling, even after the re-organisation of the police system implemented by the Police Act 1964. It is still not clear whether anyone is entitled to give him instructions as to the performance of any of his duties,[10] or to what extent the Home Secretary is answerable for decisions taken by chief constables outside the Metropolis.[11]

The Police Act 1996 reasserts that chief constables are responsible for the direction and control of their respective police forces. However, when making operational and other decisions, he or she must have regard to the local policing plan mentioned above. In *R v Commissioner of Police for the Metropolis ex p Blackburn* (1968), at 135, Lord Denning MR gave the following guidance regarding the legal status of chief officers of police:

> The office of Commissioner of Police within the Metropolis dates back to 1829, when Sir Robert Peel introduced his disciplined force. The commissioner was a justice of the peace specially appointed to administer the police force in the Metropolis. His constitutional status has never been defined either by statute or by the courts. It was considered by the Royal Commission on the Police in their report (Cmnd 1728). I have no hesitation, however, in holding that, like every constable in the land, he should be, and is, independent of the executive. He is not subject to the orders of the Secretary of State, save that, under the Police Act 1964, the Secretary of State can call on him to give a report, or to retire in the interests of efficiency. I hold it to be the duty of the Commissioner of Police, as it is of every chief constable, to enforce the law of the land. He must take steps so to post his men that crimes may be detected and that honest citizens may go about their affairs in peace. He must decide whether or not suspected persons are to be prosecuted and, if need be, bring the prosecution or see that it is brought but, in all these things, he is not the servant of anyone, save of the law itself. No Minister of the Crown can tell him that he must or must not keep observation on this place or that; or that he must or must not prosecute this man or that one. Nor can any police authority tell him so. The responsibility for law enforcement lies on him. He is answerable to the law and to the law alone. That appears sufficiently from *Fisher v Oldham Corporation* (1930) and the Privy Council case of *Attorney General for New South Wales v Perpetual Trustee Co Ltd* (1955).

---

10   This statement is increasingly open to question in view of recent reforms of the police service, especially those under the Police Reform Act 2002.

11   de Smith, S and Brazier, R, *Constitutional and Administrative Law* (7th edn, London: Penguin, 1994).

In the light of many reforms of the police service since this case was decided, does this guidance have the same relevance at the present time?

Chief constables have the responsibility for appointing, promoting and, where necessary, disciplining (including dismissing) all officers below the rank of assistant chief constable. The appointment of special constables and other police auxiliaries, as well as police cadets, also falls within the responsibility of chief constables under the Police Act 1996, which also requires that they submit annual reports to the Home Secretary and their police authority, as well as any additional reports as requested by either, including the submission of criminal statistics to the Home Secretary. Although there are now fairly exhaustive mechanisms in place regarding the accountability of chief constables, the fact remains that no one can give such a person direct orders in terms of operational matters. Even the judiciary have shown great reluctance in interfering with the decisions of police chiefs, particularly with regard to the deployment of manpower and resources,[12] although the judges have warned that the exercise of police discretion is reviewable in the courts.[13] This was demonstrated in *R v Commissioner of Police for the Metropolis ex p Free Tibet Campaign and Others* (2000), where it was held that the Metropolitan Police had acted unlawfully by, *inter alia*, removing banners and using vans to block peaceful protestors from the view of the visiting Chinese President during an official visit to London.

Under s 2 of the Police Reform Act 2002, the Home Secretary may issue and revise codes of practice regarding the discharge of any functions by chief officers of police. A draft of this document must be formulated in conjunction with the Central Police Training and Development Authority, who in turn must consult with certain other bodies such as the Association of Police Authorities and the Association of Chief Police Officers; the codes of practice must then be laid before Parliament. It should be noted that there are similar provisions under s 39 of the Police Act 1996 with regard to codes of practice for police authorities; also, the Home Secretary has a duty to issue other codes of practice regarding the policing of this country. These include provisions under s 51 of the Police Reform Act 2002 where he is under a duty to issue and revise codes of practice in respect of independent custody visitors who inspect custody suites at police stations. However, the most voluminous codes of practice are those applicable to the operation of the Police and Criminal Evidence Act 1984, which will be mentioned at many stages throughout this book.

The Home Secretary and the police

As mentioned above, a new Metropolitan Police Authority was instituted in July 2000 under the Greater London Authority Act 1999. Until this time, the Home Secretary retained his role as the police authority for the Metropolis of London, assisted by the

---

12 See *Harris v Sheffield United Football Club Ltd* (1987), where Neill LJ stated: 'I see the force of the argument that the court must be very slow before it interferes in any way with a decision of a chief constable about the disposition of his forces.' See also *R v Chief Constable of Sussex ex p International Trader's Ferry Ltd* (1997).

13 See *R v Commissioner of Police for the Metropolis ex p Blackburn (No 1)* (1968) and *R v Commissioner of Police for the Metropolis ex p Blackburn (No 3)* (1973).

transitional Metropolitan Police Committee. Even though the new authority has commenced its duties, the Home Secretary is still in a position to exert some influence regarding the policing of the capital. This includes having the ultimate say regarding the appointment of new commissioners. It was noted above that the Metropolitan Police Authority is, in essence, very similar to the police authorities elsewhere in England and Wales. There is one important exception to this statement and this relates to the fact that the Metropolitan Police Service plays an important role in matters which go beyond merely policing the capital. As mentioned earlier, the Metropolitan Police perform national as well as international functions, which are of a very sensitive nature, both politically and otherwise. This has constituted a powerful argument in the past against it having its own police authority. In order to ensure the effective performance of its national and international policing functions, para 104 of Sched 27 to the Greater London Authority Act 1999 provides that if the Home Secretary is not satisfied with the standard of performance of the Metropolitan Police in its national and international functions, then he may direct the Metropolitan Police Authority to take such measures as may be specified in that direction. The definition of such functions under these provisions includes the personal protection of VIPs, as well as their property, national security, counter-terrorism or 'the provision of services for any other national or international purpose'.

Notwithstanding the overall effects of these changes, the Home Secretary is still the most singularly prominent figure in respect of the policing of this country. Under the Police Act 1996 (as amended), which has preserved many of the powers held by him under the Police Act 1964, the Home Secretary may determine policing objectives in all areas, having made prior consultations with the relevant police authorities and their police chiefs. This may also include him requiring police authorities to set performance targets in order to achieve this end. However, under s 1 of the Police Reform Act 2002, which inserts a new s 36A into the Police Act 1996, the Home Secretary is under a duty to prepare an annual National Policing Plan. This must include a wide range of policing objectives such as performance targets, making regulations under the 1996 Act and the Criminal Justice and Police Act 2001 regarding police training, as well as issuing various codes of practice and dealing with complaints and misconduct. Under s 42 of the 1996 Act (as amended by s 33 of the Police Reform Act 2002), the Home Secretary may require a police authority to suspend and dismiss a chief constable following an inquiry and, if representations are made by that officer, a hearing must be convened by the Home Secretary. See *Ridge v Baldwin* (1964), where the principle of the right to a fair hearing was extended to a former chief constable, who had been dismissed from his post by a borough police authority, and that committee had not initially given him the opportunity to present his case in defence. The right to make representations to a police authority where that body dismisses a chief constable is also provided for under the 1996 Act.

Other provisions under the 1996 Act include the Home Secretary's power to order inquiries into specific incidents (the Scarman Report on the Brixton riots, for example), the appointment of inspectors of constabulary in order to assess the efficiency of individual forces, the making of regulations regarding the administration of the police service as a whole, including matters affecting national pay and conditions, as well as issuing Home Office circulars for the guidance of the police service. Under Pt 4 of the Criminal Justice and Police Act 2001, the Home Secretary has been given extensive powers to regulate police training. Among other things, he has the power to set objectives and performance targets for the Central Police Training and Development

Authority, which has the overall responsibility for providing and promoting police training in this country. The Home Secretary may also give specific and general directions to the authority in the performance of its functions.

In *R v Secretary of State for the Home Department ex p Northumbria Police Authority* (1988), police authorities in several areas, including Northumbria, sought to challenge the Home Secretary's actions regarding the issue of certain riot control equipment. Following the inner city riots in 1981, it had been apparent that the police could no longer effectively control serious disturbances using their existing standard equipment, which was largely confined to truncheons and long shields, especially when dealing with rioters throwing missiles, including fire bombs. This was acknowledged in the Scarman Report, and it was recommended that the police should be issued with stand-off weaponry, such as CS gas and plastic bullets. The police authorities mentioned above objected to such devices being issued to their police officers and refused to authorise their purchase. The Home Secretary then issued a circular to all chief constables, advising them of the availability of such equipment on permanent loan, in the event of their police authorities refusing to authorise the purchase of CS gas and plastic bullets. The Court of Appeal held that the Home Secretary had acted lawfully on two grounds. First, under ss 4 and 5 of the Police Act 1964, powers to effect the supply of equipment to the police were vested in chief constables and police authorities. However, under s 41, the Home Secretary also had powers to supply central or common services to the police service as a whole. It was held that the Home Secretary had lawfully exercised this power, as riot control equipment fell within this definition. Secondly, it was held that, in acting in this manner, the Home Secretary had correctly exercised the prerogative power to keep the Queen's peace, which was unaffected by the 1964 Act.

With regard to the present powers of the Home Secretary to regulate the standard of equipment used by the police, s 6 of the Police Reform Act 2002 enables the Home Secretary to make regulations so that all police forces in England and Wales will use certain equipment approved by him, and in the way prescribed. The reason for this power is to ensure that whenever police forces are deployed on mutual aid, they will all be using the same or similar equipment. Examples will include vehicles, IT systems, batons, incapacitant sprays, headgear or protective clothing.[14] Before making such regulations, the Home Secretary is under a duty to consult with the representative bodies of chief officers of police and police authorities. In order to create greater rationalisation between police forces, especially when engaged in joint operations, s 7 of the Police Reform Act 2002 makes provision for the Home Secretary to make regulations regarding police procedures and practices. However, the consultation process required before such regulations may be made is much wider than those pertaining to the regulation of police equipment.

Her Majesty's Inspectorate of Constabulary

With regard to all police forces in England and Wales, many decisions of any Home Secretary and, indeed, chief police officers, are likely to be influenced by the findings of Her Majesty's Inspectorate of Constabulary, a body first instituted in 1856, which

---

14   Police Reform Act 2002 'Explanatory Notes' (The Stationery Office, 2002).

inspects the efficiency and effectiveness of all police forces. The Inspectorate currently consists of inspectors of constabulary, who are mainly former chief police officers, plus a chief inspector of constabulary, who, among other things, are responsible for laying an annual report on the Inspectorate's work before Parliament. Her Majesty's inspectors of constabulary are appointed by the Queen, on the recommendation of the Home Secretary, and are empowered to inspect all police forces in England and Wales, including the Metropolitan Police which, up until fairly recently, were exempt from their scrutiny. Some inspectors are non-police officers with relevant management experience. This is a relatively new innovation that started in 1993. Under s 93 of the Criminal Justice and Police Act 2001, inspectors of constabulary may be required to inspect the Central Police Training and Development Authority on the instructions of the Home Secretary. Their inspection powers also include the National Criminal Intelligence Service and the National Crime Squad as well as any police force maintained for any police area. In addition to routine inspections of all these bodies, under s 3 of the Police Reform Act 2002, the inspectorate may be specifically required by the Home Secretary to inspect any such body in whole or part. The scope of the Inspectorate has been further enhanced by s 84 of the 2002 Act, which enables the Home Secretary's power to approve the appointment of assistant commissioners, deputy assistant commissoners, commanders, deputy chief constables and assistant chief constables to be delegated to the chief inspector of constabulary. However, it should be noted that Her Majesty's chief inspector of constabulary will reach such decisions in accordance with a special panel.

General operational policing in England and Wales

All recruits to the police service are initially attested as constables (including part time voluntary police officers in the special constabulary, who are discussed below). This is the rank in which all police men and women must begin, regardless of educational attainment or other qualities which may result in promotion during their service. This constitutes one of the many features of the police service in England and Wales, distinct from the armed forces, where there is an officer class to which suitable new entrants may immediately enter. As a consequence, all senior officers within the police service, including those who head such forces, have progressed through all the ranks, starting with the rank of constable. The first Metropolitan Police Commissioner to have risen through all the ranks was Sir Joseph Simpson, who took office as Commissioner in 1958. This is now the normal route for all police chiefs throughout England and Wales. However, there is a fast-stream promotion scheme for police officers who demonstrate exceptional abilities after joining. This, among other things, involves attendance at the Police Staff College, where promising police officers are taught advanced management practices, as well as learning senior command skills.

All new recruits must satisfactorily complete their initial two-year probationary period as constables, which provides all police officers with an essential introduction to police duties (see Appendix 2, which depicts the overall rank structure within the police service in England and Wales). Certain aspects of the police rank structure were reformed around the early 1990s as a result of the Sheehy Report,[15] which

---

15 Sheehy Commission, *Inquiry into Police Responsibilities and Rewards*, Cm 2280 (London: HMSO, 1993).

endeavoured, *inter alia*, to streamline the management of the police service by removing some of the more senior ranks. In the end, the ranks of chief superintendent and deputy chief constable were removed, although some existing holders of those ranks were allowed to keep them. Eventually, it was intended that these posts would cease to exist, as well as deputy assistant commissioners in London. However, all these substantive ranks have now been restored.

The general requirements for entry into the police service are contingent upon good health, character, education and appearance. Entry is no longer confined to British nationality, certain Commonwealth citizens and citizens of the Irish Republic. Section 82 of the Police Reform Act 2002 now enables the police to be recruited from any nationality, although subject to regulations regarding such matters as competency in written and spoken English and residential qualification in the UK. Efforts are being made in an endeavour to make the police service more representative of the overall population in this country by focusing more recruitment on the ethnic community, which is still generally under-represented within this service.

The training of recruits initially requires about five months' full time attendance at one of the police training centres, located in regions throughout the country. Training remains a prevalent feature throughout the two-year probationary period, which takes the form of practical street experience under varying degrees of supervision, but interspersed with classroom instruction.

In terms of specialist opportunities, the police service possibly has no parallel. A constable having satisfactorily completed his or her probationary period is given the opportunity to either continue working in uniform at a local police station (divisional or sub-divisional level) or to enter any of a range of specialist areas immediately or at some other stage in their career. These include the Criminal Investigation Department, traffic division, the mounted police, the drugs squad, communications, the vice squad, dog handlers, Special Branch, VIP protection, the National Crime Squad, the National Criminal Intelligence Service, internal investigations, public order control, training, youth and community work and many more. However, many prefer to remain as uniformed officers in the basic command units of local police divisions, believing that policing at this level can provide all the variety and opportunities that specialist work can bring. There is considerable merit in this assertion, since police work is equally dependent upon both specialist, as well as 'routine', police duties.

The command structure of each police force varies from area to area, although there are certain characteristics that all forces have in common. The headquarters and local command structure of a typical provincial police force is depicted in basic form in Appendix 3, whereas the more complex organisation of the Metropolitan Police Service is represented in Appendix 1.

Whatever rank a police officer holds, the numerous statutes covering police powers refer to all police officers as holders of the office of 'constable', unless specific ranks are stipulated for certain procedural purposes. The fundamental tenet that all police officers hold the office of constable also applies to voluntary, part time police officers, who are members of the special constabulary, which will be discussed in the next section.

The special constabulary

Fairly extensive coverage of this aspect of the police service will be made here, since it is a relatively understudied subject[16] and, it is submitted, warrants discussion here. The special constabulary is a very old institution which, in its original form, pre-dates the formation of the Metropolitan Police in 1829 by over 150 years. Although the early justices of the peace and lords of the manor were expected to appoint officers to enforce the law, they frequently neglected this duty and, in 1673, a statute was passed, which enabled two magistrates to appoint special constables within their respective districts. However, it was the Special Constables Act 1831 which placed this force on the general footing upon which the modern special constabulary is now based. Since then, the 'specials', as they are commonly termed, have achieved notable places within the history of the modern police service. For example, in 1848, the largest single enrolment of special constables occurred in response to fears of serious disorder arising from the Chartist movement. This resulted in no fewer than 170,000 specials being deployed in central London. The anticipated trouble was averted, since the number of specials outnumbered the protestors by over three to one. It was during both World Wars that the specials particularly excelled and often formed the bulwark of operational policing throughout many parts of the country. However, they were also involved in other high profile roles during certain events between the war years. From 1919 to 1926 they assisted in maintaining order during a series of major industrial disputes, including the General Strike, and during the early 1930s they were used extensively during a series of demonstrations in London resulting from mass unemployment.[17]

In more modern times, the special constabulary is an auxiliary force within the police service, which consists of men and women who serve as part time, unpaid police officers who work in a voluntary capacity. Specials receive no payment for their services,[18] although they receive limited out of pocket expenses, such as travel and meal allowances, together with a boot or shoe allowance. They also receive reimbursement for any loss of earnings, for example, where they attend court. Their police work is confined to whatever spare time they can devote to this end. This often involves a significant sacrifice in certain cases, since many have demanding commitments elsewhere but, in any event, they are generally expected to perform at least 16 hours' voluntary duty per month.

It is important to note that specials have full police powers, the same as regular police officers, but with one variation. Whereas members of the regular police service may exercise their powers anywhere in this country, specials are restricted to the use of police powers within their respective police areas and within those police areas which immediately border on to their own. The exception to this general rule are specials in

---

16 There are some exceptions. These include Gill, M and Mawby, R, *A Special Constable: A Study of the Police Reserve* (Aldershot: Avebury, 1990); and also Barron, T, 'The Special Constable's Manual' (London: Police Review, 1997).

17 *The Metropolitan Special Constabulary: An Illustrated History from 1831 to Today* (London: New Scotland Yard, 1981).

18 In previous years some police forces have introduced limited payment schemes for their specials, but these appear to have had little impact on recruitment and retention. Such schemes have therefore been abandoned.

the City of London, who may exercise their police powers in the Metropolitan Police area as well as the counties which border onto the Greater London boundaries. In addition, if specials are seconded to a different police area under mutual aid, they will have full police powers within that area. With some variations, specials are basically equipped with the same uniform as regular full time police officers, as well as certain protective clothing and equipment. The latter are necessary, because specials, as well as regular police officers, often face the same risks when on duty.

A grade structure exists within the special constabulary for those given additional responsibility for its management. This places graded officers within the special constabulary in authority above specials without or with lower grades. Some specials join the regular force having initially served in a voluntary capacity and feel that they wish to make a full time career within the police service. In this respect, a person joining the special constabulary acquires an excellent introduction to operational policing. As mentioned above, special constables, as well as regular police officers, are appointed by chief officers of police, and it is important to note that s 35 of the Police Reform Act 2002 places special constables within the jurisdiction of the Independent Police Complaints Commission.

In more recent years, there has been a significant drop in the number of special constables compared with about 30 or 40 years ago when their numbers were much higher. Although in some areas they exist in fairly large numbers, this is not reflected generally, and in some parts of the country the ratio of specials in relation to regular police officers is quite low. Despite recruitment campaigns at local and national level, the main difficulty appears to be the retention of those who do join. There are many reasons for the relatively large number of resignations from the special constabulary every year,[19] including the fact that some join the regular force. Meanwhile, the Government is committed to a number of initiatives designed to increase the overall strength of the special constabulary and to improve its overall effectiveness.

THE 'EXTENDED POLICE FAMILY'

A major change in the structure of policing in England and Wales has recently been effected through Part 4, Chapter 1, and Scheds 4 and 5 to the Police Reform Act 2002. These provisions have created the concept of the 'extended police family' that is designed to give certain civilians a selected range of police powers. The 2002 Act creates five main classes of civilians who can be conferred with these powers, namely community support officers, investigating officers, detention officers, escort officers and accredited civilians. This new and controversial scheme is discussed in Chapter 7 under the heading 'Civilians given police powers'.

---

19 For a discussion on a suggested scheme that, *inter alia*, could improve recruitment and retention rates in the special constabulary, see Jason-Lloyd, L, 'Police reform – a better way?' (2003) 167 JP 805.

COMPLAINTS AGAINST THE POLICE

Introduction

The foregoing coverage has endeavoured to provide an insight into the foundations of the modern police service. The following chapters will provide an introductory guide to the key issues affecting the exercise of police powers that should assist in giving a broad picture of the increasingly complex nature of policing in this country. Inevitably, a book of this nature tends to present the subject in a rather sanitised manner, with little reference to the stark realities of the overall environment in which such powers are exercised, both from the public, as well as the police, standpoint. However high the standards of the police service may be, there must be appropriate mechanisms of accountability at all levels in order to maintain credibility. The latter is most important, for it is upon this that the concept of policing by consent depends. One of the ways in which any modern police service in a democratic society can preserve public support is by having a fair and efficient police complaints system.

The development of the complaints system

Prior to the enactment of the Police and Criminal Evidence Act 1984, which significantly reformed this process, the police complaints system in this country had become the subject of increasing criticism. The earlier system inspired little public confidence because, *inter alia*, the complaints procedure was the same regardless of whether a complaint was serious or trivial, and this often wasted the time of senior police officers where the matter could be dealt with less formally. In addition, there were doubts about the independence of the body responsible for investigating complaints enacted under the Police Act 1976, namely, the Police Complaints Board, especially in view of reports that investigating officers had sometimes tried to persuade complainants to withdraw their allegations.[20] Therefore, Pt IX of the Police and Criminal Evidence Act 1984, headed 'police complaints and discipline', contained measures which constituted an overhaul of the earlier system. One of its principal reforms was the forming of the Police Complaints Authority, which replaced the Police Complaints Board.

In response to calls for further reforms, the provisions of the 1984 Act were replaced initially by the relevant measures under the Police and Magistrates' Courts Act 1994, but were subsequently recast under the Police Act 1996, together with accompanying regulations. In April 1999, that new system of police complaints and discipline was put into force, but since then there has been increasing pressure from numerous sources to reform the complaints system even further. Among other things, this was based on the belief that the Police Complaints Authority was not sufficiently independent of the police and that the system did not reflect the impartiality expected of it. Furthermore, in *Govell v UK* (Application No 27237/95), it was held that the

---

20 Zander, M, *The Police and Criminal Evidence Act 1984* (4th edn, London: Sweet & Maxwell, 2003).

police complaints system did not provide an adequate remedy for the purposes of Art 13 of the European Convention on Human Rights;[21] and in *Khan v UK* (2000) 31 EHRR 45, it was held that the Police Complaints Authority was not a sufficiently independent body and this led to a violation of Arts 13 and 8 of the European Convention. A further major influence in changing the police complaints system was the findings of the Stephen Lawrence Inquiry. All this has now led to the formation of the Independent Police Complaints Commission (the IPCC) under Pt 2 and Sched 3 to the Police Reform Act 2002. The provisions of the 2002 Act are augmented by regulations and various sources of guidance. The IPCC has been in operation since 1 April 2004, and an overview of this new body, as well as the new system of police complaints generally, will now be given.

The new police complaints system

There are several mechanisms within the structure and functions of the IPCC that are designed to increase public confidence in the new system. Under the Police Reform Act, there must be at least 10 members of the IPCC plus a chairperson. The chairperson is appointed by the Queen and the other commissioners are appointed by the Home Secretary, but none of them should be appointed if at any time they have held the office of constable or have been a member of the National Criminal Intelligence Service or the National Crime Squad. The independence of the IPCC is further reinforced by the provisions under s 9 of the Police Reform Act 2002 which, *inter alia*, states that it 'shall be a body corporate' and it 'shall not be regarded as the servant or agent of the Crown or enjoy any status, privilege or immunity of the Crown, and the Commission's property shall not be regarded as property of, or property held on behalf of, the Crown'. In other words, it is a free-standing public body that is independent of the Government.

It should be mentioned that complaints against the police regarding incidents that occurred prior to 1 April 2004 will be dealt with by the IPCC in accordance with the earlier system. This provision has been made by the Independent Police Complaints Commission (Transitional Provisions) Order 2004.

The scope of persons who are subject to the new system is much wider than previously. At one time it was only regular police officers who were subject to the complaints process. Now, however, it includes many more classes of persons within the police service. These include not only regular police officers but also special constables and civilian employees. The latter will also include civilians who are part of the extended police family, namely community support officers, investigating officers, detention officers and escort officers. (Separate arrangements exist for dealing with complaints against accredited civilians.) The scope of complaints in this context does not include general matters of discontent such as the way that police resources are allocated and the deployment of patrols in certain areas. Complaints must relate to specific conduct by police officers. Under s 12 of the Police Reform Act, the persons who may make a complaint are the victims, witnesses and those who are adversely affected by the alleged police misconduct. The latter includes persons who have been

---

21   Article 13 is the 'Right to an Effective Remedy'. Although this Article is not one of those included under the Human Rights Act 1998, the UK courts are obliged to take case law into account that has arisen from Convention jurisprudence.

placed in danger or have suffered loss or been caused distress or inconvenience. If the complaint is against a police officer above the rank of chief superintendent, that officer's police authority should record it, otherwise the chief officer of police should record the complaint if it involves an officer below that rank. The complainant should receive a copy of the complaint and an appeal may be made to the IPCC in the event of a refusal to record it. If a complaint is sent direct to the IPCC, this will be transferred to the police with the consent of the complainant, although this will be done anyway if it is considered to be in the public interest. Serious complaints such as those involving death, serious injury, serious sexual offences, serious race, sex or religious discrimination, serious corruption and any serious arrestable offence must be referred by the police to the IPCC, otherwise they have a discretion to refer cases. In certain instances, the IPCC may 'call-in' a specific case that requires the police to refer it for their consideration.

Schedule 3, para 8 to the Police Reform Act 2002 preserves the earlier practice of resolving less serious complaints through a relatively informal procedure. Under the previous system, this was called 'informal resolution', but under the new regime, it is named 'local resolution'. The complainant must consent to this procedure and may appeal if it is not followed. Incidents that have often proved appropriate for this procedure include a general lack of politeness that may be resolved through a simple apology, or other informal methods such as the officer providing an explanation for his or her conduct. However, the IPCC must decide how a complaint will be dealt with in more serious cases which, in turn, may be referred back to the police for investigation. The new rules enable the police to conduct investigations without the supervision of the IPCC or this may be done under its supervision. The latter constitutes a new procedure under the complaints system whereby the IPCC may actually manage or direct an investigation. This is another change compared with the earlier system that is intended to engender greater public confidence in the way in which complaints against the police are dealt with. It is submitted that this may have been modelled on the way that the Criminal Cases Review Commission review alleged miscarriages of justice under the Criminal Appeal Act 1995. This enables them in certain cases to adopt a 'hands on' approach in which the police are under their direct supervision rather than being allowed to deal with the investigation at their own discretion, although the latter may still apply where appropriate. Alternatively, they may conduct investigations using their own staff, which is also a procedure sometimes used by the Criminal Cases Review Commission.

One of the key changes in the new system is that complainants will have greater involvement in this process compared with the earlier regime. These include the IPCC having to take into account the complainant's views as to whether an investigation should be managed or conducted using in-house staff. Complainants will also be entitled to regular progress reports and to notification of decisions taken, as well as having access to several routes of appeal at different stages in the investigation, including the outcome. In addition, complainants are permitted to be present during disciplinary hearings and may be accompanied by up to three friends. However, complainants do not have any right to legal representation.

Whether the police or the IPCC have investigated the complaint, on its completion the relevant body must decide whether to forward the matter to the Director of Public Prosecutions in order to consider any criminal charges. If the matter is not referred to the DPP or the decision is taken not to prosecute, consideration must be given regarding any disciplinary action. In certain circumstances, the IPCC may direct that a disciplinary hearing is conducted in public.

The Police Appeals Tribunal

As a result of a complaint, a police officer may be subject to dismissal from the force, be required to resign or be reduced in rank. These (and other sanctions) may also apply in consequence of other misconduct where this is identified by a person within the police service or where the officer's performance of his or her duties is unsatisfactory. A police officer may ultimately appeal against any of the three specific sanctions listed above to the new Police Appeals Tribunal, which replaces the earlier system whereby police officers could appeal to the Home Secretary. This body has a slightly different composition depending upon whether the appellant is a senior officer or not. The common ground is that there must always be a legally qualified chairperson, a member of a police authority and a former or serving chief officer from another police force. On the conclusion of the proceedings, the Police Appeals Tribunal will either uphold the original decision or make an order which is less severe than the original decision.

The Code of Conduct under Sched 1 to the Police (Conduct) Regulations 2004, which came into force on 1 April 2004, sets out the standards expected of police officers, which, if not reached, can lead to disciplinary action being taken, whether or not a complaint is involved. All police officers are subject to the regulations, regardless of rank, and they now also apply to special constables. The regulations not only state the procedures involved in cases of misconduct, they also contain the Code of Conduct, which is reproduced as follows:

SCHEDULE 1

Code of Conduct

Honesty and integrity

1   It is of paramount importance that the public has faith in the honesty and integrity of police officers. Officers should therefore be open and truthful in their dealings, avoid being improperly beholden to any person or institution and discharge their duties with integrity.

Fairness and impartiality

2   Police officers have a particular responsibility to act with fairness and impartiality in all their dealings with the public and their colleagues.

Politeness and tolerance

3   Officers should treat members of the public and colleagues with courtesy and respect, avoiding abusive or deriding attitudes or behaviour. In particular, officers must avoid: favouritism of an individual or group; all forms of harassment, victimisation or unreasonable discrimination; and overbearing conduct to a colleague, particularly to one junior in rank or service.

Use of force and abuse of authority

4   Officers must never knowingly use more force than is reasonable, nor should they abuse their authority.

Performance of duties

5   Officers should be conscientious and diligent in the performance of their duties. Officers should attend work promptly when rostered for duty. If absent through sickness or injury, they should avoid activities likely to retard their return to duty.

Lawful orders

6   The police service is a disciplined body. Unless there is good and sufficient cause to do otherwise, officers must obey all lawful orders and abide by the provisions of Police Regulations. Officers should support their colleagues in the execution of their lawful duties and oppose any improper behaviour, reporting it where appropriate.

Confidentiality

7   Information which comes into the possession of the police should be treated as confidential. It should not be used for personal benefit and nor should it be divulged to other parties, except in the proper course of police duty. Similarly, officers should respect as confidential, information about force policy and operations, unless authorised to disclose it in the course of their duties.

Criminal offences

8   Officers must report any proceedings for a criminal offence taken against them. Conviction of a criminal offence or the administration of a caution may, of itself, result in further action being taken.

Property

9   Officers must exercise reasonable care to prevent loss or damage to property (excluding their own personal property, but including police property).

Sobriety

10   Whilst on duty, officers must be sober. Officers should not consume alcohol when on duty, unless specifically authorised to do so or it becomes necessary for the proper discharge of police duty.

Appearance

11   Unless on duties which dictate otherwise, officers should always be well turned out, clean and tidy whilst on duty in uniform or in plain clothes.

General conduct

12   Whether on or off duty, police officers should not behave in a way which is likely to bring discredit upon the police service.

Notes

(a)   The primary duties of those who hold the office of constable are the protection of life and property, the preservation of the Queen's peace and the prevention and detection of criminal offences. To fulfil these duties, they are granted extraordinary powers; the public and the police service therefore have the right to expect the highest standards of conduct from them.

(b)   This Code sets out the principles which guide police officers' conduct. It does not seek to restrict officers' discretion; rather, it aims to define the parameters of conduct within which that discretion should be exercised. However, it is important to note that any breach of the principles in this Code may result in action being taken by the organisation, which, in serious cases, could involve dismissal.

(c)   Police behaviour, whether on or off duty, affects public confidence in the police service. Any conduct which brings or is likely to bring discredit to the police service may be the subject of sanction. Accordingly, any allegation of conduct which could, if proved, bring or be likely to bring discredit to the police service should be investigated in order to establish whether or not a breach of the Code has occurred and whether formal disciplinary action is appropriate. No investigation is required where the conduct, if proved, would not bring or would not be likely to bring, discredit to the police service.

Other forms of redress

'Probably the strongest means of enforcement of good conduct by the police is the exclusion of improperly obtained evidence under ss 76 and 78 of the Police and Criminal Evidence Act 1984.'[22] Apart from this potent sanction (discussed in subsequent chapters), there are other ways in which misconduct by the police may be dealt with. In the more extreme cases where, for instance, property may have been damaged unnecessarily by officers during a search or where excessive or unnecessary force was used in the exercise of their powers, a criminal prosecution could ensue, especially where the damage or any injury was severe or, in the latter instance, even fatal. With regard to fatalities, it is mandatory for a coroner to empanel a jury for an inquest where a person has died as a result of injuries inflicted by the police or where a person has died in police custody. In more recent years, a small number of police officers have faced homicide charges arising from such proceedings. However, such cases are comparatively rare. In situations where non-fatal harm is inflicted, it is more common for civil action to be taken against the police. Whilst breaches of the provisions of the Police and Criminal Evidence Act or the Codes of Practice do not necessarily give rise to criminal or civil liability, a breach may be relevant in other actions and taken into account by the courts.

A fairly common civil action taken against the police is the tort of trespass to the person, the two main forms of which are an assault and battery, and false imprisonment. An assault and battery constitutes the unlawful application of force against another person, no matter how slight. Therefore, no injury need be inflicted, although the case will attract greater damages if personal injury resulted from the conduct in question. The court will also take into account any actions by the claimant which may have contributed to the incident. An assault and battery would apply in instances where excessive force was used by the police in exercising their powers or where a person was unlawfully searched or detained, even if very little restraint was applied against that person. False imprisonment will apply in cases where a person has been unlawfully deprived of his or her liberty, even if this was for a short time. This does not only mean unlawful detention in a police station, but will apply if a person was unlawfully detained elsewhere. Although there is no single tort of wrongful arrest or detention, this conduct usually falls under the heading of false imprisonment and, if any measure of force was used, an assault and battery as well.

The police may also be subject to an action under trespass to land where, for instance, they have entered property without lawful authority. If damage has been done to the property or anything in it, then they could also be liable for an action under trespass to goods. Other civil actions may include negligence and malicious prosecution. However, many cases are settled out of court – a common feature of the civil law process.

---

22 Cape, E and Luqmani, J, *Defending Suspects at Police Stations: The Practitioners' Guide to Advice and Representation* (3rd edn, London: Legal Action Group, 1999). See also *R v Fennelley* (1989).

Before departing from the issue of police misconduct, it is submitted that a very candid and realistic view of this subject can be found in the following extract from a comparatively little-known publication:[23]

> In its various ugly forms, violence is all too prevalent a part of the hurly burly of the police officer's daily life in some areas. Many assaults take place. Every day, police officers are injured in London. All these incidents are hurtful and unpleasant and, occasionally, some are very serious indeed, leading to grave incapacity and, tragically, even to death. Rightly, there is always public concern about these assaults; much is said, and many new initiatives are proposed, in the quest to reduce the level of violence in our society though, alas, progress seems painfully slow to those of us who have to face it daily. And when things go badly awry, on an individual or on a Force basis, and police are accused of assault or brutality, the spotlight rightly falls on us. Out of even relatively simple cases, great debates arise. Accusation and counter-accusation abound.
>
> The actions of individual officers are probed again and again. Explanations, though they be true or false, are hoisted up to the light and penetrated and shaken, sometimes with scant regard to the fact that, at the time, the officer had not the facility of this fine hindsight and was obliged to judge things in an instant, to react immediately. But that is the way of police life, of course, and it is proper and right that there should be careful public invigilation of our use of force. And the more so since, on a number of occasions, we have been found wanting; incidents ranging from careless over-reaction and burly excess to deliberate and wicked assault have been levelled, and proved, against individual officers. All the more important, then, that we should develop our ability to remain calm and restrained, and to apply force economically and humanely.
>
> You should regard it as a matter of personal pride to be able to arrest a violent offender, quell a breach of the peace or deal expeditiously with a disturbed or drunken man quietly, skilfully and with the minimum of fuss. Your training has just that in view and it is important that police officers should develop the expertise and maintain their physical fitness to do these things well. Your experience will show you that, as your skills improve, so your confidence grows and the chances of your receiving an injury diminish … You should strive to exhibit those attitudes, whatever the pressures and the provocation. The more often you succeed in doing this, the greater will be your resolution when next faced with violence, and the more impressive your example to other officers.

It may be appropriate at this point to mention briefly some specific offences which can be committed *against* the police. Two of the most well known are those of assault and obstructing police under s 89(1) and (2) of the Police Act 1996. Assault on police under sub-s (1) is triable summarily and is usually confined to cases which fall within the ambit of a common assault, although it has been known for the prosecution to downgrade rather more serious cases to this level. As will be seen in succeeding chapters, it is essential that the police officer in question is acting in the execution of his or her duty for this offence to be committed, and this offence extends to persons who are assisting police officers. The maximum sentence on conviction for assault on police is 51 weeks'[24] imprisonment and/or a fine not exceeding £5,000. The offence under

---

23   Metropolitan Police, *The Principles of Policing and Guidance for Professional Behaviour* (London: Metropolitan Police, 1985).

24   This apparently odd figure is the new maximum sentence imposed for shorter custodial sentences under the Criminal Justice Act 2003.

sub-s (2) of wilfully obstructing police includes resisting a constable in the execution of his or her duty. Whilst resisting may involve such acts as tearing away from a police officer's hold, obstructing police may not always necessitate physical contact. It has been held that any act which makes it more difficult for the police to perform their duty can amount to obstruction. This includes providing deliberately misleading information and warning persons committing offences of approaching police officers. Persons assisting the police also fall within the ambit of these offences, which are triable summarily and punishable by a maximum of 51 weeks' imprisonment and/or a fine not exceeding £1,000.

CHAPTER 2

POLICE POWERS OF STOP AND SEARCH

INTRODUCTION

The powers of the police to stop and search, particularly in public, has been the subject of particular scrutiny in recent years. The excessive and arbitrary use of such powers was held to have been a major contributory factor to the underlying resentment, notably between younger people and the police, which led to the inner city riots in 1981. It is important to note that this chapter will examine the law and procedures governing stops and searches by the police who have not, at that stage, made an arrest. Police powers to search either persons or premises, once an arrest has been effected, will be discussed in Chapters 4 and 5.

The Royal Commission on Criminal Procedure,[1] as part of its remit, examined the then-existing laws governing police powers of stop and search. These largely consisted of a patchwork of local Acts of Parliament, which lacked any standard procedures or uniform application nationally:

> The Philips Royal Commission identified two main defects in the existing law. First, police powers to stop and search varied from one part of the country to another. In London, for instance, the police could use the powers under s 66 of the Metropolitan Police Act 1839 to stop and search for stolen goods and similar local powers existed in Birmingham, Manchester, Liverpool and Rochdale, but equivalent powers did not exist in most other parts of the country. Secondly, existing powers were either inadequate or, at best, uncertain and required clarification or redefinition.[2]

As a result, the Royal Commission recommended that uniform powers of stop and search should be given to the police throughout England and Wales, although the Government rejected the idea of a single or general power covering every eventuality. In consequence, a major reform of police powers of stop and search, as well as other powers, was enacted under the Police and Criminal Evidence Act 1984.

THE POLICE AND CRIMINAL EVIDENCE ACT 1984 ('PACE')

This statute (commonly known as PACE) constituted the greatest single reform of police powers, certainly during the 20th century, to the extent that the bulk of police powers are either contained or consolidated within this statute. The main elements of PACE are: powers to stop and search (Pt I); powers of entry, search and seizure (Pt II); arrest (Pt III); detention (Pt IV); questioning and treatment of persons by police (Pt V); Codes of Practice – general (Pt VI); documentary evidence in criminal proceedings (Pt VII); and evidence in criminal proceedings – general (Pt VIII), together with general police matters and miscellaneous provisions. This is followed by several schedules

---

1   Philips Royal Commission.
2   Zander, M, *The Police and Criminal Evidence Act 1984* (4th edn, London: Sweet & Maxwell, 2003).

ranging from detailed procedures in seeking evidence, the listing of certain arrestable offences, and various technical amendments to other statutes. Since its original enactment, a number of provisions under PACE have been subject to amendment by other statutes, as well as clarification resulting from judicial decisions. These will be explained at the appropriate stages in this book, which will cover the relevant aspects of this Act.

PACE took almost two years to be passed. Certain clauses in the Police and Criminal Evidence Bill attracted fierce opposition, both within and outside Parliament, and its passage was further delayed by the general election in May 1983. Although enacted in October 1984, most of PACE did not come into effect until 1986, such was the extent of preparation needed for the operation of its new provisions. As far as the police service itself was concerned, all police officers had to be retrained under the new provisions and procedures of PACE, in time for its implementation.

As mentioned above, statutes affecting police powers refer to police officers in general as constables. This is because all police officers hold the office of constable, whether they be a police constable, chief constable or special constable, as well as the relevant ranks between them. The exception to this rule is where certain ranks are stipulated for specific procedures. For example, under s 4 of PACE, only a police superintendent or above may authorise road blocks (see later in this chapter for further coverage of this topic).

It must be stressed that whilst the bulk of police powers are enshrined under PACE, not all of them are. A number of statutes have been enacted before and after PACE which affect police powers that have not been included under its provisions. However, many of them are linked to certain procedures under PACE and, in effect, work through it, the common link being the Codes of Practice (see below). These affect, for example, the power to stop and search for controlled drugs under s 23 of the Misuse of Drugs Act 1971 and the power to stop and search for firearms under s 47 of the Firearms Act 1968. Although these specific powers to stop and search are contained within those statutes and not PACE, these powers are still subject to the various safeguards under the Codes of Practice. This will be discussed in more detail later in this chapter (see also Appendix 4, which illustrates some of the principal police powers, both under PACE and other statutes, as well as the common law).

A major development regarding the structure of PACE occurred in May 2002, when it was announced that the Home Office and the Cabinet Office would conduct a joint review of this statute. The aim of this review was to streamline certain procedures and make the operation of PACE more appropriate for policing in the 21st century. In November 2002 the Joint Review made a number of recommendations that had implications for the Codes of Practice that came into force in April 2003, followed by Codes of Practice that came into force in August 2004 (see below). The latest codes have taken into account the continuing development of the Human Rights Act 1998 (see Chapter 8), as well as several changes to PACE that have been made under the Criminal Justice Act 2003. Other legislation has also been enacted recently, namely the Domestic Violence, Crime and Victims Act 2004, and some of the changes brought by this have been incorporated within this book at the relevant stages.

THE CODES OF PRACTICE

It has already been noted that PACE is accompanied by the Codes of Practice, mentioned above under Pt VI (more specifically, under ss 66 and 67 (as amended), as well as ss 60 and 60A under Pt V). The Codes of Practice exist as a separate publication and are designed to assist in the interpretation and clarification of the relevant provisions of PACE, in addition to providing essential guidance to those who use its powers. For this reason, they will be referred to extensively throughout most of this book.

The Codes of Practice have also been subject to many changes. The first edition took effect on 1 January 1986 and the second on 1 April 1991 but, since then, further changes have necessitated the publication of more editions, particularly the Codes affecting powers of stop and search. One of the more recent editions was published in 1999 and consisted of the following five Codes under a single consolidated booklet: (A) Code of Practice for the exercise by police officers of statutory powers of stop and search (this took effect from 1 March 1999); (B) Code of Practice for the searching of premises by police officers and the seizure of property found by police officers on persons or premises; (C) Code of Practice for the detention, treatment and questioning of persons by police officers; (D) Code of Practice for the identification of persons by police officers; and (E) Code of Practice on tape recording of interviews with suspects (the last four Codes took effect on 10 April 1995). Codes of Practice were then published in 2003,[3] but certain parts of these codes were then amended in August 2004. It is anticipated that revised codes may be drafted by the summer of 2005, reflecting the ongoing review of police powers.

Certain police powers and duties are enshrined only in the Codes of Practice and do not appear in PACE. The prime examples are Codes E and F. Code E, which makes provision for the tape recording of interviews, is merely mentioned under s 60 of PACE. The video taping of interviews, however, has only recently been introduced into PACE under s 60A and the provisions governing these procedures fall under Code of Practice F.

The way in which the Codes of Practice are now produced has been substantially changed. Initially, reforms were effected through s 77 of the Criminal Justice and Police Act 2001, but more recently s 11 of the Criminal Justice Act 2003 has streamlined this process further by reducing the extent of consultation prior to any changes. One of several reasons for the frequent updating of the codes in recent years is the increasing effect of the Human Rights Act 1998 on policing in this country (see Chapter 8).

Powers of stop and search under PACE

Under s 1 of PACE, if a constable has reasonable grounds for suspecting that stolen or prohibited articles are being carried, that police officer may stop, detain and search persons or vehicles (including anything or anyone in the vehicle or anything on it), and seize such items if found (see Appendix 5). This power may be exercised in any public place. It should be noted that if persons within a vehicle are searched, there

---

3   Home Office, *Police and Criminal Evidence Act 1984 (s 60(1)(a) and s 66(1)): Codes of Practice A–E* (revised edn, London: The Stationery Office, 2003).

must be reasonable grounds for suspecting that they are personally carrying such items in order to justify searching them.

The above paragraph provides a general statement of s 1. We now have to examine the following points, namely: what constitutes 'reasonable grounds for suspecting', what is the definition of stolen or prohibited articles and what is a public place?

Reasonable grounds for suspecting (or reasonable suspicion)

The term 'reasonable grounds for suspecting' is mentioned in PACE under a number of provisions and not just s 1, but this statute does not define its meaning. Therefore, we have to examine a variety of sources in order to ascertain both its definition and how it should be applied. To begin with, the question of reasonable suspicion is tested objectively, meaning: '... facts and circumstances which would lead an impartial third party to form the belief or suspicion in question.'[4] One of the main complaints from particularly young people in the areas affected by the inner city riots of 1981, especially those from the ethnic community, was that the police had arbitrarily or randomly exercised their stop and search powers simply by virtue of the fact that those persons were on the street. In some cases, the police were alleged to have made statements that they merely had a feeling that those suspects were generally 'up to no good'. The latter constitutes a purely *subjective* approach to suspicion, which is forbidden under PACE and the Codes of Practice.

Guidance as to what constitutes the *objective* test of suspicion is given in Code A, in paras 2.2–2.11 (*searches requiring reasonable grounds for suspicion*),[5] which state:

> 2.2   Reasonable grounds for suspicion depend on the circumstances in each case. There must be an objective basis for that suspicion based on facts, information, and/or intelligence which are relevant to the likelihood of finding an article of a certain kind or, in the case of searches under section 43 of the Terrorism Act 2000, to the likelihood that the person is a terrorist. Reasonable suspicion can never be supported on the basis of personal factors alone without reliable supporting intelligence or information or some specific behaviour by the person concerned. For example, a person's race, age, appearance, or the fact that the person is known to have a previous conviction, cannot be used alone or in combination with each other as the reason for searching that person. Reasonable suspicion cannot be based on generalisations or stereotypical images of certain groups or categories of people as more likely to be involved in criminal activity.

> 2.3   Reasonable suspicion can sometimes exist without specific information or intelligence and on the basis of some level of generalisation stemming from the behaviour of a person. For example, if an officer encounters someone on the street at

---

4   Clark, D, *Bevan and Lidstone's The Investigation of Crime: A Guide to the Law of Criminal Investigation* (3rd edn, London: Butterworths, 2004).

5   The upshot of these provisions is that, *normally*, the police cannot justify stopping and searching a person just because of his or her appearance. However, the situation may be different where the police receive reliable information or intelligence that a group or gang habitually and unlawfully carries knives, weapons or controlled drugs, and membership of it is denoted by the wearing of distinctive clothing or other means of identification. This may still constitute an objective ground for suspecting that a person wearing such identification may be carrying such items unlawfully (see Code 2.6).

night who is obviously trying to hide something, the officer may (depending on the other surrounding circumstances) base such suspicion on the fact that this kind of behaviour is often linked to stolen or prohibited articles being carried. Similarly, for the purposes of section 43 of the Terrorism Act 2000, suspicion that a person is a terrorist may arise from the person's behaviour at or near a location which has been identified as a potential target for terrorists.

2.4 However, reasonable suspicion should normally be linked to accurate and current intelligence or information, such as information describing an article being carried, a suspected offender, or a person who has been seen carrying a type of article known to have been stolen recently from premises in the area. Searches based on accurate and current intelligence or information are more likely to be effective. Targeting searches in a particular area at specified crime problems increases their effectiveness and minimises inconvenience to law-abiding members of the public. It also helps in justifying the use of searches both to those who are searched and to the general public. This does not however prevent stop and search powers being exercised in other locations where such powers may be exercised and reasonable suspicion exists.

2.5 Searches are more likely to be effective, legitimate, and secure public confidence when reasonable suspicion is based on a range of factors. The overall use of these powers is more likely to be effective when up to date and accurate intelligence or information is communicated to officers and they are well-informed about local crime patterns.

2.6 Where there is reliable information or intelligence that members of a group or gang habitually carry knives unlawfully or weapons or controlled drugs, and wear a distinctive item of clothing or other means of identification to indicate their membership of the group or gang, that distinctive item of clothing or other means of identification may provide reasonable grounds to stop and search a person [see Note 9].

2.7 A police officer may have reasonable grounds to suspect that a person is in innocent possession of a stolen or prohibited article or other item for which he or she is empowered to search. In that case the officer may stop and search the person even though there would be no power of arrest.

2.8 Under section 43(1) of the Terrorism Act 2000 a constable may stop and search a person whom the officer reasonably suspects to be a terrorist to discover whether the person is in possession of anything which may constitute evidence that the person is a terrorist. These searches may only be carried out by an officer of the same sex as the person searched.

2.9 An officer who has reasonable grounds for suspicion may detain the person concerned in order to carry out a search. Before carrying out a search the officer may ask questions about the person's behaviour or presence in circumstances which gave rise to the suspicion. As a result of questioning the detained person, the reasonable grounds for suspicion necessary to detain that person may be confirmed or, because of a satisfactory explanation, be eliminated [see Notes 2 and 3]. Questioning may also reveal reasonable grounds to suspect the possession of a different kind of unlawful article from that originally suspected. Reasonable grounds for suspicion, however, cannot be provided retrospectively by such questioning during a person's detention or by refusal to answer any questions put.

2.10 If, as a result of questioning before a search, or other circumstances which come to the attention of the officer, there ceases to be reasonable grounds for suspecting that an article is being carried of a kind for which there is a power to stop and search, no search may take place [see Note 3]. In the absence of any other lawful power to detain, the person is free to leave at will and must be so informed.

2.11 There is no power to stop or detain a person in order to find grounds for a search. Police officers have many encounters with members of the public which do not involve detaining people against their will. If reasonable grounds for suspicion emerge during such an encounter, the officer may search the person even though no grounds existed when the encounter began. In an officer is detaining someone for the purpose of a search, he or she should inform the person as soon as detention begins.

The issue of reasonable suspicion has been subject to judicial interpretation in a number of cases, which include the following. In *Black v DPP* (1995), the police entered premises belonging to the defendant's brother in accordance with a search warrant under the Misuse of Drugs Act 1971. While the search was in progress, the defendant arrived, carrying a bag and was suspected by the police of attending the premises in order to buy or sell drugs. The police wished to search the defendant and asked him to enter the premises for this purpose, but he became aggressive, threw the bag down and then attempted to leave the premises. He was charged and later convicted of obstruction under s 23(4)(a) of the 1971 Act. The Divisional Court held that a person merely arriving at the address of a known drug dealer did not amount to conduct which constituted reasonable grounds for suspecting that person of possessing a controlled drug and that the defendant's behaviour after he was detained could not retrospectively provide such grounds. The defendant's conviction was quashed.

In *Samuels v Commissioner of Police for the Metropolis* (1999), S sued the police for damages under what may generally be termed unlawful detention. Earlier, he had been acquitted of the charge of assault on police. S was stopped by a police officer whilst walking home and was asked where he was going. S did not venture any significant information and stated that he had the right to go where he wanted. He then continued his journey but, when he was nearly home, the police officer stated that he wished to search S, because he suspected him of being in possession of a prohibited article. The officer later gave evidence that he thought S may have been carrying a screwdriver and his manner of walking was suspicious. It was ruled by the trial judge that the stop and search of S was based on reasonable grounds. The Court of Appeal, however, had to consider whether that suspicion was reasonable. In allowing the appeal, the court held that if the police officer did not have the prerequisite reasonable suspicion before he approached S, then the conduct of S immediately afterwards could not transform an unreasonable suspicion into one which was reasonable. The issue of reasonable suspicion was also considered in *O'Hara v Chief Constable of the RUC* (1997), although this was in the context of police powers of arrest and is therefore discussed in Chapter 3.

It is important to note that a police officer does not have the power to stop a person against their will in order to establish any grounds for suspicion; neither may a person's refusal to answer questions constitute reasonable suspicion. In *Rice v Connolly* (1966), it was held that citizens are under no *general* legal duty to answer questions put to them by the police. However, such refusal may reinforce a police officer's existing suspicion, but this may not singularly justify stopping and detaining a person. The essence of reasonable suspicion, within the context of PACE, is that there must be a tangible and positive condition present to justify the use of police powers of stop and search under s 1.

Under other legislation, namely s 60 of the Criminal Justice and Public Order Act 1994 (as amended) and s 44 of the Terrorism Act 2000, a number of stop and search powers have been conferred upon the police which do not require reasonable suspicion as a prerequisite for these powers to be exercised. These important developments will be discussed later in this chapter, together with more recent provisions under s 60AA of the Criminal Justice and Public Order Act 1994.

Another important term used frequently in PACE is 'reasonable grounds for believing'. What is the difference between reasonable grounds to *believe* and reasonable grounds to *suspect*? First, a much higher criteria is set when the exercise of certain police powers require reasonable belief, rather than suspicion. This is because many of the powers requiring reasonable belief generally impose a greater restriction on the liberty of those against whom they are being used. Belief is therefore much closer to certainty than suspicion:

> If, therefore, there are 10 steps from mere suspicion to a state of certainty, or an acceptance that something is true, then reasonable suspicion may be as low as step two or three, whilst reasonable belief may be as high as step nine.[6]

Secondly, it has been propounded that many of the powers under PACE that require reasonable belief are often exercised following decisions made as a result of consultation and reflection, whereas many powers requiring reasonable suspicion are often made in street situations, requiring quick, if not instant, decisions.[7]

Stolen and prohibited articles

The definition of *stolen articles* not only includes property actually stolen by the suspect, but also property being dishonestly handled by him or her. In effect, any property dishonestly obtained falls within the scope of s 1, whether or not obtained in this country.[8]

Prohibited articles fall under two main categories, namely offensive weapons as well as certain other dangerous instruments, and articles for use in theft, cheat or criminal damage. The definition of offensive weapons is best explained by referring to the three main classes of articles which fall under this heading. First, there are items which are made specifically for the purpose of inflicting physical harm, such as bayonets and knuckledusters. Secondly, there are weapons which have been adapted in order to cause injury, where an ordinary object has been transformed into something capable of achieving this purpose. Examples include a broom handle with a nail or spike driven through it or a metal comb being sharpened at one end to produce a razor-sharp edge. Finally, there is the third category of offensive weapons, which are neither *made* nor *adapted*, but are simply *intended* to be used to cause injury. Such items are ordinary

---

6   *Op cit*, Clark, fn 4.
7   *Op cit*, Clark, fn 4.
8   *Op cit*, Clark, fn 4.

objects, which are intended to cause physical harm, even though they have not had their substance or form altered. Examples include bunches of keys, belts and walking sticks.[9] In summary, offensive weapons may either be *made*, *adapted* or may fall into neither category but may be *intended* to be used as a weapon.

Having an offensive weapon in a public place, without lawful authority or reasonable excuse, is an offence under s 1 of the Prevention of Crime Act 1953. The meaning of 'public place' is defined below, but the interpretation of the terms 'lawful authority' and 'reasonable excuse' will now be discussed. Lawful authority simply includes certain classes of persons who are allowed to carry what would otherwise be regarded as offensive weapons, but for their professional duty. This includes the carrying of axes by firefighters and batons by police officers. The defence of reasonable excuse covers a variety of situations where the circumstances under which a person carries an offensive weapon negates any intention to cause harm. Since the introduction of s 1 of the Prevention of Crime Act 1953, there has been a considerable build up of case law in an endeavour to clarify what constitutes 'reasonable excuse'. These cases indicate that the courts interpret this term very narrowly in order to, *inter alia*, deter citizens taking the law into their own hands. For example, in *Houghton v Chief Constable of Greater Manchester* (1987), it was held that carrying a police truncheon only to authenticate a police uniform being worn on the way to or from a fancy dress party fell within the definition of reasonable excuse. However, in *R v Peacock* (1973), the court warned that where a weapon was being carried for self-defence purposes, generally, only those fearing immediate attack would be able to rely on the defence of reasonable excuse. This obviates those who carry offensive weapons in response to a general or widespread fear of being attacked, such as people carrying knives while walking the streets, because of a high number of muggings in their neighbourhood, or taxi drivers carrying coshes in their cabs, because of colleagues being robbed. However, in *Evans v Hughes* (1972), it was held that the carrying of a weapon a week after an attack could constitute a reasonable excuse.[10]

The above provisions have been augmented by s 139 of the Criminal Justice Act 1988, which created the offence of having articles with blades or sharp points in public places without lawful authority or reasonable excuse. In effect, this extended the law regarding possession of offensive weapons, although it does not apply to folding pocket knives with a blade less than three inches in length when exposed. Blades and sharp points prohibited under s 139 are also included under the heading of prohibited articles for the purposes of s 1 of PACE.

The second meaning of the term 'prohibited articles' applies to articles made, adapted to be used or intended to be used in burglary, theft, taking a motor vehicle without consent, obtaining property by deception, or destroying or damaging property. These have included a variety of objects such as housebreaking implements, jemmies, screwdrivers and skeleton keys, although it has also included less obvious items such as gloves, adhesive tape (to muffle the sound of breaking glass) and credit cards (to open locks as well as to commit offences of deception). The inclusion of objects used to destroy or damage property is a more recent addition through s 1(2) of

---

9   Jason-Lloyd, L, 'The Offensive Weapons Act 1996 – an overview' (1996) 160 JP 931.
10   *Ibid.*

the Criminal Justice Act 2003 that amended s 1(8) of PACE accordingly. Although criminal damage covers a wide variety of vandalism, one of the main purposes behind this recent inclusion is to combat graffiti.

Definition of 'public place'

Under s 1(1) of PACE, police powers of stop and search may be exercised as follows:

(a) in any place to which, at the time when he proposes to exercise the power, the public or any section of the public has access, on payment or otherwise, as of right or by virtue of express or implied permission; or

(b) in any other place to which people have ready access at the time when he proposes to exercise the power, but which is not a dwelling.

The above generally includes the streets, parks and garage forecourts, as well as museums, cinemas, supermarkets, football grounds and public houses. It has also been subscribed that any open ground or fenced land with an open gate, or even a building which is not a dwelling, with an unlocked, unattended door, can fall under the description of a public place. In effect, these are places where ready access can be gained rather than right of access although, ultimately, it is for the courts to decide in such cases.[11] However, this does not include schools and universities.[12] It was largely because of the exclusion of schools from the ambit of public places that the Offensive Weapons Act 1996 was enacted, in order to give the police powers to search such places and persons in them for offensive weapons and knives (see the coverage of the 1996 Act in Chapter 4).

It has been generally mentioned above that police stop and search powers under s 1 of PACE may not be exercised in a dwelling. This includes persons or vehicles in any garden, yard, land or building which constitutes a dwelling, unless the police have reasonable cause to *believe*[13] that the person or individual in charge of the vehicle does not reside there, and that the resident has not given his or her express or implied permission for the person or the vehicle to be there; in other words, being or driving there without the resident's consent. This is designed to prevent suspects randomly fleeing into a person's residence or driving into a garden or yard belonging to a residence, in order to avoid being searched.

Definition of a 'vehicle'

Some obvious, and even amusing, definitions have arisen as to what constitutes a vehicle for the purposes of police stop and search powers. The most well known are motor vehicles such as cars, vans, lorries, coaches, buses and motorcycles. As a result of case law, 'vehicles' have also included aircraft, hovercraft, ships, boats, rafts, trams, bicycles, horse-drawn carts, handcarts and trailers. The definition has even included

---

11 Levenson, H, Fairweather, F and Cape, E, *Police Powers: A Practitioner's Guide* (London: Legal Action Group, 1996).

12 Zander, M, *The Police and Criminal Evidence Act 1984* (4th edn, London: Sweet & Maxwell, 2003).

13 See the discussion above regarding the difference between reasonable suspicion and reasonable belief.

perambulators and an empty poultry shed drawn by a tractor![14] In essence, it is assumed that a vehicle would be known when one saw it.

SEARCH PROCEDURE

The conduct of a search under PACE is governed by ss 2 and 3, as well as paras 2, 3 and 4 of Code A. As far as persons are concerned, the first step is to *stop* that person or the vehicle in which he or she is being carried. The second stage is to *detain* him or her. It does not always follow that a *search* is then made because, according to para 2.9 of Code A already mentioned earlier:

> An officer who has reasonable grounds for suspicion may detain the person concerned in order to carry out a search. Before carrying out a search the officer may ask questions about the person's behaviour or presence in circumstances which gave rise to the suspicion. As a result of questioning the detained person, the reasonable grounds for suspicion necessary to detain that person may be confirmed or, because of a satisfactory explanation, be eliminated [see Notes 2 and 3]. Questioning may also reveal reasonable grounds to suspect the possession of a different kind of unlawful article from that originally suspected. Reasonable grounds for suspicion, however, cannot be provided retrospectively by such questioning during a person's detention or by refusal to answer any questions put.

In other words, if the suspect has been stopped and detained, the procedure may be aborted at any stage if it subsequently comes to light that a search is unnecessary. Under para 2.9 of the Code, this will often occur as a result of satisfactory answers being given as to the suspect's conduct, which gave rise to the police officer's initial suspicion. However, it goes on to warn that reasonable grounds for suspicion cannot be retrospectively provided by such questioning or refusal to answer any questions at all. The power to abort the procedure where a search becomes unnecessary is to be found under s 2(1) of PACE and the duty to inform the suspect accordingly exists under para 2.10 of Code A mentioned earlier, as follows (see also Appendix 5):

> If, as a result of questioning before a search, or other circumstances which come to the attention of the officer, there cease to be reasonable grounds for suspecting that an article is being carried of a kind for which there is a power to stop and search, no search may take place [see Note 3]. In the absence of any other lawful power to detain, the person is free to leave at will and must be so informed.

SEARCHING OF PERSONS

Following the stopping and subsequent detention of a person on foot or in a vehicle, if the police officer still contemplates a search, then, under s 2(2) of PACE, it is the duty of that officer to do the following:

(1) if the police officer is not in uniform, he or she must produce documentary evidence (usually a warrant card), confirming their status as a police officer; or

---

14 *Op cit*, Clark, fn 4.

(2) even if the police officer is in uniform (which must be the case if a moving vehicle is stopped), that officer must then state the following to the suspect (s 2(3)):

(a) the police officer's name and station to which attached (in cases linked to terrorism, for personal safety reasons, the police officer does not have to give his or her name, but their number instead);

(b) the object of the proposed search;

(c) the grounds for making the search;

(d) that the person is entitled to a record of the search if applied for within a year following the incident. However, para 4.2 of Code A stipulates that if a record is made at the time, this must be given immediately to the suspect. Under s 2(4), the requirement to make a record on the spot may be waived in the circumstances mentioned below under 'the completion of the search procedure'.

Any search which then follows must be conducted strictly in accordance with the provisions under s 2(9)(a) of PACE and para 3 of Code A, augmented by Annex A to Code C. Under s 2(9)(a), a suspect must not be required to remove any clothing in public other than an outer coat, jacket or gloves.[15] Paragraph 3 of the Code gives essential guidance as follows:

3.1 All stops and searches must be carried out with courtesy, consideration and respect for the person concerned. This has a significant impact on public confidence in the police. Every reasonable effort must be made to minimise the embarrassment that a person being searched may experience [see Note 4].

3.2 The co-operation of the person to be searched must be sought in every case, even if the person initially objects to the search. A forcible search may be made only if it has been established that the person is unwilling to co-operate or resists. Reasonable force may be used as a last resort if necessary to conduct a search or to detain a person or vehicle for the purposes of a search.

3.3 The length of time for which a person or vehicle may be detained must be reasonable and kept to a minimum. Where the exercise of the power requires reasonable suspicion, the thoroughness and extent of a search must depend on what is suspected of being carried, and by whom. If the suspicion relates to a particular article which is seen to be slipped into a person's pocket, then, in the absence of other grounds for suspicion or an opportunity for the article to be moved elsewhere, the search must be confined to that pocket. In the case of a small article which can readily be concealed, such as a drug, and which might be concealed anywhere on the person, a more extensive search may be necessary. In the case of searches mentioned in paragraph 2.1(b), (c), and (d), which do not require reasonable grounds for suspicion, officers may make any reasonable search to look for items for which they are empowered to search [see Note 5].

3.4 The search must be carried out at or near the place where the person or vehicle was first detained [see Note 6].

---

15 However, Note for Guidance 7 under Code A states: '... Although there is no power to require a person to do so, there is nothing to prevent an officer from asking a person to voluntarily remove more than an outer coat, jacket or gloves (and headgear or footwear under section 45(3) of the Terrorism Act 2000) in public.'

3.5 There is no power to require a person to remove any clothing in public other than an outer coat, jacket or gloves except under section 45(3) of the Terrorism Act 2000 (which empowers a constable conducting a search under section 44(1) or 44(2) of that Act to require a person to remove headgear and footwear in public) and under section 60AA of the Criminal Justice and Public Order Act 1994 (which empowers a constable to require a person to remove any item worn to conceal identity) [see Notes 4 and 6]. A search in public of a person's clothing which has not been removed must be restricted to a superficial examination of outer garments. This does not, however, prevent an officer from placing his or her hand inside the pockets of the outer clothing, or feeling round the inside of collars, socks and shoes if this is reasonably necessary in the circumstances to look for the object of the search or to remove and examine any item reasonably suspected to be the object of the search. For the same reasons, subject to the restrictions on the removal of headgear, a person's hair may also be searched in public [see paras 3.1 and 3.3].

3.6 Where on reasonable grounds it is considered necessary to conduct a more thorough search (eg by requiring a person to take off a T-shirt), this must be done out of public view, for example, in a police van unless paragraph 3.7 applies, or police station if there is one nearby [see Note 6]. Any search involving the removal of more than an outer coat, jacket, gloves, headgear or footwear, or any other item concealing identity, may only be made by an officer of the same sex as the person searched and may not be made in the presence of anyone of the opposite sex unless the person searched specifically requests it [see Notes 4, 7 and 8].

3.7 Searches involving exposure of intimate parts of the body must not be conducted as a routine extension of a less thorough search, simply because nothing is found in the course of the initial search. Searches involving exposure of intimate parts of the body may be carried out only at a nearby police station or other nearby location which is out of public view (but not a police vehicle). These searches must be conducted in accordance with paragraph 11 of Annex A to Code C except that an intimate search mentioned in paragraph 11(f) of Annex A to Code C may not be authorised or carried out under any stop and search powers. The other provisions of Code C do not apply to the conduct and recording of searches of persons detained at police stations in the exercise of stop and search powers [see Note 7].

Strip searches

Under para 10 of Annex A to Code C, the justifications for making strip searches are as follows:

10 A strip search may take place only if it is considered necessary to remove an article which a detainee would not be allowed to keep, and the officer reasonably considers that the detainee might have concealed such an article. Strip searches shall not be routinely carried out where there is no reason to consider that articles have been concealed.

Where a strip search is necessary and involves the exposure of intimate parts of the body, the following rules under para 11 of Annex A to Code C will apply:

11 When strip searches are conducted:

(a) a police officer carrying out a strip search must be the same sex as the detainee;

(b) the search shall take place in an area where the detainee cannot be seen by anyone who does not need to be present, nor by a member of the opposite sex except an appropriate adult who has been specifically requested by the detainee; [See Chapter 6 for the definition of 'appropriate adult'.]

(c) except in cases of urgency, where there is a risk of serious harm to the detainee or to others, whenever a strip search involves exposure of intimate body parts, there must be at least two people present other than the detainee, and if the search is of a juvenile or a mentally disordered or otherwise mentally vulnerable person, one of the people must be the appropriate adult. Except in urgent cases as above, a search of a juvenile may take place in the absence of the appropriate adult only if the juvenile signifies in the presence of the appropriate adult that they do not want the adult to be present during the search and the adult agrees. A record shall be made of the juvenile's decision and signed by the appropriate adult. The presence of more than two people, other than an appropriate adult, shall be permitted only in the most exceptional circumstances;

(d) the search shall be conducted with proper regard to the sensitivity and vulnerability of the detainee in these circumstances and every reasonable effort shall be made to secure the person's co-operation and minimise embarrassment. Detainees who are searched should not normally be required to have all their clothes removed at the same time, eg a person should be allowed to remove clothing above the waist and redress before removing further clothing;

(e) if necessary, to assist the search, the detainee may be required to hold their arms in the air or to stand with their legs apart and to bend forward, so a visual examination may be made of the genital and anal areas provided that no physical contact is made with any body orifice;

(f) if articles are found, the detainee shall be asked to hand them over. If articles are found within any body orifice other than the mouth, and the person refuses to hand them over, their removal would constitute an intimate search, which must be carried out as in Part A;

(g) a strip search shall be conducted as quickly as possible, and the detainee allowed to dress as soon as the procedure is complete.

Where a strip search is carried out, a record shall be made which must include the reason for it, those present during the search and any result accruing from it.

Intimate searches

It should be emphasised that a strip search is distinct from an *intimate* search, the latter being more intrusive, since it involves the searching and examination of the body orifices except the mouth. Intimate searches can only take place at a police station or in medical premises following an arrest and where certain items may be concealed in a person's body; therefore, this subject is covered in Chapter 5. The above rules regarding strip searches also apply to persons who have been detained by the police following an arrest and are also applicable to Chapter 5.

VEHICLES

Moving vehicles

Under s 2(9)(b), only a police officer in uniform may stop a moving vehicle. With regard to motor vehicles, this, *inter alia*, has a practical application, since a plain clothes officer would be indistinguishable from any other citizen and drivers of such conveyances would be unlikely to stop. Section 2(9)(b), however, does not prevent a vehicle being searched by a non-uniformed police officer once it has already stopped or is parked unattended. There is a general power for uniformed police officers to stop motor vehicles under s 163 of the Road Traffic Act 1988 and, once a vehicle has been stopped, the powers of s 1 of PACE can then be applied. It should be noted that if reasonable suspicion is focused on something which the vehicle may be carrying, the power to search should be confined to the vehicle and anything in or on it. This should not extend to anyone in the vehicle, unless they are reasonably suspected of carrying stolen or prohibited articles themselves. This being the case, the same search procedures mentioned above will apply as they do to persons who are not in vehicles. Whether or not just the vehicle is searched, the person in charge of the vehicle (usually the driver) should also be given the same information as persons who are about to be searched namely, the officer's name and station, the grounds and object of the search and the availability of a record of the search if applied for within a year, or an on the spot record (subject to the exceptions mentioned below). Apart from the overall requirement under Code A that any search should be conducted with reasonable expedition (para 3.3), it was held in *Lodwick v Saunders* (1985) that a police officer is entitled to detain a vehicle for a reasonable time in order to carry out the necessary procedures, so as to make an arrest if the vehicle is suspected of being stolen.

Unattended vehicles

Unattended vehicles may be searched but, since the person in charge of it will not be present, it is, of course, not possible for the police to convey to that person the name of the officer conducting the search, his or her station to which attached and the grounds and object of the search. In such circumstances, s 2(6) of PACE states that, if possible, a notice should be left inside or on the vehicle, in which the officer should identify him or herself and the station to which attached and information that the vehicle has been searched. There should also be mention that an application for compensation in respect of any damage caused by the search may be made and to where it should be directed, and that the person in charge of the vehicle is entitled to a record of the search (s 3(8) and (9) of PACE and para 4.9 of Code A). Under para 4.10 of Code A, the vehicle must, if practicable, be left secure.

Road blocks

For a number of years, the police have had powers under both the common law and statute to stop vehicles, including the use of road blocks. The most frequently used is s 163 of the Road Traffic Act 1988, which gives a constable in uniform the power to stop any vehicle for a variety of reasons, although this is often confined to road traffic matters, such as the need to check on driving documents or the vehicle's general roadworthiness. More specifically, s 4 of PACE enables the police to conduct such a procedure in order to carry out road checks using the power under s 163 if the following conditions exist: where a serious arrestable offence is reasonably believed to have been or is likely to be committed and there are reasonable grounds for suspecting that the culprit is or will be in the area (the definition of a serious arrestable offence can be found in Chapter 3); where there are reasonable grounds for believing that witnesses to a serious arrestable offence are likely to be traced; and where it is reasonably suspected that a person unlawfully at large is or about to be in the area.

The authorisation of road checks must be made in writing by a police officer of at least the rank of superintendent and such authority lasts for up to seven days, but can be renewed, where appropriate, although not for periods exceeding seven days. Every written authorisation shall specify the name of the officer giving it, the purpose of the road check and the locality in which the vehicles are to be stopped. In an emergency, a police officer below that rank may make such an authorisation, but is under a duty to make a written record of the time at which it is given and to inform an officer of at least the rank of superintendent that it has been given as soon as is practicable. That officer may then either continue or discontinue the road check. Persons in charge of vehicles stopped in the course of road checks are entitled to a written statement of the purpose of the check.

Section 49 of the Police Reform Act 2002 has amended s 163 of the Road Traffic Act 1988, and now confers a power of arrest on the police regarding those who commit the offence of failing to stop a vehicle (whether in the course of a road block or for other purposes). Section 49 has also amended s 17 of PACE so that the police may enter and search premises without warrant in order to arrest a person for this offence (see Chapter 4).

The police also have powers under the common law to stop vehicles. In *Moss v McLachlan* (1985), it was held that the police had acted lawfully in setting up road blocks and turning vehicles away, in order to prevent a breach of the peace (see Chapter 3). This case was decided in the wake of the miners' strike during the winter of 1984–85, where the police stopped pickets travelling to a colliery whose purpose was to reinforce the strength of pickets already there. Such places were often the scenes of violent confrontations between the police and striking miners and, therefore, a breach of the peace was apprehended.

FURTHER SEARCH PROCEDURES

The use of force

Section 117 of PACE states:

> Where any provision of this Act:
>
> (a) confers a power on a constable; and
>
> (b) does not provide that the power may only be exercised with the consent of some person, other than a police officer, the officer may use reasonable force, if necessary, in the exercise of the power.

This means that, if necessary, a person may be forcibly searched, although the degree of force used must always be reasonable in all the circumstances. Section 117 applies to all coercive powers under PACE, including the power to make arrests (see Chapter 3).

The issue of what constitutes reasonable force is decided on its own merits, although some guidance has been derived from a build-up of case law discussed in Chapters 1 and 8.

The completion of the search procedure

Any stolen or prohibited article found in the course of a search under s 1 may be seized (s 1(6)) and an arrest usually follows (see Chapter 3). In any event, under s 3(1), the police officer must make a written record of the search, unless it is impracticable to do so. The latter will include instances where a large number of persons have been searched in a short space of time, such as at a major sporting event. This may also apply in situations involving public disorder or where the officer has been called away urgently (para 4.1 of Code A). Wherever possible, the record should be written contemporaneously with the incident, and given immediately to the suspect (para 4.2); if this is not practicable, the record should be completed as soon as possible afterwards (s 3(2) of PACE and para 4.1).

Under s 3(3), the police officer must include the suspect's name in the record if known, but there is no compulsion for his or her name to be given and, therefore, the suspect must not be detained for this purpose. Failure to obtain the name of the suspect must be substituted by a description of him or her (s 3(4)) and, under s 3(5), a description of any vehicle searched must also be included. Paragraphs 4.2–4.4 of Code A state that a suspect's date of birth should also be sought in addition to his or her name and that the following information must also be recorded, even if some of the details are not forthcoming: a description of the suspect if the name is withheld; a note of the person's self-defined ethnic origin; the registration number of any vehicle searched; the grounds (or authorisation) and purpose of the search; the date, time and place of the search; the results of the search; any injury or damage to property resulting from it; and, finally, the police officer's identity and duty station, except in cases linked to terrorism, where, usually, the officer's warrant number is recorded instead of his or her name. This may include other circumstances where police officers reasonably believe that recording names might endanger themselves (para 4.4 of Code A).

Under s 3(7)–(9) of PACE, any person searched or the owner or person in charge of any vehicle searched may obtain a copy of any record made within 12 months of the incident. However, as mentioned above, paras 4.1 and 4.2 of Code A state that wherever possible, a record should be made at the time and given immediately to the suspect. If a person is stopped where initially there was reasonable suspicion, but as a result of questioning is not searched, para 4.7 of Code A requires the police to make a record of the incident.

Informal police procedures

Up until 1 April 2003, the police were not strictly bound to resort to their substantive powers of stop and search in every instance. The following notes for guidance under the *earlier* Code A made it very clear that less formal police procedures were permissible at that time, but subject to certain safeguards:

1D Nothing in this Code affects:

...

(b) the ability of an officer to search a person in the street with his consent where no search power exists. In these circumstances, an officer should always make it clear that he is seeking the consent of the person concerned to the search being carried out by telling the person that he need not consent and that, without his consent, he will not be searched.

1E   If an officer acts in an improper manner, this will invalidate a voluntary search. Juveniles, people suffering from a mental handicap or mental disorder and others who appear not to be capable of giving an informed consent should not be subject to a voluntary search.

There were some misgivings regarding the use of voluntary or consensual searches by the police. It had been pointed out, *inter alia,* that a person who provided such consent was not covered by the procedural safeguards that applied in the case of searches under s 1 of PACE. There were also some suggestions that even where a substantive power to search did exist, the police would still try and obtain the consent of the suspect in order to avoid 'the procedural burdens of a statutory search', notwithstanding the Note for Guidance under Note 1D(b) stated above.[16] This has now changed as a result of para 1.5 of the new Code A, which states as follows:

An officer must not search a person, even with his or her consent, where no power to search is applicable. Even where a person is prepared to submit to a search voluntarily, the person must not be searched unless the necessary legal power exists, and the search must be in accordance with the relevant power and the provisions of this Code. The only exception, where an officer does not require a specific power, applies to searches of persons entering sports grounds or other premises carried out with their consent given as a condition of entry.

Voluntary or consensual searches have therefore been completely banned, except where a person consents to a search as a condition of entry to premises such as places where certain sporting events are held.

It is still quite common for the police to speak to or even question people on a general basis in the course of everyday patrol duties, and this can sometimes even be used as an informal and subtle means to confirm or repudiate any form of suspicion, rather than resort to the more authoritarian use of substantive powers. This is made clear by para 1 under the Notes for Guidance in Code A, which states:

This Code does not affect the ability of an officer to speak to or question a person in the ordinary course of the officer's duties without detaining the person or exercising any element of compulsion. It is not the purpose of the code to prohibit such encounters between the police and the community with the co-operation of the person concerned and neither does it affect the principle that all citizens have a duty to help police officers to prevent crime and discover offenders. This is a civic rather than a legal duty; but when a police officer is trying to discover whether, or by whom, an offence has been committed he or she may question any person from whom useful information might be obtained, subject to the restrictions imposed by Code C. A person's unwillingness to reply does not alter this entitlement, but in the absence of a power to arrest, or to detain in order to search, the person is free to leave at will and cannot be compelled to remain with the officer.[17]

---

16   *Op cit*, Clark, fn 4.

17   The following provisions under para 2.11 of Code A should be borne in mind regarding informal encounters with the police: 'There is no power to stop or detain a person in order to find grounds for a search. Police officers have many encounters with members of the public which do not involve detaining people against their will. If reasonable grounds for suspicion emerge during such an encounter, the officer may search the person, even though no grounds existed when the encounter began. If an officer is detaining someone for the purpose of a search, he or she should inform the person as soon as detention begins.'

As mentioned above, under the section dealing with reasonable suspicion, there is no *general* legal duty for citizens to answer questions put to them by the police.[18] This was held in *Rice v Connolly* (1966), where two police officers approached a man in the street and asked him questions regarding his movements that night. He gave an incomplete answer and walked away. His conviction for wilfully obstructing police was quashed, on the grounds that whilst there was a moral obligation to assist the police, he was under no legal obligation to answer their questions. This is in contrast to *Ricketts v Cox* (1982), where, in a similar scenario, the suspect was asked questions by the police, but he responded with hostility and abuse instead of passive silence, and his conviction for wilfully obstructing police was subsequently upheld. A number of cases have been decided which confirm that unless the police have a specific power to detain a person (such as under s 1 of PACE or where they have made an arrest), they will be acting outside the scope of their powers if they restrict a person's liberty. In *Kenlin v Gardiner* (1967), a youth in company with another attempted to run away when being questioned by the police He was restrained and a police officer was assaulted in the ensuing scuffle. Both youths were convicted of assault on police, but their convictions were quashed, on the grounds that the police had unlawfully detained the youth; therefore, the police officer was not acting in the course of his duty. In *Collins v Wilcock* (1984), a woman police officer spoke to another female in the street who was suspected of soliciting for prostitution. The suspect walked away when questioned and the police officer took her by the arm in order to compel her to remain. The female scratched the police officer's arm and was charged with assault on a police officer. Her conviction was quashed, on the grounds that the police officer did not have the power to forcibly detain the suspect in order to answer questions and that, in scratching the officer's arm, she was using reasonable force to free herself from what amounted to false imprisonment. Also, in *Bentley v Brudzinski* (1982), it was held to have been unlawful where a police officer stated 'just a minute' whilst placing his hand on the person's shoulder at the same time. Both this case and *Collins v Wilcock* illustrate the fact that where a police officer touches a person in such a manner as to indicate that officer's intention to delay or detain that person, such action will be unlawful.[19] However, the courts have been prepared to exclude trivial interference with a person's liberty from the ambit of these cases, as in *Donnelly v Jackman* (1970), where it was held that the police may take reasonable steps to attract a person's attention, for instance, by tapping them on the shoulder. Also, in *Mepstead v DPP* (1996), it was held that a police officer was not acting unlawfully by briefly holding a person's arm in order to draw his attention to another police officer, who was talking to him to try to calm him down. This constituted the police officer acting within the execution of his duty, even though he was not making an arrest at the time.

---

18 There are some specific provisions that impose a legal duty to answers questions, for instance, the requirement under s 169 of the Road Traffic Act 1988, where there is a legal duty for a person to provide their name and address, and also under the Criminal Justice Act 1987, where there is the requirement for answers to be given during certain investigations into serious fraud, as well as similar provisions under the Companies Act 1985.

19 Stone, R, *Entry, Search and Seizure: A Guide to Civil and Criminal Powers of Entry* (3rd edn, London: Sweet & Maxwell, 1997).

Police/public encounters

The distinction between the various encounters that the police may have with the public has been somewhat blurred by the introduction of paras 4.11–4.20[20] of Code A entitled 'Recording of encounters not governed by statutory powers', which state:

4.11 It is up to individual forces to decide when they implement paragraphs 4.12 to 4.20 of this Code. However, there must be full implementation across every force prior to 1 April 2005. Consequently, if an officer requests a person in a public place to account for themselves prior to 1 April 2005 and in an area where the force has not at that time implemented these provisions, no record will be completed.

4.12 When an officer requests a person in a public place to account for themselves, ie their actions, behaviour, presence in an area or possession of anything, a record of the encounter must be completed at the time and a copy given to the person who has been questioned. The record must identify the name of the officer who has made the stop and conducted the encounter. This does not apply under the exceptional circumstances outlined in paragraph 4.1 of this Code.

4.13 This requirement does not apply to general conversations such as when giving directions to a place, or when seeking witnesses. It also does not include occasions on which an officer is seeking general information or questioning people to establish background to incidents which have required officers to intervene to keep the peace or resolve a dispute.

4.14 When stopping a person in a vehicle, a separate record need not be completed when an HO/RT/1 form, a Vehicle Defect Rectification Scheme Notice, or an Endorsable Fixed Penalty ticket is issued. It also does not apply when a specimen of breath is required under section 6 of the Road Traffic Act 1988.

4.15 Officers must inform the person of their entitlement to a copy of a record of the encounter.

4.16 The provisions of 4.4 of this Code apply equally when the encounters described in 4.12 and 4.13 are recorded.

4.17 The following information must be included in the record:

   (i) the date, time and place of the encounter;

   (ii) if the person is in a vehicle, the registration number;

   (iii) the reason why the officer questioned the person; [see Note 18]

   (iv) a note of the person's self-defined ethnic background; [see Note 19]

   (v) the outcome of the encounter.

4.18 There is no power to require the person questioned to provide personal details. If a person refuses to give their self-defined ethnic background, a form must still be completed, which includes a description of the person's ethnic background [see Note 19].

---

20 See Jason-Lloyd, L, 'Police and Criminal Evidence Act 1984 – Code A: some proposed changes' (2002) 166 JP 542.

4.19 A record of an encounter must always be made when a person requests it, regardless of whether the officer considers that the criteria set out in 4.12 have been met. If the form was requested when the officer does not believe the criteria were met, this should be recorded on the form.

4.20 All references to officers in this section include police staff designated as Community Support Officers under section 38 of the Police Reform Act 2002.

A slightly differently worded version of the above was originally included in paras 4.11–4.18 under Code A, which took effect on 1 April 2003. Those provisions were piloted by a limited number of police forces until August 2004 when the latest Codes came into force. The main reason for piloting these latest provisions is that during the consultation process in 2002, serious concerns were expressed regarding, *inter alia*, the increased bureaucracy this would cause the police service. These additions to Code A were motivated by the Report of the Inquiry into the Matters Arising from the Death of Stephen Lawrence (1999) (Recommendation 61). The arrangements regarding the recording of police/public encounters under paras 4.11–4.20 will clearly fall within many occurrences involving the police (and community support officers as in Chapter 7) stopping, but not searching persons in public places. It is not surprising that there was considerable criticism of this requirement during the consultation process that preceded its provisional introduction. On the other hand, the circumstances under which such encounters may occur could fall within the scope of the exemptions to this requirement, such as large numbers of persons involved, especially within a public order setting.

Other stop and search powers

Section 1 of PACE is by no means the only stop and search power available to the police, although it is the most widely used. A number of statutory provisions conferring such powers on the police for other purposes existed before PACE and some have been enacted since 1984. The former include s 6 of the Public Stores Act 1875, which empowers a constable to stop, detain and search any vessel, boat or vehicle where, *inter alia*, there is reason to suspect that any of Her Majesty's stores may be found which have been stolen or unlawfully obtained; also, s 23 of the Misuse of Drugs Act 1971 empowers the police to search a person and any vessel or vehicle where he or she suspects that a person is in possession of a controlled drug; s 47 of the Firearms Act 1968 has also been preserved by PACE. This power enables the police to stop and search persons or vehicles where they have reasonable cause to suspect that a firearm is being carried in a public place or elsewhere, with the intention to commit certain unlawful acts.

Statutory stop and search powers conferred on the police since PACE include s 7 of the Sporting Events (Control of Alcohol, etc) Act 1985, which empowers the police to search certain vehicles for alcohol *en route* to or from football matches; also, s 4 of the Crossbows Act 1987 enables the police to search persons or vehicles reasonably suspected of unlawfully carrying crossbows or parts of such devices, although there is an age restriction in such cases, where the suspect must be under 17 years of age.

MORE RECENT POWERS TO STOP AND SEARCH VEHICLES AND PEDESTRIANS

During and since the 1990s, a number of other stop and search powers have been conferred upon the police in response to increasing concerns regarding public safety. These are to be found under the Criminal Justice and Public Order Act 1994, the Terrorism Act 2000 and also the Offensive Weapons Act 1996, although the latter will be covered in Chapter 4, since the stop and search powers in this instance are contingent upon entry into school premises.

Sections 60 and 60AA of the Criminal Justice and Public Order Act 1994 – an overview

The provisions of s 60 of the Criminal Justice and Public Order Act 1994, as originally enacted, have since been amended by s 8 of the Knives Act 1997, s 25 of the Crime and Disorder Act 1998 and expanded into a new s 60AA of the Criminal Justice and Public Order Act 1994, which was an amendment created by s 94 of the Anti-terrorism, Crime and Security Act 2001. The overall purpose of s 60 of the 1994 Act is to prevent incidents of serious violence by providing the police with additional stop and search powers, over and above those which exist under s 1 of PACE (see Appendix 6). The new s 60AA of the 1994 Act is intended to prevent and deal with a range of offences that constitute a threat to public safety, particularly those where face coverings and possibly other items are used to disguise the identities of persons engaged in violent protests.

Section 60 of the Criminal Justice and Public Order Act 1994

Since the enactment of PACE, the police had complained that the s 1 requirement of reasonable suspicion that persons were carrying dangerous articles, such as offensive weapons and knives, constituted a serious impediment in preventing violent crime. This was a particular problem where large numbers of potential suspects were in a particular locality and reasonable suspicion could be attributed to some, but not all, of them. In response to this difficulty, s 60 of the Criminal Justice and Public Order Act 1994 (as amended) enables police inspectors or above to make a written authorisation enabling *uniformed* police officers to exercise stop and search powers in places within their police area where incidents of serious violence are anticipated or where potential troublemakers are passing through. However, inspectors must inform a police officer of at least the rank of superintendent that such an authorisation has been made by them as soon as is practicable. These authorisations must be based on reasonable belief that such action is necessary to prevent serious violence, or that persons are carrying dangerous instruments or offensive weapons in any part of that police area without good reason. The authorisation should specify the grounds on which it is given, the locality where these powers may be exercised and the timescale during which these powers may be used. The preconditions regarding such authorisations are echoed in paras 2.12–2.14 of Code A, although paras 11–13 under the Notes for Guidance state that authorising officers should also observe the following:

11 Authorisations under section 60 require a reasonable belief on the part of the authorising officer. This must have an objective basis, for example: intelligence or relevant information such as a history of antagonism and violence between particular groups, previous incidents of violence at, or connected with, particular events or locations; a significant increase in knife-point robberies in a limited area; reports that individuals are regularly carrying weapons in a particular locality; or in the case of section 60AA previous incidents of crimes being committed while wearing face coverings to conceal identity.

12 It is for the authorising officer to determine the period of time during which the powers mentioned in paragraph 2.1(b) and (c) may be exercised. The officer should set the minimum period he or she considers necessary to deal with the risk of violence, the carrying of knives or offensive weapons, or terrorism. A direction to extend the period authorised under the powers mentioned in paragraph 2.1(b) may be given only once. Thereafter further use of the powers requires a new authorisation. There is no provision to extend an authorisation of the powers mentioned in paragraph 2.1(c); further use of the powers requires a new authorisation.

13 It is for the authorising officer to determine the geographical area in which the use of the powers is to be authorised. In doing so the officer may wish to take into account factors such as the nature and venue of the anticipated incident, the number of people who may be in the immediate area of any possible incident, their access to surrounding areas and the anticipated level of violence. The officer should not set a geographical area which is wider than that he or she believes necessary for the purpose of preventing anticipated violence, the carrying of knives or offensive weapons, acts of terrorism or, in the case of section 60AA, the prevention of commission of offences. It is particularly important to ensure that constables exercising such powers are fully aware of where they may be used. If the area specified is smaller than the whole force area, the officer giving the authorisation should specify either the streets which form the boundary of the area or a divisional boundary within the force area. If the power is to be used in response to a threat or incident that straddles police force areas, an officer from each of the forces concerned will need to give an authorisation.

It will be observed that the above guidance also refers to terrorism. The application of this aspect of Code A to the prevention of acts of terrorism will be covered below under ss 44–47 of the Terrorism Act 2000.

The maximum period that an authorisation under s 60 may be in force is 24 hours, although this may be extended by up to a further 24 hours, but only by a police officer of at least the rank of superintendent. This may be done only once, since a new authorisation has to be made if further use of these powers is necessary.

When an authorisation is in force, it confers wide powers of stop and search upon uniformed police officers in those locations specified in it. Under s 60(4) of the 1994 Act, those powers enable uniformed police officers at the scene to do the following:

(a) stop any pedestrian and search him or anything carried by him for offensive weapons or dangerous instruments; or

(b) stop any vehicle and search the vehicle, its driver and any passenger for offensive weapons or dangerous instruments.

They also have powers:

(a) to require any person to remove any item which the constable reasonably believes that person is wearing wholly or mainly for the purpose of concealing his identity;

(b) to seize any item which the constable reasonably believes any person intends to wear wholly or mainly for that purpose.

The powers to require the removal of disguises and to seize them under the last two provisions above now exist under s 60AA(2) of the 1994 Act. Prior to this change, these powers existed under s 60(4A), which was inserted by s 25(1) of the Crime and Disorder Act 1998, in order to overcome the problem of people who wear masks to avoid being identified when carrying out violent offences. It is important to note that there is no power for the police to search for such items, although they can be seized in the course of other search powers being exercised at the time.[21] Likewise, offensive weapons and dangerous instruments may also be seized, although, of course, there is the express power for the police to search for such items.

However, it is s 60(5) that provides the most controversial aspect of these powers:

(5) A constable may, in the exercise of those powers, stop any person or vehicle *and make any search he thinks fit, whether or not he has any grounds for suspecting that the person or vehicle is carrying weapons or articles of that kind* [emphasis added].

At first sight, the above provisions would seem to confer almost unfettered stop and search powers upon the police within the times and locations specified in an authorisation. This begs the following questions: does this mean that the police can effect random searches?; are there limits as to the extent of a search in view of the words '... and make any search he thinks fit'?; can these powers be exercised anywhere, since no mention is made of their restriction to public places?; does the power to require the removal of face coverings extend to those wearing them for religious purposes?; and, since there are no express powers to detain for the purposes of a search or to use force if necessary, as in ss 1 and 117 of PACE respectively, can persons simply walk or drive away when stopped?[22] The answers to the first four

---

21 In *DPP v Avery* (2001), a demonstration was in progress within a locality covered by an authorisation under s 60. A police officer at the scene asked the defendant to remove a mask which he believed was being worn to conceal her identity. This was not complied with, so the police officer attempted to remove it but was struck by the defendant. She was subsequently charged with assaulting a police officer in the execution of his duty. At the summary trial, magistrates acquitted the defendant on the grounds that the officer was not acting in the course of his duty. They accepted the argument that the powers under the then-s 60(4A) of the Criminal Justice and Public Order Act 1994 had to conform to the procedures under s 2(2)(b) and (3) of PACE. These include the requirement for the police officer to state his or her name and station, as well as the reasons for the request. The prosecutor appealed successfully to the Divisional Court, which held that the power under the then-s 60(4A) did not give rise to a search, therefore it was not necessary to comply with the PACE procedures. No reason had to be given for the requirement to remove the mask as 'A request to a person to remove a mask is self-explanatory'. A number of commentators have remarked that it would be advisable for the police to give some explanation where possible, as this generally falls in line with the requirements of the exercise of other police powers. However, it is submitted that the facts of this case clearly show that the power exercised by the police officer was a power of seizure rather than a search power.

22 For a useful discussion on most of these issues, see Card, R and Ward, R, *The Criminal Justice and Public Order Act 1994* (Bristol: Jordans, 1994).

questions can be found in several parts of Code A, which state that such searches must conform to the same general procedures as those applicable to ss 1, 2 and 3 of PACE. These include the requirement for police officers to state their name (except in terrorist investigations and other instances where it would be dangerous to do so), their station, the legal power justifying the search and the purpose of it (para 3.8); that, regardless of the power being exercised, stops and searches must be exercised in a fair, responsible manner with respect for those being searched and without unlawful discrimination (Note for Guidance 1); searches *in public* must be restricted to a superficial examination of outer clothing and that there is no power to require the removal of any clothing *in public*, other than an outer coat, jacket or gloves (para 3.5); if there may be religious sensitivities where a person is asked to remove a face covering (such as a Muslim woman wearing a face covering for religious purposes), the item should be removed away from public view and, where practicable, in the presence of an officer of the same sex and out of sight of anyone of the opposite sex (Note for Guidance 4).

Nearly all of the above guidance applies to all searches, including those under ss 1, 2 and 3 of PACE, as well as those applicable to s 60 of the 1994 Act and (subject to certain modifications) searches to prevent acts of terrorism, which will be discussed below. The importance of correct stop and search procedures being complied with by the police is shown in the following case. In *Osman v DPP* (1999), a fair was being held in a public park and two police officers, acting under a s 60 authorisation, asked the defendant if he was going to attend the fair and, if so, they were going to search him for weapons. None of the officers stated their names or stations and then proceeded to take the defendant by the arms. He responded by swearing and then demanded to be taken to the police station in order to be searched. Fearing that he may have had a weapon, the police officers continued to search him and were assaulted. The defendant's conviction for assault on police was quashed on the grounds that the search was unlawful by virtue of the officers' failure to comply with the correct search procedure. They were therefore not acting in the course of their duty.

With regard to detaining for the purposes of a search, it has been subscribed that to stop for the purposes of a search should also mean to detain as well. Also, failure to remain for the purposes of a search could amount to the offence of obstructing police in the execution of their duty and further resistance, resulting in the use of unlawful force against them, could lead to a charge of assault on police.[23] There is also a specific offence under s 60(8) of failing to stop when required to do so for a constable in the exercise of these powers. This could also be construed as failing to remain; furthermore, it is an offence under s 60AA(7) to fail to remove an item (a face covering for instance) when required to do so by a police officer. The maximum penalty on summary conviction for these offences is 51 weeks' imprisonment and/or a level 3 fine on the standard scale (currently £1,000).

Oddly, whilst failure to remove a mask or other item constitutes an arrestable offence (see Chapter 3 as to the meaning of this term), there is no specific arrest power attached to failing to stop for the police. It is submitted that in such circumstances, the police may resort to their powers under s 25 of PACE where appropriate ('general arrest conditions', which are discussed in Chapter 3), or arrest the suspect for the

---

23 *Ibid.*

offence of obstructing police or for any other matters that may emerge in the course of the incident for which there may be an arrest power.

As a result of an amendment to the original s 60 by s 8 of the Knives Act 1997, all persons searched (whether pedestrians or those in vehicles) and drivers of vehicles stopped are entitled to a written statement covering the incident if applied for within 12 months of its occurrence. Previously, only drivers of vehicles and pedestrians fell within the ambit of these provisions. However, paras 4.1 and 4.2 of Code A state that whenever a police officer carries out a search which is subject to that code, a record of the incident must be made at the time, unless this is wholly impracticable. Where such exceptional circumstances exist, a record must be completed as soon as practicable afterwards. Whilst every reasonable effort should be made to obtain the information necessary for a record to be completed, it is acknowledged that this may not always be possible. Where a record is made at the time of the incident, the suspect must be given a copy immediately.

Section 60AA of the Criminal Justice and Public Order Act 1994

Section 94 of the Anti-terrorism, Crime and Security Act 2001 inserted a new s 60AA into the Criminal Justice and Public Order Act 1994 which runs parallel to s 60. As described above, s 60 makes provision for a police inspector or above to authorise the stopping and searching of pedestrians and/or vehicles in specified locations within their police area. The duration of such authorisations must not exceed 24 hours, and the stop and search powers must be conducted by police officers in uniform. The broad criteria for such action is the reasonable belief on the part of an inspector or above that either incidents of serious violence may occur, or that dangerous instruments or offensive weapons are being carried within his or her police area. The important point to be emphasised here is that uniformed police officers exercising these powers under s 60 may also require a person to remove any item which they reasonably believe is being worn wholly or mainly for the purpose of concealing that person's identity; they may also seize items reasonably believed to be intended to be worn wholly or mainly for that purpose (see Appendix 6). Failure to remove such an item constitutes an arrestable offence under s 24(2) and Sched 1A to PACE.

The power to require the removal of disguises has been extended into a new s 60AA of the Criminal Justice and Public Order Act 1994 by s 94 of the Anti-terrorism, Crime and Security Act 2001. This provides a further criteria justifying the requirement for a person to remove any item which is reasonably believed to be worn wholly or partly for the purposes of concealing that person's identity. This is possible where an inspector or above reasonably believes:

(a) that activities may take place in any locality in his police area that are likely (if they take place) to involve the commission of offences, and

(b) that it is expedient, in order to prevent or control the activities, to give an authorisation ...

The duration of such authorisations must not exceed 24 hours initially, and these may apply to any locality within the respective police area. Section 94 then goes on to make virtually identical provisions to those under s 60 regarding the procedures for making such authorisations, as well as those applicable to extending their time limit. Also, in parallel with s 60, failure by a person to remove a disguise worn by them when demanded by a uniformed police officer is an offence. This is also punishable on summary conviction by a maximum of 51 weeks' imprisonment and/or a fine not exceeding level 3 on the standard scale (currently £1,000). Section 94(3) of the 2001 Act has included this offence within the range of arrestable offences which are to be found under s 24(2) and Sched 1A to PACE. In contrast to s 60, there is no specific power under s 60AA to stop vehicles. However, it has been stated that the general power to stop vehicles under s 163 of the Road Traffic Act 1988 could be used in view of the fact that uniformed police officers will be acting under an authorisation.[24] It should also be noted that the new power under s 60AA does not extend to searching for such items, although this does not mean that they cannot be seized if found in the course of lawful searches conducted under other powers.

It appears that the original s 60 provisions regarding disguises were directed mainly towards persons who wore masks and other face coverings. Section 60AA seems to go much further as indicated by the following statement:

> The expression 'item' is very wide and would clearly include balaclavas, scarves and crash helmets. It is not specifically restricted to face coverings and would appear to extend to anything that could be worn wholly or mainly for the purpose of concealing identity (eg where offenders swap clothing after an offence). Although the purpose of the legislation is primarily to ensure that people are not allowed to commit offences anonymously in situations of public disorder, it is unclear whether other methods that hinder identification – such as face paint – would be caught by this new power as it may be difficult to show that such materials amounted to 'an item' which is capable of being seized.[25]

Sections 44–47 of the Terrorism Act 2000 (power to stop and search)

The genesis of the current provisions under ss 44–47 of the 2000 Act is rather complicated. Section 81 of the Criminal Justice and Public Order Act 1994 created new police powers to stop and search vehicles and persons in order to prevent acts of terrorism. These were inserted into the Prevention of Terrorism (Temporary Provisions) Act 1989 under a new s 13A. The new powers applied to vehicles and their occupants as well as pedestrians. Section 1 of the Prevention of Terrorism (Additional Powers) Act 1996 expanded the provisions under s 81 by, *inter alia*, amending s 13A and creating a new s 13B under the 1989 Act. As a result, s 13A applied to stop and search powers relating to vehicles and their occupants, and s 13B applied to pedestrians only. These powers are now contained under ss 44–47 of the Terrorism Act 2000. These provisions share a number of features in common with s 60 of the 1994 Act, although there are also some marked differences, since the anti-terrorist provisions are more wide-ranging and, subsequently, more accountable (see Appendix 7).

The exercise of stop and search powers under ss 44–47 is contingent upon an authorisation being made by a police officer of at least the rank of assistant chief

---

24 Sampson, F, *Blackstone's Police Manual. Volume 4. General Police Duties* (Oxford: OUP, 2005).
25 *Ibid.*

constable (outside London) or by a commander or above (in London) (see Appendix 2). An authorisation, not exceeding 28 days, may be issued if it appears that this action is expedient in order to prevent acts of terrorism, and this may be given orally or in writing, although oral authorisations must be confirmed in writing as soon as is reasonably practicable. The authorisation should stipulate the place or locality where the stop and search powers may be exercised, which must be within the senior officer's police area.

There are, however, certain additional procedures that must be followed. Whenever an authorisation has been made, the Home Secretary must be informed. He may then allow the authorisation to continue for its full duration (but not exceeding 28 days) or substitute a shorter period or cancel it at any time. If the Home Secretary does not confirm the authorisation within 48 hours of it being made, then it will automatically cease to have effect. Authorisations can be renewed where necessary for a further 28 days by an officer of at least the rank of assistant chief constable or commander.

The effects of the above authorisations are that they confer on *uniformed* police officers the power to stop and search vehicles and persons in them and pedestrians, as well as anything carried by them, for articles that could be used in the commission, preparation or instigation of acts of terrorism. In common with the powers under s 60 of the 1994 Act, the police may conduct such searches without having any prerequisite reasonable suspicion. However, the Codes of Practice have also ameliorated the effects of what would otherwise be almost unfettered police powers to stop and search by largely applying the same general constraints on the exercise of these powers as in s 60. These include Notes for Guidance 12 and 13 (minimum periods of time and geographical areas to be set by authorising officers), Note for Guidance 1 (objective and non-prejudicial grounds for stopping and searching) and para 3.8 (uniformed police officers to identify themselves, their station and the object and grounds for the search to be given). Since these powers are related to terrorist investigations, note that the officers are only required to give their warrant numbers, for instance, rather than their names. However, unlike the powers under s 60, these powers under ss 44–47 enable uniformed police officers in public to remove headgear and footwear as well as outer coat, jacket and gloves. Removal of footwear and headgear in public does not apply to s 60 and is expressly excluded from the ambit of s 1 of PACE. One of the reasons why the removal of headgear in public is excluded from PACE is that certain religious groups would find this very offensive, such as Sikhs being required to remove their turbans. In recognition of this, Note for Guidance 8 states:

> Where there may be religious sensitivities about asking someone to remove headgear using a power under s 45(3) of the Terrorism Act 2000, the police officer should offer to carry out the search out of public view (for example, in a police van or police station if there is one nearby).

Drivers of vehicles and also pedestrians stopped under these powers are entitled to a written statement covering the incident, provided any application is made within 12 months of its occurrence. However, the police are now under a duty to comply with paras 4.1 and 4.2 of Code A, which stipulate that, wherever possible, records of searches should be made on the spot and given immediately to the persons searched. Anyone who fails to stop for the police when required under ss 44–47, or who wilfully obstructs them in the exercise of such powers, commits a summary offence. The maximum penalty for each offence is 51 weeks' imprisonment and/or a fine not exceeding level 5 on the standard scale (currently £5,000). Note the significant difference in the maximum penalties between failing to stop under s 60 powers and those under ss 44–47.[26]

As a conclusion to the discussion on ss 44–47 of the 2000 Act as well as s 60 of the 1994 Act, the following caveat under Code A has been made by para 1.4 regarding the usage of these and other search powers:

> The primary purpose of stop and search powers is to enable officers to allay or confirm suspicions about individuals without exercising their powers of arrest. Officers may be required to justify the use or authorisation of such powers, in relation both to individual searches and the overall pattern of their activity in this regard, to their supervisory officers or in court. Any misuse of the powers is likely to be harmful to policing and lead to mistrust of the police. Officers must also be able to explain their actions to the member of the public searched. The misuse of these powers can lead to disciplinary action.

This advice was echoed in *R (on the Application of Gillan and Another v Commissioner of Police of the Metropolis and the Secretary of State for the Home Department* (2003), where it was stated *obiter* that: 'It behoves the police to take particular care to ensure that these powers are not used arbitrarily or against any particular group of people.' In this case the police used their powers under s 44 of the Terrorism Act 2000 to search protestors at an arms fair in London. This action was challenged by way of judicial review, but the judges ruled that this power had been used lawfully and this was proportionate to the risk of terrorism. They also held that in response to a general threat of terrorism on a substantial scale, a stop and search authorisation under s 44 could cover the whole of a police area. An appeal to the Court of Appeal was largely unsuccessful, although the court severely criticised the lack of police training in the exercise of this power. However, leave has been given for this case to be heard by the House of Lords.

Section 43 of the Terrorism Act 2000 (search of persons)

The police power to stop and search persons under s 43 of the 2000 Act is a more directly applied power compared with those under ss 44–47 which have a broader application. Section 43 provides that a constable may stop and search a person whom he or she reasonably suspects to be a terrorist, in order to discover if that person is in possession of anything that may be evidence of their being a terrorist. This possibly may apply to private property as well as public places, although there should be some other legal basis for the police to be on private property in order to conduct the search.[27] These searches must be carried out by an officer of the same sex as the person who is searched, who may seize and retain anything reasonably suspected to constitute evidence that the suspect is a terrorist. Section 43 is augmented by s 116 of the Terrorism Act 2000 which, *inter alia*, provides that a constable may stop a person by stopping a vehicle (except an aircraft in flight!). Failure to stop a vehicle is an offence punishable by a maximum of 51 weeks' imprisonment and/or a level 5 fine. Section 114 of the 2000 Act provides that reasonable force may be used in the exercise of any of these powers.

---

26 For further discussion on this point, see Jason-Lloyd, L, 'Some recent changes in police powers and their effect on road users' (1997) 2 Road Traffic Indicator 1, 27 May.

27 Walker, C, *Blackstone's Guide to the Anti-Terrorism Legislation* (Oxford: OUP, 2002).

Powers to stop and search for drugs

As mentioned above, in the introduction to PACE and the section entitled 'Other stop and search powers', a number of pre-existing police powers to stop and search were preserved by PACE. This includes s 23 of the Misuse of Drugs Act 1971, which provides the power for the police to stop, detain and search for controlled drugs.

It should be emphasised that this power is concerned with *controlled* drugs and not just drugs in general. Therefore, what is a controlled drug? These are substances listed under the Misuse of Drugs Act, which are either addictive or otherwise socially harmful when misused. Most of them have medicinal properties and, when prescribed and used properly for that purpose, are designed to be therapeutic. However, when used for the wrong purpose, they can have the opposite effect. The Misuse of Drugs Act 1971 specifically lists about 300 named substances (together with many chemical variations) which are classed as controlled drugs and places each substance under one of three classes. Class A controlled drugs are the most harmful when misused and these include heroin, cocaine, 'ecstasy', methadone, LSD, pethidine and dipipanone. Class B controlled drugs are less harmful compared with those under Class A, but are still subject to strict legal controls to prevent misuse. This class includes substances such as amphetamine, codeine and methylphenobarbitone. Class C controlled drugs include mild sedatives which, although less potentially harmful than Class A or B drugs, can have addictive qualities. These include diazepam (once marketed under the well-known brand name of 'valium'), nitrazepam (mogadon), temazepam, and chlordiazepoxide (librium). A number of anabolic steroids are also included under Class C, as well as cannabis and cannabis resin that were downgraded from Class B in January 2004.[28]

Section 23(2) of the Misuse of Drugs Act provides that where a police officer has reasonable grounds to suspect than any person is unlawfully in possession of a controlled drug, that officer may:

(a) search that person and detain him for the purpose of searching him;

(b) search any vehicle or vessel in which the constable suspects that the drug may be found and, for that purpose, require the person in control to stop it;

(c) seize and detain, for the purpose of proceedings under the Act, anything found in the course of the search which appears to the constable to be evidence of an offence under the Act.

The search should be conducted in accordance with the relevant rules and guidance under Code A, including the officer giving his or her name and police station, as well as stating the grounds and object of the search. If the officer is not in uniform, then he or she should produce some identification. These rules are reinforced by Note for Guidance 6 of Code A, which makes the following provisions:

A person may be detained under a stop and search power at a place other than where the person was first detained, only if that place, be it a police station or elsewhere, is nearby. Such a place should be located within a reasonable travelling distance using

---

28 For further discussion, see Jason-Lloyd, L, *Drugs, Addiction and the Law* (9th edn, Cambridgeshire: ELM, 2004).

whatever mode of travel (on foot or by car) is appropriate. This applies to all searches under stop and search powers, whether or not they involve the removal of clothing or exposure of intimate parts of the body (see paragraphs 3.6 and 3.7) or take place in or out of public view. It means, for example, that a search under the stop and search power in section 23 of the Misuse of Drugs Act 1971 which involves the compulsory removal of more than a person's outer coat, jacket or gloves cannot be carried out unless a place which is both nearby the place they were first detained and out of view, is available. If a search involves exposure of intimate parts of the body and a police station is not nearby, particular care must be taken to ensure that the location is suitable in that it enables the search to be conducted in accordance with the requirements of paragraph 11 of Annex A to Code C.

This illustrates, among other things, the common link between certain stop and search powers enacted before (and after) PACE.

General points

It is important to note that if any of the procedures under any powers of stop and search are not conducted properly, then the relevant stop and search could be rendered unlawful (see *R v Fennelley* (1989), which is discussed in Chapter 3). Also, the police are not by any means totally reliant upon the stop and search powers covered in this chapter in order to detect crime. A variety of other search powers are available to the police once an arrest has been made, as well as certain other powers conferred on them under anti-terrorist legislation.

SOME MISCELLANEOUS POWERS OF STOP AND SEARCH

The powers of stop and search discussed above are among those most widely known and used within this sphere. A number of other powers exist, which may not be so well known but are significant constituents within the battery of powers held by the police. Some examples of these powers are as follows.

Powers to search unaccompanied goods

The Terrorism Act 2000 (as amended) includes a number of additional police powers of stop and search as well as those discussed above under ss 43–47 of that Act. Schedule 7, paras 9–12 to the 2000 Act enable the police (and others) to search unaccompanied goods in order to determine whether they are or have been involved in the commission, preparation or instigation of terrorist acts. Under these provisions, a police officer, immigration officer or customs and excise officer (classed as an 'examining officer' under the Act)[29] may search any goods, such as baggage or stores, for instance, which have arrived in or are about to leave England, Scotland, Wales or Northern Ireland on any ship or vehicle. They may also search goods which have

---

29 Under s 97 of the Terrorism Act 2000, the Secretary of State may, by order, assign members of HM Forces to specified duties performed by examining officers, although this applies to Northern Ireland only.

arrived at, or are about to leave, any place in Great Britain or Northern Ireland on an aircraft (whether the place they have come from or going to, is within or outside Great Britain or Northern Ireland). An examining officer may board any ship, aircraft or vehicle in pursuance of this power and may use reasonable force if necessary. Interestingly, an examining officer may delegate these powers to another person who is not necessarily a police, immigration or Customs and Excise officer. It is submitted that these delegated search powers may be vested in ordinary citizens, including persons from the private security industry, although the bodies which appeared to have been the main focus of this power when it was first introduced include persons employed within organisations such as the Dover Harbour Board Police.[30]

All persons entitled to exercise these search powers may detain anything found for up to seven days for the purpose of further examination. Should this later be required as evidence in criminal proceedings, the goods may be detained until no longer needed. Anyone who wilfully obstructs or seeks to frustrate the object of a search commits a summary offence, punishable by a maximum of 51 weeks' imprisonment and/or a level 4 fine on the standard scale (currently £2,500).[31]

Police cordons

This is another power conferred on the police under the auspices of prevention and detection of terrorism under the Terrorism Act 2000 although, in this instance, it contains a mixture of provisions which include powers of entry into premises, as well as some search powers (see Appendix 8). Sections 33–36 of the 2000 Act enable a police superintendent or above to authorise the imposing of a cordon in a specified area if it appears expedient for the purposes of a terrorist investigation. This may be given in written or oral form, although verbal authorisations must be put into writing as soon as is reasonably practicable. A police officer below the rank of superintendent may make an authorisation, but only in matters of great urgency. In such circumstances, the officer must record this in writing and inform a superintendent or above of his or her action as soon as is reasonably practicable. The senior officer receiving this information may then either confirm or cancel the authorisation in writing.

Under this power, police cordons may be in force for up to 14 days initially, although a superintendent or above may renew it but, in aggregate, the total period for which an authorisation is in force must not exceed 28 days. Whilst an authorisation is operative, the area specified must be indicated as clearly as possible, involving the use of police tape or other means. *Uniformed* police officers have the power to order any person to leave the cordoned area immediately, including persons in premises within or adjacent to it, and persons in charge of vehicles within the cordoned area must remove them if ordered to do so by the police. Failure to comply with any of these orders without lawful authority or reasonable excuse constitutes a summary offence punishable by a maximum of 51 weeks' imprisonment and/or a fine not exceeding

---

30 See Jason-Lloyd, L, 'The Prevention of Terrorism (Additional Powers) Act 1996 – a commentary' (1996) 160 JP 503.

31 These penalties apply to other powers exercisable under the Terrorism Act 2000 in respect of port and border controls. These include powers conferred on examining officers under Sched 7, paras 7 and 8, enabling them to search ships, vehicles and aircraft, as well as persons, in connection with their powers to detain and question suspected terrorists.

level 4 on the standard scale. This same maximum penalty also applies to persons who disobey directions by uniformed police officers whilst they are are exercising their power to prohibit or restrict access to the cordoned area to pedestrians or vehicles. Anyone who wilfully obstructs the police in the execution of any of these powers also commits an offence punishable by the same maximum penalties.

Under Sched 5, para 3 to the 2000 Act, written authority by a superintendent or above can extend police powers within cordoned areas even further. This will enable premises wholly or partly within that area to be searched if the authorising officer has reasonable grounds to believe that material is to be found there that is likely to be of substantial value to a terrorist investigation, excluding items subject to legal privilege or excluded or special procedure material (see Chapter 4 for the definition of these terms). For as long as such premises are subject to a police cordon, entry may be effected at any time and on more than one occasion. In addition to the power to enter and search such premises, the police may also search any person found there and may seize anything which is reasonably believed to be of substantial value to the terrorist investigation (except items subject to legal privilege). Persons found in such premises who are subsequently searched *in public* may not be required to remove any of their clothing other than any headgear, footwear, outer coat, jacket or gloves. Anyone who wilfully obstructs such a search commits a summary offence punishable by the same maximum sentence as mentioned above.

Apart from this power to impose cordons under anti-terrorism legislation, a recent case has highlighted the curious fact that the police have no general power to impose cordons to preserve crime scenes, especially on private property. In *DPP v Morrison* (2003), the Divisional Court upheld the conviction of a man who defied an order by the police not to enter a cordoned area in a private shopping mall, where a stabbing had occurred. The court held, *inter alia*, that the police were entitled to assume that the owner of the private land would have consented to their imposing a cordon on that occasion.[32]

'Raves' and prohibited assemblies

Under ss 65 and 71 of the Criminal Justice and Public Order Act 1994, the police have been given powers to prevent persons going to certain gatherings, although this has provided them with powers to stop, but not search. Section 65 of the 1994 Act provides that police officers *in uniform* may stop persons who are reasonably believed to be travelling to a 'rave', where such a gathering has already been disbanded under the direction of a police superintendent or above. This power may only be exercised within a five-mile radius of the gathering and the police have a further power to direct the persons stopped not to proceed in the direction of the 'rave'. There is no specific power under s 65 to stop motor vehicles for this purpose and therefore it appears that the police may rely on their general power to stop motor vehicles under s 163 of the Road Traffic Act 1988. The police may arrest without warrant anyone who disregards such a direction and that person will be liable on summary conviction to a fine not exceeding level 3 on the standard scale (£1,000). These powers may not be exercised on

---

32 See the commentary on this case in [2003] Crim LR 727.

an 'exempt person', who is described under the Act as the occupier of the land where a 'rave' has been disbanded, any member of that person's family, any employee or agent of that person and any person whose home is on that land.

Section 71 of the 1994 Act is almost identical to s 65, except that it is applied in order to stop and turn back persons reasonably believed to be going to the venue of a prohibited assembly. As mentioned above, no power of search applies under the provisions of s 65 or 71, although the police may draw upon search powers from other legal sources where appropriate. For example, if any persons are reasonably suspected of carrying stolen property or offensive weapons, the police may exercise their search powers under s 1 of PACE. Neither is there a specific power under s 71 to stop motor vehicles, thereby placing reliance on s 163 of the Road Traffic Act 1988 for this purpose.

Police powers to stop harassment of persons in their homes

Section 42 of the Criminal Justice and Police Act 2001 creates provisions designed to prevent the harassment of persons in their homes. These measures have been included here because they also involve the lawful restriction on the freedom of movement of certain persons by the police. These provisions came into force on the day that the Criminal Justice and Police Act 2001 received Royal Assent (11 May 2001), and were enacted in response to the increase in incidents involving the harassment of persons in their homes by certain protestors. Section 42 provides that the most senior police officer who is at the scene of a protest may direct any person outside or in the vicinity of any premises used as a dwelling to move to a different location. Various conditions and modifications may be attached to these directions, but anyone who knowingly contravenes a direction commits an offence which is punishable by a maximum of 51 weeks' imprisonment and/or a fine not exceeding level 4 on the standard scale (currently £2,500). A constable *in uniform* may arrest without warrant any person whom he or she reasonably suspects is committing this offence. Note that this power of arrest applies only to a uniformed police officer, whereas a police officer does not have to be in uniform in order to make a direction in the first instance.

Police powers to combat anti-social behaviour

A number of measures have been introduced in recent years in order to combat the increase in anti-social behaviour. One of these is s 1 of the Crime and Disorder Act 1998 (as amended), which enables local authorities, the police and social landlords to apply to the courts for anti-social behaviour orders. These are preventative orders which are designed to deal with persons who act in an anti-social manner that causes, or is likely to cause, harassment, alarm or distress to one or more persons not of the same household. Section 50 of the Police Reform Act 2002 empowers a police officer in uniform to require the name and address of a person whom that officer has reason to believe has been acting, or is acting, in an anti-social manner within the meaning of s 1 of the Crime and Disorder Act 1998. It will be an offence for that person to fail to provide his or her name and address or to give false or inaccurate particulars. This attracts a fine not exceeding level 3 on the standard scale (currently £1,000).

Another power that has recently been given to the police under the Police Reform Act 2002 is under s 59. This is mentioned here as it is related to anti-social behaviour and also involves stopping vehicles. Section 59 empowers a police officer in uniform to order the driver of a motor vehicle to stop, after which the officer may then seize and remove the vehicle, using reasonable force if necessary. This power may be exercised where that police officer has reasonable grounds for believing that the motor vehicle is being used on any occasion in a manner which constitutes the offences of careless or inconsiderate driving, or off-road driving, and is causing, or is likely to cause alarm, distress or annoyance to the public. There is also the police power to enter any premises where the motor vehicle is reasonably believed to be in order to seize the vehicle, using reasonable force where necessary. However, a motor vehicle must not be seized unless the person using it in the above manner has been given prior warning by the police officer or any other constable on a separate occasion within the last 12 months that it will be seized if he or she continues to use it or another vehicle in the prohibited manner. If the circumstances make it impracticable for a police officer to give a warning, the motor vehicle may then be seized and removed. Section 60, however, provides that the Home Secretary may make regulations regarding the removal and retention of motor vehicles under s 59, as well as their release or disposal.

CHAPTER 3

POLICE POWERS OF ARREST

DEFINITION OF 'ARREST'

One of the most popularised conceptions of an arrest is the scenario whereby a police officer takes a suspect by the arm who is then led to a waiting police car having first been cautioned. In the American style, one would expect the suspect to be 'read his rights' whilst being handcuffed. These arrests usually occur in the street or other public places, or even in private property, but this is not the only situation under which a person may be arrested. A person may already be at a police station voluntarily, in order to 'assist the police with their enquiries', but could later be arrested. Under what other circumstances can a person be arrested? What powers are available to the police? What are the correct arrest procedures? To what extent may ordinary citizens make arrests? These, among other questions, will be discussed throughout this chapter, but first it is necessary to define the word 'arrest'. An arrest may be defined as the lawful deprivation of a citizen's liberty, using whatever degree of lawful force is reasonably necessary and proportionate, in order to assist in the investigation and prevention of crime, to ensure that a citizen is brought before a court or to preserve a person's safety or others or their property. From this definition, an insight may already be gained regarding the complexity of this subject. This is not by chance, since it is a fundamental tenet of our basic rights and freedoms that no person shall be deprived of their liberty without lawful reason.[1]

An overview of police powers of arrest

As well as recognising the need to reform police powers of stop and search (see Chapter 2), the Philips Royal Commission were also aware of a similar need to rationalise police powers of arrest which, likewise, consisted of a patchwork of statutory and common law provisions:

> There is a lack of clarity and an uneasy and confused mixture of common law and statutory powers of arrest, the latter having grown piecemeal and without any consistent rationale.[2]

The Government accepted this point in principle, but did not accept all of the Commission's proposals as to how this problem could be remedied.[3] In the end, the

---

1   'The right to personal liberty as understood in England ... means, in substance, a person's right not to be subjected to imprisonment, arrest or other physical coercion in any manner that does not admit of legal justification.' Dicey, A, *An Introduction to the Study of the Law of the Constitution* (10th edn, London: Macmillan, 1959), cited in Hood-Phillips, O and Jackson, P, *Constitutional and Administrative Law* (8th edn, London: Sweet & Maxwell, 2001), Chapter 24. This is reinforced by Art 5 (right to liberty and security) under the European Convention for the Protection of Human Rights and Fundamental Freedoms (see Chapter 8).

2   Philips Royal Commission, para 3.68.

3   See Zander, M, *The Police and Criminal Evidence Act 1984* (4th edn, London: Sweet & Maxwell, 2003).

enactment of the Police and Criminal Evidence Act 1984 (PACE), among a number of other things, rationalised and preserved many statutory police powers of arrest that existed prior to its enactment. All such powers work through PACE, especially in terms of its procedures. These statutes include the Prison Act 1952, the Bail Act 1976, the Criminal Law Act 1977, the Public Order Act 1936, the Children and Young Persons Act 1969 and the Mental Health Act 1983 (see Sched 2 to PACE for the complete list). These were preserved basically because of the need to take certain vulnerable persons into police custody or to apprehend persons unlawfully at large. A substantial number of statutes conferring arrest powers on the police have been enacted since PACE. These include the Sporting Events (Control of Alcohol, etc) Act 1985, the Public Order Act 1986, the Criminal Justice and Public Order Act 1994, the Terrorism Act 2000, the Criminal Justice and Police Act 2001 and the Police Reform Act 2002 to name but a few.

At this stage, it is important to distinguish between the different categories of arrest powers that are available to the police. The two *main* categories are arrests *without* warrant and arrest *with* warrant. Arrests with warrant are far less common than those which are made without; therefore, the former will be discussed later in this chapter.

Arrests *without* warrant

As far as arrests without warrant are concerned, these fall under five *main* subheadings as follows:

(1) Offences where the police only are given an arrest power under the statutes which created these offences. This is known as a 'power of arrest'. A number of these, which existed before 1984, were preserved by PACE. For example, under s 1 of the Public Order Act 1936, it is an offence to wear a political uniform in public. Section 7(3) of the 1936 Act states:

> A constable may, without warrant, arrest any person reasonably suspected by him to be committing an offence under s 1 of this Act.

An example of a power of arrest conferred on the police for a specific offence since PACE was enacted is s 3 of the Public Order Act 1986, which created the offence of affray. Section 3(6) provides that:

> A constable may arrest without warrant anyone he reasonably suspects is committing affray.

A power of arrest actually created by PACE can be found under s 27. Under s 27(1), a person convicted of a 'recordable offence' (see Chapter 6, fn 21 for the definition) who has not been in police detention for the offence and, subsequently, has not been fingerprinted may be required by a constable to attend a police station to have this done. Section 27(3) then states:

> Any constable may arrest without warrant a person who has failed to comply with a requirement under sub-s (1) above.

Also, s 63A(7) of PACE, which was inserted by s 56 of the Criminal Justice and Public Order Act 1994, has given the police a further power of arrest. This applies to persons who do not comply with a request to attend a police station to have a body sample taken (see Chapter 6).

It should be mentioned that s 41 of the Terrorism Act 2000 enables a constable to arrest, without warrant, a person whom he or she reasonably suspects to be a terrorist. Special procedures apply regarding the suspect's detention, treatment, review and extension of the review period. Under s 114 of the 2000 Act, reasonable force may be used to make the arrest.

The exercise of a 'power of arrest', as in all arrests made by the police, is subject to the general rules governing arrest procedures under PACE, as will be illustrated later in this chapter.

(2) Statutory powers of arrest without warrant conferred upon 'any person' for specific offences. These fall under a rather grey area and are therefore covered towards the final part of this chapter.

(3) Offences classed as 'arrestable offences', which are defined and listed under s 24 of and Sched 1A to PACE where the police and (subject to certain limitations) ordinary citizens may make an arrest (see Appendix 9). Running alongside these provisions are those under s 116 of and Sched 5 to PACE, which create 'serious arrestable offences', although these have greater significance to police powers of detention rather than arrest. Arrestable offences will be discussed in greater detail below.

(4) Any offences to which there is no direct police power of arrest or which are not arrestable offences, but the circumstances surrounding their commission justify invoking 'general arrest conditions' under s 25 of PACE. These offences are normally dealt with by way of summons, such as nearly all motoring offences, but, under s 25, the police may arrest if certain adverse conditions or potential obstructions are present. Further coverage of this subject is included below.

(5) The common law power to arrest for a breach of the peace. This is the only common law power that was not repealed by PACE and is available to both the police and ordinary citizens. The definition of what constitutes a breach of the peace, together with the relevant case law, will be discussed below.

Arrestable offences

Arrestable offences are covered under s 24 of PACE, which is divided into seven sub-sections. Sub-sections (1)–(3) define arrestable offences and sub-ss (4)–(7) provide the conditions under which these arrest powers may be exercised. Section 24(1) provides that:

(1) The powers of summary arrest conferred by the following sub-sections shall apply:

    (a) to offences for which the sentence is fixed by law;

    (b) to offences for which a person of 21 years of age or over (not previously convicted) may be sentenced to imprisonment for a term of five years (or might be so sentenced, but for the restrictions imposed by s 33 of the Magistrates' Courts Act 1980); and

    (c) to the offences to which sub-s (2) below applies and, in this Act, 'arrestable offence' means any such offence.

Section 24(1)(a) simply means that murder is an arrestable offence because it is now the only offence for which the sentence is fixed by law. The only sentence that can be given on a murder conviction is mandatory life imprisonment (or its equivalent for young offenders). Up until 1998, technically at least, the offences of treason and piracy actually attracted the death sentence. However, s 36 of the Crime and Disorder Act 1998 has replaced this with discretionary (but not mandatory) life imprisonment; therefore, the sentences for these offences are no longer fixed by law.

Section 24(1)(b) is much wider in terms of the number of offences which fall under its provisions. It includes any offence which can attract a five-year term of imprisonment or more if committed by a person aged 21 or over (due to be reduced to 18 years or over) who has not been previously convicted. Examples of substantive offences which fall under this category, together with their maximum custodial terms, are: assault occasioning actual bodily harm (five years); wounding/grievous bodily harm (five years); blackmail (14 years); burglary of a dwelling (14 years); burglary of a non-dwelling (10 years); theft (seven years); obtaining property by deception (10 years); obtaining services by deception (five years); forgery (10 years); counterfeiting (10 years); ordinary criminal damage (10 years); rioting (10 years); violent disorder (five years); bomb hoax (seven years); contamination of goods (10 years); witness/juror intimidation (five years); perjury (seven years); possession of a Class A controlled drug (seven years); possession of a Class B controlled drug (five years) and many more.[4]

Section 24(2) is more complex than the preceding provisions. It lists a number of specific offences which do not themselves attract the five year or more custodial sentences, as in sub-s (1)(b), but are considered serious enough to be classed as arrestable. This list has changed significantly since it was originally enacted in 1984 and has been subject to some deletions as well as many additions. Section 24(2) of and Sched 1A to PACE provide that the following are arrestable offences – the words in square brackets have been inserted for clarification where necessary:

Customs and Excise Acts

1   An offence for which a person may be arrested under the customs and excise Acts (within the meaning of the Customs and Excise Management Act 1979 (c 2).

[This basically includes smuggling offences. Although enforcement of these provisions falls primarily on Customs and Excise officers, the police sometimes become involved in the enforcement of this aspect of the law. Note that the specific offence of importing indecent or obscene articles under s 170 of the Customs and Excise Management Act 1979 is a serious arrestable offence.]

Official Secrets Act 1920

2   An offence under the Official Secrets Act 1920 (c 75) which is not an arrestable offence by virtue of the term of imprisonment for which a person may be sentenced in respect of them.

[Some offences under the 1920 Act attract terms of imprisonment which fall under s 24(1)(b) of PACE; therefore, they automatically become arrestable offences. Others do not, but are considered serious enough to justify making them arrestable under the above.]

Criminal Justice Act 1925

2ZA An offence under section 36 of the Criminal Justice Act 1925 (untrue statement for procuring a passport).

---

4   A more complete list can be gained from authoritative works such as *Blackstone's Criminal Practice* (London: Blackstone) and *Archbold's Criminal Pleadings, Evidence and Practice* (London: Sweet & Maxwell). See also Cape, E and Luqmani, J, *Defending Suspects at Police Stations* (4th edn, London: Legal Action Group, 2003).

[This was inserted under Sched 1A to PACE by s 3(2) of the Criminal Justice Act 2003.]

Wireless Telegraphy Act 1949

2A An offence mentioned in section 14(1) of the Wireless Telegraphy Act 1949 (offences under that Act which are triable either way).

Prevention of Crime Act 1953

3 An offence under section 1(1) of the Prevention of Crime Act 1953 (c 14) (prohibition of carrying offensive weapon without lawful authority or excuse).

[4 Repealed by s 140 of and Sched 7 to the Sexual Offences Act 2003.]

Obscene Publications Act 1959

5 An offence under section 2 of the Obscene Publications Act 1959 (c 66) (publication of obscene matter).

Firearms Act 1968

5A An offence under section 19 of the Firearms Act 1968 (carrying firearm or imitation firearm in public place) in respect of an air weapon or imitation firearm.

Theft Act 1968

6 An offence under –

(a) section 12(1) of the Theft Act 1968 (c 60) (taking motor vehicle or other conveyance without authority etc); or

(b) section 25(1) of that Act (going equipped for stealing etc).

Misuse of Drugs Act 1971

6A An offence under section 5(2) of the Misuse of Drugs Act 1971 (having possession of a controlled drug) in respect of cannabis or cannabis resin (within the meaning of that Act).

[This inclusion was made under s 3(3) of the Criminal Justice Act 2003. This has been made in conjunction with the reclassification of cannabis and cannabis resin from Class B to Class C controlled drugs. Ordinary possession of a Class B drug is automatically arrestable because the maximum sentence for this offence is five years' imprisonment, whereas possession of a Class C drug does not constitute an arrestable offence because this attracts a maximum custodial penalty of no more than two years. However, it has been decided that possession of cannabis and cannabis resin should remain arrestable offences and have therefore been placed under Sched 1A. However, the police have been issued with guidance stating that possession of these two drugs should not be subject to arrests except under aggravated circumstances, for example, being openly smoked in the street or in close proximity to children.]

Theft Act 1978

7 An offence under section 3 of the Theft Act 1978 (c 31) (making off without payment).

Protection of Children Act 1978

8 An offence under section 1 of the Protection of Children Act 1978 (c 37) (indecent photographs and pseudophotographs of children).

Wildlife and Countryside Act 1981

9 An offence under section 1(1) or (2) or 6 of the Wildlife and Countryside Act 1981 (c 69) (taking, possessing, selling etc of wild birds) in respect of a bird included in Schedule 1 to that Act or any part of, or anything derived from, such a bird.

10 An offence under –

    (a) section 1(5) of the Wildlife and Countryside Act 1981 (disturbance of wild birds);

    (b) section 9 or 13(1)(a) or (2) of that Act (taking, possessing, selling etc of wild animals or plants); or

    (c) section 14 of that Act (introduction of new species etc).

Civil Aviation Act 1982

11 An offence under section 39(1) of the Civil Aviation Act 1982 (c 16) (trespass on aerodrome).

11A An offence of contravening a provision of an Order in Council under section 60 of that Act (air navigation order) where the offence relates to –

    (a) a provision which prohibits specified behaviour by a person in an aircraft towards or in relation to a member of the crew, or

    (b) a provision which prohibits a person from being drunk in an aircraft, in so far as it applies to passengers.

[These offences were made arrestable by the Aviation (Offences) Act 2003.]

Aviation Security Act 1982

12 An offence under section 21C(1) or 21D(1) of the Aviation Security Act 1982 (c 36) (unauthorised presence in a restricted zone or on an aircraft).

Sexual Offences Act 1985

13 An offence under section 1 of the Sexual Offences Act 1985 (c 44) (kerb-crawling).

Public Order Act 1986

14 An offence under section 19 of the Public Order Act 1986 (c 64) (publishing etc material likely to stir up racial or religious hatred).

Criminal Justice Act 1988

14A Common assault.

[This was inserted by s 10 of the Domestic Violence, Crime and Victims Act 2004.]

15 An offence under –

    (a) section 139(1) of the Criminal Justice Act 1988 (c 33) (offence of having article with a blade or point in public place); or

    (b) section 139A(1) or (2) of that Act (offence of having article with a blade or point or offensive weapon on school premises).

Road Traffic Act 1988

16 An offence under section 103(1)(b) of the Road Traffic Act 1988 (c 52) (driving while disqualified).

17 An offence under subsection (4) of section 170 of the Road Traffic Act 1988 (failure to stop and report an accident in respect of an accident to which that section applies by virtue of sub-section (1)(a) of that section (accidents causing personal injury)).

17A An offence under section 174 of the Road Traffic Act 1988 (false statements and withholding material information).

[This was included under Sched 1A by s 3(4) of the Criminal Justice Act 2003. This offence applies to a person making false statements and withholding information in order to obtain a driving licence.]

Official Secrets Act 1989

18 An offence under any provision of the Official Secrets Act 1989 (c 6) other than sub-section (1), (4) or (5) of section 8 of that Act.

[These offences are concerned with the unauthorised disclosure of official information, but do not attract custodial sentences of sufficient length to place them under s 24(1)(b); however, they are considered serious enough to be classed as arrestable offences. Offences falling within s 8(1), (4) and (5) of the 1989 Act are offences which are triable summarily only and have been excluded from the ambit of arrestable offences.]

Football Spectators Act 1989

19 An offence under section 14J or 21C of the Football Spectators Act 1989 (c 37) (failing to comply with requirements imposed by or under a banning order or a notice under section 21B).

Football (Offences) Act 1991

20 An offence under any provision of the Football (Offences) Act 1991 (c 19).

[These are the offences of throwing missiles, indecent or racialist chanting, or pitch invasion during designated football matches.]

Criminal Justice and Public Order Act 1994

21 An offence under –

(a) section 60AA(7) of the Criminal Justice and Public Order Act 1994 (c 33) (failing to comply with requirement to remove disguise);

(b) section 166 of that Act (sale of tickets by unauthorised persons); or

(c) section 167 of that Act (touting for car hire services).

Police Act 1996

22 An offence under section 89(1) of the Police Act 1996 (c 16) (assaulting a police officer in the execution of his duty or a person assisting such an officer; this also includes any person who is a member of an international joint investigation team who is led by a member of a police force or the National Criminal Intelligence Service or the National Crime Squad).

[The latter was inserted by s 104 of the Police Reform Act 2002.]

Protection from Harassment Act 1997

23 An offence under section 2 of the Protection from Harassment Act 1997 (c 40) (harassment).

[Although the above offence includes harassment of different kinds, the most well known aspect of the Protection from Harassment Act is that it is designed to deal with 'stalking'.]

Crime and Disorder Act 1998

24 An offence falling within section 32(1)(a) of the Crime and Disorder Act 1998 (c 37) (racially or religiously aggravated harassment).

Criminal Justice and Police Act 2001

25 An offence under –

(a) section 12(4) of the Criminal Justice and Police Act 2001 (c 16) (failure to comply with requirements imposed by constable in relation to consumption of alcohol in public place); or

(b) section 46 of that Act (placing of advertisements in relation to prostitution).

Licensing Act 2003

26 An offence under section 143(1) of the Licensing Act 2003 (failure to leave licensed premises etc).

Sexual Offences Act 2003

27   An offence under –

    (a)   section 66 of the Sexual Offences Act 2003 (exposure);

    (b)   section 67 of that Act (voyeurism);

    (c)   section 69 of that Act (intercourse with an animal);

    (d)   section 70 of that Act (sexual penetration of a corpse);

    (e)   section 71 of that Act (sexual activity in public lavatory).

In relation to the above list of arrestable offences under sub-s (2) and Sched 1A, s 24(3) of PACE provides:

Without prejudice to s 2 of the Criminal Attempts Act 1981, the powers of summary arrest conferred by the following sub-sections shall also apply to the offences of:

(a)   conspiring to commit any of the offences listed in Schedule 1A;

(b)   attempting to commit any such offence [other than one which is a summary offence];

(c)   inciting, aiding, abetting, counselling or procuring the commission of any such offence,

and such offences are also arrestable offences for the purposes of this Act.

These provisions mean that aiding, abetting, counselling or procuring any of the offences listed in s 24(2) of PACE (in other words, being an accomplice to any of them) are also arrestable offences. This also applies to the inchoate offences of inciting, conspiring or attempting to commit them, although there are some exceptions regarding attempts. Section 24(3)(b) states that an attempt does not apply to any of those offences under Sched 1A that are summary offences. This is because s 1(4) of the Criminal Attempts Act 1981 provides that there is no such offence as attempting to commit an offence which is triable summarily only.[5]

An important point regarding the issue of arrestable offences is that certain wide investigative powers are available to the police where an offence is arrestable. These include powers of entry and search of premises without warrant, which will be covered in Chapter 4. This is one of the principal reasons for the inclusion of certain offences under s 24(2) of PACE. Whilst some of these are not particularly serious, several being triable summarily only, and a few are not even imprisonable, they can lead or be connected to more serious crimes.

Under what circumstances can an arrest be made for an arrestable offence? This is dealt with under s 24(4)–(7) of PACE, which provides:

(4)   Any person may arrest without a warrant:

    (a)   anyone who is in the act of committing an arrestable offence;

    (b)   anyone whom he has reasonable grounds for suspecting to be committing such an offence.

---

5   The insertion of Sched 1A under PACE and the amendment of s 24(3)(b) to its present form were effected by s 48 of the Police Reform Act 2002. For a full discussion of the reasons for these changes, see Jason-Lloyd, L, 'Section 24(2) of the Police and Criminal Evidence Act 1984 – codification or complication?' (1999) 163 JP 944; 'New arrest powers under the Criminal Justice and Police Act 2001' (2001) 165 JP 536; and 'Arrestable offences – an update' (2002) 166 JP 736.

(5) Where an arrestable offence has been committed, any person may arrest without a warrant:

   (a) anyone who is guilty of the offence;

   (b) anyone whom he has reasonable grounds for suspecting to be guilty of it.

(6) Where a constable has reasonable grounds for suspecting that an arrestable offence has been committed, he may arrest without a warrant anyone whom he has reasonable grounds for suspecting to be guilty of the offence.

(7) A constable may arrest without a warrant:

   (a) anyone who is about to commit an arrestable offence;

   (b) anyone whom he has reasonable grounds for suspecting to be about to commit an arrestable offence.

See also Appendix 9 which should assist in understanding the following discussion.

Section 24(4) of PACE

Under sub-s (a), any person, including the police, may arrest without a warrant anyone who is caught in the act of committing an arrestable offence. If a suspect is arrested on that basis and if he or she is not committing an arrestable offence, then the arrest is unlawful. However, if an arrest is made under sub-s (b) on the basis that the police officer or an ordinary citizen has reasonable grounds for suspecting a person to be committing an arrestable offence, the arrest will be lawful, even if the suspect was not committing such an offence. This is illustrated in *R v Brosch* (1988), where a store manager had lawfully arrested a man seen in the toilets who was looking dazed and had a syringe in his possession. The store manager asked him some questions about drugs and then took hold of him when he tried to leave and said 'You are not going anywhere'. In this case, the store manager had reasonable grounds for suspecting the defendant to be unlawfully in possession of controlled drugs, which is an arrestable offence. However, if, for instance, the suspect did not unlawfully have drugs in his possession, the arrest would have still been lawful, because the store manager had reasonable grounds for suspecting that an arrestable offence *was being committed*. This constitutes the well known 'citizen's arrest' power, which is often relied upon by security professionals, such as store detectives, since the focus of their attention is on theft, which is an arrestable offence, as it can attract a maximum seven year prison sentence. However, such powers should always be exercised with care, since an arrest which is declared unlawful can result in civil or even criminal action being taken against the arrestor. If the police make an unlawful arrest, as far as the former is concerned, they are usually protected by the vicarious liability mentioned in Chapter 1. Others may not have the same legal protection and may suffer the punitive effects of being sued for making an unlawful arrest (see the coverage below regarding the consequences of such action).

Section 24(5) and (6) of PACE

This applies to situations where an arrestable offence *has been* committed, in contrast to s 24(4), where the offence *is being* committed. Under s 24(5)(a), any person may arrest anyone who is guilty of having committed an arrestable offence or, under sub-s (b), is reasonably suspected of being guilty of it. In both instances, the lawfulness of an arrest by an *ordinary citizen* under these provisions is contingent upon the suspect being found guilty in court. If not, then the arrest is unlawful. This is illustrated in *R v Self* (1992), where a store detective and a shop assistant allegedly saw the defendant take a bar of chocolate and leave the store without paying. He then threw it under a car and was challenged by the store detective. Following a scuffle, the defendant ran away and was pursued and later arrested by a man who had seen the earlier incident. The defendant was charged with theft (shoplifting) and assault with intent to resist arrest. He was acquitted of the shoplifting charge, but was found guilty of two counts of assault with intent to resist arrest. These two charges were overturned on appeal, because he had been acquitted of theft; therefore, no arrestable offence had been committed and this invalidated the arrest power that was used.[6] It should be noted that this was a scenario affecting just one defendant. There is one redeeming feature under these provisions where more than one suspect is allegedly involved. This is illustrated as follows:

> The legality of the arrest is not affected by the fact that the person arrested did not commit the arrestable offence if there were such reasonable grounds, provided that the offence was committed by someone. For example, security officers arrested three men reasonably suspected of theft from their employer. Two were subsequently acquitted; the third was convicted. The conviction made it clear than an arrestable offence had been committed; therefore, the arrest of those acquitted was lawful under s 24(5)(b). The acquittal of all three would not render the arrest unlawful.[7]

However, sub-s (6) significantly extends this arrest power to the *police only*, where they have reasonable grounds to suspect that an arrestable offence has been committed in the first place, even if it is later disclosed that one has not occurred. This may seem to militate somewhat harshly against public spirited citizens who make arrests when an arrestable offence has not been committed at the outset, but the rationale for this is that Parliament believed that wider powers are best left in the hands of trained police officers.

Section 24(7) of PACE

This arrest power applies only to the police, who may arrest a person about to commit an arrestable offence or anyone whom they have reasonable grounds for suspecting to be about to commit an arrestable offence. This would cover the situation where, for example, a police officer sees a person about to throw a brick through a window, but restrains the suspect at the last moment. In this case, the suspect is reasonably suspected of being about to commit criminal damage. This principle would also apply where a police officer sees a person about to stab someone, but manages to hold the suspect down before any harm is done to the intended victim. However, what if an ordinary citizen sees the same things about to happen? It would be absurd to leave the general public with no legal provision for dealing with such situations; therefore, there is the power under s 3(1) of the Criminal Law Act 1967, which states:

> A person may use such force as is reasonable in the circumstances in the prevention of crime or in effecting or assisting in the lawful arrest of offenders or suspected offenders or of persons unlawfully at large.

---

6   See Stannard, J, 'The store detective's dilemma' (1994) 58 JCL 393, November.
7   Clark, D, *Bevan and Lidstone's The Investigation of Crime: A Guide to the Law of Criminal Investigation* (3rd edn, London: Butterworths, 2004).

Note that this provision applies to 'a person', which includes all citizens, including the police. With regard to the latter, this empowers them to use reasonable force if necessary in the exercise of their powers outside of PACE (note that s 117 of PACE only empowers them to use reasonable force in the exercise of the coercive powers under that statute). Whether s 3(1) of the 1967 Act is used by the police or members of the public, it is essential that any force used must be reasonable and necessary. This is a question of fact which is left to the jury to decide. Another point which must be borne in mind is that any force used must be proportionate to the harm threatened. In the somewhat dramatic case of *Cockcroft v Smith* (1705), it was held that excessive violence should not be returned in response to a minor assault. Cockcroft, a clerk in a court, became involved in an altercation with Smith, an attorney. In the course of the scuffle, Cockcroft pointed his finger towards Smith's eye and Smith promptly bit it off. In this case, Holt CJ said:

> ... in a case of a small assault, [a man ought not to] give a violent or an unsuitable return. For hitting a man a little with a little stick is not a reason for him to draw a sword and cut and hew the other.

Serious arrestable offences

Certain offences are so grave that, by virtue of their nature and consequences, the Philips Royal Commission felt that these should attract additional police powers in order to enhance their chances of detection.[8] These include additional powers to detain those suspected of having committed such crimes, the authorising of road blocks and delaying a suspect's access to legal advice or notification to another of his or her arrest. The definition of serious arrestable offences is rather complicated, as is the case with those which are simply arrestable. We therefore have a list of offences which are always classed as serious arrestable offences, as well as a formula for converting arrestable offences into the serious variety. The latter operates under s 116 of PACE, which provides that an arrestable offence becomes a serious arrestable offence where it has led to any of the following consequences or is intended or likely to lead to any of them, namely:

(a) serious harm to the security of the State or to public order;

(b) serious interference with the administration of justice or with the investigation of offences or of a particular offence;

(c) the death of any person;

(d) serious injury to any person;

(e) substantial financial gain to any person; and

(f) serious financial loss to any person.

If an arrestable offence involves making a threat which, if carried out, would be likely to lead to any of the consequences in (a)–(f) above, that will also be classed as a serious arrestable offence (see Appendix 10).

An example of where an arrestable offence may become serious can be illustrated in the following scenarios.

---

8   Royal Commission on Criminal Procedure, 1981, para 3.5.

A person is caught whilst committing a burglary, which is an arrestable offence. However, this could be transformed into a serious arrestable offence if the premises constituted the home of an important government official and the suspect was about to break into a safe where secret documents were kept (see (a)). If the suspect was caught in official premises where important evidence was being held and was in the process of trying to destroy it, then the provisions under (b) may apply. Also, (e) may apply if the suspect was caught in premises whilst stealing valuable jewellery and art treasures, and (f) may apply if the burglar was caught stealing £1,000 from the home of a pensioner and this constituted the victim's life savings. However, (f) may not apply if the same amount of money was stolen from a bank, as this would not constitute a great loss to that organisation.

Crimes which are always classed as serious arrestable offences are listed under s 116 of and Sched 5 to PACE. These include treason, murder, manslaughter, kidnapping, importing indecent or obscene articles, causing an explosion likely to endanger life or property, possession of a firearm with intent to injure, use of firearms and imitation firearms to resist arrest, carrying firearms with criminal intent, hostage-taking, hijacking, torture, causing death by dangerous driving, causing death by careless driving when under the influence of drink or drugs, endangering safety at aerodromes, hijacking of ships, seizing or exercising control of fixed platforms, hijacking of Channel Tunnel trains, seizing or exercising control of the tunnel system, offences relating to indecent photographs and pseudo-photographs of children, publication of obscene matter, rape, assault by penetration, causing sexual activity without consent involving penetration, rape of a child under 13, assault of a child under 13 by penetration, causing/inciting a child under 13 to engage in sexual activity involving penetration, sexual activity with a mentally disordered person involving penetration, causing/inciting a mentally disordered person to engage in sexual activity involving penetration, and causing or allowing the death of a child or vulnerable adult, as well as drug trafficking and certain money laundering offences. See Appendix 10, which depicts the relationship between arrestable and serious arrestable offences.

General arrest conditions

The provisions under s 25 of PACE were among some of the most controversial under the Police and Criminal Evidence Bill during its passage through Parliament. This is because it empowers the police to arrest persons who have committed offences which are not arrestable. At first sight, this would appear to be a rather draconian power, but deeper analysis into the purposes behind these provisions discloses sound practical reasons for this arrest power being conferred upon the police.

Non-arrestable offences include literally dozens of minor offences, which are usually dealt with at summary level before magistrates. The bulk of these constitute motoring offences, apart from some of the most serious, such as causing death by dangerous driving. However, there are also a substantial number of other offences which are non-arrestable, in view of their less serious nature, but which fall within the scope of law enforcement duties that fall upon the police. These include common assault, highway obstruction, litter dropping, unlawful street trading and many more. A common procedure for prosecuting offences under this category is to issue a summons for the defendant to attend court. This procedure is known as 'reporting' rather than 'arresting'. The effectiveness of this method in bringing suspects to court is largely contingent upon the correct name and address being given. In the past, substantial numbers of summonses were 'unserved' on such persons, because of incorrect particulars being given to the police at the time, as well as other reasons.

Section 25 of PACE enables the police to arrest a person in connection with a non-arrestable offence which they have reasonable cause to suspect is being or has been committed or attempted, and where it appears that the service of a summons is impracticable or inappropriate 'because any of the general arrest conditions are satisfied'. Section 25(3) then defines what the general arrest conditions are (the words in square brackets have been added for clarification where appropriate):

(3) The general arrest conditions are:

(a) that the name of the relevant person is unknown to, and cannot be readily ascertained by, the constable;

[This includes situations where a suspect simply refuses to provide a police officer with his or her name, or gives an absurd name which is obviously not real, such as 'Mickey Mouse'!]

(b) that the constable has reasonable grounds for doubting whether a name furnished by the relevant person as his name is his real name;

[Sometimes, a name is given which does not sound quite as absurd as above, but the police officer has reasonable grounds for doubting that this is the suspect's real name.]

(c) that:

(i) the relevant person has failed to furnish a satisfactory address for service; or
(ii) the constable has reasonable grounds for doubting whether an address furnished by the relevant person is a satisfactory address for service;

[In both the above situations, a police officer may arrest a suspect who either refuses to give his or her address (or gives one which is obviously very doubtful, such as 10 Downing Street) or provides an address which would be unsatisfactory for the service of a summons, for instance, a large gypsy encampment.]

(d) that the constable has reasonable grounds for believing that arrest is necessary to prevent the relevant person:

(i) causing physical injury to himself or any other person;
(ii) suffering physical injury;
(iii) causing loss of or damage to property;
(iv) committing an offence against public decency; or
(v) causing an unlawful obstruction of the highway;

(e) that the constable has reasonable grounds for believing that arrest is necessary to protect a child or other vulnerable person from the relevant person.

[The above conditions may generally apply where a minor assault has been committed and the suspect is still in a very aggressive mood, despite the presence of the police, or if the suspect threatens self-harm or if that person is at risk of being harmed by others involved in the incident. Also, the suspect may threaten to damage property out of revenge or there may be a risk of evidence being destroyed. Where an offence involves generally indecent behaviour and the condition in sub-s (5) below applies, an arrest will be appropriate in order to remove such a person. If a person obstructs the highway and refuses to move the source of that obstruction, then an arrest may be a correct course of action. Finally, the protection of children and other vulnerable persons could apply where, for instance, an aggressive man involved in a road traffic accident with a female driver, threatens her, and there are also children or very elderly passengers in her car.]

(4) For the purposes of sub-s (3) above, an address is a satisfactory address for service if it appears to the constable:

    (a) that the relevant person will be at it for a sufficiently long period for it to be possible to serve him with a summons; or

    (b) that some other person specified by the relevant person will accept service of a summons for the relevant person at it.

[Even if a suspect provides a correct address, if that abode happens to be an overnight hostel or a holiday address, for instance, and a more suitable alternative address is not given or the suspect is unable to specify someone living at a suitable address who is able to accept the summons on his or her behalf, that suspect will be arrested.]

(5) Nothing in sub-s (3)(d) above authorises the arrest of a person under sub-paragraph (iv) of that paragraph, except where members of the public going about their normal business cannot reasonably be expected to avoid the person to be arrested.

In *Nicholas v DPP* (1987), it was held that the correct approach to arresting a person under s 25 is to inform the suspect of the offence for which he or she is being arrested and the general arrest condition which exists, such as failing to provide a name and address. As a matter of good practice, the police are advised that the suspect should be told the consequences of meeting the general arrest conditions before arresting that person, for example, by saying 'If you do not provide me with your name and address, then you will be arrested'. Under s 30(7) of PACE, there is a power to de-arrest a person before reaching a police station who co-operates and provides a name and address (see below for further coverage of this power).

Common law power to arrest for a breach of the peace

This is a common law power of arrest that was preserved by PACE and is available to ordinary citizens as well as the police. As far as the police are concerned, it has not been widely used by them in more recent times because of the array of public order offences created by the Public Order Act 1986 and the Criminal Justice and Public Order Act 1994. Also, the police have specific powers under s 17 of PACE, for instance, to effect entry into premises in order to deal with incidents which can sometimes be placed under the heading of breaches of the peace (see Chapter 4). These have made the exercise of their powers more certain, in view of the availability of statutory provisions, rather than relying on the interpretation of the common law in individual cases. However, this power has proved to be useful in circumstances where the other powers may not be used.

What is a breach of the peace? It is important to note that a breach of the peace is not simply noisy or exuberant behaviour, but there must be violent conduct or the apprehension of it. In *R v Howell* (1981), a breach of the peace was defined by the Court of Appeal as follows:

We are emboldened to say that there is a breach of the peace whenever harm is actually done or is likely to be done to a person or in his presence to his property, or a person is in fear of being so harmed through an assault, an affray, a riot, an unlawful assembly or other disturbance.

Any citizen (including the police) may arrest another where a breach of the peace has been committed in his or her presence, or where there is reasonable cause to believe that unless a person is arrested, a breach will be committed in the immediate future, or where a breach has occurred and there are reasonable grounds to believe that it will be repeated if the person is not arrested (*R v Howell* (1981); see also *R v Kelbie* (1996)). The law permits the temporary restraint and detention of persons breaching or threatening to breach the peace, although this falls short of making an arrest. This is to enable the person to calm down, so that no further action will be necessary.[9] This was held in *Albert v Lavin* (1982), where Lord Diplock stated:

> Any person, in whose presence a breach of the peace is being or reasonably appears to be about to be committed, has the right to take reasonable steps to make the person who is breaking or threatening to break the peace refrain from doing so; and those reasonable steps in appropriate cases will include detaining him against his will. At common law, it is not only the right of every citizen, it is also his duty, although, except in the case of a citizen who is a constable, it is a duty of imperfect obligation.

In *Chief Constable of Cleveland Police v McGrogan* (2002), it was held that the following applied where a person has been arrested for a breach of the peace:

- the power to detain that person in order to prevent a further breach of the peace must be based on a real apprehension that the arrested person will commit or restart the breach of the peace within a short time;

- there must be a real apprehension that this will occur and not merely a fanciful one;

- the police officer making the decision for the continued detention of the arrested person must have an honest belief that further detention is necessary to prevent a breach of the peace, and there must be reasonable grounds for this belief;

- the arrested person cannot be subjected to continued detention on the ground that sooner or later that person is likely to breach the peace if released;

- as a person detained for a breach of the peace should be regularly reviewed in order to decide whether continued detention is justified, the rules under PACE should apply in such cases.

This common law power also extends to the entering of premises, public or private, in order to deal with breaches of the peace. As far as the police are concerned, they have relied to a certain extent on the law as stated in *Thomas v Sawkins* (1935), which empowers them to enter and remain on any premises in order to prevent a breach of the peace. In this case, two police officers were present during a meeting held on private premises, although the public were invited. The presence of these officers at the meeting was unwelcome and a steward attempted to eject one of them. Sergeant Sawkins prevented this and a private prosecution was brought against him. It was held by the Divisional Court, *inter alia*, that the police were entitled to enter and remain on premises if they reasonably anticipated a breach of the peace (see also *Lamb v DPP* (1990), regarding the power to enter premises where a breach of the peace is actually occurring).

Ordinary citizens should exercise great caution when intervening in matters concerning breaches of the peace, whether or not they enter premises for this purpose. It has been stated that even the police may be reluctant to use this power in private

---

9   *Op cit*, Clark, fn 7.

premises unless a breach of the peace is actually occurring.[10] The problems inherent when acting in anticipation of a breach of the peace are illustrated in *McLeod v Commissioner of Police for the Metropolis* (1994). In this case, in anticipation of a dispute, two police officers, together with a solicitor, accompanied a man to the home of his former wife in order to collect property under a court order. All four of them were admitted by the wife's mother in the absence of the wife and the property was duly removed. In later proceedings, the wife alleged that although her mother opened the door, she had not given actual permission for them to enter; therefore, they were all trespassers. Whilst the Court of Appeal held that this applied to the husband and his solicitor, it did not apply to the two police officers whose presence was legitimised by s 17(6) of PACE, which preserved the common law power to deal with breaches of the peace. The court went on to issue a warning that police officers must be sure that, before they enter private premises against the will of the owner or occupier, a real and imminent risk of a breach of the peace exists. This case was later referred to the European Court of Human Rights (*McLeod v UK* (1999)), where it was held that the police officers should not have entered the applicant's home, as there were insufficient grounds to apprehend a breach of the peace. Subsequently, there had been a violation of Art 8 of the European Convention on Human Rights (the right to respect for private and family life, as discussed in Chapter 8).

In *Moss v McLachlan* (1985), discussed in Chapter 2, it was held that the police had correctly exercised their powers to prevent a breach of the peace by turning vehicles away four miles from a colliery. It was suspected that the occupants were intending to join fellow striking miners and that a breach of the peace was likely. The defendants were arrested for obstruction following refusal to comply with the direction to turn back. However, in *R (on the Application of Laporte) v Chief Constable of the Gloucestershire Constabulary* (2004), the judges took a rather different view in the light of the following facts. Three coaches containing about 120 passengers were travelling from London. The passengers were intending to take part in a protest at an airbase in Gloucestershire. The coaches were stopped by the police a short distance from the intended destination as there had been recent incidents there. The police found articles that included masks, shields, scissors, spray paint and a smoke bomb, and concluded that the intended protest was not a peaceful one. They escorted the coaches back to London on a journey that took about two hours, and without a break. One of the passengers brought an action for judicial review on the grounds that the police had acted unlawfully by preventing her from travelling to the demonstration, and forcing her to return to London that involved a two-hour period of detention. She contended that this constituted a breach of Art 11 of the European Convention on Human Rights (the right to freedom of peaceful assembly), Art 10 (freedom of expression) and Art 5 (the right to liberty). It was held that although the police had acted lawfully in preventing the coaches from reaching the airbase, they were not entitled to cause the detention of the passengers whilst being escorted back to London. A restriction on their liberty for this period of time could only be justified if an immediate breach of the peace was apprehended and they were under arrest at the time and due to be brought before a court.

---

10   Stone, R, *Entry, Search and Seizure: A Guide to Civil and Criminal Powers of Entry* (2nd edn, London: Sweet & Maxwell, 1989).

ARREST PROCEDURE

Information that must be given on arrest

An arrest is the lawful deprivation of a person's liberty. In order for an arrest to be lawful, it must be based on a legal power to do so and must also be conducted in the correct manner. Part of the arrest procedure is that the suspect must be informed that he or she is under arrest and the correct grounds for the arrest must also be given. This was held in *Christie v Leachinsky* (1947), where it was stated, *inter alia*, that an arrest would be unlawful if such a procedure was not followed. The grounds for an arrest need not be in precise technical terms, but should be given in such a manner that the suspect 'knows in substance the reason why it is claimed that this restraint should be imposed'.[11] This common law principle was later enacted under s 28 of PACE (entitled 'information to be given on arrest'), which makes the following provisions:

(1) Subject to sub-s (5) below, when a person is arrested otherwise than by being informed that he is under arrest, the arrest is not lawful, unless the person arrested is informed that he is under arrest as soon as is practicable after his arrest.

(2) Where a person is arrested by a constable, sub-s (1) above applies, regardless of whether the fact of the arrest is obvious.

(3) Subject to sub-s (5) below, no arrest is lawful unless the person arrested is informed of the ground for the arrest at the time of or, as soon as is practicable after, the arrest.

(4) Where a person is arrested by a constable, sub-s (3) above applies, regardless of whether the ground for the arrest is obvious.

(5) Nothing in this section is to be taken to require a person to be informed:

(a) that he is under arrest; or

(b) of the ground for the arrest,

if it was not reasonably practicable for him to be so informed, by reason of his having escaped from arrest before the information could be given.

The requirements under sub-ss (2) and (4) that the fact that an arrest is being made and the grounds for it must be conveyed to the suspect, even if those facts are obvious, only applies to the police. Sub-section (5) states, somewhat obviously, that this requirement does not apply where the suspect escapes before this information can be given. The words 'as soon as practicable after his/the arrest' in sub-ss (1) and (3) cover the contingency where the suspect may be incapable of knowing what is happening, for example, where he or she is drunk, or may be violent to the extent that the police are compelled to immediately restrain the suspect. The police may later inform him or her of the arrest and the grounds for it when the person has either sobered up or calmed down at the police station.

It should be noted that the grounds for making an arrest as communicated to the suspect must constitute the correct reasons. If not, then the arrest is unlawful and a third party would also be legally entitled to intervene to prevent the arrest. This was confirmed in *Edwards v DPP* (1993), where Evans LJ stated:

---

11 *Per* Simon V in *Christie v Leachinsky* (1947). See also *Clarke v Chief Constable of North Wales Police* (2000), where it was stated that terms such as 'You're nicked for handling this gear' are sufficient.

... it has to be borne in mind that giving correct information as to the reason for an arrest is a matter of the utmost constitutional significance in a case where a reason can be and is given at the time.

Apart from the ethical implications of giving reasons for depriving a person of his or her liberty, there are also practical reasons for this course of action. An arrested suspect may be able to provide an explanation which could have the effect of reducing the charges against him or her (see *R v Fennelley* (1989), discussed below). In addition, in *Wilson v Chief Constable of Lancashire Constabulary* (2000), the Court of Appeal stated that one of the reasons for stating the grounds of an arrest is to enable an innocent suspect to repudiate the allegation. The importance of this procedure is underlined by the inclusion of a new para 10.3 of Code C, which states that: 'A person who is arrested, or further arrested, must be informed at the time, or as soon as practicable, thereafter, that they are under arrest and the grounds for their arrest, see Note 10B.' This requirement is especially important in view of Art 5(2) of the European Convention on Human Rights, which states: 'Everyone who is arrested should be informed promptly, in a language which he understands, of the reasons for his arrest and of any charge against him.'

An illustration of the application of Article 5(2) can be seen in *Taylor (A Child Proceeding by his Mother & Litigation Friend CM Taylor) v Chief Constable of Thames Valley* (2004). In this case, the respondent, Taylor, was arrested by a police officer who informed him that he was being arrested on suspicion of violent disorder, having been seen throwing rocks during a demonstration. This occurred in 1998 when Taylor was 10 years old. He was then taken to a police station and later released, having been given a formal caution. He subsequently claimed damages for false imprisonment on the grounds that his arrest was unlawful. The judge awarded him damages on the grounds that, *inter alia*, insufficient words were spoken to him lawfully to effect his arrest under s 28(3) of PACE, because more information was reasonably required, such as mentioning the throwing of stones. The chief constable appealed against the judgment in which the respondent Taylor was awarded £1,500 damages for false imprisonment. The Court of Appeal referred to *Fox, Campbell and Hartley v UK* (1990), which was considered on Art 5(2) of the European Convention on Human Rights. The issue was whether adequate information was given under s 28(3) of PACE, which had to be assessed objectively in respect of the information which was reasonably available to the arresting officer. The court went on to state that, in this instance, the offence of violent disorder was committed by a large number of people and it was not practicable for the police to give precise details of the case against each arrested person. In allowing the appeal and setting aside the £1,500 damages, the court held that Taylor's arrest was lawful and complied with s 28(3) of PACE and Art 5(2) of the European Convention on Human Rights, on the grounds that it was sufficient to inform him that he was being arrested for violent disorder.

In *Dhesi v Chief Constable of the West Midlands Police* (2000), it was held that the reason for an arrest does not necessarily have to be given by the arresting officer. An arrest is lawful, provided the suspect is given the reason at the time or as soon as is practicable thereafter, even if this is done by a police officer other than the one making the arrest.

The act of legal restraint

When an arrest is being made, it is necessary to convey to the suspect a clear indication that he or she is under legal restraint. This may be done by words (see *Alderson v Booth* (1969)), although the suspect must submit to the arrest, which must then be followed by informing him or her of the reasons for it. If the suspect does not submit or circumstances militate against the use of mere words, an arrest may consist of taking hold of the suspect. In cases where a person about to be arrested is not showing any signs of hostility or likelihood of escaping, it is usual police procedure to take a firm hold of the suspect's arm whilst giving the reason for the arrest and administering the caution. In a more volatile situation, the police may use more physical force if necessary, but this must always be reasonable in all the circumstances (s 117 of PACE, s 3(1) of the Criminal Law Act 1967 and s 114 of the Terrorism Act 2000 regarding, *inter alia*, the arrest of suspected terrorists). It is largely for this reason that the requirement to give certain information on arrest may be delayed until it is practicable to do so. It is not uncommon for the police to meet with such strong resistance when making arrests that this information cannot be conveyed until the suspect has ceased to behave in a violent and noisy manner or when other potential dangers have passed.

As a general rule, the use of handcuffs to effect restraint is confined to cases where the suspect may become violent or attempt to escape. This falls within the ambit of using reasonable force, as is the case where the police use batons, CS spray or other incapacitants, in accordance with police guidelines.

The caution

A further arrest procedure is the giving of the caution to the suspect. This is not covered under PACE, but under paras 10.4, 10.5 and 10.7 of Code C, which provide:

10.4 A person who is arrested, or further arrested, must also be cautioned upon arrest unless:

    (a) it is impracticable to do so by reason of their condition or behaviour at the time; or

    (b) they have already been cautioned immediately prior to arrest ...

10.5 The caution which must be given on arrest ... should ... be in the following terms:

'You do not have to say anything. But it may harm your defence if you do not mention when questioned something which you later rely on in court. Anything you do say may be given in evidence.'

10.7 Minor deviations from the words of any caution given in accordance with this Code do not constitute a breach of this Code, provided that the sense of the relevant caution is preserved ...

Voluntary attendance at a police station

What is the position where a person is voluntarily at a police station and is 'helping the police with their inquiries'? This issue is covered under s 29 of PACE, but is a subject which has attracted much controversy. According to Professor Zander: 'The police frequently find it convenient to blur the line between freedom and arrest. The newspaper phrase "a man is helping the police with their inquiries" has become a polite euphemism to describe this shadowy area.' Professor Zander then goes on to make the following point: 'But, in law, the position has not been in doubt. A person is either under arrest or he is not. If he is not technically under arrest, he is free to go.'[12] Section 29 of PACE makes the following provisions:

29 Where, for the purpose of assisting with an investigation, a person attends voluntarily at a police station or at any other place where a constable is present or accompanies a constable to a police station or any such other place without having been arrested:

(a) he shall be entitled to leave at will, unless he is placed under arrest;

(b) he shall be informed at once that he is under arrest if a decision is taken by a constable to prevent him from leaving at will.

During the passage of the Police and Criminal Evidence Bill through Parliament, it was suggested that such individuals should be protected by certain safeguards, such as expressly informing them that they were free to leave at any time or asking if they wished to have a solicitor. Lord Denning even described such attendance at a police station as 'half way to making an arrest'.[13] This was rejected by the Government on the grounds that so many people attend police stations for a variety of reasons that to introduce such a scheme would cause the police severe administrative burdens. There is one safeguard under para 10.2 of Code C, which states:

Whenever a person not under arrest is initially cautioned, or reminded they are under caution, that person must at the same time be told that they are not under arrest and are free to leave if they want to ...

Further guidance is given under paras 3.21 and 3.22 of Code C, as follows:

3.21 Any person attending a police station voluntarily to assist with an investigation, may leave at will unless arrested. If it is decided they shall not be allowed to leave, they must be informed at once that they are under arrest and brought before the custody officer, who is responsible for making sure that they are notified of their rights in the same way as other detainees. If they are not arrested, but are cautioned ... the person who gives the caution must, at the same time, inform them they are not under arrest, they are not obliged to remain at the station, but if they remain at the station, they may obtain free and independent legal advice if they want. They shall be told the right to legal advice includes the right to speak with a solicitor on the telephone and be asked if they want to do so.

3.22 If a person attending the police station voluntarily, asks about their entitlement to legal advice, they shall be given a copy of the notice explaining the arrangements for obtaining legal advice ...

However, it will be observed that these safeguards only apply when a suspect is under caution and not before then. A suspect can, of course, be arrested at any time during his or her voluntary attendance at a police station once the police have the required grounds for making it.

---

12 *Op cit*, Zander, fn 3.
13 House of Lords, *Hansard*, 5 July 1984, col 502.

Arrests made elsewhere than at police stations

Most arrests occur away from police stations and there is the *general* rule under s 30(1) of PACE that arrested persons shall be taken to a police station as soon as practicable following their arrest. Sub-section (10), however, provides that a constable may delay this procedure if the arrested person's presence is needed elsewhere in order to further the investigation, if it is reasonable to do this immediately. Sub-section (11) provides that in the event of such a delay, the reasons for it must be recorded on arrival at the police station. Normally arrested persons should be taken to a 'designated' police station, namely, a station where there are facilities for the purpose of detaining arrested persons (s 35 of PACE), although there are exceptions to this general rule under sub-ss (3)–(6) inclusive. These provide that unless the suspect will have to be detained for longer than six hours, police officers operating within an area covered by a non-designated police station may take an arrested person there. If it is necessary to keep that person for longer than six hours, that person must then be transferred to a designated police station. These rules also apply to constables employed by bodies which do not fall under the mainstream police forces, such as the British Transport Police. The other exception is where a police officer has arrested a suspect on his or her own (or taken charge of a person arrested by someone else, such as a store detective), no assistance is available from other officers and it appears to the arresting officer that the suspect may injure him or herself or anyone else (including the constable) if taken to a designated police station. This covers the contingency where a non-designated police station in proximity to an arrest may be closer than one which is designated, and the constable carrying out the arrest without police assistance is having difficulty restraining the suspect. This situation is more likely to occur in rural areas, where a local police station may be considerably closer than the nearest designated police station.

There is provision under s 30(7) for a police officer to release a suspect before arriving at a police station, where the constable is satisfied that there are no grounds for keeping that person under arrest. This can occur under a number of situations, but let us assume, for instance, that a man has been arrested under the general arrest conditions under s 25 of PACE because he has committed a minor road traffic offence and has refused to give the police officer his name and address. If the arrested person decides to co-operate before being taken to the police station or whilst en route and provides the police officer with the required details, that person may be released, as there are no grounds for keeping him or her under arrest. However, sub-ss (8) and (9) provide that a record must be made as soon as is practicable if this is done. The power to release a suspect without taking that person to a police station has been extended under the new 'street bail' scheme. This may apply, for instance, where a shoplifter has been arrested by a police officer. The shoplifter is well known to the arresting officer, who knows where the suspect lives. In those circumstances, the police officer has the discretion to give 'street bail' to that person that requires his or her attendance at a police station, but at a later date. However, if the shopkeeper then approaches the officer and expresses a willingness not to press charges if the goods are paid for, and the suspect agrees, the suspect may be released on the spot. The suspect is therefore not taken to a police station or even given street bail, but is released unconditionally. The new procedure where bail may be given in places other than police stations is discussed further below. However, it should be noted at this stage that s 4 of the Criminal Justice Act 2003 has made provision that a person given street bail may be required to attend *any* type of police station and not necessarily a designated police station. The same also applies if that person is arrested and taken to a police station if he or she fails to attend voluntarily.

Arrest for one or more further offences

Section 31 of PACE provides that where a person is at a police station as a result of being arrested and one or more further offences come to light, that person shall be arrested at the police station for those offences. This is to prevent an arrested person being released and then immediately re-arrested for further offences where this could have been done in the course of the original period of detention. In Chapter 5, the full significance of this procedure will be apparent; suffice it to say here that there are strict limitations on the times that an arrested suspect may be detained without being charged. Section 31, *inter alia*, prevents an arrested person being released without charge for one offence when the detention time becomes exhausted, and then being immediately re-arrested for another alleged crime, where fresh detention time will begin.

Searches on arrest

When a person has been arrested away from a police station under any arrest power, s 32 of PACE empowers the police to search the suspect and, if the arrest is for an offence, any premises the person was in at the time of the arrest or immediately before it, whether or not the premises are occupied or controlled by the suspect. The power of entry into premises must be confined to searching for evidence relating to the offence in question and can only be exercised if it is reasonably believed that such evidence will be found there. In *R v Beckford* (1991), it was stated that s 32 must not be used to initiate 'fishing expeditions'. The police must have genuine belief that the premises contain evidence of the offence for which the suspect has been arrested; this will be a matter of fact for the jury to decide. If a person is arrested in premises which consist of two or more separate dwellings, such as a block of flats, the police may only search the premises in which the suspect was arrested or was in immediately beforehand, as well as any common parts shared with others, such as stairways and balconies.

Section 32 of PACE shares certain similarities with s 18, in so far as both empower the police to search premises following the arrest of a suspect, although s 18 applies to premises occupied or controlled by the suspect, whether or not the suspect was in such places at the time of the arrest; also, s 18 is confined to arrestable offences only. Furthermore, the power to enter and search premises under s 32 has to be applied either immediately or very soon after the arrest. In *R v Badham* (1987), it was held that a lapse of four hours between an arrest and the subsequent entry and search of premises under s 32 was unacceptable (see also *Hewitson v Chief Constable of Dorset Police* (2003)). Section 18 is covered in more detail in Chapter 4, since all of it falls within the ambit of police powers of entry and search of premises. At this stage, it may be useful to mention s 17 of PACE, which is also covered in detail in Chapter 4. Part of this section empowers the police, *inter alia*, to enter and search premises in order to execute an arrest warrant issued in connection with criminal proceedings, as well as make an arrest for an arrestable offence or for certain other offences.

Under s 32, an arrested person may be searched on arrest if there are reasonable grounds for believing that the suspect may present a danger to him or herself, or to others. This will often be focused on the suspect carrying any weapons, as is the power to search an arrested person for anything which might be used to effect an escape from lawful custody. Section 32 also permits the searching of an arrested person for any evidence relating to an offence but, in all the foregoing circumstances, sub-ss (3) and (4) provide that a search must be confined to the extent that is reasonably required in order to find such objects. Where an arrested person is searched in public under these powers, sub-s (4) provides that such persons shall not be required to remove any clothing other than outer coat, jacket or gloves. Also, under s 59(2) of the Criminal Justice and Public Order Act 1994, the mouth of an arrested suspect may be searched in public. Arrested suspects could be required to remove other clothing if there are reasonable grounds for this requirement, but this should not be done in public, although such items may be removed in public with the suspect's genuine consent.

Police discretion in making arrests

In *Holgate-Mohammed v Duke* (1984), a woman was suspected of having stolen jewellery and was arrested by a detective on the basis that not only did he have reasonable grounds to suspect that she had committed this offence, but he also believed that she would be more ready to confess if she were arrested and questioned at the police station. This action was upheld by the House of Lords which, *inter alia*, held that a decision to arrest constitutes an executive discretion expressly conferred on the police, which can only be questioned in the courts on the grounds that no reasonable police officer would make such a decision. In other words, such an executive discretion can only be questioned if it was manifestly absurd (see *Associated Provincial Picture Houses Ltd v Wednesbury Corp* (1948)).

It is also useful to mention here the issue of reasonable suspicion with regard to police discretion to make arrests. The leading case, as mentioned earlier in Chapter 2, is *O'Hara v Chief Constable of the RUC* (1997), where the House of Lords considered the entitlement of a police officer to arrest a terrorist suspect. In this case, the officer had acted on information received during a briefing by a senior police officer who instructed him to make the arrest. Their Lordships held that a police officer may make an arrest based on information received from another, *although* this must cause that officer to have suspicion based on reasonable grounds. This issue was later considered in *Hough v Chief Constable of the Staffordshire Constabulary* (2001), where police officers effected their arrest powers based on information received from the Police National Computer. The Court of Appeal held that, depending on the nature of such information, a police officer could base his or her reasonable suspicion on information received from that source.[14] There are instances where a crime has been committed for which only one person could be responsible, but the suspect is in a small group and the police do not know who the culprit is. In *Cumming v Chief Constable of Northumbria Police* (2003), it was held that in those circumstances, each member or all of the group may be arrested.

---

14   See Parpworth, N, 'Reasonable suspicion and the power of arrest' (2002) 166 JP 702.

Street bail

Section 4 of the Criminal Justice Act 2003 has substantially amended s 30 of PACE, as well as inserting new ss 30A, 30B, 30C and 30D. Collectively, these have created a new scheme commonly called 'street bail' (although the Act officially names it as 'Bail elsewhere than at police station'). The purpose behind this new procedure is to obviate the need to take every arrested suspect to a police station where this is clearly unnecessary. In such cases, the arresting officer has the discretion not take the suspect into custody but will require the suspect to attend a specific police station at a later date and time. This will either be recorded at the scene on the appropriate document, or notified to the suspect at some future date. Where a person has been arrested and then taken elsewhere for identification purposes, for instance, street bail may then be given at the arresting officer's discretion; otherwise that person would normally be taken to a police station at that stage. No conditions may be attached to street bail other than the requirement for the suspect to attend the relevant police station as required in order to participate in the police investigation. The time, date or police station specified in the original or a subsequent notice may be varied by a later notification. A police officer may arrest without warrant anyone who fails to attend the police station at the specified time. Although no criminal sanctions are attached to a failure to attend, this is to be treated as an arrest for an offence for the purposes of ss 30 and 31 of PACE.

Unlawful arrests

The consequences on the police in making unlawful arrests are varied. Such incidents can be the subject of formal complaints against the police (see Chapter 1) and may also involve civil and even criminal action being taken against those responsible. In *Holgate-Mohammed v Duke* (above), the arrest of the appellant was initially challenged before the county court and she was awarded £1,000 damages for false imprisonment. The chief constable for that police area appealed against this decision which, as already discussed above, resulted in the House of Lords finding in his favour. Although a civil action under the tort of false imprisonment is available in cases of wrongful arrest, sometimes, an action for assault and battery may also brought in the same case; this can apply where some degree of force was used in effecting that arrest (see Chapter 1 for further discussion of the consequences of unlawful police action). However, it should be noted that in *Simpson v Chief Constable of South Yorkshire Police* (1991), it was held that the use of excessive force in making an arrest will not automatically render the arrest unlawful.

A further consequence of the police making wrongful arrests or otherwise unlawfully detaining a person can be the exclusion of any evidence obtained as a result of such improper conduct, thereby leading to the collapse of the case. Section 78 of PACE, headed 'exclusion of unfair evidence', makes the following provisions:

(1) In any proceedings, the court may refuse to allow evidence on which the prosecution proposes to rely to be given if it appears to the court that, having regard to all the circumstances, including the circumstances in which the evidence was obtained, the admission of the evidence would have such an adverse effect on the fairness of the proceedings that the court ought not to admit it.

(2) Nothing in this section shall prejudice any rule of law requiring a court to exclude evidence.

In *R v Fennelley* (1989), the defendant was stopped and searched in the street and then arrested. In the course of the searches, including a strip search at the police station, some jewellery was found and two packets of heroin were discovered in his underpants. Since the prosecution were unable to establish that the defendant was given reasons for the stop, search and subsequent arrest, the evidence of the search was excluded at the Crown Court trial under s 78 of PACE. This was done on the grounds that, had he been informed of the reasons for being stopped, he would have had the opportunity to provide an early explanation; it would therefore be unfair to admit evidence obtained in this matter where he was denied that opportunity. However, the decision in this case was criticised in *R v McCarthy* (1996), where the Court of Appeal stated that it was difficult to understand why the evidence was excluded in *Fennelley*. There was no denial by the defendant that the evidence was on him and the drugs would have been discovered by the police in any event, although the matter may be different where a confession is made. In *Jarrett v Chief Constable of the West Midlands Police* (2003), it was held that a police officer must have reasonable grounds for being suspicious that a person is guilty of an offence and must also have genuine suspicion. The latter denotes that a partly subjective element exists within the test as to whether an arrest is lawful. In *DPP v L and S* (1998), it was held by the Divisional Court that even where an initial arrest is unlawful, it does not necessarily mean that everything which follows is also unlawful. An arrest which is flawed may be rectified later by complying with the relevant provisions of PACE. In this case, a person was arrested, but without being informed as such, despite the fact that it was reasonably practicable to do so. The arrest was therefore unlawful. However, the court took the view that it is well established that the custody officer (see Chapter 5) must comply with a set of procedures when a person is detained at a police station; therefore, at some stage after the arrested person's arrival, she must have been told the reason for the arrest. A custody officer receiving a prisoner at a police station may assume that the prisoner has been lawfully arrested. If that person then assaults the custody officer, this will constitute an assault on police, even though the initial arrest may have been unlawful.

Arrests *with* warrant

Arrests under warrant account for a minority of arrests and are applied in relatively limited circumstances. Under s 1 of the Magistrates' Courts Act 1980, an arrest warrant may be issued against a person who is suspected of having, or has committed, an indictable offence or an offence which is otherwise punishable by imprisonment, or whose whereabouts are unknown. This method of arresting a suspect may be used, *inter alia*, where the suspect's identity is known, but not his or her location, or it may be too dangerous or otherwise inexpedient to make an arrest immediately. Section 13 of the 1980 Act enables warrants to be issued where a defendant fails to attend court when required to do so in answer to a summons or other official notification. Arrest warrants may also be issued in a number of other circumstances. These include instances where an offender has breached certain community sentences and has to be brought before the court to be re-sentenced, where a member of Her Majesty's armed forces has deserted, or the arrest of a reluctant witness, to name but a few.

For a number of practical reasons, it is not always essential for the arresting officer to be in actual possession of the warrant when executing it; this depends on the type of warrant in question. One example where the warrant must be in the officer's possession on arrest is for non-payment of a fine, but where the warrant is for a person's arrest in order to enquire into his or her ability to pay, rather than for non-payment. In *DPP v Peacock* (1989), it was held that in such cases, the officer must be in possession of the warrant as this can enable the defaulter to pay the outstanding fine. If the warrant does not have to be in the officer's possession at the time of the arrest, the arrested person must be shown the warrant as soon as is practicable if sight of it is requested. Where an arrest is made under a warrant, the procedure for making it is essentially the same as an arrest without one, although it seems that a suspect is entitled to be informed that he or she is being arrested under a warrant.[15] However, this should be done as a matter of good practice in view of the wording of s 28(3) of PACE (the giving of reasons for the arrest).

Under s 117 of the Magistrates' Courts Act 1980, arrest warrants are endorsed with or without bail. Where the latter applies, the arrested person must be held in custody until that person is brought before the court. If the former applies, the arrested person must be released from the police station as directed. As will be discussed immediately below, some fairly recent provisions have been made regarding the cross-border enforcement of arrests, which includes those made under warrant.

Under Pt V of the Access to Justice Act 1999 (amended by the Domestic Violence, Crime and Victims Act 2004), certain arrest warrants may be served by civilian enforcement officers and not just the police. The use of civilians in the exercise of other policing functions is discussed in Chapter 7.[16]

Cross-border enforcement

Section 136 of the Criminal Justice and Public Order Act 1994 enables arrest warrants issued in England and Wales or Northern Ireland against persons charged with an offence to be executed in Scotland. Similarly, arrest warrants issued in Scotland or Northern Ireland may be executed in England and Wales, and warrants issued in England and Wales or Scotland may be executed in Northern Ireland.[17] Warrants may be executed by any constable from within the country where the warrant was issued or the country where it is to be executed, or by any other person within the directions of the warrant.

Section 137 of the 1994 Act provides that any police officer in England and Wales who has reasonable grounds to suspect that an arrestable offence has been committed or attempted in England and Wales, where the suspect is in Scotland or Northern Ireland, may arrest that person within any of those countries without warrant. The same reciprocal measures will apply to police officers in Scotland and Northern Ireland. This power also applies to non-arrestable offences, provided the service of a summons would be impracticable or inappropriate.[18] In effect, the same conditions will apply as in s 25 of PACE (general arrest conditions).

---

15 Levenson, H, Fairweather, F and Cape, E, *Police Powers: A Practitioner's Guide* (3rd edn, London: Legal Action Group, 1996).

16 See Jason-Lloyd, L, *Quasi-Policing* (London: Cavendish Publishing, 2003). See also Jason-Lloyd, L, 'Civilian enforcement officers: enhancement of their powers' (2005) 169 JP 88.

17 See Jason-Lloyd, L, *The Criminal Justice and Public Order Act 1994: A Basic Guide for Practitioners* (London: Frank Cass, 1996).

18 *Ibid*.

Persons arrested should be taken by the arresting officer, as soon as is reasonably practicable, to the nearest convenient designated police station where the alleged offence is being investigated. Reasonable force may be used where necessary in the execution of the above powers, and s 139 of the 1994 Act provides almost the same search powers and procedures as those prescribed under s 32 of PACE on the arrest of a suspect, with or without warrant. However, s 139(1) and (5) provides that in the case of suspects wanted in Northern Ireland or suspects from elsewhere in the UK being arrested in Northern Ireland, police powers to search such suspects in public may not extend beyond the removal of headgear and footwear as well as outer coat, jacket and gloves (but may include searching a person's mouth). Section 140 of the 1994 Act covers reciprocal powers of arrest and provides that police officers from one part of the UK who are exercising arrest powers under the above provisions in another part of the UK may conduct the arrest using the same powers applicable to that local jurisdiction.[19]

POWERS UNDER THE CRIME AND DISORDER ACT 1998

Sections 14, 15 and 16 of the Crime and Disorder Act 1998 confer two powers on the police which can be usefully be considered in this chapter, since they, technically at least, involve actions which come close to making arrests. These are powers to remove children from areas which are subject to local child curfews and the removal of truants from public places.

Local child curfews

Under ss 14 and 15 of the 1998 Act, local authorities or chief officers of police have the power to give notice of local child curfew schemes in certain areas. This will enable them to apply a ban on children under the age of 16 from being in specific public places between the hours of 9 pm and 6 am, unless under the effective control of a parent or a responsible person aged at least 18. These notices may specify different hours in relation to different age groups and the total period of such bans may not exceed 90 days. The curfew notices may be effected by posting them in one or more conspicuous places within the specified area and in any other such manner as the local authority or chief police officer considers to be desirable in order to publicise the notice. This could include distributing circulars through letter boxes or advertising in local newspapers. These curfews will be imposed if the relevant local authority or chief officer of police considers it necessary for the purpose of maintaining order in response to complaints from local residents. These measures have been enacted because of increasing concerns regarding young people engaging in generally disruptive behaviour by being allowed to roam the streets unsupervised at night and placing themselves at risk. Whether a child curfew scheme is being considered by a local authority or a police chief, each is under a duty to consult with the other prior to putting such a scheme into effect. They are also under a duty to consult with such

---

19 *Ibid.*

other persons or bodies as they consider appropriate. However, a local child curfew scheme must ultimately be approved by the Secretary of State.

Where a police officer has reasonable cause to believe that an unaccompanied child is contravening a ban imposed by a curfew notice, that officer may take the child to his or her place of residence, unless there is reasonable cause to believe that the child would be likely to suffer significant harm if taken there. In such circumstances, the officer may take the child into police protection, in order to be accommodated elsewhere. Where the child is returned home immediately after having been found in contravention of a curfew, the police have a duty to inform the relevant local authority as soon as is practicable. Although not expressly regarded as an arrest, the removal of a child from the street in this manner is technically a deprivation of that person's liberty and, therefore, reasonable force may be used where necessary. This matter is discussed further below when considering the power of the police to remove truants from public places.

Under the original provisions of the Crime and Disorder Act 1998, only local authorities had the power to initiate local child curfew schemes, but there seemed to be great reluctance to use this power. Subsequently, s 49 of the Criminal Justice and Police Act 2001 has made the necessary amendment that enables chief officers of police also to exercise this power. It was also an amendment under s 48 of the 2001 Act that increased the upper age limit of young people subject to child curfews from 10 to 16. On the subject of police discretion in enforcing these curfews, the 1998 Act requires that they may only exercise their powers based on reasonable *belief* that a child is under the age of 16. Unless the officer actually knows each child's age, it may be extremely difficult to enforce this power, especially where a curfew notice specifies different age groups under the age of 16. It will also become very difficult to enforce where an officer has definite knowledge that one or more children are under the age of 16, but others in the group are not or the officer is unsure. It appears that in such circumstances, the police will have to leave the others in the prohibited area, unless they have cause to exercise their powers under public order law, for instance.

Under the Anti-social Behaviour Act 2003, designated community support officers (see Chapter 7) may be given police powers to remove a child or young person to his or her place of residence when in contravention of a local child curfew. They will also be under the same duty as the police to inform the relevant local authority when such a contravention occurs (see below under 'Powers under the Anti-social Behaviour Act 2003' and 'Police powers to issue fixed penalties under the Criminal Justice and Police Act 2001' for further details regarding community support officers).

Power to remove truants

In order to prevent under 16 year olds from committing criminal and anti-social acts whilst truanting from school, s 16 of the 1998 Act has empowered the police to remove them from public places and to take them to designated premises or back to their respective schools. A local authority may designate certain premises where children and young persons of compulsory school age who are caught playing truant may be taken by the police. These premises may include offices in social services departments, for instance, or schools, although the Home Office has stressed that it is not appropriate to take such persons to police stations, unless they have committed an offence. The chief officer of police for that area should then be notified that such premises are available and a police officer of at least the rank of superintendent may authorise police officers to exercise their powers within specific areas and periods of time. Those powers are to remove a child or young person to designated premises, or return him or her to school if found in a public place within the geographical and time parameters mentioned above. The police may do this if they have reasonable cause to believe that the child or young person is of compulsory school age and is absent from school without lawful authority.

The provision of designated premises by a local authority (which are not intended to be permanent), plus the requirement of a police superintendent's authority, indicate that these powers are likely to be used following consultations with specific schools and other agencies. In other words, it appears that these powers may be intended to be used as part of an organised police 'swoop' on known trouble spots, involving truanters who are also known. The latter would seem necessary, since the police may only act on the grounds of reasonable belief that a child or young person is of compulsory school age and is absent from school without lawful authority.

Since the exercise of this power is not strictly an arrest, there has been some debate regarding the need to use reasonable force in the case of unco-operative children or young persons. It has been suggested that the common law principles governing the use of force will apply here, but with the caveat that it is essential that anyone deprived of their liberty should be given the reasons for doing so (*Christie v Leachinsky* (1947)).[20] However, it has been suggested that the use of force in exercising this power should be less than that when making an arrest, because of the general rule that juveniles should be handled with particular care wherever possible (including avoiding the use of handcuffs), plus the risk of endangering relations between the police and the younger community.[21] However, the possible long term consequences of allowing young people to 'cock a snook' at the police when exercising these powers could outweigh the utility of this argument, despite it being soundly based on the balance of social interest. Among other things, it could become common knowledge that a child or young person playing truant merely had to walk away from the police to avoid further action, thus rendering these powers useless.

Section 75 of the Police Reform Act 2002 empowers police superintendents or above from the British Transport Police to issue directions regarding the removal of truants from specified areas which are within are partly within places which fall under their jurisdiction. This is one of many examples of the recent inclusion of the British Transport Police within a greater range of overall policing activities in this country beyond their own specialised duties.

POWERS UNDER THE ANTI-SOCIAL BEHAVIOUR ACT 2003

Powers to impose local child curfews and remove truants under the Crime and Disorder Act 1998 are among many measures taken recently to combat both crime as well as sub-criminal behaviour. The latter has been described as such because it falls

---

20 Card, R and Ward, R, *The Crime and Disorder Act 1998: A Practitioner's Guide* (Bristol: Jordans, 1998).
21 Leng, R, Taylor, R and Wasik, M, *Blackstone's Guide to the Crime and Disorder Act 1998* (London: Blackstone, 1998).

short of actual criminal acts but still causes harm to victims. This has led to the now widely used term 'anti-social behaviour' which, in its broadest sense, could be described as a form of nuisance that causes significant discomfort to others. Part 4 of the Anti-social Behaviour Act 2003 has provided the police with further powers to deal with conduct that is placed under the heading of anti-social behaviour. Under this Part of the 2003 Act, anti-social behaviour is defined as 'behaviour by a person which causes or is likely to cause harassment, alarm or distress to one or more other persons not of the same household as the person'. If members of the public have been intimidated, harassed, alarmed or distressed by the presence or behaviour of groups of at least two persons in public places within a locality, and that anti-social behaviour is a significant and persistent problem in that locality, the following action may be taken.

To begin with, a police officer of at least the rank of superintendent who reasonably believes that such conduct has occurred may give an authorisation enabling police officers in uniform to disperse these groups in public places. This must be preceded by consultation with the relevant local authority, followed by giving advance notice regarding the locality affected by the authorisation and its duration. This notice should be posted in one or more conspicuous places within that locality and/or published in a local newspaper. An authorisation must be in writing, stating the grounds justifying it, and the period when it will be in force, which must not exceed six months. The senior police officer who made the authorisation, or another officer of at least the same rank, may withdraw it, but only when there has been prior consultation with the relevant local authority. If the authorisation is withdrawn or it simply expires, fresh authorisations may be made regarding all or part of the relevant locality.

Uniformed police officers in public places within the relevant locality will have a number of powers available to them when an authorisation is in force. These constitute a power to disperse troublesome groups in a number of ways, provided they have reasonable grounds for believing that the presence or behaviour of a group of two or more persons has, or is likely to result in, members of the public being intimidated, harassed, alarmed or distressed. If these conditions are present, the police may give one or more directions as follows:

- direct persons in the group to disperse either immediately or at a later specified time and in a way specified by the police;
- direct any within the group who do not reside in the relevant locality to leave that area or any part of it. They will be directed to do this either immediately or at a later specified time and in the way as directed by the police;
- further direct those who are dispersed but who live outside the relevant locality not to re-enter that area or part of it for any period not exceeding 24 hours.

Flexibility is introduced into these provisions by enabling directions to be given verbally and to individuals as well as groups of two or more, and the police officer who gives a direction may withdraw or vary it. There are two circumstances where a direction may not be given, namely where a group is lawfully assembled during an industrial dispute or participating in a public procession. Police officers in uniform have the power to arrest anyone defying a direction, which constitutes a summary offence that is punishable by a maximum of three months' imprisonment and/or a fine not exceeding level 4 on the standard scale (currently £2,500). It should be noted that the maximum custodial sentence for this offence could be changed at some future date. Section 281(1) and (2) of the Criminal Justice Act 2003 enables the Home Secretary to increase maximum custodial sentences of five months or less to 51 weeks, or make those offences no longer punishable with imprisonment.

When an authorisation applicable to a relevant locality is in force, and any under 16 year olds are engaged in the prohibited conduct within that area, the police have a further power to deal with such situations. Instead of dispersing them as described above, the police have the power to remove them to their normal places of abode. There are, however, a number of restrictions on the use of this power. Police officers in uniform may return persons under 16 to where they normally live, and this should only be done where they are within the relevant locality between 9 pm and 6 am. In addition, this power may not be exercised if the under 16 year old is under the effective control of a parent or a responsible person aged 18 or above. Nor should the child or young person be taken to his or her normal place of residence if the officer has reasonable grounds for believing that the young person would suffer harm if taken there. If an under 16 year old is removed under this power, the police are under a duty to inform the relevant local authority accordingly. Authorising officers conferring powers of dispersal and removal applicable to any relevant locality, as well as uniformed officers exercising any of these powers, will have to comply with a code of practice that may be issued by the Home Secretary. It should be noted that all of the above powers are also available to the British Transport Police.

These new powers have been included here because although they do not constitute arrest powers (except where there is a contravention of a direction), they do involve a restriction on the liberty of citizens. In this case, the restriction involves compelling them to move rather than remain. Part 4 of the Anti-social Behaviour Act has extended the exercise of these powers to include designated community support officers, as well as the power to remove young persons who contravene local child curfews as mentioned above (see Chapter 7).[22]

'ANY PERSON' ARREST POWERS

Section 3 of the Theft Act 1978 created the offence of making off without payment. This covers activities described as 'bilking' where, for instance, a person arrives at his or her destination in a taxi, then runs off in order to avoid paying the fare or has a meal and then leaves the restaurant, intending to avoid paying the bill. Sub-section (4) states that:

> Any person may arrest without warrant anyone who is, or whom he, with reasonable cause, suspects to be, committing or attempting to commit an offence under this section.

Note the inclusion of the words 'any person', meaning that both the police and ordinary citizens have this power of arrest without warrant. However, this was made an arrestable offence by virtue of s 48 of the Police Reform Act 2002, which placed it under para 7 of Sched 1A to PACE. This enhances the powers of the police to deal with such an offence, but it also preserves the right of the ordinary citizen to intervene, although subject to the restrictions discussed earlier in this chapter. Once again, it is suggested that ordinary citizens exercise great caution if considering using this power. Apart from the physical dangers inherent in making arrests, there may be potential

---

22 For a full discussion of these, and other powers conferred upon civilians, see Jason-Lloyd, L, 'Community support officers – more powers in the pipeline' (2003) 167 JP 637.

legal traps, bearing in mind the instantaneous nature of this specific offence. A suspect may be able to convince magistrates or a jury that it was his or her intention to pay for the goods later, since it has to be proved beyond reasonable doubt that there was the intention never to pay the amount due. This offence is triable either way and, when tried on indictment, carries a maximum prison sentence of two years.

A number of other statutes have created arrest powers for specific offences where 'any person' or 'anyone' may arrest without a warrant (see Appendix 11), for example, s 91 of the Criminal Justice Act 1967 (arrest of a person who is drunk and disorderly in a public place). See also s 1 of the Licensing Act 1902, s 11 of the Prevention of Offences Act 1851 and s 6 of the Vagrancy Act 1824. According to some commentators,[23] these arrest powers have not strictly been removed from the police by s 26(1) of PACE, which repealed all statutory powers of arrest without warrant previously held by them, except those recast under Sched 2. The general line of argument is that since the above arrest powers may be exercised by any person, this also includes the police (although, with specific reference to s 3 of the Theft Act 1978, a contrary view has been expressed).[24] However, in *DPP v Kitching* (1989) and *Gapper v Chief Constable of Avon and Somerset* (1998), the matter seems to have been clarified as far as offences under s 91 of the Criminal Justice Act 1967 and s 6 of the Vagrancy Act 1824 are concerned. In both these cases, it was held that 'any person' also included the police. It has been suggested in Home Office guidance, *inter alia*, that it may be prudent for the police to take into account the criteria in the general arrest conditions under s 25 of PACE before exercising such powers of arrest.

Section 41 of the Sexual Offences Act 1956 had the specific requirement attached to it under para 9 of Sched 6 to PACE that the police should only make an arrest for this offence using their powers under s 25. This has now been repealed by Sched 7 of the Sexual Offences Act 2003, thus reducing the number of offences subject to arrest by 'any person' to a mere handful.

POLICE POWERS TO ISSUE FIXED PENALTIES UNDER THE CRIMINAL JUSTICE AND POLICE ACT 2001

Increasingly, the police are being given powers to use alternative methods in enforcing the law without arresting the persons concerned or even reporting them for a summons. Apart from giving 'street bail' as mentioned earlier, the police are now empowered to issue fixed penalty notices, where appropriate, for a range of offences that obviate the need to make arrests. The issue of fixed penalties is therefore no longer confined to road traffic offences but has been extended to include other offences as follows.

---

23 *Op cit*, Zander, fn 3. See also *op cit*, Clark, fn 7.
24 *Op cit*, Levenson, Fairweather and Cape, fn 15. See also *op cit*, Cape and Luqmani, fn 4.

Part 1, Chapter 1 of the Criminal Justice and Police Act 2001 gives the police a discretion to issue a fixed penalty notice to a 10 year old and above[25] where there is reason to believe that he or she has committed any of the following offences:

(a) being drunk in a highway, other public place or licensed premises (s 12 of the Licensing Act 1872);

(b) throwing fireworks in a thoroughfare (s 80 of the Explosives Act 1875) (prospectively repealed by s 15 of the Fireworks Act 2003 from a date to be appointed);

(c) knowingly giving a false alarm to a fire and rescue authority (s 49 of the Fire and Rescue Services Act 2004);

(d) trespassing on a railway (s 55 of the British Transport Commission Act 1949);

(e) throwing stones etc at trains or other things on railways (s 56 of the British Transport Commission Act 1949);

(f) buying or attempting to buy alcohol for a person under 18 or for consumption on licensed premises (s 169C(2) of the Licensing Act 1964 and s 149(4) of the Licensing Act 2003);

(g) disorderly behaviour while drunk in a public place (s 91 of the Criminal Justice Act 1967);

(h) wasting police time or giving false report (s 5(2) of the Criminal Law Act 1967);

(i) using public electronic communications network in order to cause annoyance, inconvenience or needless anxiety (s 127(2) of the Communications Act 2003);

(j) consumption of alcohol in designated public place (s 12 of the Criminal Justice and Police Act 2001);

(k) behaviour likely to cause harassment, alarm or distress (s 5 of the Public Order Act 1986).[26]

More recently, the following fixed penalty offences have been created as follows:

(l) sale of alcohol to a person under 18 years (s 169A of the Licensing Act 1964);

(m) consumption of alcohol by a person under 18 years or allowing such consumption (s 169E of the Licensing Act 1964);

(n) delivery of alcohol to a person under 18 years or allowing such delivery (s 169F of the Licensing Act 1964);

---

25 Originally, under the Criminal Justice and Police Act 2001, the minimum age was 18 years, but this was lowered to 16 as a result of an amendment under the Anti-social Behaviour Act 2003. Then, on 26 December 2004, the Penalties for Disorderly Behaviour (Amendment of Minimum Age) Order 2004 came into force. That reduced the lower age limit to 10 years. This also makes the parent or guardian of an under 16 year old who receives a penalty notice, liable to pay the financial penalty. This means that they must receive written notification plus a copy of the penalty notice originally given to the under 16 year old (the 'young penalty recipient'). There is also the provision for the police to cancel the original notification and issue a fresh one where the original version was issued to the wrong person. This includes the situation where the original notification was issued to someone who is not the parent or guardian of the young penalty recipient, or where the notification would be more appropriately sent to another person. Initially, this scheme is being piloted by a limited number of police forces.

26 The offence under s 5 of the Public Order Act 1986 was not included in the original list under s 1(1) of the Criminal Justice and Police Act 2001. This was subsequently added by means of the power held under s 1(2) of the 2001 Act which enables the Home Secretary to make changes to this range of offences.

(o) theft (s 1 of the Theft Act 1968) [in practice this is mainly directed towards shoplifting];

(p) destroying/damaging property (s 1(1) of the Criminal Damage Act 1971) [this should apply to relatively minor acts of vandalism];

(q) depositing and leaving litter (s 87 of the Environmental Protection Act 1990);

(r) prohibition/failure to comply regarding fireworks regulations/making false statements (s 11 of the Fireworks Act 2003).

Where a fixed penalty notice is issued in a place other than at a police station, such as in the street, it must be given by a police officer in uniform. Only police officers authorised by their chief officer of police may issue fixed penalty notices at a police station, and these officers need not be in uniform. This will occur, for instance, where a drunken person has been taken to a police station and, on sobering up, is given a fixed penalty notice before being released.

For a number of years, the police have been given the discretion to issue a range of fixed penalty notices instead of initiating a prosecution in each case. The reason for introducing fixed penalties for the above offences under the 2001 Act is to combat low-level disorder in a simple and swift manner. In return for the saving of police and the courts' time, the alleged offender does not acquire a criminal conviction for the offence in question. However, a person risks a conviction if he or she opts for trial before a court, as well as receiving a higher financial penalty. This will also apply in cases where the alleged offender refuses to pay the fixed penalty sum. This fixed penalty scheme is discretionary and does not prevent the police from exercising their arrest powers where they consider it appropriate.

Under the Police Reform Act 2002, the power to issue fixed penalties with some possible exceptions is also held by designated community support officers. This has been extended by the Anti-social Behaviour Act 2003 to include 'accredited civilians', but with the exception of the offences of being drunk, or drunk and disorderly, in a public place (see Chapter 7).[27]

27　*Op cit*, Jason-Lloyd, fn 22.

CHAPTER 4

POLICE POWERS OF ENTRY AND SEARCH OF PREMISES, AND SEIZURE OF EVIDENCE

INTRODUCTION

As discussed in Chapters 2 and 3, the Royal Commission on Criminal Procedure recognised that police powers of stop and search, as well as those affecting arrests, were both fragmented and unclear. This also applies to the Commission's findings regarding police powers of entry and search of premises, and the seizure of any evidence found there. A number of recommendations were made, some of which, but by no means all, were later enacted under the Police and Criminal Evidence Act 1984 (PACE).

The relevant provisions under s 8 of PACE, described below, constitute a *general* power to obtain search warrants. Sections 17 and 18 of PACE also include certain powers to enter and search premises, but without warrant, as well as s 32 (entry and search of premises which an arrested person was in at the time of their arrest or immediately before it, as considered in the previous chapter).

It should be noted that PACE is not the only legal source enabling the police to enter and search premises. A number of statutes conferring specific police powers to obtain search warrants also exist, although the procedures involved in issuing search warrants and executing them must comply with the standard procedures and safeguards contained in PACE and Code of Practice B. Some examples of these specific powers are included under the following statutes: s 26 of the Theft Act 1968 (warrant to enter premises to search for stolen goods); s 23(3) of the Misuse of Drugs Act 1971 (warrant to enter and search premises for controlled drugs or documents relating to unlawful drug transactions); s 2(4) of the Criminal Justice Act 1987 (warrant to enter and search for evidence of serious fraud), and many more.[1]

There are also further specific statutory powers of entry and search without warrant included under the following examples: s 23(1) of the Misuse of Drugs Act 1971 (power of entry into premises of a person carrying on business as a producer or supplier of controlled drugs in order to examine records and stocks of drugs); s 13 of the Aviation Security Act 1982 (power to enter any building, etc, at airports to search for firearms, explosives or other dangerous articles).[2] More recently, the Terrorism Act 2000 has given the police further powers of entry and search without warrant in order to combat terrorism. These will be discussed later in this chapter. Mention should be made at this stage of powers under ss 4(7) and 6(6) and the Road Traffic Act 1988. These empower the police to enter premises in order to arrest persons for drink-drive offences or for the purpose of making breath tests where road traffic accidents involving personal injury have occurred. There is also a common law power of entry into premises which has been unchanged by PACE and that is the power to enter

---

1   Stone, R, *Entry, Search and Seizure: A Guide to Civil and Criminal Powers of Entry* (3rd edn, London: Sweet & Maxwell, 1997).

2   *Ibid.*

premises to deal with or prevent a breach of the peace. However, as discussed earlier, this common law power is largely superseded by s 17 of PACE.

Definition of 'premises'

For the purposes of the exercise of police powers of entry and search, the word 'premises' applies to a wide variety of public and private places. Section 23 of PACE provides only a partial definition by stating:

23   In this Act – 'premises' includes any place and, in particular, includes:

(a) any vehicle, vessel, aircraft or hovercraft;

(b) any offshore installation; and

(c) any tent or movable structure; and

'offshore installation' has the meaning given to it by s 1 of the Mineral Workings (Offshore Installations) Act 1971.

Apart from those specific examples mentioned above, what constitutes 'any place'? Using case law, the term 'premises' has also been held to include buildings, caravans, houseboats, non-residential premises, such as unattended garages, and land. In *Palmer v Bugler* (1988), it was held that a field used on a regular basis for car boot sales constituted 'a place'.[3] It is interesting to note that s 25(1) of the Private Security Industry Act 2001 defines premises as including '... any vehicle or moveable structure and any other place whatever, whether or not occupied as land'. These very broad definitions under both PACE and the 2001 Act could, *inter alia*, include virtually any open-air location but, according to Professor Zander, Home Office guidance that originally accompanied PACE stated that such places 'should be a distinct piece of land in single occupation or ownership'.[4]

ENTRY AND SEARCH BY WARRANT

As already discussed, s 8 of PACE has introduced a general power under which magistrates may issue warrants enabling the police to enter premises and search for items not covered by the specific Acts mentioned above. However, according to Professor Stone:

There is no evidence that these more specific powers are used any less now that the police have the general power to obtain a search warrant under s 8 of PACE. This power only applies to 'serious arrestable offences' and, in some cases (perhaps where it is proposed to use other procedures under an Act, for example, the forfeiture procedures under the Obscene Publications Act 1959), the specific powers may anyway be thought more appropriate.[5]

---

3   Levenson, H, Fairweather, F and Cape, E, *Police Powers: A Practitioner's Guide* (3rd edn, London: Legal Action Group, 1996).

4   Zander, M, *The Police and Criminal Evidence Act 1984* (4th edn, London: Sweet & Maxwell, 2003).

5   *Op cit*, Stone, fn 1.

Section 8 provides that a police officer may apply in writing for a warrant from a justice of the peace if there are reasonable grounds for believing that there is material on premises relating to the committing of a serious arrestable offence[6] which is likely to be of substantial value to the investigation and admissible as evidence in court, and that this is the only means to obtain such evidence; in other words, where it would be impracticable to try to gain entry without a search warrant. This will include instances where the purpose of the search may be frustrated or seriously prejudiced unless the police effect immediate entry. It will also include circumstances where no one can be contacted who has the authority to grant access to the premises or to the required material on those premises, or where consent to enter those premises has already been refused. It therefore follows that a justice of the peace should not issue a search warrant if entry can be gained through the consent of the occupier. Certain items may not be obtained by a search warrant under s 8, but may be obtained through other provisions. These are items subject to legal privilege, excluded material or special procedure material.

Meaning of 'items subject to legal privilege'

This is defined under s 10 of PACE as follows, with explanations in square brackets where appropriate:

(1) Subject to sub-s (2) below, in this Act, 'items subject to legal privilege' means:

(a) communications between a professional legal adviser and his client or any person representing his client made in connection with the giving of legal advice to the client;

[First, what is meant by the term 'professional legal adviser'? This includes qualified barristers and solicitors. A solicitor in this context does not have to be employed by a solicitors' practice. This will therefore include a solicitor working from an advice centre, for instance. Solicitors' clerks are also included, since they act under the direction of solicitors. Unqualified advisers may possibly claim that communications fall under this heading if acting as agents for barristers or solicitors, but generally the advice from unqualified persons does not fall under legally privileged material, although it could receive some protection as 'excluded material' (see below). The legally privileged material must be in the possession of a person who is entitled to possess it, and communications subject to legal privilege can be written or verbal, including tape recordings of interviews.][7]

(b) communications between a professional legal adviser and his client or any person representing his client or between such an adviser or his client or any such representative and any other person made in connection with or in contemplation of legal proceedings and for the purposes of such proceedings; and

(c) items enclosed with or referred to in such communications and made:

(i) in connection with the giving of legal advice; or

---

6   Or a 'relevant offence' as defined under s 28D(4) of the Immigration Act 1971 (added by s 169(1), Sched 14, para 80(1), (2)).

7   *Op cit*, Levenson, Fairweather and Cape, fn 3.

      (ii) in connection with or in contemplation of legal proceedings and for the purpose
          of such proceedings,
     when they are in the possession of a person who is entitled to possession of
     them.

  (2) Items held with the intention of furthering a criminal purpose are not items subject
     to legal privilege.

What is meant by 'the intention of furthering a criminal purpose'? Within the context
of sub-s (2), this can perhaps be illustrated by the following scenarios.

Mr X is thinking of committing a crime and writes a letter to his solicitor, asking
what the consequences would be. His solicitor writes and tells him that he could go to
prison, say, for five years if convicted. These letters would be subject to legal privilege.
However, if Mr Y writes to his solicitor and tells him of a crime he intends to commit
and asks how he can avoid being detected and his solicitor replies and gives him this
information, this would not be subject to legal privilege, as this constitutes furthering a
criminal purpose.

In *R v Central Criminal Court ex p Francis and Francis* (1989), the exclusion of legal
privilege immunity was given a broad interpretation by the House of Lords which
excludes from such immunity not only the criminal intentions of legal advisers or their
clients, but also anyone using a client as an innocent agent.[8] Material which is legally
privileged cannot be subject to a search, except under rare circumstances, where it can
be obtained under written authority other than a warrant. Examples include the
powers under s 73 of the Explosives Act 1875 and s 9(2) of the Official Secrets Act 1911,
where a police superintendent may, in extremely urgent cases, make a written order to
enter and search specified premises for explosives or for certain material in the
interests of State security. Legally privileged material is therefore highly protected and
in *R v Guildhall Magistrates' Court ex p Primlaks Holdings Co* (1989), it was stressed that
great care should be exercised by those applying for search warrants to ensure that the
material sought after did not include anything that was subject to legal privilege.
However, in *R v Customs and Excise Commissioners ex p Popely* (1999), it was held that
even though a search warrant cannot authorise the seizure of legally privileged
material, the inadvertent seizure of such material during a search under a warrant did
not render the execution of the warrant unlawful. In *R v Chesterfield Justices ex p
Bramley* (1999), it was held that the police will not be acting unlawfully if they seize
items subject to legal privilege, providing they do not have reasonable grounds for
believing that the material is privileged; however, 'violation of the legal privilege by
making use of the privileged information would be unlawful'. It was this case that
necessitated the enactment of ss 50–66 of and Scheds 1 and 2 to the Criminal Justice
and Police Act 2001, in order to create a new power to seize and sift property following
the execution of a search warrant.

Meaning of 'excluded material'

The term 'excluded material' is defined under s 11 of PACE as follows, with
explanations included in square brackets where appropriate. Such material falls under

---

8   Cited in Jason-Lloyd, L, *The Law on Money-Laundering: Statutes and Commentary* (London:
    Frank Cass, 1997).

three categories, namely, personal records, human tissue or tissue fluid and journalistic material. It is important to note that there must always be an element of confidentiality in the holding of excluded material, whichever category it falls under:

(1) Subject to the following provisions of this section, in this Act, 'excluded material' means:

(a) personal records which a person has acquired or created in the course of any trade, business or profession or other occupation or for the purposes of any paid or unpaid office and which he holds in confidence;

['Personal records' are defined under s 12 of PACE and consist of documents and other records regarding a person, whether living or dead, which relate to the following: (1) documentary or other records regarding physical and mental health (this also includes dental records);[9] (2) personal records in relation to spiritual counselling or assistance, which includes information kept by members of the clergy and other religious ministers; (3) personal records regarding counselling or assistance given to a person for personal welfare purposes by any voluntary organisation or by any person who, 'by reason of his office or occupation, has responsibilities for his personal welfare'. This may include careers advice records in educational establishments, records of social workers, records in advice centres and so on.[10]

Also included are personal records regarding counselling or assistance given to a person for his or her welfare by any voluntary organisation or individual who, 'by reason of an order of a court, has responsibilities for his supervision'. This was originally designed to protect personal records held by probation officers, but this must now clearly extend to local authority social workers and, more recently, to members of Youth Offending Teams and, under Pt I of the Youth Justice and Criminal Evidence Act 1999, to members of Youth Offender Panels.]

(b) human tissue or tissue fluid which has been taken for the purposes of diagnosis or medical treatment and which a person holds in confidence;

[This category of excluded material is not defined in PACE, but such material will include blood samples, for instance.]

(c) journalistic material which a person holds in confidence and which consists:

(i) of documents; or

(ii) of records other than documents.

(2) A person holds material other than journalistic material in confidence for the purposes of this section if he holds it subject:

(a) to an express or implied undertaking to hold it in confidence; or

(b) to a restriction on disclosure or an obligation of secrecy contained in any enactment, including an enactment contained in an Act passed after this Act.

(3) A person holds journalistic material in confidence for the purposes of this section if:

(a) he holds it subject to such an undertaking, restriction or obligation; and

(b) it has been continuously held (by one or more persons) subject to such an undertaking, restriction or obligation since it was first acquired or created for the purposes of journalism.

[The protections afforded to journalistic material apply to the media generally and not exclusively to professional journalists. The material may be in the form of maps,

---

9   *R v Singleton* [1995] Crim LR 236, cited in Levenson, Fairweather and Cape, *op cit*, fn 3.

10   *Op cit* Levenson, Fairweather and Cape, fn 3.

plans, photographs, discs, tapes, films or microfilms. If journalistic material is not continuously held in confidence, then it does not constitute excluded material, but falls under 'special procedure material', which will be discussed below. Media coverage of certain public demonstrations involving the photographing or filming of those events has been regarded as special procedure material, since this material, although journalistic, was not held in confidence. See, for example, *R v Bristol Crown Court ex p Bristol Press and Picture Agency Ltd* (1987).]

Unless they are able to gain access to such evidence with the appropriate co-operation and consent from the person concerned, if the police need access to excluded material, they must apply to a circuit judge for a 'production order'. This avoids the police having to search premises to find and obtain such evidence because a production order requires the person in possession of this material to either give it to the police or allow them access to it. In exceptional circumstances, such as where this evidence is likely to be tampered with, a circuit judge may issue a warrant instead of a production order or may even issue both.

Meaning of 'special procedure material'

The provisions regarding the definition of special procedure material are contained under s 14 of PACE. As mentioned above, such material includes that of a journalistic nature, but which is not continuously held in confidence (or the material may not be in the prescribed form required under the Act). The second type of special procedure material is that which is not legally privileged or excluded material, but which is in 'the possession of a person who acquired or created it in the course of any trade, business, profession, or other occupation or for the purposes of any paid or unpaid office' and holds it in confidence.

Examples of special procedure material have included bank accounts, stock records, the accounts of a youth association and photographs held by the media (see *R v Bristol Crown Court ex p Bristol Press and Picture Agency Ltd* (1986)). The most important sources of special procedure material are banks and building societies, as well as accountants, estate agents, financial brokers, insurance brokers, telecommunications organisations, journalists and solicitors (excluding legally privileged material).[11] Access of the police to special procedure material can be gained in several ways. First, such access can be voluntarily given by the person who holds this material. However, where such consent cannot be obtained, the police may apply for a search warrant from a justice of the peace or, depending on the nature of the material in question, they may apply for a production order from a circuit judge. In the exceptional circumstances mentioned above, a judge may grant a search warrant instead of a production order or may issue both.

The importance of the provisions under PACE regarding such material is illustrated by the following:

In England and Wales, more than 2,000 orders for the production of special procedure material or warrants to search for and seize such material were granted in the first three

---

11   Clark, D, *Bevan and Lidstone's The Investigation of Crime: A Guide to the Law of Criminal Investigation* (3rd edn, London: Butterworths, 2004).

years of PACE 1984. These have enabled the police to investigate crimes which they were previously unable to investigate and to obtain evidence in respect of other crimes which they were previously unable to obtain, or were able to obtain only after a charge had been laid under the Bankers' Books Evidence Act 1879.[12]

Section 9 of PACE, in conjunction with Sched 1, makes detailed provision regarding special procedures when applying for production orders or search warrants from circuit judges in respect of excluded or special procedure material. These finer points will not be covered in detail within this chapter, as they are largely applicable to those working within specialist areas of criminal investigation. It is also for this reason that not all police powers pertaining to the prevention of terrorism are included either, except those which are likely to be enforced by the police in the course of routine duties, rather than by specialised squads. However, some mention will be made at this stage of several methods used to obtain evidence in cases connected with terrorism in view of the increasing importance of this subject.

Powers of entry and search in the prevention of terrorism

Terrorism within its general meaning falls within the definition of a number of different crimes, including firearms and explosives offences to name but a few. These will often necessitate the use of entry and search powers of premises, since many of them also fall under the heading of serious arrestable offences. The Prevention of Terrorism (Additional Powers) Act 1996, which substantially amended the Prevention of Terrorism (Temporary Provisions) Act 1989, conferred wide-ranging powers on the police in order to deal with and prevent acts of terrorism. Those provisions augmented specific and more general powers already held by the police in England and Wales to deal with terrorist activities. These have now been recast under the Terrorism Act 2000 which, *inter alia*, has consolidated earlier anti-terrorism law that had developed piecemeal over a number of years. Several amendments to the 2000 Act were later made by the Anti-terrorism, Crime and Security Act 2001, although these largely fall outside the scope of this book (one notable exception being the extended power to require the removal of disguises as discussed in Chapter 2). Some of the powers under the 2000 Act to enter and search premises have also been discussed in Chapter 2, since those provisions also involve the stopping and searching of vehicles and persons. However, s 42 of the 2000 Act, which deals with police powers to enter and search premises to arrest suspected terrorists, should be noted for the purposes of this chapter.

Provisions are made under s 37 of and Sched 5 to the Terrorism Act 2000, whereby the police may apply to magistrates and circuit judges for a variety of court orders and warrants relating to terrorist investigations. For instance, a constable may apply to a justice of the peace for a warrant to enter and search specified premises, as well as any person found there, and to seize and retain any relevant material discovered in the course of the search. This excludes items subject to legal privilege as well as special procedure or excluded material as defined in ss 10, 11 and 14 of PACE. The powers under ss 50–66 of and Scheds 1 and 2 to the Criminal Justice and Police Act 2001

---

12 *Ibid.*

enabling the police, where necessary, to seize and then sift through articles elsewhere also applies here. Note the inclusion of the power to search any persons found on the premises and also note that there is a restriction on the extent of such searches in public. Where such persons have not been arrested, the overall conduct of those searches should also be in accordance with the provisions under Code of Practice A (see para 2.4 of Code B). In view of the nature of terrorism in modern times, there is provision under Sched 5 whereby a search warrant may be dispensed with, but only in cases of 'great emergency'. In such circumstances, a superintendent or above may make a written order conferring the entry and search powers on police officers as stated above provided 'that immediate action is necessary'. However, where a senior police officer makes such an order, there is a duty to inform the Home Secretary of the particulars of the case as soon as is reasonably practicable.

There is also provision under para 2 of Sched 5 to the 2000 Act that enables the police to search non-residential premises where an officer of at least the rank of superintendent applies to a magistrate for a warrant to search one or more premises named in the application, and this is granted accordingly. This may be done where a terrorist investigation is taking place and there are reasonable grounds for believing that it is likely that material of substantial value to that investigation will be found there (although this excludes items subject to legal privilege, excluded material or special procedure material). A search warrant issued under para 2 of Sched 5 must be executed within 24 hours and empowers the police to enter and search any of the premises named in it and anyone found there. Anything found on the premises or found on anyone discovered there may be seized and retained if there are reasonable grounds for believing that it is likely to be of substantial value to the investigation and it is necessary to prevent it from being concealed, lost, damaged, altered or destroyed. These provisions enable the police to search any number of non-residential premises specified in the warrant, whereas under the earlier provisions, separate warrants had to be issued for each of them. It is important to note that these powers do not apply to premises which the applicant has reasonable cause to believe are used wholly or mainly as a dwelling. An example of the type of premises to which these powers may apply is given by Professor Walker as follows:

> The purpose is to allow for mass searches, such as lock up premises in a given area where it is suspected that bomb-makers are active but without sufficient knowledge as to the location of their premises.[13]

Instead of applying for a warrant, a police superintendent or above may make a written order for the entry and search of one or more unattended premises if there are reasonable grounds for believing that this is a case of great emergency and immediate action is necessary. Where such an order has been made, there is a legal duty to notify the particulars of the case to the Home Secretary as soon as is reasonably practicable.[14]

---

13 Walker, C, *Blackstone's Guide to the Anti-Terrorism Legislation* (Oxford: OUP, 2002).

14 For a complete commentary on all the provisions of the Prevention of Terrorism (Additional Powers) Act 1996, from which these and other powers originated, see Jason-Lloyd, L, 'The Prevention of Terrorism (Additional Powers) Act 1996: a commentary' (1996) 160 JP 503, although note the changes where appropriate.

As mentioned in Chapter 2, Sched 5 to the 2000 Act enables a police officer of at least the rank of superintendent to authorise police officers to enter and search premises, residential or otherwise, that are located wholly or partly within a cordoned area. This includes the power to seize articles found on the premises that are likely to constitute evidence of terrorist activity, including such articles found on any person who is searched within those premises at the time. However, this does not apply to items subject to legal privilege; nor does it apply to excluded or special procedure material. The powers under ss 50–66 of and Scheds 1 and 2 to the Criminal Justice and Police Act 2001 to seize materials and sift them elsewhere may be applied where necessary. In particularly urgent situations, an authorisation to use these powers may be given by an officer below the rank of superintendent, even to the extent as stated as follows by Professor Walker: '... perhaps within the first few minutes of cordoning off, any constable may give an authorisation (presumably to himself) if he considers it necessary by reason of urgency.'[15] One effect of the Anti-terrorism, Crime and Security Act 2001 is that this power, under certain circumstances, has been extended to the Ministry of Defence Police and also the British Transport Police Force.

Where the police wish to obtain or gain access to excluded or special procedure materials, Sched 5 enables a constable to apply to a circuit judge for an order compelling a specified person to produce or give information regarding such items. Where necessary, a warrant may be obtained from a circuit judge to enable the police to enter premises in order to search for excluded or special procedure material; this also includes the power to search any person found on those premises at the time. A circuit judge may issue a search warrant, not only because the material may be of substantial value to a terrorist investigation, but also because of difficulties in communicating with any person entitled to produce or give access to the material, or to give access to the premises in question. There is the further ground that a warrant is necessary because a terrorist investigation may be seriously prejudiced unless the police can secure immediate access to the material. A search warrant may also be issued on the grounds that an order has previously been made for the production of, or access to, the required material, but this order has not been complied with. However, para 3.4(b) of Code B states that an application to a circuit judge for a search warrant or any court order mentioned above must be supported by signed written authority from a superintendent or above. In cases of 'great emergency' and where 'immediate action is necessary', a superintendent or above may issue a written order giving police officers the powers normally conferred by a warrant to enter and search premises as well as search anyone found there. This provision is identical to that described above regarding search warrants obtained from magistrates, including the requirement to inform the particulars of the case to the Home Secretary.

The requirement of prior authority before certain action can be taken, whether under anti-terrorism powers or more general provisions, is an important issue. This is mentioned under para 2.7 of Code B, which states:

> When this Code requires the prior authority or agreement of an officer of at least inspector or superintendent rank, that authority may be given by a sergeant or chief inspector authorised to perform the functions of the higher rank under PACE, section 107.

---

15 *Op cit*, Walker, fn 13.

In the *previous* version of para 6.14 of Code B, it was stipulated that the person in charge of a search under Sched 5 to the 2000 Act had to be a police officer of at least the rank of inspector. This also applied to Sched 1 to PACE, which empowers circuit judges to issue production orders or warrants regarding excluded or special procedure material in respect of serious arrestable offences. The latest para 6.14 has removed the requirement for an inspector to be in charge of the search and largely reflects para 2.10, which states that: 'The "officer in charge of the search" means the officer assigned specific duties and responsibilities under this Code. Whenever there is a search of premises to which this Code applies one officer must act as the officer in charge of the search ...' This requirement is discussed in further detail under Note for Guidance 2F to Code B, which provides the following guidance:

> For the purposes of paragraph 2.10, the officer in charge of the search should normally be the most senior officer present. Some exceptions are:
>
> (a) a supervising officer who attends or assists at the scene of a premises search may appoint an officer of lower rank as officer in charge of the search if that officer is:
>
> • more conversant with the facts;
>
> • a more appropriate officer to be in charge of the search;
>
> (b) when all officers in a premises search are the same rank. The supervising officer if available must make sure one of them is appointed officer in charge of the search, otherwise the officers themselves must nominate one of their number as the officer in charge;
>
> (c) a senior officer assisting in a specialist role. This officer need not be regarded as having a general supervisory role over the conduct of the search or be appointed or expected to act as the officer in charge of the search.
>
> Except in (c), nothing in this Note diminishes the role and responsibility of a supervisory officer who is present at the search or knows of a search taking place.

The latest para 6.14 includes the following provision that repeats the earlier version regarding officers in charge of searches: '... They are responsible for making sure the search is conducted with discretion and in a manner that causes the least possible disruption to any business or other activities carried out on the premises.'

Other general search provisions under PACE and Code B will now be discussed immediately below.

General search provisions

Notwithstanding the multiplicity of legal powers enabling the police to enter and search premises, whether enacted before or after 1984, PACE has established a common procedure regarding applications for all search warrants, as well as establishing a uniform set of procedures in respect of the conduct of such searches. This is in addition to applications for search warrants under PACE itself, whether obtained from circuit judges or justices of the peace, and the subsequent searches. These procedures are covered under ss 15 and 16 of PACE which, if breached, will render the entry and search unlawful. These provisions are supplemented by Code B, although, under para 2.3(a), this Code does not apply to police searches of premises following bomb threats, or when answering burglar alarm or fire calls, or the discovery of insecure premises, or when making routine investigations at the scenes of crimes, including burglaries. Neither do they apply where it is unnecessary to seek the consent of a person entitled to grant entry, because this would cause disproportionate inconvenience to that person, or where there is a statutory power to enter premises to inspect goods, equipment or procedures where no offence is suspected. It is submitted that the latter may apply to s 23(1) of the Misuse of Drugs Act 1971, where the police may routinely examine the records and stocks of a person carrying on the business of producing or supplying controlled drugs such as pharmaceutical manufacturers and distributors. Any breaches of the Codes of Practice, whilst not necessarily rendering police action unlawful, may constitute evidence in civil or even criminal proceedings and also in internal disciplinary proceedings.

Paragraph 3 of Code B, entitled 'Search warrants and production orders – (a) Before making an application', states that the following must be complied with prior to any action under s 15 of PACE. First, any information which appears to justify an application for a search warrant must be checked for accuracy and that it is not out of date. Reasonable steps must also be taken to ensure that the information has not been provided maliciously or irresponsibly. Corroboration must also be sought in cases where the information comes from an anonymous source. Note for Guidance 3A to Code B states the following with regard to such information:

3A   The identity of an informant need not be disclosed when making an application, but the officer should be prepared to answer any questions the magistrate or judge may have about:

- the accuracy of previous information from that source;
- any other related matters.

Secondly, the officer concerned in the application must ascertain, as specifically as possible, the nature of the articles sought and their location. This provision is echoed in Note for Guidance 3B to Code B, which states:

The information supporting a search warrant application should be as specific as possible, particularly in relation to the articles being sought and where in the premises it is suspected they may be found. The meaning of 'items subject to legal privilege', 'special procedure material' and 'excluded material' are defined by PACE, sections 10, 11 and 14 respectively.

Thirdly, the officer shall be expected to make reasonable inquiries to see if anything is known about the likely occupier of the premises in question, as well as the nature of the premises, and to obtain any other information which may be relevant to the application. This will include whether the premises have been searched before and, if so, how recently. Fourthly, no application to a magistrate for a search warrant, or to a circuit judge for a search warrant or production order under Sched 1 of PACE, may be made without the accompanying written authority of a police officer of at least the rank of inspector although, in urgent cases, the senior officer on duty may do this. However, as mentioned earlier, applications for production orders or search warrants under Sched 5 to the Terrorism Act 2000 must be made on the written authority of a police officer of at least the rank of superintendent.[16] Finally, if there is reason to believe that the execution of a search warrant might have an adverse effect on relations

---

16   A police officer of the next lower rank may be allowed to give prior authority if they are acting in the capacity of an inspector or superintendent (apart from the provision regarding urgent cases). See s 107 of PACE and para 2.7 of Code B.

between the police and the community, the local police/community liaison officer must be consulted beforehand. The exception to this rule is in cases of urgency where such persons should be informed of the search as soon as practicable after the event (see para 3.5 of Code B).

Safeguards regarding applications for search warrants

The provisions governing applications for search warrants are contained under s 15 of PACE, which are augmented by Code B. Section 15 will now be reproduced, with annotations in square brackets where appropriate, accompanied by the relevant information and guidance under Code B in each instance:

Search warrants – safeguards

(1) This section and s 16 below have effect in relation to the issue to constables under any enactment, including an enactment contained in an Act passed after this Act of warrants to enter and search premises, and an entry on or search of premises under a warrant is unlawful, unless it complies with this section and s 16 below.

[Sub-section (1) states that the provisions under this section and s 16 apply to applications for warrants under any enactment, whether it was passed before or after PACE, including applications made under PACE itself. It also provides that any non-compliance with these provisions will render the entry and search unlawful.]

(2) Where a constable applies for any such warrant, it shall be his duty:
    (a) to state:
        (i) the ground on which he makes the application; and
        (ii) the enactment under which the warrant would be issued;
    (b) to specify the premises which it is desired to enter and search; and
    (c) to identify, so far as is practicable, the articles or persons to be sought.

[Code B, under the subheading 'Before making an application', reiterates much of what is already stated in sub-s (2), although para 3.8 makes the following statement which is absent from the above provisions: 'If a search warrant application is refused, a further application may not be made for those premises unless supported by additional grounds.']

(3) An application for such a warrant shall be made *ex parte* and supported by an information in writing.

(4) The constable shall answer on oath any question that the justice of the peace or judge hearing the application asks him.

[See also Note for Guidance 3A to Code B (see above, with regard to sub-s (4)).]

(5) A warrant shall authorise an entry on one occasion only.

[The reason for this safeguard will be obvious. Unlimited entry to premises in this context would be viewed as too draconian and challengable on constitutional and human rights grounds. This rule is also repeated in para 6.3 of Code B. There are, however, exceptions under prevention of terrorism legislation, which are discussed in this chapter. In addition, para 6.3 makes reference to the new seize and sift powers which may be considered where a search is likely to take a long time due to the complexity or extent of a search.]

(6) A warrant:
    (a) shall specify:
        (i) the name of the person who applies for it;
        (ii) the date on which it is issued;

(iii) the enactment under which it is issued; and

(iv) the premises to be searched; and

(b) shall identify, so far as is practicable, the articles or person to be sought.

[In *R v South Western Magistrates' Court and Metropolitan Police Commissioner ex p Cofie* (1996), it was held that where a property is in multi-occupancy, the warrant should state to which part of those premises the search should be directed. In this case, a search warrant was obtained in which the number of the house was 78. The police did not make it clear that they only needed to search Flat 78F and the common parts of the building. The court held that the warrant was unlawful, as it did not comply with s 15(6)(a)(iv) of PACE.]

(7) Two copies shall be made of a warrant.

(8) The copies shall be clearly certified as copies.

The execution of search warrants

Section 16 of PACE, together with the relevant provisions under Code B, cover the important issue of the conduct of entry and search of premises. The provisions under s 16 are as follows, together with appropriate annotations and quotations from the Code of Practice:

Execution of warrants

16(1) A warrant to enter and search premises may be executed by any constable.

[This means that any constable may execute a search warrant, in so far as that officer need not be the person named in it. It also means that the constable may be of any rank, although note the provisions mentioned above, whereby an inspector or above must take charge and be present during a search under Sched 1 to PACE and Sched 5 to the Terrorism Act 2000.]

(2) Such a warrant may authorise persons to accompany any constable who is executing it.

(2A) A person so authorised has the same powers as the constable whom he accompanies in respect of –

(a) the execution of the warrant, and

(b) the seizure of anything to which the warrant relates.

(2B) But he may exercise those powers only in the company, and under the supervision, of a constable.

[Occasionally, other persons may accompany the police during the search of premises. This may include an expert witness,[17] a social worker, a community leader where the search may adversely affect police/community relations or even a carpenter to lift floorboards.[18] Sub-sections (2A) and (2B) were inserted by s 2 of the Criminal Justice Act 2003, and this enables certain civilians to play a more direct role in the execution of search warrants. Previously they were confined to a more passive role as ruled in *R v Reading Justices ex p South West Meats Ltd* (1992), where it was held, *inter alia*, that the police must exercise care in order to avoid delegating their authority to non-police officers who may accompany them. Although it appears that this is now overruled by the new sub-ss (2A) and (2B), it is submitted that any civilian assistance must still be under the control of the police who are ultimately responsible for the execution of search warrants; but note the provisions under the Police Reform Act 2002 as discussed in

17 *Op cit*, Levenson, Fairweather and Cape, fn 3.
18 *Op cit*, Clark, fn 11. See also Note for Guidance 3C in Code B.

Chapter 7 where civilian investigating officers have been given certain police powers to enter and search premises.]

(3) Entry and search under a warrant must be within one month from the date of its issue.

(4) Entry and search under a warrant must be at a reasonable hour, unless it appears to the constable executing it that the purpose of a search may be frustrated on an entry at a reasonable hour.

[The provisions under sub-ss (3) and (4) are repeated in paras 6.1 and 6.2 of Code B. These are designed to prevent warrants lasting indefinitely and to ensure that 'dawn raids' on premises are restricted to cases where this is essential. Paragraph 6.3 of Code B, inserted in the Codes of Practice in April 2003, offers the following guidance with regard to the time of searches:

> A warrant authorises an entry on one occasion only. When the extent or complexity of a search mean it is likely to take a long time, the officer in charge of the search may consider using the seize and sift powers referred to in section 7.

Again, the new powers of seize and sift under ss 50–66 and Scheds 1 and 2 to the Criminal Justice and Police Act 2001 are referred to in the Codes of Practice. This indicates the potential usefulness of these powers with regard to police powers of entry, search and seizure, even though it has been predicted that such cases may be fairly rare.]

(5) Where the occupier of premises which are to be entered and searched is present at the time when a constable seeks to execute a warrant to enter and search them, the constable:

    (a) shall identify himself to the occupier and, if not in uniform, shall produce to him documentary evidence that he is a constable;

    (b) shall produce the warrant to him; and

    (c) shall supply him with a copy of it.

[In *R v Chief Constable of Lancashire ex p Parker and Magrath* (1993), the police executed search warrants to which a schedule listing the articles sought was attached when the application was made. Following the search and subsequent seizure of documents, the police supplied the applicants with a copy of the authorisation, but not the schedule. The court held that since there had been a breach of s 16(5)(c) of PACE, the police had no legal right to retain the documents seized in the course of this unlawful entry and search.]

(6) Where:

    (a) the occupier of such premises is not present at the time when a constable seeks to execute such a warrant; but

    (b) some other person who appears to the constable to be in charge of the premises is present,

sub-s (5) above shall have effect as if any reference to the occupier were a reference to that other person.

(7) If there is no person present who appears to the constable to be in charge of the premises, he shall leave a copy of the warrant in a prominent place on the premises.

[Paragraphs 6.4 to 6.6 of Code B cover 'Entry other than with consent' and fill certain gaps uncovered by s 16 of PACE by making the following provisions:

6.4 The officer in charge of the search shall first try to communicate with the occupier, or any other person entitled to grant access to the premises, explain the authority under which entry is sought and ask the occupier to allow entry, unless:

(i) the search premises are unoccupied;

(ii) the occupier and any other person entitled to grant access are absent;

(iii) there are reasonable grounds for believing that alerting the occupier or any other person entitled to grant access would frustrate the object of the search or endanger officers or other people.

6.5 Unless sub-paragraph 6.4(iii) applies, if the premises are occupied the officer, subject to paragraph 2.9, shall, before the search begins:

(i) identify him or herself, show their warrant card (if not in uniform) and state the purpose of and grounds for the search;

(ii) identify and introduce any person accompanying the officer on the search (such persons should carry identification for production on request) and briefly describe that person's role in the process.

[In *R v Longman* (1988), police officers obtained a search warrant under s 23(3) of the Misuse of Drugs Act 1971 and went to the defendant's address in plain clothes. One of them posed as a delivery lady, since there had been difficulty executing a warrant there in the past. Once the door was opened by the defendant, the police entered the premises and one of them shouted who they were and that they had a warrant. In the course of the search, the defendant lunged at a police officer with a knife and was subsequently convicted of attempted wounding and obstructing the police. During his appeal, it was contended that, under ss 15 and 16 of PACE, the police officer should have announced his identity and produced his warrant card as well as the search warrant prior to entry. The Court of Appeal held that these procedures could be bypassed if there were reasonable grounds for believing that this would frustrate the object of the search or endanger the police or others.

However, in *R v Linehan* (1999), the police attended the defendant's address, intending to conduct a search under s 18 of PACE, having previously arrested his son (this power to enter and search premises is covered below). When they identified themselves and requested entry, he responded by asking them to push their warrant under the door; instead, the police offered to display it at the window, but this offer was rejected. The defendant was then warned by the police that the door would be forced, which they subsequently did, and he then threw liquid through the door, which struck two of the officers in the face. The defendant was later convicted of two charges of assault on police. In allowing his appeal against conviction, the Divisional Court held that as it was unclear as to whether the police had given a proper explanation regarding the reason for their intention to enter and search the premises, the officers were not acting in the execution of their duty.]

6.6 Reasonable and proportionate force may be used if necessary to enter premises if the officer in charge of the search is satisfied that the premises are those specified in any warrant, or in exercise of the powers described in paragraphs 4.1 to 4.3, and 16 if:

(i) the occupier or any other person entitled to grant access has refused entry;

(ii) it is impossible to communicate with the occupier or any other person entitled to grant access; or

(iii) any of the provisions of paragraph 6.4 apply.

[Apart from specific mention of the use of reasonable force in the Codes of Practice, it should also be remembered that s 117 of PACE applies this to all the coercive powers under PACE; also, the provisions of s 3(1) of the Criminal Law Act 1967 should be borne in mind in the exercise of other powers.]

Section 16 of PACE continues as follows:

(8) A search under a warrant may only be a search to the extent required for the purpose for which the warrant was issued.

[This is a safeguard which prevents unfettered search powers being exercised by the police. If, for instance, a warrant is issued to search for a large power drill suspected of being used to break into a bank, police officers executing a search warrant would not be justified in sifting through clothing in a small drawer in a dressing table, unless they were also seeking documents relating to ownership of the drill. This is confirmed in para 6.9 of Code B, which states: *'Premises may be searched only to the extent necessary to achieve the object of the search, having regard to the size and nature of whatever is sought.'*

But, in the other extreme, it does not mean that the police should ignore the presence of a dead body when looking for something else! (See sub-s (9)(b), below, which covers such eventualities.) Sub-section (8) should also be read in conjunction with s 15(2)(c) and (6)(b), which states that the warrant should state, as far as is practicable, the articles or persons to be sought. In *R v Reading Justices ex p South West Meats Ltd* (1992), cited above, a search warrant was applied for by the police at the request of the Intervention Board for Agricultural Produce. However, the warrant was not executed correctly, as the actual search was conducted by members of the Board, instead of the police, and the warrant did not identify the persons likely to enter the premises with the police. Also, the objects and documents sought were not described in sufficient detail and an inappropriate enactment was cited. The Divisional Court held the warrant to be invalid and the subsequent entry and search unlawful to the extent that exemplary damages were awarded against the police and the board.

Also relevant to sub-s (8) is *R v Chesterfield Justices ex p Bramley* (1999), where it was held that, when executing warrants under s 8(1) of PACE, the police are not entitled to remove items from the premises in order to 'sift through' them for the purpose of ascertaining whether or not they fall within the scope of the warrant. Items seized unlawfully during a search must be returned, although the search remains valid regarding any items that were properly seized. As a result of this judgment, law enforcement bodies were placed in a difficult position, especially those who needed to sift through large quantities of materials, such as during a fraud investigation. According to Mr Justice Turner, whilst expressing reluctance in making his judgment: '... I agree that further statutory power has to be provided to cover the situation which I have considered above. For my part, I doubt whether anything short of primary legislation would suffice to meet the stringency of the requirements of the European Convention. Having regard to the practical implications of the result of this case, it may be thought that the authorities should consider this matter with a degree of urgency.' In other words, it was necessary to pass an Act of Parliament in order to resolve this difficult situation. In limited circumstances, the removal of disputed legally privileged (and other) material for sifting may now be permissible, provided it cannot be ascertained on the spot whether any item falls within this definition. This, and other measures, are now possible through ss 50–66 of and Scheds 1 and 2 to the Criminal Justice and Police Act 2001 (Part 2), which will be discussed later in this chapter.]

(9) A constable executing a warrant shall make an endorsement on it, stating:

    (a) whether the articles or persons sought were found; and

    (b) whether any articles were seized other than articles which were sought.

(10) A warrant which:

    (a) has been executed; or

    (b) has not been executed within the time authorised for its execution, shall be returned:

        (i) if it was issued by a justice of the peace, to the clerk to the justices for the petty sessions area for which he acts; and

(ii) if it was issued by a judge, to the appropriate officer of the court from which he issued it.

(11) A warrant which is returned under sub-s (10) above shall be retained for 12 months from its return:

(a) by the clerk to the justices, if it was returned under para (i) of that sub-section; and

(b) by the appropriate officer, if it was returned under para (ii).

(12) If, during the period for which a warrant is to be retained, the occupier of the premises to which it relates asks to inspect it, he shall be allowed to do so.

Finally, in *DPP v Meaden* (2003), it was held that when executing search warrants, the police may restrict the movement of persons within those premises, using reasonable force if necessary, in order to enable the search to be effective. In this case, the warrant authorised the searching of the premises and persons for controlled drugs, as well as documents connected with drug offences.

ENTRY AND SEARCH WITHOUT WARRANT

Introduction

At the beginning of this chapter, it was stated that there are a number of statutory powers available to the police enabling them to enter and search premises without warrant (apart from executing arrest warrants). One of those cited was s 23(1) of the Misuse of Drugs Act 1971, which empowers the police to enter premises where a person is carrying on business as a producer or supplier of controlled drugs, in order to examine their records and stocks of drugs. Others include s 13 of the Aviation Security Act 1982, s 15(3) of the Theatres Act 1968 and s 2 of the Performing Animals (Regulation) Act 1925 to name but a few.[19] Many of these provisions are essentially regulatory by nature and often specialised in their enforcement since, *inter alia*, certain premises are excluded from their ambit.

The three *main* statutory sources of police powers to enter and search premises without warrant are to be found under ss 17, 18 and 32 of PACE, although the search powers in these instances are limited.[20] There is also a common law power which has been preserved by PACE, namely the power for the police to enter premises in order to deal with or prevent a breach of the peace. Finally, there are a number of specific entry and search powers conferred on the police in order to prevent acts of terrorism, under the Terrorism Act 2000, and also powers to enter school premises in order to search those premises and any person on them for knives and any offensive weapons. The latter provisions are to be found in the Offensive Weapons Act 1996. All the statutory sources of police powers to enter and search premises mentioned in this paragraph will now be discussed.

---

19 For a comprehensive list of such statutory powers, see *op cit*, Levenson, Fairweather and Cape, fn 3, Appendix 6.

20 Code B, paras 4.1 to 4.3 refer to entry without warrant under PACE, ss 17, 18 and 32.

Section 17 of PACE – entry for purpose of arrest, etc

Section 17 applies to any premises (which, *inter alia,* includes vehicles for this purpose) and permits entry for a number of purposes, including making arrests. As far as the latter is concerned, a constable may enter and search premises in order to execute a warrant for an arrest in connection with or arising out of criminal proceedings, or to execute a warrant of commitment (these are issued in response to non-payment of fines, compensation orders or maintenance orders). The police may also enter and search premises in order to arrest a person for an arrestable offence or for the following offences:

(a) s 1 of the Public Order Act 1936 – prohibiting the wearing of uniforms in connection with political objects;

(b) any enactment under ss 6–8 or 10 of the Criminal Law Act 1977 – offences relating to entering and remaining on property (squatting);

(c) s 4 of the Public Order Act 1986 – causing fear or provocation of violence;

(d) s 163 of the Road Traffic Act 1988 – failure to stop a vehicle when required to do so by a police officer in uniform;

(e) s 76 of the Criminal Justice and Public Order Act 1994 – failure to comply with interim possession order (squatters failing to leave).

Note that, with regard to (b) and (e), these police powers of entry and search may only be exercised by officers in uniform.

Section 17 also empowers the police to enter and search premises for the purposes of recapturing persons unlawfully at large. Under sub-ss (1)(ca) and (cb), this includes any child or young person remanded or committed to local authority accommodation under s 23(1) of the Children and Young Persons Act 1969 and persons unlawfully at large from a prison, remand centre, young offender institution or secure training centre. Also included are children or young persons guilty of 'grave crimes' who are unlawfully at large from any place designated by the Home Secretary for their detention. 'Grave crimes' are defined under s 91 of the Powers of Criminal Courts (Sentencing) Act 2000, which refers to particularly serious offences which, if committed by any 10–17 year old, can justify long term detention (although ss 226 and 228 of the Criminal Justice Act 2003, when in force, will modify this criteria).

Persons unlawfully at large who do not fall under any of the aforementioned categories are covered under sub-s (1)(d), which provides that the police may enter and search premises in order to recapture any person 'whatever' who is unlawfully at large. This appears to include those who escape from such places as police stations, court cells and police vehicles, and compulsory patients who abscond from psychiatric hospitals. However, it is important to note that, with regard to this miscellaneous category under sub-s (1)(d), the police may only exercise these powers when in actual pursuit of the person unlawfully at large.

The meaning of the word 'pursuing' means actually 'chasing' or being in 'hot pursuit', according to the House of Lords in *D'Souza v DPP* (1992). In this case, Mrs D'Souza was compulsorily admitted to a psychiatric unit, but absconded shortly afterwards. Three police officers, acting on information received, later arrived at her home, together with two nurses, intending to return her to hospital, although they did not have a warrant. Other members of the family refused to admit the police to the premises; therefore, they forced entry. A struggle ensued between the family and the police, and subsequently the daughter, Miss D'Souza, was charged and later convicted of assault on police. Her conviction was quashed by the House of Lords on the grounds that whilst her mother was unlawfully at large, the police had no legal right to enter her home, since they were not actively pursuing her at the time and, therefore, they were not acting in the course of their duty. Subsequently, there could be no assault on police. In this decision, Lord Lowry stated:

> There must be an act of pursuit – a chase – however short in time and distance. It was not enough for the police to form an intention to arrest, which they put into practice by resorting to the premises where they believed the person whom they sought might be found. Entry without warrant under s 17(1)(d) of PACE could be made for the purpose of recapturing a person who was unlawfully at large, but could be made only if the constables were 'pursuing' that person and not in any other circumstances. Therefore, a constable, acting on information received, but not being in possession of a warrant, who simply goes to a house where he reasonably (and correctly) believes that the person he is seeking can be found, cannot conceivably say that he is 'pursuing' that person. To do so would empty the word 'pursuing' of all meaning.[21]

Up until the passing of the Prisoners (Return to Custody) Act 1995, the recapture of all persons unlawfully at large was subject to the 'hot pursuit' requirement. This no longer applies to those mentioned above in sub-ss (1)(ca) and (cb), although it is still an essential requirement regarding those who fall under sub-s (1)(d), which includes formally detained psychiatric patients who abscond, as illustrated in the above case.[22]

Section 17 further empowers the police to enter and search premises without warrant in order to save life or limb or to prevent serious damage to property (sub-s (1)(e)). A number of situations which may fall under this broad heading could also constitute a breach of the peace for which a common law power of entry exists and has been preserved under sub-s (6). In addition to this overlapping of powers, it has been suggested that the potential for intervention under sub-s (1)(e) can create even further inroads into other police powers; for example, entry in order to deal with or prevent a child or wife being battered by a violent partner, entry into the premises of an extreme political organisation where it is believed that weapons are being kept for imminent use and entry into premises where it is alleged that a drunken brawl is taking place.[23] In view of the infinite variety of dangerous situations that sub-s (1)(e) is designed to prevent or alleviate, it may come as no surprise that this is not subject to the following procedural requirements under sub-s (2), which restrict all the other entry and search powers under s 17. These are that they are only exercisable if the police have reasonable grounds for believing that the person being sought is on the premises, and confining the entry and search to communal parts of premises where they consist of more than one dwelling. Since this limitation does not apply to sub-s (1)(e), the scope for its application is even wider, as illustrated in the following statement:

---

21 *The Guardian*, 17 November 1992.

22 The legal situation, however, is not entirely clear on this issue. See Jason-Lloyd, L, 'Prisoners (Return to Custody) Act 1995 – a review' (1995) 159 JP 754; Jason-Lloyd, L, 'Escape from lawful custody and the Prisoners (Return to Custody) Act 1995 – are they reconcilable?' (1997) 161 JP 354.

23 *Op cit*, Clark, fn 11.

Furthermore, there is no requirement that the threat to life, limb or property should concern the premises in question, eg the police can enter if they believe that the premises contain material such as burglary or arson equipment which may be used against other premises or if a person who has planted a bomb elsewhere is on the premises.[24]

Section 17 goes on to state that all search powers within its ambit must be confined to searching premises to the extent that is reasonably required to find who or what the police are seeking. Since most of this section applies to searching for persons, this means, *inter alia*, that it would not be permissible to search a dressing table for a fully grown adult, although it may be permissible to open a wardrobe which could be large enough to conceal such a person. Section 17 ends by abolishing all the earlier common law rules governing entry of premises without warrant but, at the same time, it preserves the common law power of entry to deal with or prevent a breach of the peace (see sub-s (6), mentioned above). However, in *R (Rottman) v Metropolitan Police Commissioner and the Secretary of State for the Home Office* (2002), the House of Lords confirmed that s 17 did not abolish the common law power for the police to enter the home of a person arrested on warrant and search for evidence and seize property. This applied to extradition cases as well as domestic crimes.

Inevitably, the police will sometimes have to use force in effecting their powers under s 17, but this is always subject to s 117 of PACE, which requires the use of any force to be reasonable and necessary. In *Smith (Peter John) v DPP* (2001), it was held that police officers had the power to use reasonable force where they moved a man from the front door of a house where an abandoned 999 call had been made, in order to gain entry under s 17.

Section 18 of PACE – entry and search after arrest

Section 18 provides that the police may enter and search premises occupied or controlled by a person who has been arrested for an arrestable offence. This is contingent upon them having reasonable grounds for suspecting that there is evidence on those premises which relates to the offence in question or some other arrestable offence connected with, or similar to it, although this excludes items subject to legal privilege. The power to search premises under this section may only be exercised to the extent that is reasonably required to discover any evidence just mentioned. If the arrested suspect is already at the police station, a police officer of at least the rank of inspector must make written authorisation before these entry and search powers are exercised. In *R v Badham* (1987), it was held that this authorisation must be made on an independent document and not a mere entry in a notebook as confirmation of verbal instructions. On this issue, para 4.3 of Code B states that, if possible, that authority shall be given on the notice of powers and rights (see below).

If the presence of the arrested person is necessary for the effective investigation of the offence, the police may exercise their powers under s 18 *before* the suspect is taken to the police station and without an inspector or above giving prior written authorisation. Where this is done, the officer conducting the search must inform the inspector as soon as practicable following its completion. Where an inspector or above

---

24   *Op cit*, Clark, fn 11.

either authorises a search under s 18 or has been informed that one has been conducted prior to the suspect being brought to the police station, that officer shall record, in writing, the grounds for the search and the nature of evidence that was sought. This will be part of the custody record if the person who was in occupation or control of the premises during the search is under police detention at the time the record is being made. Otherwise, the relevant entry should be made in the officer's pocket book or the search record.

Section 32 of PACE – search upon arrest

The provisions under s 32 were discussed in Chapter 3, since searches under this section can apply to suspects themselves as well as premises they were in at the time of the arrest or immediately beforehand (see above).

Notice of powers and rights

Whenever a search of premises is made under Code B, para 6.7 states that, unless it is impracticable to do so, the occupier shall be given a copy of a notice in a standard format, which contains the following information:

(a) whether the search is made under a warrant or with the occupier's consent, or under s 17, 18 or 32 of PACE;

(b) a summary of the extent of the powers of search and seizure conferred under PACE;

(c) an explanation of the occupier's rights, and those of the owner of any property seized;

(d) notification that compensation may be available in appropriate cases where damage has been caused by entering and searching premises, together with the address to which such claims may be directed;

(e) a statement that a copy of this Code may be consulted at any police station.

Paragraph 6.8 provides that copies of the notice of powers and rights shall be given to the occupier and any warrant, where applicable, if he or she is present. This shall, if practicable, be given to the occupier prior to the commencement of the search, unless the officer in charge reasonably believes that this would frustrate the object of the search or endanger police officers present or other people. Where the occupier is not present, a copy of the notice and warrant, where appropriate, shall be left in a prominent place on the premises. This shall be endorsed with the name of the officer in charge (or warrant number, where the search is linked to a terrorist investigation), the name of the police station where that officer is attached and the date and time of the search. Any warrant shall be endorsed to the effect that this has been done.

With regard to compensation under (b) above, Note for Guidance 6A to Code B provides the following advice where forced entry occurs:

> Whether compensation is appropriate depends on the circumstances in each case. Compensation for damage caused when effecting entry is unlikely to be appropriate if the search was lawful, and the force used can be shown to be reasonable, proportionate and necessary to effect entry. If the wrong premises are searched by mistake everything possible should be done at the earliest opportunity to allay any sense of grievance and there should normally be a strong presumption in favour of paying compensation.

Consensual entry and search of premises

Paragraph 6.4 of Code B provides that, wherever possible, the police are obliged to seek the co-operation of the occupier to enter premises, even where they have the power to enter without his or her consent. The exceptions to this rule are where the premises are known to be unoccupied or the occupier or any other person entitled to grant access is absent, or where attempting to communicate with such persons would frustrate the object of the search or endanger police officers or others present. Paragraph 6.6 states that reasonable and proportionate force may be used if necessary to enter premises under the authority of a warrant or where entry is required under s 17, 18 or 32 of PACE. This may be done where any of the above-mentioned conditions are present, or where the occupier or other person entitled to grant access has refused to allow entry to the premises, or where it is not possible to communicate with such persons.

Searches with consent are covered under paras 5.1–5.4 of Code B, together with Notes for Guidance 5A, 5B and 5C as follows. Unless it would cause disproportionate inconvenience to the person concerned,[25] the police should seek the consent of that person in the following manner. First, the officer in charge should make necessary inquiries to ensure that the person is in a position to give consent. Secondly, the officer should state the purpose and the extent of the search and inform the person that he or she is not obliged to co-operate and that anything seized may be produced in evidence. If the person is not suspected of an offence at the time, the officer shall tell that person when stating the purpose of the search. Thirdly, where consent is given, this should be put into writing if practicable on the notice of powers and rights before the search takes place. The police cannot enter and search premises, or continue to do so once a search has started, if the consent has been given under duress or the person withdraws their consent before completion of the search. For an interesting perspective on the issue of consensual entry to premises by the police, see *Hobson and Others v Chief Constable of the Cheshire Constabulary* (2004), and the article 'Police officers entering private property: the issue of consent' by Neil Parpworth, in (2004) 168 JP, 28 February.

Searches of lodging houses or similar accommodation should not be made solely on the basis of the landlord's consent, unless the matter is urgent and the tenant, lodger or occupier is not available.

Police powers of entry and search of school premises[26]

In response to a series of incidents involving the use of knives and similar weapons both in and around school premises, the Offensive Weapons Act 1996 was passed, in

---

25 Note for Guidance 5C states that this applies where it is reasonable to assume that innocent occupiers would not object to the police taking action where, eg, a suspect is fleeing from the police and they need to quickly check surrounding gardens and readily accessible places to see if that person is hiding there or the police have arrested someone and wish to briefly check gardens nearby for any discarded evidence.

26 For further discussion on this subject, as well as other issues arising from the enactment of the Offensive Weapons Act 1996, see Jason-Lloyd, L, 'The Offensive Weapons Act 1996 – an overview' (1996) 160 JP 931; and 'The Offensive Weapons Act 1996 and the Knives Act 1997 – how effective will they be?' (1997) 161 JP 572, 599.

order to combat the increasing knife culture that has been particularly prevalent among teenagers in recent times. One of the provisions under the 1996 Act is the power under s 4, enabling the police to enter school premises in order to search such places and any person in them for any article with a blade or point, or any offensive weapon. The definition and general search powers to find such dangerous articles have been covered in Chapter 2, although it should be noted that these apply to public places. Prior to the passing of the Offensive Weapons Act, there was some contention as to whether these general stop and search powers applied to school premises. This was subsequently resolved when s 4 made express provision for school premises to be included within the ambit of police powers to search for articles such as knives (except folding pocket knives with cutting edges of no more than three inches) and offensive weapons.

In addition, s 1 of the 1996 Act created the new offences of unlawful possession of an offensive weapon or an article with a blade or point in school premises, and made them arrestable offences under s 24 of PACE (see Chapter 3). This is subject to a number of defences, which include instances where the person in possession of such an article has it with good reason, with lawful authority or where it was for use at work or for educational purposes, religious reasons or as part of a national costume. 'School premises', for the purposes of the 1996 Act, include main and secondary buildings, playgrounds, sports fields, and even extend to school buses.[27] However, dwellings used by persons employed at schools are excluded from these provisions. This will include the homes of caretakers and groundsmen, for instance.

Entry by the police in school premises for the purposes of searching for such dangerous articles is contingent upon them having reasonable grounds to believe that someone is in unlawful possession of them. The requirement of reasonable belief, rather than reasonable suspicion, seems rather anomalous. If a police officer has reasonable *suspicion* that someone on school premises is unlawfully in possession of a prohibited article under the 1996 Act, that officer has the power to enter those premises in order to make an arrest under s 17 of PACE and may then search the premises and that individual under s 32. This is possible because such offences are arrestable. Also, subject to the constraints mentioned above under the coverage of s 18 of PACE, the police may then search the suspect's home. Why rely on the much higher requirement of reasonable *belief* to enter and search school premises or any person there for weapons when the lesser requirement of reasonable *suspicion* avails the police far greater powers? The position is even more puzzling when considering that the 1996 Act, as applied in Scotland, requires police officers there to have only reasonable suspicion in this context.

Where any suspected person in school premises is below the age of criminal responsibility (10 years), the police cannot exercise this arrest power, because those under 10 years old are not criminally liable; therefore, they cannot commit this or any other offence. In such cases, the police may even have difficulty in relying on their entry and search powers conferred under the 1996 Act where *any* person may be searched, because, according the wording of the Act, an offence has to be involved. Primary schools therefore appear to be excluded from the ambit of the 1996 Act. It could be argued, however, that weapons offences are more likely to be committed in

---

27 *Hansard*, Parliamentary Debates, HC Standing Committee C, 6 March 1996, 15.

secondary schools; therefore, these potential legal difficulties may not present a serious problem. A further anomaly seems apparent under the 1996 Act. Although it enables the police to use reasonable force where necessary in order to effect entry into school premises, it makes no express provision regarding force in order to search persons. However, it is submitted that the courts may imply such a power, notwithstanding the absence of any precise provision under the Act. Any resistance could be regarded as obstructing police, thereby constituting an offence, albeit a non-arrestable one.

Up until April 2003, there was no specific guidance in the Codes of Practice regarding the power to enter and search school premises, and any person in such places. This has now been rectified by the inclusion of the following new provisions under Code A:

> 2.27 The following powers to search premises also authorise the search of a person, not under arrest, who is found on the premises during the course of the search:
>
> > (a) section 139B of the Criminal Justice Act 1988 under which a constable may enter school premises and search the premises and any person on those premises for any bladed or pointed article or offensive weapon; and
> >
> > (b) under a warrant issued under section 23(3) of the Misuse of Drugs Act 1971 to search premises for drugs or documents but only if the warrant specifically authorises the search of persons found on the premises.
>
> 2.28 Before the power under section 139B of the Criminal Justice Act 1988 may be exercised, the constable must have reasonable grounds to believe that an offence under section 139A of the Criminal Justice Act 1988 (having a bladed or pointed article or offensive weapon on school premises) has been or is being committed. A warrant to search premises and persons found therein may be issued under section 23(3) of the Misuse of Drugs Act 1971 if there are reasonable grounds to suspect that controlled drugs or certain documents are in the possession of a person on the premises.
>
> 2.29 The powers in paragraph 2.27(a) or (b) do not require prior specific grounds to suspect that the person to be searched is in possession of an item for which there is an existing power to search. However, it is still necessary to ensure that the selection and treatment of those searched under these powers is based upon objective factors connected with the search of the premises, and not upon personal prejudice.

It will be seen that paras 2.27–2.29 of Code A also apply to searches under s 23(3) of the Misuse of Drugs Act 1971, but only when the warrant to search premises also includes the power to search any persons found there. As is the case regarding searches in schools, the new Code of Practice now places some constraints on searching persons in the exercise of specific powers to enter and search premises.

General provisions under Code B

Some miscellaneous provisions under Code B, most of which have not yet been discussed, will now be mentioned. Paragraphs 6.10 and 6.11 make provision regarding certain aspects of the conduct of searches and para 6.13 covers police conduct when leaving premises that have been searched. These are cited as follows, with annotations in square brackets where appropriate:

> 6.10 Searches must be conducted with due consideration for the property and privacy of the occupier and with no more disturbance than necessary. Reasonable force may be used only when necessary and proportionate because the co-operation of the occupier cannot be obtained or is insufficient for the purpose ...

6.11 A friend, neighbour or other person must be allowed to witness the search if the occupier wishes unless the officer in charge of the search has reasonable grounds for believing the presence of the person asked for would seriously hinder the investigation or endanger officers or other people. A search need not be unreasonably delayed for this purpose. A record of the action taken should be made on the premises search record including the grounds for refusing the occupier's request.

[This provision exists for a number of reasons, including reducing fears of evidence being 'planted' in the course of a search, as well as having a witness to any damage done to property.]

6.13 If premises have been entered by force, before leaving the officer in charge of the search must make sure they are secure by:

- arranging for the occupier or their agent to be present
- any other appropriate means.

Note for Guidance 6A, mentioned earlier, gives the following important advice when errors have been made:

6A Whether compensation is appropriate depends on the circumstances in each case. Compensation for damage caused when effecting entry is unlikely to be appropriate if the search was lawful, and the force used can be shown to be reasonable, proportionate and necessary to effect entry. If the wrong premises are searched by mistake everything possible should be done at the earliest opportunity to allay any sense of grievance and there should normally be a strong presumption in favour of paying compensation.

Paragraphs 8.1 to 8.3 and 9.1 provide the action to be taken after police searches and the maintenance of search registers at police stations as follows:

8.1 If premises are searched in circumstances where this Code applies, unless the exceptions in *paragraph 2.3(a)* apply [note that these exceptions cover scenes of routine crime searches, calls to fires or burglaries, bomb threat calls and searches where it would cause disproportionate inconvenience if consent was sought] on arrival at a police station the officer in charge of the search shall make or have made a record of the search to include:

(i) the address of the searched premises;

(ii) the date, time and duration of the search;

(iii) the authority used for the search:

- if the search was made in exercise of a statutory power to search premises without warrant, the power which was used for the search:
- if the search was made under a warrant or with written consent:
  - a copy of the warrant and the written authority to apply for it, *[see para 3.4; refer to earlier coverage regarding prior authority of inspectors and superintendents before warrants can be applied for]* or
  - the written consent;

shall be appended to the record or the record shall show the location of the copy warrant or consent.

(iv) subject to *[para 2.9]*, the names of:

- the officer(s) in charge of the search:
- all other officers who conducted the search;

[Paragraph 2.9 referred to above exempts officers from disclosing their names in terrorist investigations, or where it is reasonably believed that this might put them in danger for other reasons such as where serious organised crime is being investigated, or where particularly violent suspects have been arrested. Paragraph 2.9 is augmented by Note for Guidance 2E which, *inter alia*, advises that where there is any doubt, an inspector or above should be consulted. In appropriate cases, instead of disclosing their names, they should use their warrant or other identification numbers and the name of their police station.]

(v) the names of any people on the premises if they are known;

(vi) any grounds for refusing the occupier's request to have someone present during the search;

[See para 6.11 above.]

(vii) a list of any articles seized or the location of a list and, if not covered by a warrant, the grounds for their seizure;

(viii) whether force was used, and the reason;

(ix) details of any damage caused during the search, and the circumstances;

(x) if applicable, the reason it was not practicable:

(a) to give the occupier a copy of the Notice of Powers and Rights;
[See para 6.7, discussed above.]

(b) before the search to give the occupier a copy of the Notice;
[See para 6.8 above.]

(xi) when the occupier was not present, the place where copies of the Notice of Powers and Rights and search warrant were left on the premises.

[See para 6.8, discussed above.]

8.2 Where premises are searched under warrant, the warrant shall be endorsed to show:

(i) if any articles specified in the warrant were found;

(ii) if any other articles were seized;

(iii) the date and time it was executed;

(iv) subject to paragraph 2.9, the names of the officers who executed it;

(v) if a copy, together with a copy of the Notice of Powers and Rights was:

• handed to the occupier; or
• endorsed as required by paragraph 6.8 *[see above]*, and left on the premises and where.

8.3 Any warrant shall be returned within one calendar month of its issue, if it was issued by a:

• justice of the peace, to the clerk to the justices for the petty sessions area concerned;

• judge, to the appropriate officer of the court concerned.

[Note that para 8.2 constitutes an extension of the provisions contained under s 16(9) of PACE, and para 8.3 is identical to s 16(10).]

9.1 A search register will be maintained at each sub-divisional or equivalent police station. All search records required under paragraph 8.1 [see above] shall be made, copied or referred to in the register ...

Somewhat ironically, this discussion will end with key extracts from the introduction to Code B. Rather than set the tone for this subject at the beginning, it is perhaps equally useful to conclude by citing these important provisions at this stage. Paragraphs 1.3–1.5 of Code B make the following points regarding powers of entry, search and seizure:

1.3 The right to privacy and respect for personal property are key principles of the Human Rights Act 1998. Powers of entry, search and seizure should be fully and clearly justified before use because they may significantly interfere with the occupier's privacy. Officers should consider if the necessary objectives can be met by less intrusive means.

1.4 In all cases, police should:

- exercise their powers courteously and with respect for persons and property;
- only use reasonable force when this is considered necessary and proportionate to the circumstances.

1.5 If the provisions of PACE and this Code are not observed, evidence obtained from a search may be open to question.

Common law power of entry to prevent or deal with a breach of the peace

This was the only common law power to enter premises which survived PACE. The power to arrest in order to deal with or prevent a breach of the peace has been discussed in Chapter 3, along with the power to enter public and private premises to do this.

Powers to enter and close drug houses under the Anti-social Behaviour Act 2003

Since 20 January 2004, Pt 1 of the Anti-social Behaviour Act 2003 has given the police a wide-ranging power to close premises associated with certain drug activities where this is also causing serious public nuisance. Although intended principally to deal with 'crack houses', the provisions under Pt 1 of the 2003 Act also have a wider application. The first stage in the process is where a police superintendent or above has a reasonable belief that during a three-month period, specific premises have been used for certain drug activities. These activities are the unlawful production, supply or use of any Class A controlled drugs. There must also be a reasonable belief that those premises have been associated with disorder or serious nuisance to the public.

During this three-month period, the relevant local authority must be consulted and reasonable steps must be taken in order to establish the identity of anyone who lives on, controls, or is otherwise responsible for those premises. A superintendent or above may then authorise a closure notice, which prohibits *public* access to those premises. In other words, only those who habitually reside on those premises may remain, and any other persons there at the time must leave. The serving of a closure notice involves the police fixing copies of it in several parts of the premises as well as any outbuildings; copies must also be given to persons affected by the notice. The contents of this document must explain the effects of this closure power as well as state that non-compliance is an offence. Information must also be given as to where any person affected by this action can obtain legal and housing advice.

A very important component of a closure notice is that it has to contain a warning that an application will be made for a closure *order* against the premises as well as give the date, time and venue of the hearing. Magistrates are under a duty to consider the application within 48 hours of the closure notice being served. If a closure order is granted, this will have the effect of denying *anyone* access to the premises for up to three months that may, in turn, be extended by up to a further three months. Part 1 of the 2003 Act also contains a number of safeguards in order to comply with the Human

Rights Act 1998. This includes detailed provisions enabling the relevant parties to request modifications to any of the closure powers, as well as an appeals process and provision for compensation, where appropriate.

Where necessary, reasonable force may be used whilst entering and securing the premises and, although the premises will be fully secured against entry throughout the closure period, the police and/or contractors may enter at any time to effect essential repairs and maintenance. It is an offence for any person unlawfully to remain on or enter into premises in defiance of *any* power of closure, or to obstruct the police or authorised persons such as contractors when entering and securing the premises. Any of these offences are punishable by a maximum of 51 weeks' imprisonment and/or a fine not exceeding level 5 on the standard scale (currently £5,000). Police officers in uniform may arrest without warrant anyone reasonably suspected of committing, or having committed, any of these offences.[28]

POLICE POWERS OF SEIZURE

Introduction

A number of sections under PACE have given the police specific and general powers to seize evidence, and a number of other statutes passed before and after PACE provide the police with a variety of powers of seizure in respect of certain categories of property. These include the Betting, Gaming and Lotteries Act 1963, the Biological Weapons Act 1974, the Misuse of Drugs Act 1971, the Theft Act 1968, the Financial Services Act 1986 and the Criminal Justice (International Co-operation) Act 1990 to name but a few. Further examples of specific police powers of seizure under statutes enacted since PACE will be illustrated later in this chapter, including the new power to 'seize and sift' under the Criminal Justice and Police Act 2001.

General powers of seizure under PACE, other statutes and the common law

Under s 19 of PACE, a constable may seize anything if he or she has reasonable grounds for believing that it constitutes evidence in relation to any offence or that it has been obtained as a result of an offence being committed, and that it is necessary to seize such items to prevent them being concealed, lost, altered or destroyed. The general power of seizure only applies when the constable is on premises lawfully, namely, where the officer is executing a search warrant or any other search under written authority, is dealing with or preventing a breach of the peace, is entering premises under s 17, 18 or 32 of PACE or has entered premises with the consent of a person entitled to give it. It is submitted that this may also apply where the police are

---

28 For a full commentary on the provisions of Pt 1 of this Act, see Jason-Lloyd, L, 'Controlled Drugs and the Anti-social Behaviour Bill' (2003) 167 JP 32, 9 August.

on premises under the authority of any statutory power to enter premises without a warrant.[29]

It is irrelevant that the police did not have the express authority to search for a particular item which is seized. This will include situations where the police may be searching premises for a murder weapon, for instance, but find illicit drugs in the course of the search. It will be for the trial judge to decide whether such articles should be admitted as evidence in accordance with s 78 of PACE.

Paragraph 7.4 of Code of Practice B makes provision for the scenario where an officer has entered premises and has reasonable grounds for believing that property there has been obtained as a result of the commission of a criminal offence, but decides that it is inappropriate to seize that property, because of an explanation by the person holding it. In those circumstances, that officer shall inform the holder of his suspicions and explain that he may be liable to civil or criminal proceedings if he or she disposes of that property.

It should be noted at this stage that whilst excluded or special procedure may be seized under these provisions, material subject to legal privilege may not be seized under any power under PACE or any other statute. The exception to this rule is where it is inextricably linked with material for which there is a power of seizure (see the coverage below of the new seize and sift power under the Criminal Justice and Police Act 2001). Any items that have been seized unlawfully during a search must be returned, although this will not invalidate the search regarding any other items that were properly seized.

Specific powers of seizure under PACE and the Terrorism Act 2000

Property may be seized by the police under the following circumstances:

- articles obtained as a result of a search under s 1 of PACE which are reasonably suspected to be stolen or prohibited;

- material obtained as a result of a warrant issued by magistrates under s 8 regarding evidence of a serious arrestable offence, or anything obtained in the execution of a search warrant authorised by a circuit judge under Sched 1 to PACE;

- any object found as a result of searches under ss 18 and 32 of PACE;

- items found under ss 54 and 55 of PACE as a result of the search of a suspect while detained by the police; and

- material discovered as a result of searches under the Terrorism Act 2000.

Information held on computer

Section 19(4) of PACE makes provision for access to information stored in any electronic form. This is put into more simplified form under para 7.6 of Code B, which states:

---

29 In *Cowan v Metropolitan Police Commissioner* (2000), it was held that ss 18(2) and 19(2) of PACE include the power to seize everything, even the premises themselves! In this case, a car, which was held to constitute 'premises', was seized by the police, since it was alleged that a number of indecent assaults had taken place in it and the car was needed as evidence.

7.6 If an officer considers information stored in any electronic form and accessible from the premises could be used in evidence, they may require the information to be produced in a form:

- which can be taken away and in which it is visible and legible; or
- from which it can readily be produced in a visible and legible form.

This, for example, will cover the police obtaining a printout, as opposed to a disk,[30] and such procedures may be applied under the following powers: powers of seizure under any enactment before or after PACE; powers of seizure under s 8 of PACE; powers of entry and search under s 18 of PACE; searches under Sched 1 to PACE; and the power under s 19 of PACE to seize evidence discovered when the police are lawfully on premises, but which is not the object of the search. It has been stated that in order to avoid a computer being destroyed or tampered with, the police may secure it in order to ensure the production of a print out.[31] See also the coverage of the new seize and sift powers below.

Access to and the copying of seized articles

Access to all property seized and subsequently held by the police under any power of seizure is provided for under s 21 of PACE. Where a person can show that he or she was the occupier of the premises from which the police have seized property, or had custody or control of the property immediately before it was seized, that person may request a record of the items taken, which must be provided within reasonable time. Such a person, or someone acting on their behalf, may be granted supervised access to the property by the investigating officer and may photograph or copy it; alternatively, this may be done by the police and given to the person concerned. However, these provisions will not apply where there are reasonable grounds for believing that this would prejudice that or any other criminal investigation or proceedings.

Retention of articles seized

Under s 22 of PACE, the police may retain any property seized (including information obtained from a computer) for as long as is necessary in all the circumstances. This will include retaining it for use as evidence at a trial, for forensic examination, for investigation into any criminal offence or to establish the rightful owner of the property where applicable. However, the police should not retain any property which can be photographed or otherwise copied for their purposes. In some circumstances, the police may not be under an obligation to return the property at all, for example, drugs which have been unlawfully possessed.[32] However, they should return anything seized from a person where it may have been used to cause physical injury or damage to property, to interfere with evidence or to assist in escape from police detention or

---

30 Levenson, H, Fairweather, F and Cape, E, *Police Powers: A Practitioner's Guide* (3rd edn, London: Legal Action Group, 1996).

31 Zander, M, *The Police and Criminal Evidence Act 1984* (4th edn, London: Sweet & Maxwell, 2003).

32 *Op cit*, Levenson, Fairweather and Cape, fn 30.

lawful custody, if that person is no longer in police detention or the custody of a court or is in the custody of a court, but has been released on bail.

At this stage, further mention should be made of *R v Chesterfield Justices ex p Bramley* (1999), discussed earlier, where it was held, *inter alia*, that it was unlawful to remove items from premises in order to 'sift through' them, so as to find out if they fall within the scope of the search warrant. In this case, it was stated that:

> ... if the material is taken from the premises searched other than by agreement, it is 'seized' ... and the only right to seize is that to be found in s 8(2) of the [1984] Act which, subject to s 19(2)(iii) and (iv),[33] is restricted to items for which a search has been authorised by the warrant. If a constable executing a warrant seizes items which, when examined, are found to be outside the scope of the warrant and not covered by s 19, even if he acts in good faith, I find in the statute no defence to an action for trespass to goods based on that unjustified seizure ...

This decision has since been overturned by Pt 2 of the Criminal Justice and Police Act 2001, which will be mentioned below.

'Seizure and sift' powers under the Criminal Justice and Police Act 2001

Part 2 of the Criminal Justice and Police Act 2001 (which includes ss 50–66 and Scheds 1 and 2) deals with situations where the police are lawfully on premises in order to search for certain material, but it is not practicable to examine the items there and then. This may be due, for instance, to the length of time it would take for the material to be examined because of its sheer bulk, or where material cannot be separated from other items on the spot, such as computerised information. In such cases, 'inextricably linked material' on the hard drive may be seized and retained, which may include legally privileged material. A further example would include the discovery of a safe which the police reasonably believed contained material that could be seized, but it would not be possible to open the safe whilst on the premises. This new power has been created under the 2001 Act in response to the decision in *R v Chesterfield Justices ex p Bramley* (1999) as mentioned earlier, and may also be exercised by designated civilian investigating officers (see Chapter 7). Furthermore, these new provisions apply to existing powers of seizure available to other law enforcement bodies such as the Department of Trade and Industry, HM Customs and Excise, and the Serious Fraud Office to name but a few. These are listed under Pt 1 of Sched 1 to the 2001 Act, which includes no fewer than 73 such powers of seizure in addition to those applicable under PACE.

Although the police (and others) have the power to remove material elsewhere for examination, they may not retain items that they do not normally have the power to seize unless it is inextricably linked material. The criteria that will justify the removal of items and their subsequent examination elsewhere is when it is not 'reasonably practicable' to determine or separate the material that is being sought. 'Reasonably practicable' includes the length of time it would take to determine or separate the material on the premises, or whether such action would cause alteration or damage to

---

[33] It is respectfully submitted that this should have been quoted as s 19(2)(a) and (b).

other relevant material. As mentioned above, this new power enables legally privileged material to be seized where it is inextricably linked with material for which there would normally be a power of seizure. This is the exception to s 19(6) of PACE, which forbids the seizure of material which is reasonably believed to be legally privileged. Therefore, if the police are seeking certain information which is on a computer disk, and that same disk also contains legally privileged material, that would be classed as inextricably linked material which can justify removing the computer disk for examination or analysis elsewhere.

Seizure of suspect cash

Under Pt II of the Drug Trafficking Act 1994, provision was made to prevent the import or export of cash being used as part of the drug trafficking process. The police (or customs) officers were empowered to seize and detain imported or exported cash that directly or indirectly represented the proceeds of drug trafficking which could later be forfeited to the courts. Chapter 3 of the Proceeds of Crime Act 2002 has now replaced these provisions with a much wider scheme that empowers police or customs officers to seize cash inland as well as at the borders. This power may be exercised where that officer has reasonable grounds for suspecting that the cash is recoverable property or is intended for use in unlawful conduct. This not only includes drug trafficking but also any criminal offence, whether committed in this country or abroad under a corresponding law, and applies to cash obtained through such criminal activity. The cash may not be detained for more than 48 hours unless a magistrate makes an order that can extend this period up to three months; further extensions may be given up to a period not exceeding two years. A magistrate may order the further detention of the cash on the following grounds:

- that there are reasonable grounds for the officer's suspicion;
- that the continued detention of the cash is justified in order to investigate its origin or intended use; or
- if criminal proceedings are being considered, or have already commenced but have not been concluded.

The person from whom the cash was seized may apply to the magistrates' court to have it released on the grounds that it is not recoverable property and is not intended for use in unlawful conduct. The cash may also be returned where the officer notifies the court that it can no longer be justified. However, if the court is satisfied on the balance of probabilities, that the cash is recoverable property or is intended for use in unlawful conduct, it may order its forfeiture. Victims connected with the cash, such as where it was stolen from them, and other owners may also apply for its release. Otherwise any aggrieved party may appeal to the Crown Court against the forfeiture of the cash. Compensation may be applied for, although it is expected that the seized cash will be placed into an interest-bearing account at the first opportunity after the initial 48-hour period of detention. The minimum amount of cash held that is liable to seizure is currently £10,000, although there is provision for this amount to be changed by an order made by the Secretary of State.

SPECIFIC POWERS OF SEIZURE UNDER OTHER STATUTES

Some examples of specific police powers of seizure will be provided below. These will include provisions under the Criminal Justice and Public Order Act 1994, the Terrorism Act 2000, the Offensive Weapons Act 1996 and the Confiscation of Alcohol (Young Persons) Act 1997.

The Criminal Justice and Public Order Act 1994

Section 60(6) of the 1994 Act provides the police with the power to seize any offensive or dangerous weapons found in the course of a search under written authority in anticipation of serious violence (see Chapter 2); and s 60AA, inserted by s 94 of the Anti-terrorism, Crime and Security Act 2001, empowers the police to seize any item which it is reasonably believed any person intends to wear wholly or mainly to conceal his or her identity whilst such a written authority is in force. Under s 64(4) of the 1994 Act, the police may seize vehicles and/or sound equipment used for 'raves' under specific circumstances, and s 62 provides them with the power to seize vehicles which have not been removed from land in accordance with a direction under s 61 (power to remove trespassers on land).

The Terrorism Act 2000

Under Sched 5 to the 2000 Act, the police are provided with the power to seize and retain items (except those subject to legal privilege) which are found in residential and non-residential premises and on persons within them, in the course of a search. This may be done where any item is reasonably believed to be of substantial value to a terrorist investigation and that it is necessary to prevent it from being concealed, lost, damaged, altered or destroyed. Also under Sched 5, the police may seize and retain anything found on premises or on any person found there which are within a police cordon and are subject to a search under the written authority of a superintendent or above, or lesser rank in an emergency. Any property seized must not be subject to legal privilege and it must be reasonably believed that it is likely to be of substantial value to a terrorist investigation and that seizure is necessary to prevent its concealment, loss, damage, alteration or destruction. It should be noted that the new seize and sift powers discussed above also apply to searches under the Terrorism Act 2000.

The Offensive Weapons Act 1996

Police officers, using their powers to search school premises and persons on them for offensive weapons and articles with blades or points, may seize and retain such articles if found in the course of a search under the Offensive Weapons Act. This same power of seizure will also apply, of course, where such items have been discovered as a result of a stop and search in a public place under s 1 of PACE.

The Confiscation of Alcohol (Young Persons) Act 1997

Although there is no direct power of seizure or search under this statute, the 1997 Act is considered here because it empowers the police to require under 18 year olds to surrender any alcohol in their possession when in a public place, other than in licensed premises. Failure to do so without reasonable excuse and to state name and address when requested constitutes a summary only offence and confers a power of arrest on the police, which is a powerful inducement for the youngster to hand over the alcoholic drink.[34] The power to require the surrender of alcohol has been extended to include a sealed container for such liquor, although under s 155 of the Licensing Act 2003, there must be reasonable belief that the person has been drinking, or intends to consume the drink.

A similar power to that under the 1997 Act can also be found in the Criminal Justice and Police Act 2001, under ss 12–16. This empowers the police to require a person who is, or has been, drinking in a designated public place, or intends to do so, to refrain from doing so, and to surrender the drink or a container which contains alcohol. Designated public places are places designated by local authorities as virtual no-go areas for drinkers due to their association with general disorder. Failure to comply with such directions within a designated place is an arrestable offence.

34 For a full commentary on the 1997 Act, see Jason-Lloyd, L, 'The Confiscation of Alcohol (Young Persons) Act 1997 – an overview' (1997) 161 JP 871; Jason-Lloyd, L, 'The Confiscation of Alcohol (Young Persons) Act 1997: implications for the police service' (1997) LXX(4) Police Journal 287, October–December.

CHAPTER 5

POLICE POWERS OF DETENTION

INTRODUCTION

Section 30 of the Police and Criminal Evidence Act 1984 (PACE) (already discussed above in Chapter 3) provides that, following the arrest of a person by the police away from a police station or the taking into custody of a suspect arrested by a non-police officer (a store detective, for example), there is a duty to convey the suspect to a police station as soon as practicable unless, of course, if street bail has been given by the police. *Normally*, that police station will be one designated for the purposes of detaining suspects, although there are exceptions, as discussed earlier. What is a designated police station, as distinct from one which is not?

DESIGNATED POLICE STATIONS

Section 35 of PACE places a statutory duty on all chief officers of police to provide designated police stations within their respective police areas. These may not necessarily function in that capacity all the time. For instance, a designated police station may operate as such for certain days of the week, although they may not be restricted to just certain times of the day.[1] Police stations falling within this category are places where custody areas are provided for the detention and subsequent questioning of suspects, and where at least one 'custody officer' is present.

THE CUSTODY OFFICER

Under s 36(3) of PACE, a custody officer must be a sergeant or above, although, under s 36(4), if a custody officer is not readily available at a designated police station, a police officer of any rank may perform this duty. However, in any event, such an officer must not be involved in the investigation of the case. A person appointed as a custody officer may not necessarily perform such duties all the time and may be assigned to other tasks although, in particularly busy police stations, custody officers are invariably full time. Under s 36(7) of PACE, where a suspect is taken to a non-designated police station, any police officer may assume the role of custody officer although, wherever possible, it should not be done by the officer investigating the case. If this cannot be avoided, due to shortage of manpower, for instance, then the officer who took the suspect to the police station or any other police officer may assume the role of custody officer; however, the arresting officer must, under s 36(9) and (10), inform an officer of at least the rank of inspector at a designated police station, as soon as practicable, that this is being done.

---

1 Zander, M, *The Police and Criminal Evidence Act 1984* (4th edn, London: Sweet & Maxwell, 2003).

The custody officer, including anyone acting in that capacity under any of the circumstances mentioned above, is the person primarily responsible for ensuring the proper treatment of persons held in police detention (s 36(8)). This is in accordance with the relevant provisions of PACE and the Codes of Practice (s 39(1)). Custody officers are also under a duty to record all relevant matters which have to be included in the 'custody record'. Where it is necessary to transfer the suspect to the investigating officer or to an officer who has charge of that person outside the police station, the responsibilities of the custody officer are then incumbent upon them (s 39(2)). Where a suspect is subsequently returned by the investigating officer, he or she must account to the custody officer for the proper treatment of that person whilst in their charge. Section 39(6) deals with the potentially difficult situation where a higher ranking officer than the custody officer gives directions which are at a variance with those of the custody officer. In such circumstances, the custody officer must immediately refer the matter to a police officer of at least the rank of superintendent who is responsible for that police station.

Section 34(1)–(5) of PACE contains important provisions regarding the overall responsibilities of custody officers towards detained suspects, whether arrested at the police station or elsewhere. However, para 1.10 of Code C makes the important point that the Code also applies to persons in custody at police stations, whether or not they have been arrested for an offence, as well as those removed to police stations as a place of safety under ss 135 and 136 of the Mental Health Act 1983 (mentally ill persons removed to police stations as an interim measure, prior to examination by medical practitioners); but para 1.12 excludes the following from the ambit of the Code, whilst providing that they should still be subject to the same minimum standards on conditions and treatment as other detainees (see also Chapter 6): persons arrested by police officers from Scotland exercising their detention powers under cross-border powers of arrest (see Chapter 3); persons arrested under s 142(3) of the Immigration and Asylum Act 1999 for fingerprinting, those whose detention is authorised by an immigration officer under the Immigration Act 1971; convicted or remanded prisoners held in police cells on behalf of the Prison Service; persons detained for examination under the Terrorism Act 2000; and persons detained for searches under stop and search powers except as required by Code A.

For the sake of simplicity, the remainder of this chapter will concentrate on arrested persons.

The provisions under s 34(1)–(4) of PACE are as follows:

(1) A person arrested for an offence shall not be kept in police detention except in accordance with the provisions of this Part of this Act.

(2) Subject to sub-s (3) below, if, at any time, a custody officer:

    (a) becomes aware, in relation to any person in police detention, that the grounds for the detention of that person have ceased to apply; and

    (b) is not aware of any other grounds on which the continued detention of that person could be justified under the provisions of this Part of this Act,

it shall be the duty of the custody officer, subject to sub-s (4) below, to order his immediate release from custody.[2]

---

2   Code C, para 1.1 reinforces this duty by stating that: 'All persons in custody must be dealt with expeditiously, and released as soon as the need for detention no longer applies.'

(3) No person in police detention shall be released, except on the authority of a custody officer at the police station where his detention was authorised or, if it was authorised at more than one station, a custody officer at the station where it was last authorised.

(4) A person who appears to the custody officer to have been unlawfully at large when he was arrested is not to be released under sub-s (2) above.

Sub-section (5) states that where a suspect is released from police detention, this must be unconditional, except where there is the need to impose bail because it appears to the custody officer that proceedings may be taken against the suspect in respect of the case or that further investigation is needed into the matter, or that the suspect may be reprimanded or warned under s 65 of the Crime and Disorder Act 1998. However, what are the provisions for holding suspects before any of these circumstances may apply? These will now be discussed.

THE FIRST STAGES AT THE POLICE STATION

The custody record

On arrival at a police station, an arrested person has the benefit of a considerable number of rights and safeguards, many of which either did not exist or were not clearly defined before the enactment of PACE. These provisions also apply to persons already at the police station prior to being arrested or to those who attend in order to answer bail. Once an arrested person has arrived at the police station (or once a person has been arrested at the police station or answers bail), that person should be brought before the custody officer, who will normally open a custody record for each individual. In strict accordance with procedure, the custody officer should do this once he or she has decided whether or not to authorise the detention of the suspect having heard the reasons for the arrest from the arresting officer. However, para 2.1A of Code C, which came into force on 1 August 2004, makes the following provisions regarding the bringing of persons before the custody officer without delay:

2.1A When a person is brought to a police station:

- under arrest;
- is arrested at the police station having attended there voluntarily; or
- attends a police station to answer bail,

they should be brought before the custody officer as soon as practicable after their arrival at the station or, if appropriate, following arrest after attending the police station voluntarily. This applies to designated and non-designated police stations. A person is deemed to be 'at a police station' for these purposes if they are within the boundary of any building or enclosed yard which forms part of that police station.

Under s 37 of PACE, the custody officer must determine if there is enough evidence to charge the suspect and, if so, may detain that person for as long as is necessary for that purpose. If not, the suspect must be released either on bail or without bail,[3] or the

---

3   If a person is arrested on warrant which is endorsed for bail, that person must be released on bail accordingly.

custody officer may authorise the suspect being detained without charge if there are reasonable grounds for believing that this is necessary to secure or preserve evidence relating to the offence in question, or to obtain such evidence by questioning the suspect. However, since custody officers rarely refuse to authorise detention, the custody record for the arrested suspect is usually opened on their arrival at the police station or very soon afterwards.

Where detention without charge is authorised, the grounds must be noted on the custody record and the suspect informed accordingly, unless incapable of understanding what is said, or is asleep, or is violent or likely to be so, or is in urgent need of medical attention. According to para 2.1 of Code C: '... Any audio or video recording made in the custody area is not part of the custody record.' Paragraphs 2.3, 2.6 and 2.7 provide that the custody officer is responsible for the accuracy and completeness of the custody record. All of its entries must be signed and timed by the persons making them, together with their appropriate identification, although para 2.6A states that police or civilian support staff may not disclose their names if this is reasonably believed that this might put them in danger, such as where a terrorist investigation is involved. Instead they may record their appropriate identification numbers and the name of their police station. If any detainee refuses to sign an entry in the custody record when required to do so, this fact must be recorded as well as the time of the refusal. When a detained person is transferred to another police station, it is the duty of the custody officer to ensure that the custody record or a copy of it accompanies the suspect.

The initial and continuing three rights of arrested persons

Under para 3.1 of Code C, the custody officer must inform the arrested person of the following rights which may be exercised at any stage throughout his or her detention, although this is subject to certain exceptions under Annex B, which is discussed below. In practice, unless those exceptions apply, arrested persons are usually notified of them at a very early stage in the detention process. These rights are to have someone informed of the arrest; to consult privately with a solicitor who may, if required, provide independent legal advice free of charge under the duty solicitor scheme; and to consult the Codes of Practice. Under para 3.2, the arrested person should then be served with a written notice, setting out these rights, together with the entitlement to a copy of the custody record, an explanation of the caution and the arrangements for obtaining legal advice. A further written notice must also be given to that person, which briefly sets out his or her entitlements whilst being held in custody. These include reasonable standards of physical comfort, adequate food and drink, access to toilets and washing facilities, clothing, medical attention and exercise when practicable. Note for Guidance 3B to Code C states that: 'In addition to notices in English, translations should be available in Welsh, the main minority ethnic languages and the principal European languages, whenever they are likely to be helpful. Audio versions of the notice should also be made available.' The last sentence of 3B was added under the latest Codes, which came into force on 1 August 2004. The arrested person should then be asked to sign the relevant part of the custody record which acknowledges receipt of these notices and any refusal to sign should be noted on it. In the case of the right to legal advice, posters advertising this right should be displayed in prominent places within police stations and in different languages where it is practicable and likely to be helpful.

Legal advice

The provisions regarding access to legal advice are contained under s 58 of PACE, augmented by procedures covered under s 6 of Code C. Apart from specific exceptions which will be dealt with later, arrested persons held in police custody (whether or not they have been arrested for an offence) have the fundamental right to consult a solicitor in private at any time. This may be in person, in writing or by telephone, unless the design and layout of the custody area or the positioning of the telephones make the latter impracticable. In *Roques v Metropolitan Police Commissioner* (1997), a successful action for breach of statutory duty was brought where the police had insisted on being present during the time that a suspect was speaking on the telephone to his solicitor. The right to private consultation with a solicitor is even more important in order to comply with Art 6(3) of the European Convention on Human Rights; see *R (on the Application of M (A Child)) v Commissioner of the Police of the Metropolis* (2002).

Persons voluntarily attending police stations ('helping police with their inquiries') also have the same right and this cannot be subject to any delay as long as they remain unarrested. Persons detained under prevention of terrorism legislation may have access to legal advice (subject to any postponement), although they may not consult with a solicitor privately if the relevant provisions of Sched 8 to the Terrorism Act 2000 apply. In such cases, an assistant chief constable (or a commander in London) may give a direction authorising a uniformed officer of at least the rank of inspector to be within the sight and hearing of a solicitor giving legal advice to a person detained under the relevant terrorism provisions.

As previously stated, arrested persons are usually informed of the right to legal advice at an early stage during their detention (or voluntary attendance at a police station), but this right must also be notified to them at other stages during the detention period where appropriate. This includes: the stage before a review of detention is made; the stage just prior to the commencement of any interview or continuation of an interview; where further questions are put to, or answers are invited from, a person already charged or notified of possible prosecution; where a person is asked to provide an intimate sample; and the stage before an identification parade or a group identification or video identification is arranged. If the presence of a solicitor is declined, the detained person should be informed that he or she may consult with a solicitor on the telephone. If this is also declined, that person must be asked to state the reason which, if given, must then be recorded in the custody or interview record. If this is not given, the detained person should not be pressed to explain any reasons for declining legal advice, but no police officer shall do or say anything intended to dissuade a person from obtaining legal advice. It should be noted that in *Rixon and Others v Chief Constable of Kent* (2000), it was held, *inter alia*, that if a detained person has the right to legal advice, a solicitor does not automatically have the right to see his or her client. This right only applies if the detained client is entitled to legal advice and requests it. Provided access to legal advice is not denied under s 58 of PACE (see below), the police should not delay in calling a solicitor unless there is justification. In *Kirkup v DPP* (2003), it was held that even a delay of seven minutes constituted a breach of s 58 of PACE and the Codes of Practice. However, the evidence in this case was not excluded under s 78 of PACE because the delay was very short.

How may a solicitor be obtained? It is important that the detained person be informed that he or she has the right to free legal advice and of the availability of the

Duty Solicitor Scheme. This scheme operates in each locality where a 24-hour rota system is organised by local legal practitioners who attend police stations on a 'call out' basis. However, detained persons who request legal advice should be given the opportunity to consult with a specific solicitor of their choice or another solicitor from the same firm. If legal advice is not available by these means or the services of the duty solicitor are declined, a list may be provided, containing solicitors willing to provide legal advice, from which the detained person may select a legal adviser and up to two alternatives if the first choice is not available. Even then, the custody officer has a discretion to make further efforts to obtain a solicitor if these attempts to secure legal advice are unsuccessful, although specific advice by the police about particular firms of solicitors must be avoided. In *R v Vernon* (1988), the defendant, who was arrested for assault, nominated a solicitor of her choice who was not available, due to the lateness of the hour. She was not informed of the Duty Solicitor Scheme and agreed to be interviewed without legal representation, which she would not have done had she known that a solicitor would have attended. The record of the interview was subsequently excluded under s 78 of PACE.

Can only fully qualified solicitors provide this service? Paragraph 6.12 of Code C clarifies the position as follows: 'solicitor' means a solicitor who holds a current practising certificate, a trainee solicitor, a duty solicitor representative or an accredited representative included on the register of representatives maintained by the Legal Services Commission. Under para 6.12A, if a solicitor sends a non-accredited or probationary representative to provide advice on his behalf, then that person shall be admitted to the police station for this purpose, unless an officer of the rank of inspector or above considers that such a visit will hinder the investigation of crime and directs otherwise.

Paragraph 6.14 states that any refusal of access to a non-accredited or probationary representative must be followed by the inspector notifying the solicitor who sent such a person, in order that alternative arrangements may be made. The custody record should then be noted and the detainee informed accordingly. Note for Guidance 6F provides that if a police officer of at least the rank of inspector considers that a particular solicitor or firm is persistently sending non-accredited or probationary representatives who are not suited to provide legal advice, that officer should make this known to a superintendent or above for consideration as to whether this matter should be taken up with the Law Society.

The above provisions clarify the position arising from *R v Chief Constable of Avon and Somerset ex p Robinson* (1989). In this case, an instruction was issued by the deputy chief constable to police officers in that area regarding the suitability of certain solicitors clerks, with particular reference to some unqualified clerks who were employed by a solicitor to be present during the interviewing of clients in police stations. This related to their background and conduct, with particular reference to four of them. The Divisional Court held that a police inspector or above is entitled to deny access if that officer knew or believed that a clerk was not capable of providing legal advice. This would not apply if such a person was capable of giving advice, even though it was of poor quality, and that a clerk could be denied entry if that person had a criminal record or was criminally orientated. This decision was applied in *R v Chief Constable of Northumbria ex p Thompson* (2001), where the Court of Appeal held that it is not permissible to impose blanket bans on persons who are not qualified as solicitors, as each case has to be judged on its own merits.

Paragraph 6.12A goes on to make the important point that hindering the investigation of crime does not include giving proper legal advice to a detained person in accordance with the provisions under Note for Guidance 6D. This stresses the right of a detained person to free legal advice and to be represented by a solicitor, and goes on to state what constitutes acceptable and non-acceptable conduct on the part of a solicitor during the questioning of a suspect. This, and other relevant provisions relating to the interviewing of suspects, will be covered in detail in Chapter 6.

Notification to another of a person's detention

Paragraph 5 of Code C sets out the basic right for detained persons not to be held incommunicado. This applies whether or not they have been arrested for an offence; for example, they might have been arrested to prevent a breach of the peace. Anyone arrested may request that one person be informed of his or her whereabouts as soon as is practicable. This will be done at public expense. Up to two alternatives may be contacted if the first attempt does not succeed and any further attempts are at the discretion of the person in charge of detention or the investigation. The detained person may also receive visits at the discretion of the custody officer. Any friend, relative or other person interested in the suspect's welfare who contacts the police station inquiring if that person is there should be informed as such, provided the suspect agrees and that the exceptions under Annex B to Code C do not apply.

There is a difference between having a person informed by the police of a suspect's whereabouts and allowing the suspect direct contact with such persons for this purpose. Whilst a suspect may be supplied with writing materials on request and allowed to speak on the telephone for a reasonable time to one person, an inspector or above may deny or delay either or both of these privileges. This will apply where an arrestable or a serious arrestable offence is involved and the consequences laid down in Annex B apply. This does not affect the right of having a person informed of the suspect's whereabouts or the suspect's entitlement to legal advice, *provided* these do not run contrary to Annex B. Before the suspect sends any letter or message, that person must be warned that any of these may be read and given in evidence; where the suspect makes a telephone call, he or she must be warned that the conversation may be listened to and also given in evidence. This does not apply to communications with a solicitor. The cost of such telephone calls can be at public expense, but this will be at the custody officer's discretion. This will take into account factors such as the distance at which a call is being made and the time involved. A telephone call may be terminated if the right is being abused.

Paragraph 5 of Code C provides that a record must be kept of all requests made under these rights and privileges, and the action taken, including any letters, messages or telephone calls made or received, or of any visits to the suspect. A record must also be kept of any refusal on the part of the suspect to have any information or the whereabouts regarding him or herself disclosed to an outside inquirer. The suspect must be asked to countersign the record to this effect and a record should be made of any refusal to sign.

Unco-operative detainees

It should be mentioned that the conduct of persons as a whole can vary considerably when confronted by the police at any point in the execution of their duties. Whether a police officer is exercising stop and search powers or effecting an arrest or detaining a suspect at a police station, it is often the case that such actions are met with verbal abuse, physical resistance and violent behaviour directed towards the police. In many cases, such conduct is drink or drug-related. In addition, arrested persons may not always be in the best physical condition when brought to the police station; for example, they might have been injured in a fight. Paragraph 1.8 of Code C therefore makes the following provisions:

> 1.8　If this Code requires a person to be given certain information, they do not have to be given it if at the time they are incapable of understanding what is said, are violent or may become violent or in urgent need of medical attention, but they must be given it as soon as practicable.

With regard to unco-operative detainees, the following case, *inter alia*, illustrates the volatile nature of working in a custody suite. This particular case was also severely criticised by the court as being a waste of public money. In *Bucher v DPP* (2003), the 16 year old appellant was with her mother in a custody suite; the latter was acting as the appropriate adult for her daughter but became abusive towards the custody officer to the extent that he was unable to perform his duties. He therefore tried to escort the mother from the custody suite, but the appellant caused injuries to the custody officer's face and was later convicted of assault on police. On appeal, however, it was argued that the custody officer was neither arresting the mother, nor preventing a breach of the peace and therefore he was not acting in the execution of his duty. The Administrative Court rejected this argument on the grounds that it is within the power of the police to remove disruptive or abusive persons from police stations in order to maintain their 'proper working'. The custody officer was therefore acting in the execution of his duty (see also Parpworth, N and Thompson, K, 'Physical contact and a police officer's execution of duty' (2003) 167 JP 426, 7 June).

General search provisions

Under s 54 of PACE, a person brought to a police station following an arrest or under other circumstances may be searched where necessary if the custody officer needs to fulfil the duty to ascertain everything that such persons have with them. This especially includes anything which could be used to: (a) cause physical injury; (b) cause damage to property; (c) interfere with evidence; (d) assist in an escape; or (e) where there are reasonable grounds for believing that it constitutes evidence of an offence. Anything which falls within any of these categories may be seized by the custody officer (except items subject to legal privilege), who must list them in the custody record. Any other property that the person may have when brought to the police station or when arrested at the police station must be ascertained by the custody officer. This includes anything found as a result of a search under ss 18 and 32 of PACE if the person was arrested away from the police station. However, s 8 of the Criminal Justice Act 2003 has amended s 54 of PACE so as to give the custody officer a discretion as to what items to list in the custody record. In other words, unlike the earlier provisions under s 54, the custody officer no longer has to record everything found on the detainee. In this connection, para 4.4 to Code C, which came into force on 1 August 2004, states that:

> 4.4 It is a matter for the custody officer to determine whether a record should be made of the property a detained person has with him or had taken from him on arrest. Any record made is not required to be kept as part of the custody record but the custody record should be noted as to where such a record exists. Whenever a record is made the detainee shall be allowed to check and sign the record of property as correct. Any refusal to sign shall be recorded.

Anyone searched at a police station should be informed of the reasons, unless this is unnecessary or impracticable; this provision could therefore render 'automatic' searches unlawful (see *Brazil v Chief Constable of Surrey* (1983)).

A detained person's clothes and any personal property, such as watches and spectacles, for example, may only be seized if the custody officer believes that the conditions mentioned in (a)–(e) above apply. If *any* property is seized, whether clothes, personal effects or otherwise, the custody officer is under a duty to give reasons to the suspect, unless that person is violent or likely to be so, or is incapable of understanding what is being said. Any cash and valuables should be removed from a detained person and held in safe custody after being recorded in the custody record. A search under s 54 must be carried out by police officers of the same sex as the individual being searched, using reasonable force if necessary (s 117), and this may be conducted to the extent that the custody officer considers necessary. This could include a strip search, but *not* an intimate search, which has to be authorised under the provisions of s 55.

Strip searches

The rules governing strip searches are to be found under Annex A to Code C. These were explained in Chapter 2, since a strip search involves more than the removal of outer clothing, but any search requiring exposure of intimate parts of the body must not be conducted in a police van. The legal source of the power to strip search detained suspects can be found under the relevant part of s 54 of PACE. This provides that in the exercise of a custody officer's duty to ascertain everything which a suspect has in his or her possession following arrest, the suspect may be searched 'to the extent that the custody officer considers necessary for that purpose'. However, para 10 of Annex A to Code C states that:

> A strip search may take place only if it is considered necessary to remove an article which a detainee would not be allowed to keep, and the officer reasonably considers that the detainee might have concealed such an article. Strip searches shall not be routinely carried out if there is no reason to consider that articles are concealed.

Intimate searches

Section 55 of PACE provides that a police inspector or above may authorise the intimate search of an arrested suspect if that officer has reasonable grounds to believe that the suspect may have concealed on him or herself any of the following: anything which the suspect could use to cause physical self-injury or injury to others while lawfully detained; or any Class A drug being smuggled out of this country, or possessed with intent to supply to another. It is important to emphasise that the drugs in question must be Class A controlled drugs listed under the Misuse of Drugs Act 1971 – the most socially harmful substances when misused. These include heroin (diamorphine), cocaine, 'ecstasy', LSD, pethidine, methadone, dipipanone and over 100 other named substances, plus numerous chemical variations. These do not include amphetamine, which is a Class B controlled drug, or cannabis, cannabis resin or temazepam, which are under Class C.[4]

Such authorisations must ultimately be put into written form if initially given orally and may not be given if the object can be obtained in some other way. Therefore, the suspect should be given the opportunity to voluntarily hand over the object and, if there is a refusal, then an intimate search may be authorised. An intimate search for a drug offence must be carried out by a registered medical practitioner or a registered nurse and may only be conducted at a hospital, a doctor's surgery or other place used for medical purposes, but not at a police station. Intimate searches for other objects covered under s 55 (which can generally be headed 'weapons') may be made at any of these premises, including police stations, and by a registered medical practitioner or nurse. However, if a police inspector or above considers this impracticable, then the search may be carried out by a constable of the same sex as the suspect. Paragraph 3A to Annex A of Code C makes the following caveat where this is being considered:

> 3A Any proposal for a search under *paragraph 2(a)(i)* to be carried out by someone other than a registered medical practitioner or registered nurse must only be considered as a last resort and when the authorizing officer is satisfied the risks associated with allowing the item to remain with the detainee outweigh the risks associated with removing it ...

Apart from medical practitioners and nurses, no person of the opposite sex shall be present or anyone whose presence is not necessary. However, a minimum of two people (excluding the suspect) must be present during an intimate search, which should be conducted with due regard to the sensitivity and vulnerability of the suspect under these conditions.

Where an intimate search involves a juvenile or a person who is mentally disordered or otherwise mentally vulnerable, this may only take place in the presence of an 'appropriate adult' (see below) who is of the same sex, unless the suspect requests a particular adult of the opposite sex who is readily available. An intimate search of a juvenile may only take place in the absence of the appropriate adult if the juvenile states that he or she prefers the search to be done in this way and the appropriate adult agrees. A record shall be made of the juvenile's decision, and this should then be signed by the appropriate adult.

An intimate search involves the examination of the bodily orifices, except the mouth;[5] in other words, the ears, nasal passages, rectum and vagina. Where such a search is carried out, the custody record must state which parts of the suspect's body were searched and why. Anything found in the course of an intimate search may be seized and retained by the custody officer where it is believed that it may be used to cause physical injury to the suspect or anyone else, cause damage to property, interfere with evidence or assist the suspect to escape. The custody officer may also seize and

---

4   For further reading on the law on controlled drugs, see Jason-Lloyd, L, *Drugs, Addiction and the Law* (9th edn, Cambridgeshire: Elm, 2004).

5   The examination of a suspect's mouth was excluded from the ambit of an intimate search by the Criminal Justice and Public Order Act 1994, s 59.

retain an article obtained in this way which, it is reasonably believed, may constitute evidence relating to an offence. The suspect must be informed of the reason for the seizure, unless he or she is violent or likely to be so, or is incapable of understanding what is being said.

The average layperson may be amazed at the number of items falling under the above description which can be concealed in the body orifices in question. Fairly substantial quantities of drugs in appropriate packaging can sometimes be concealed in a vagina or rectum and so may certain weapons:

> The types of weapon which may be concealed in a body orifice include a penknife in the mouth (*no longer an intimate search*),[6] a wrapped razor blade concealed in the vagina, a detonator or radio transmitter designed to detonate explosives elsewhere concealed in the rectum ... and a phial of poison concealed in the nose.[7]

The very intrusive nature of an intimate search justifies careful scrutiny; therefore, s 55 requires that annual reports to the Home Secretary from chief officers of police must contain details of all intimate searches carried out within their police area. However, such searches are used infrequently:

> ... only 172 were recorded in England and Wales in 2002–03. Of these 91% were for drugs. In 61 cases, Class A drugs were found and, in two cases, a harmful article was found.[8]

SEARCHES AND EXAMINATION TO ASCERTAIN IDENTITY

Section 90(1) of the Anti-terrorism, Crime and Security Act 2001 inserted a new s 54A under PACE. This is a power enabling the police to search or examine a suspect in order to establish the true identify of that person or their involvement in an offence. A search or examination of the suspect under this power may be carried out as stated under s 5 of Code D as follows:

5.1 PACE, section 54A(1), allows a detainee at a police station to be searched or examined or both, to establish:

    (a) whether they have any marks, features or injuries that would tend to identify them as a person involved in the commission of an offence and to photograph any identifying marks, see *paragraph 5.5*; or

    (b) their identity, see *Note 5A*.

A person detained at a police station to be searched under a stop and search power, see Code A, is not a detainee for the purposes of these powers.

5.2 A search and/or examination to find marks under section 54A(1)(a) may be carried out without the detainee's consent, see *paragraph 2.12*, only if authorised by an officer of at least inspector rank when consent has been withheld or it is not practicable to obtain consent, see *Note 5D*.

5.3 A search or examination to establish a suspect's identity under section 54A(1)(b) may be carried out without the detainee's consent, see *paragraph 2.12*, only if

6   Emphasis added.
7   Clark, D, *Bevan and Lidstone's The Investigation of Crime: A Guide to the Law of Criminal Investigation* (3rd edn, London: Butterworths, 2004).
8   *Ibid.*

authorised by an officer of at least inspector rank when the detainee has refused to identify themselves or the authorizing officer has reasonable grounds for suspecting the person is not who they claim to be.

5.4	Any marks that assist in establishing the detainee's identity, or their identification as a person involved in the commission of an offence, are identifying marks. Such marks may be photographed with the detainee's consent, see *paragraph 2.12*; or without their consent if it is withheld or it is not practicable to obtain it, see *Note 5D*.

5.5	A detainee may only be searched, examined and photographed under section 54A by a police officer of the same sex.

5.6	Any photographs of identifying marks, taken under section 54A, may be used or disclosed only for purposes related to the prevention or detection of crime, the investigation of offences or the conduct of prosecutions by, or on behalf of, police or other law enforcement and prosecuting authorities inside, and outside, the UK. After being so used or disclosed, the photographs may be retained but must not be used or disclosed except for these purposes, see *Note 5B*.

5.7	The powers, as in *paragraph 5.1*, do not affect any separate requirements under the Criminal Procedure and Investigations Act 1996 to retain material in connection with criminal investigations.

5.8	Authority for the search and/or examination for the purposes of *paragraphs 5.2*, and *5.3* may be given orally or in writing. If given orally, the authorising officer must confirm it in writing as soon as practicable. A separate authority is required for each purpose which applies.

5.9	If it is established a person is unwilling to co-operate sufficiently to enable a search and/or examination to take place or a suitable photograph to be taken, an officer may use reasonable force to:

(a)	search and/or examine a detainee without their consent; and

(b)	photograph any identifying marks without their consent.

5.10	The thoroughness and extent of any search or examination carried out in accordance with the powers in section 54A must be no more than the officer considers necessary to achieve the required purpose. Any search or examination which involves the removal of more than the person's outer clothing shall be conducted in accordance with Code C, Annex A, paragraph 11.

5.11	An intimate search may not be carried out under the powers in section 54A.

Although not expressly stated in s 5 of Code D, the above powers to search, examine and photograph suspects may be exercised by civilians who are designated by the chief officer of police for their area to perform such functions. This is provided under s 54A(6) of PACE, which states:

Where a search or examination may be carried out under this section, or a photograph may be taken under this section, the only persons entitled to carry out the search or examination, or to take the photograph, are:

(a)	constables; and

(b)	persons who (without being constables) are designated for the purposes of this section by the chief officer of police for the police area in which the police station in question is situated;

and section 117 (use of force) applies to the exercise by a person falling within paragraph (b) of the powers conferred by the preceding provisions of this section as it applies to the exercise of those powers by a constable.

It should also be noted that searching or examining a suspect for any marks will include, for instance, any tattoos, birthmarks, scars or other injuries that may be on that person. Further guidance in respect of s 54A of PACE is given in ss 5.12 to 5.24 and the accompanying Notes for Guidance in Code D. This is to be found in Chapter 6, as this guidance also applies to photographing suspects generally.

DETENTION WITHOUT CHARGE

The decision to authorise detention without charge is an important step in the investigation of crime. However, Art 5 of the European Convention on Human Rights, which is now incorporated into our system of law by the Human Rights Act 1998, makes it even more important to make the right decisions.

Introduction

As mentioned above, the custody officer may authorise the detention of a suspect without charge in order to secure or preserve evidence relating to the offence in question or to obtain such evidence by questioning the suspect. The suspect must then be informed of the grounds for detention, unless he or she is incapable of understanding what is being said, or is asleep, or is violent, or likely to be so, or in urgent need of medical attention. The grounds for detention should be recorded in the custody record as soon as is practicable. If a suspect is not in a fit state to be either charged or released, that person may be kept in police detention until fit. However, whether the suspect is fit or otherwise once the appropriate time limit has been reached, that person must either be released on bail, released unconditionally or charged. If released without charge, that person cannot be re-arrested unless new evidence is discovered which justifies arresting the suspect again or unless a warrant is issued for the same offence. The exception to this rule is where, under s 30D or s 46A of PACE, a person fails to surrender to police bail and is subsequently arrested without warrant and taken to the police station where the suspect should have reported at the due time and date. This is to be treated as an arrest for an offence, although this does not apply to a breach of bail conditions. The same principle applies to persons who breach court bail.

It should be noted that custody officers are now required to conduct a series of procedures designed to reduce risk to detainees and others. These are to be found under paras 3.6–3.10 to Code C as follows:

> 3.6 ... the custody officer is responsible for initiating an assessment to consider whether the detainee is likely to present specific risks to custody staff or themselves. Such assessments should always include a check on the Police National Computer, to be carried out as soon as practicable, to identify any risks highlighted in relation to the detainee. Although such assessments are primarily the custody officer's responsibility, it may be necessary for them to consult and involve others, eg the arresting officer or an appropriate health care professional, see *paragraph 9.13*. Reasons for delaying the initiation or completion of the assessment must be recorded.

> 3.7 Chief officers should ensure that arrangements for proper and effective risk assessments required by *paragraph 3.6* are implemented in respect of all detainees at police stations in their area.

> 3.8 Risk assessments must follow a structured process which clearly defines the categories of risk to be considered and the results must be incorporated in the detainee's custody record. The custody officer is responsible for making sure those

responsible for the detainee's custody are appropriately briefed about the risks. If no specific risks are identified by the assessment, that should be noted in the custody record. See *Note 3E* and *paragraph 9.14*.

3.9 The custody officer is responsible for implementing the response to any specific risk assessment, eg:

- reducing opportunities for self-harm;
- calling a health care professional;
- increasing levels of monitoring or observation.

3.10 Risk assessment is an ongoing process and assessments must always be subject to review if circumstances change.

The above Codes are augmented by Home Office Circular 32/2000 regarding detainee risk assessment.

Time limits

The general rules

Section 41 of PACE imposes strict limits on the period of detention without charge. This is *normally* 24 hours, but is subject to certain exceptions, discussed below. The 24-hour period starts from the 'relevant time', which, in most cases, is either the time that an arrested person arrives at the first police station he or she is taken to or the time that a person already at the police station is actually arrested, or initially presents him or herself in response to being given 'street bail' earlier. If a person is arrested outside England and Wales, the relevant time operates from when the suspect arrives at the first police station within the area where the alleged crime is being investigated or 24 hours after the suspect's arrival in England and Wales. It is the earlier of the two which is calculated as the relevant time. If a suspect is arrested in a different police area from the one where the alleged offence is being investigated, but within England and Wales, much depends on whether the arrested person is questioned regarding the offence at the time. If so, the relevant time operates from when the suspect arrived at the first police station following arrest. If not, the relevant time is calculated from either 24 hours after the arrest or the time of arrival at the police station where the alleged offence is being investigated, whichever is the earlier.

If a person returns to a police station in response to police bail and is detained on arrival, the relevant time is calculated from that applicable to the initial detention, and that person may be detained without charge up to the maximum of any unused detention time left from the previous occasion. If a suspect in police detention is taken to hospital, the detention clock stops running whilst he or she is in hospital and in the course of the journey, unless the suspect is being questioned during this time. No account is taken under PACE where a suspect is taken directly to hospital following arrest and then to the police station.

The reader may find it useful to consult Appendix 12 in order to follow the main stages in the detention of a suspect from arrest until eventual release from the police station.

Periodic reviews of detention

In order to ensure that no person arrested for an offence is detained any longer than can be legally justified, s 40 of PACE provides a system of periodic reviews of persons in police detention. These rules do not apply where a person is voluntarily attending a police station, but will, of course, apply if that person is later arrested for an offence. The general rule is that arrested suspects detained *without charge* are reviewed by a police officer of at least the rank of inspector who is not directly involved with the investigation of the alleged offence. These reviews must be carried out periodically from the time that the suspect's detention was authorised by the custody officer. This will be later than the relevant time which, in most cases, applies when an arrested suspect arrives at the police station. It therefore follows that two 'clocks' run alongside each other when a person is in police detention, namely, the detention clock and the review clock (see Appendix 12).

It should be noted at this stage that periodic reviews are applicable to persons in 'police detention', namely, suspects who have been arrested for an offence and have been taken to a police station (including arrests made under s 41 of and Sched 8 to the Terrorism Act 2000), or those subsequently arrested after initially attending a police station voluntarily. Therefore, they do not apply to arrested persons who have not been arrested for an offence (for example, persons arrested in order to be fingerprinted, or mentally disordered persons arrested under s 136 of the Mental Health Act 1983 in order to be taken to a place of safety). Neither do they apply to persons held by the police who are awaiting extradition or deportation. However, whilst persons detained for a breach of the peace do not expressly fall under the requirement of reviews under PACE, in practice this is done by the police and in *Chief Constable of Cleveland Police v McGrogan* (2002), such action was held to be correct. This is further confirmed by Note for Guidance 15B in Code C, which states:

> The detention of persons in police custody not subject to the statutory review requirement in paragraph 15.1 should still be reviewed periodically as a matter of good practice. The purpose of such reviews is to check the particular power under which a detainee is held continues to apply, any associated conditions are complied with and to make sure appropriate action is taken to deal with any changes. This includes the detainee's prompt release when the power no longer applies, or their transfer if the power requires the detainee be taken elsewhere as soon as the necessary arrangements are made. Examples include persons:
>
> (a) arrested on warrant because they failed to answer bail to appear at court;
>
> (b) arrested under the Bail Act 1976, section 7(3) for breaching a condition of bail granted after charge;
>
> (c) in police custody for specific purposes and periods under the Crime (Sentences) Act 1997, Schedule 1:
>
> (d) convicted, or remand prisoners, held in police stations on behalf of the Prison Service under the Imprisonment (Temporary Provisions) Act 1980, section 6;
>
> (e) being detained to prevent them causing a breach of the peace;
>
> (f) detained at police stations on behalf of the Immigration Service.
>
> The detention of persons remanded into police detention by order of a court under the Magistrates' Courts Act 1980, section 128 is subject to a statutory requirement to review that detention. This is to make sure the detainee is taken back to court no later than the end of the period authorised by the court or when the need for their detention by police ceases, whichever is the sooner.

Where a person in police detention *has been charged*, it is then the *custody officer* who is responsible for carrying out the periodic reviews. Whether the reviews are conducted by an inspector or the custody officer, either is regarded as the 'review officer'. The first review must be carried out no later than six hours following the authorisation of the suspect's detention and then at intervals of no more than nine hours. Reviews may be postponed where necessary, but must be resumed as soon as practicable; this takes into account the wide and often unpredictable nature of police duties. This will include instances where the criminal investigation would be prejudiced if the questioning of the suspect were interrupted or where a review officer is not readily available, due to a serious incident requiring his or her urgent attention. The review officer must record the reasons for any postponement in the custody record; however, a review of a suspect's detention who has not been charged may be conducted by video link, or over the telephone if this is the only practicable means by which it can be conducted (see Note for Guidance 15F to Code C).

Prior to authorising a suspect's further detention, the review officer must give the suspect or the solicitor representing that person the opportunity to make any representations. Other people may be involved in this process, at the review officer's discretion. These will be persons having an interest in the suspect's welfare, including the appropriate adult, if available. These representations may be given orally or in writing and may include such matters as whether detention without charge is necessary in order to secure or preserve evidence, or whether there is sufficient evidence for the police to charge the suspect. Any dispute between the review officer and someone of higher rank regarding a suspect's detention in police custody should be referred to an officer of at least the rank of superintendent.

The review officer is under a duty to remind the suspect of the entitlement to free legal advice prior to conducting a review and to ensure that all such reminders are entered in the custody record. Other matters should also be recorded in the custody record, including the reasons for any delay in conducting a review and the extent of the delay, as well as the result of each review and any application for a warrant of further detention and any extension of it (see below). Any representations made in writing must be retained. Paragraph 15.7 to Code C states that if the suspect is sleeping at the time of a review, that person must be informed about the decision to authorise continued detention and the reason, as soon as practicable after waking.

In *Roberts v Chief Constable of Cheshire* (1999), the claimant sued for damages for false imprisonment. Having been arrested on suspicion of burglary, he arrived at a police station at 11.25 pm, where his detention without charge was authorised. The first review should have been made at 5.25 am, but did not take place until 7.45 am. The court held that the detention was unlawful after 5.25 am, until some event occurred to make it lawful.

Significant changes have recently been made that no longer necessitate the physical presence of review officers at police stations where suspects are held. The latest changes are to be found under s 6 of the Criminal Justice Act 2003, which inserts a new s 40A(1) and (2) into PACE that enables reviews to be conducted using the telephone, although if video conferencing facilities are available, these should be used as appropriate. The provisions regarding the use of the telephone do not apply to suspects who have been charged, or to reviews under Sched 8, Pt II to the Terrorism Act 2000.

Extensions to normal detention periods

As mentioned above, the general time limit for detention without charge is 24 hours, but this is subject to the following exceptions. Sections 42, 43 and 44 of PACE make provision for the authorisation of 'continued detention' by the police and warrants of 'further detention' by magistrates and their extension.

The provisions under s 42 regarding continued detention by the police apply where it is reasonably believed that the criminal investigation is concerned with an arrestable offence (or a serious arrestable offence as defined in Chapter 3), where the investigation is being conducted diligently and expeditiously, and where continued detention without charge is necessary to secure or preserve evidence or to obtain evidence by questioning the suspect. The authorisation for continued police detention *without charge* must be given before the expiry of the 24 hour detention period and by an officer of at least the rank of superintendent if the above criteria are met. Under Note for Guidance 15C to Code C, this must be done in person and not over the telephone or by video link. The period of detention *without charge* may then be extended up to 36 hours from the relevant time; in other words, up to another 12 hours beyond the initial 24 hours that normally apply. Representations may be made by the suspect or any solicitor representing that person on grounds such as whether the investigation is proceeding with due diligence, the length of the continued detention or whether the alleged crime constitutes an arrestable offence. Representations may also be made by other persons having an interest in the welfare of the suspect, including the appropriate adult where applicable. Special provisions now exist for juveniles and mentally vulnerable persons with regard to the police power to extend detention beyond 24 hours (see below under the subheading 'Initial action' in respect of safeguards regarding vulnerable persons).

Where continued detention has been authorised, the suspect must be informed by that officer of the grounds for the decision which, in turn, must be recorded in the custody record. Unless a warrant for further detention has been granted by magistrates in the case of a *serious* arrestable offence (see below), if at the end of the 36-hour time limit the suspect has not been charged, that person must be released on bail, released unconditionally or charged. The suspect must not be re-arrested for the same offence without a warrant, except where new evidence has been discovered.

Delay in access to legal advice and notification of arrest to another

It is important to mention at this stage that access to legal advice, as well as the right for a suspect to have a person informed of their detention, can be postponed in the case of a *serious* arrestable offence where the suspect has *not been charged*. The following provisions, under ss 56 and 58 of PACE and Annex B to Code C, constitute the exceptions to the general rules discussed above.

Section 58 and Annex B provide that a police superintendent or above may delay access to a solicitor for up to 36 hours if there are reasonable grounds for believing that such access would lead to: interference with or harm to evidence connected with any serious arrestable offence; interference with or physical injury to other persons; alerting other persons not yet arrested, but suspected of having committed a serious arrestable offence; or hindering the recovery of any property obtained as a result of such an offence.

Section 58 provides a further ground under which a superintendent or above may postpone access to legal advice. This is where the person is detained for a serious arrestable offence and the suspect has benefited from his or her criminal conduct,[9] and the recovery of that property will be obstructed if access to legal advice is granted.

The rules governing the postponement of the right for a detained suspect to have a person informed of his or her detention are the same as those applicable to delaying access to legal advice, except that the postponement may be authorised by an inspector or above. These are to be found under s 56 of PACE and Annex B to Code C. However, it should be noted that if one right can be delayed, it does not mean that the other can be denied automatically (see para 5 of Annex B to Code C).

If the authorisation for a delay in giving access to legal advice or informing a person of a suspect's detention is given orally, it must be put into writing as soon as is practicable and the suspect must be informed of the postponement, together with the reasons, which must be noted in the custody record. If the grounds for the postponement cease to exist before the 36-hour time limit, the detained person must be asked if he or she requires the presence of a solicitor and sign the custody record to this effect. This will also apply where the suspect is charged during this period.

In *R v Samuel* (1987), two important points were established regarding the power to delay access to legal advice under s 58 of PACE. In this case, the defendant was arrested for armed robbery and was subsequently detained for questioning. In the course of the second interview with the police, he requested access to legal advice, but this was denied on the ground that this might inadvertently alert other suspects. He later confessed to two burglary offences, one of which constituted a serious arrestable offence, since firearms were allegedly used, and he was duly charged with both these offences. About 15 minutes later, the defendant's solicitor telephoned and was informed of this, but was still denied access to the defendant. Shortly afterwards, during the final interview, the defendant confessed to the robbery and was later charged. Eventually, he was allowed access to his solicitor 29 hours after his arrest. The Court of Appeal held that the trial judge should have ruled the evidence regarding the final interview inadmissible, since the denial of access to the solicitor was not justified. His conviction for robbery was therefore quashed. The two important points held by the Court of Appeal were that once the suspect is charged with any offence, especially if it is a serious arrestable offence, the right to legal advice cannot be delayed thereafter. Secondly, an authorising officer must believe that such access will lead to alerting other suspects and not just *may* lead to this consequence, even if this could occur inadvertently or unwittingly, and that due regard should be had as to whether legal advice could be given by another solicitor where there is such a risk. In this case, the Court of Appeal stated in passing that as far as duty solicitors were concerned, since they were well known to the police, it would be very difficult to justify delaying access to any of them if another solicitor was denied access to the suspect. In other words, denial of access to a *particular* solicitor may be justified, but denial of access to all solicitors is another matter. This is emphasised in para 3 of Annex B to Code C, which states:

---

9   Under Pt 2 of the Proceeds of Crime Act 2002, criminal conduct is conduct which constitutes an offence if committed in England and Wales, or would be an offence if it occurred in this country. Anyone who obtains property from criminal conduct benefits from it and therefore falls under this heading.

Authority to delay a detainee's right to consult privately with a solicitor may be given only if the authorising officer has reasonable grounds to believe the solicitor the detainee wants to consult will, inadvertently or otherwise, pass on a message from the detainee or act in some other way which will have any of the consequences specified under paragraph 1 or 2. In these circumstances the detainee must be allowed to choose another solicitor. See Note B3.

However, in *R v Alladice* (1988), the Court of Appeal, whilst supporting the decision in *R v Samuel*, dismissed an appeal against the defendant's conviction for robbery where a confession was obtained whilst access to legal advice was denied by a police officer of the rank of chief inspector. First, the court held that since the chief inspector was acting under the authority of an acting chief superintendent, he was to be treated as if he were the holder of the substantive rank, 'unless the appointment to the acting rank was a colourable pretence, which was not suggested in the present case'. Secondly, whilst acknowledging that there had been a breach of the defendant's right to legal advice under s 58, the court held that there was no suggestion of oppression or that the confession was given because of the absence of a solicitor and that the confession was unreliable. Subsequently, the breach did not require the court to render the confession inadmissible. The provisions of s 107 of PACE as follows should be noted at this stage:

Police officers performing duties of higher rank

(1) For the purpose of any provision of this Act or any other Act under which a power in respect of the investigation of offences or the treatment of persons in police custody is exercisable only by or with the authority of a police officer of at least the rank of superintendent, an officer of the rank of chief inspector shall be treated as holding the rank of superintendent if:

   (a) he has been authorised by an officer holding a rank above the rank of superintendent to exercise the power or, as the case may be, to give his authority for its exercise; or

   (b) he is acting during the absence of an officer holding the rank of superintendent who has authorised him, for the duration of that absence, to exercise the power or, as the case may be, to give his authority for its exercise.

(2) For the purpose of any provision of this Act or any other Act under which such a power is exercisable only by or with the authority of an officer of at least the rank of inspector, an officer of the rank of sergeant shall be treated as holding the rank of inspector if he has been authorised by an officer of at least the rank of superintendent to exercise the power or, as the case may be, to give his authority for its exercise.

The *general* provisions regarding access to legal advice, and the right to have a person informed of a suspect's arrest and subsequent detention, were discussed above. It should be noted that Pt B of Annex B contains special provisions regarding the delay of access to legal advice and notification of arrest in respect of persons detained under s 41 of or Sched 7 to the Terrorism Act 2000. One of the main differences is that only a superintendent or above may authorise delaying the notification of a terrorist suspect's detention to another. Also, as discussed below, the provisions under Annex B are modified in the case of juveniles and the mentally disordered or mentally vulnerable.

Warrants of further detention by magistrates

Under s 43 of PACE, further detention without charge beyond the 36 hour maximum may be authorised by magistrates in the case of *serious* arrestable offences only. Unless a district judge (magistrates' courts) is present in court, who may make the authorisation sitting alone, the authority to extend the 36 hour period must be made by at least two lay magistrates, although three is the usual number. Where further detention is being sought, a constable may apply on oath for their authority to keep the suspect in detention beyond 36 hours. This must be supported by 'an information', a copy of which the suspect should already have in his or her possession when attending court at the time the application is being made. The 'information', in this context, means the nature of the offence and the evidence which justified the suspect's arrest, as well as inquiries made to date and anticipated further inquiries in addition to the grounds for applying for further detention. An application for further detention will only be justified where the offence is a serious arrestable offence and the investigation is proceeding diligently and expeditiously, and this is necessary to secure or preserve evidence or to obtain it by questioning the suspect.

Where a suspect has been denied legal access under s 58 of PACE and is due to be taken before magistrates under an application for further detention, reasonable time should be allowed for the detained person to consult with a solicitor before the hearing. In any event, the detainee is entitled to legal representation during the application and an adjournment may be granted, if necessary, in order for such representation to be obtained. The legal representative may cross-examine the police applicant on oath and the application may be challenged accordingly. Particular care has to be taken in anticipating whether further detention may be necessary as, unlike many police stations, magistrates' courts are not operational 24 hours a day, seven days a week. It is therefore permissible for an application for further detention to be made prior to the expiry of the 36 hour period, in order to ensure that the court is sitting. However, where the court is not sitting at the end of the first 36 hours (and it was not reasonably practicable to have made the application before then), but the court is due to sit during the following six hours, the application for further detention may be made within that six hour period. The suspect may be kept in police detention during this time and these facts must be recorded in the custody record accordingly.

Where the application is made in court beyond the expiry of the first 36 hours and it appears to the court that it was unreasonable for the police not to have done so before, it is a mandatory requirement that the court dismiss the application. In *R v Slough Justices ex p Stirling* (1987), it was held that in failing to bring an application in good time when the police officer was in a position to do so (in this case, the application was made just eight minutes before the expiry of the first 36 hours), that officer did not act reasonably within s 43(7) of PACE. It was also confirmed that the application for further detention occurs when the police officer makes the application in court and gives evidence.

The application to magistrates for further detention is by no means a rubber stamp process. Under s 43 of PACE, magistrates may refuse the application if they feel that further detention is not justified and a further application against a refusal may only be considered by the court if new evidence is discovered. Where appropriate, the court may adjourn the hearing, but only if the 36 hour maximum period of police detention has not expired. Where there has been a refusal, the police may continue to detain the suspect without charge, but only up until the normal maximum of 24 hours, or up to 36 hours if continued authorisation was made by a police superintendent. However, if during the application for further detention the court rules that the offence is not a serious arrestable offence, it is submitted that the custody officer must ensure the release of the suspect once the first 24 hour period has elapsed, or if a superintendent has authorised continued detention, up to 36 hours. The suspect must either be charged or released (unconditionally or on bail) where the court rejects an application for any reason or where the appropriate 24 or 36 hour detention period expires.

If the court agrees to issue a warrant of further detention, it may do so for a maximum period of 36 hours, having regard to all the circumstances of the case. At the end of this maximum period (which can be less than 36 hours), the suspect must be either be charged or released unconditionally or on bail, and may not be subject to further arrest for the offence without warrant, unless new evidence has been discovered.

Extended powers of detention by magistrates

Under s 44 of PACE, the warrant of further detention may be extended (repeatedly if necessary) if the court is satisfied that there are reasonable grounds for believing that this is justified. In such cases, the same procedures apply as those governing initial applications for warrants of further detention, and include an application being made on oath by a police officer – supported by an information, a copy of the latter being given to the detained suspect – and the entitlement to legal representation. If an application to extend a warrant of further detention is refused by the court, the suspect must either be charged, immediately released on bail or released unconditionally, or any of these may be done at the end of the previous detention period authorised by magistrates. Where the court agrees to extend a warrant of further detention (or even one or more extensions since then), it may be for any period the court thinks fit, but the extension period must not exceed 36 hours. No extension may result in a total period of 96 hours' detention being exceeded from the relevant time. Also, due account should be taken of any time spent in waiting for the court to sit when the first 36 hours of police detention has expired. At the end of the period specified in an extension or further extension of a warrant of further detention, the suspect must either be charged, released on bail or released unconditionally, and may not be subject to further arrest for the offence without warrant, unless new evidence is discovered. The suspect need not be charged or released at that stage, of course, if a further extension is granted by the court, but the absolute limit of 96 hours' total detention without charge must not be exceeded.

Police detention under prevention of terrorism legislation

The time limits described above in respect of the detention of suspects without charge do not apply to certain offences under prevention of terrorism legislation. Section 41 of and Sched 8 to the Terrorism Act 2000 provide that a person arrested for being a suspected terrorist may be detained by the police without charge for up to 48 hours. This may, in turn, be extended by a 'judicial authority' for a period or periods totalling up to five days. The detention period without charge may, therefore, be up to seven days, although this may be extended by a further seven days, making a total of 14 days in all. Section 75 of the Criminal Justice and Police Act 2001 has amended Sched 8 to the Terrorism Act 2000 to enable judicial authority to use video link when conducting their proceedings regarding extended detention. The term 'judicial authority' means a district judge (magistrates' courts) appointed for this task by the Lord Chancellor.

SAFEGUARDS REGARDING VULNERABLE PERSONS

Whilst PACE and the Codes of Practice contain many provisions designed to protect the rights of persons in police custody, further measures are available to ensure that particularly vulnerable suspects are subject to additional safeguards. These are juveniles, persons who are mentally disordered or otherwise mentally vulnerable, deaf persons, blind persons, foreign suspects and those unable to understand English. It should be mentioned that in the case of juveniles, the child or young person should be of a minimum age of 10 and no older than 17 years. The most important provisions either originate from or are largely echoed in Code C, the relevant parts of which are summarised as follows.

General

Section 1 of Code C makes the following general provisions regarding vulnerable persons held in police custody. Where a police officer suspects or is informed in good faith that a person of any age may be mentally disordered or otherwise mentally vulnerable, or is mentally incapable of understanding questions put to him or her or understanding any replies, that person will fall under the scope of this Code in protecting such persons. Note for Guidance 1G endeavours to define 'mentally vulnerable' for the purposes of this Code of Practice. For the sake of brevity, the term generally means: (1) mental illness (such as schizophrenia and manic depression, to name but two); (2) psychopathic disorder; and (3) various states of mental impairment caused as a result of brain damage or an undeveloped brain (arrested or retarded development). In any event, the presence of an appropriate adult should be sought where the custody officer has any doubt regarding the mental state or capacity of a detained person.

Section 1 goes on to state that, for the purposes of this Code and in the absence of clear evidence to the contrary, persons appearing to be under the age of 17 shall be treated as juveniles, and persons appearing to be blind or seriously visually handicapped, deaf, unable to read, speak or who have difficulty orally because of a speech impediment also fall under the provisions of this Code.

With regard to juveniles and those who are mentally disordered or otherwise mentally vulnerable, provision is made for such persons to have the support of 'the appropriate adult' when in police custody. The definition as to whom the appropriate adult may be is variable, depending on the category of vulnerable person in question. The Code of Practice therefore defines the appropriate adult in each case as follows.

In the case of juveniles, the 'appropriate adult' means the child or young person's parent or guardian and, if the juvenile is in care, this will mean the relevant local authority or voluntary organisation. The term 'in care' is defined under the Code of Practice as all cases in which a juvenile is 'looked after' under the terms of the Children Act 1989. The appropriate adult may also be a social worker and, if any of the above are not available, the presence of another responsible adult aged 18 or over is permissible, provided that person is not a police officer or employed by the police service. In addition to these rules, the police should still be alert as to the general suitability of persons who may be asked to act as the appropriate adult. In *R v Morse and Others* (1991), it was held that the father of the suspect in this case should not have been asked to act as the appropriate adult, since he may have been unable to appreciate the seriousness of the situation due to being illiterate and of low intelligence.

With regard to the mentally disordered or otherwise mentally vulnerable, the appropriate adult may be a relative, guardian or other person responsible for that person's care or custody. Alternatively, that person may be someone with experience in dealing with mentally disordered or otherwise mentally vulnerable people, such as an officer of a local social services authority appointed to act as an 'approved social worker' for the purposes of the Mental Health Act 1983, or any other specialist social worker. However, the person with the relevant experience must not be a police officer or any employee within the police service. In any of these are not available, then the appropriate adult may be some other responsible person aged 18 or over, provided, as before, that the person is not a police officer or a police employee. Note for Guidance 1D states that in certain circumstances, it may be better for all concerned if the appropriate adult is someone with experience and training in the care of the mentally disordered or otherwise mentally vulnerable, rather than a relative without such qualifications. However, it goes on to state that the detained person's wishes should be respected, if practicable, where that person prefers a relative to a better qualified stranger. In *R v Aspinall* (1999), the defendant was arrested for a drug offence and, on his arrival at the police station, he informed the custody officer that he was a schizophrenic. Two doctors later confirmed that he was probably in a fit state to be interviewed; meanwhile, he asked for a solicitor, who was not obtained, due to a mistake by the police. The defendant was interviewed 13 hours later, without the presence of a solicitor or an appropriate adult. His conviction for conspiracy to supply heroin was quashed on the grounds that the custody officer knew that he was suffering from a mental illness and that there was a clear breach of para 11.15 of Code C, which stipulates that such persons must not be interviewed without an appropriate adult. The unfairness of the proceedings was also made worse by the absence of legal advice during the interview.

Notes for Guidance 1B, 1C, 1E and 1F provide further guidelines regarding appropriate adults. They begin by making the important point that no one, including a parent or guardian, should be an appropriate adult if he or she is suspected of involvement in the offence in question, or is the victim of it, or is a witness, or is involved in the investigation of the offence or has received admissions prior to attending the police station to act as the appropriate adult. In *DPP v Morris* (1990), it was held that a social worker probably should not have acted as the appropriate adult in this case, because that person had called the police. This would have led to the juvenile viewing the social worker as being biased towards the police.

If the parent of a juvenile is estranged from that child or young person, the parent should not be asked to act as the appropriate adult if the juvenile expressly objects to that parent's presence. The Notes for Guidance continue by providing that, in the interests of fairness, if a juvenile admits to an offence in the presence of a social worker, except when acting as the appropriate adult, then another social worker should act in that capacity. The guidance ends by stating that a solicitor or an independent custody visitor (formerly a lay visitor), who happens to be in the police station in that capacity at the time, may not act as the appropriate adult and that when an appropriate adult is called to a police station, a detained person should always be given an opportunity to consult privately with a solicitor in the appropriate adult's absence. However, para 6.5A to Code C, which took effect on 1 August 2004, states that:

6.5A In the case of a juvenile, an appropriate adult should consider whether legal advice from a solicitor is required. If the juvenile indicates that they do not want legal advice, the appropriate adult has the right to ask for a solicitor to attend if this would be in the best interests of the person. However, the detained person cannot be forced to see the solicitor if he is adamant that he does not wish to do so.

Normally, only one person should be designated as the appropriate adult, although in *H and M v DPP* (1997), it was held that, in certain circumstances, it may be permissible to have more than one person performing this function during a juvenile's interview. This would apply, for instance, where both the parents were present or where one parent was present but, due to language difficulties, needed someone to assist in overcoming this problem.

Custody records

Section 2 of Code C states that as soon as practicable after their arrival at the police station, a solicitor or appropriate adult must be allowed to consult the custody record of the detained person. When that person leaves police custody or is taken before a court, he or she, or the legal representative or the appropriate adult, must be supplied with a copy of the custody record if requested, as soon as practicable, provided the request is made within 12 months following that person's release. The original custody record may be examined by any of these three classes of person after the detained person has left police custody, if reasonable notice is given. If this inspection takes place, it shall be noted in the custody record.

Initial action

Section 3 makes a number of provisions affecting all classes of vulnerable persons together with references to the relevant notes for guidance.

Detained persons: normal procedure

Under this subheading, the Code provides that a citizen of an independent Commonwealth country or a national of a foreign state, including the Irish Republic, must be informed, as soon as practicable, of the right to communicate with his or her High Commission, embassy or consulate. This right is covered in detail under s 7 of this Code. At this stage, reference is made to the risk assessment procedure under para 3.5(c) and (d) and paras 3.6–3.10 as listed above in the introduction under 'Detention without charge'.

Detained persons: special groups

The custody officer must, as soon as practicable, call an interpreter if effective communication cannot be established, because it appears that a person is deaf or there is doubt about that person's hearing or ability to speak or understand English. Detailed provisions regarding interpreters are given in s 13 of Code C.

Where the detained person is a juvenile, the custody officer must, if practicable, ascertain the identity of a person responsible for the welfare of the child or young person, who may be a parent, guardian, or the care authority or voluntary organisation if in care, or any other person who has assumed responsibility for the juvenile's welfare. That person must be informed, as soon as practicable, that the juvenile has been arrested, the reason why and where they are detained. This right may be exercised in addition to the general right not to be held incommunicado. Even where Annex B to Code C applies, this action must be taken. Note for Guidance 3C makes provision where a juvenile is in care, but living with his or her parents or other adults responsible for the juvenile's welfare. In such cases, whilst there is no legal obligation to do this, it is advised that they too should normally be informed, as well as the relevant authority or organisation, unless suspected of involvement in the offence in question. Consideration should still be given to informing a juvenile's parents, even where a juvenile in care is not living with them.

Where a juvenile is detained, or a person in police custody appears to be mentally disordered or otherwise mentally vulnerable, the custody officer must, as soon as practicable, inform the appropriate adult of the reasons for and the location of the detention and request that person's presence (see *R v Aspinall* (1999), regarding those which fall under the latter category). In the case of a juvenile, the appropriate adult may or may not be a person responsible for the welfare of that individual. Again, this action must be taken, even if the provisions under Annex B to Code C apply. If a detained child or young person is known to be under a supervision order, the police must take reasonable steps to notify the probation officer or local authority social worker who is responsible for supervising that person.

Mentally disordered or otherwise mentally vulnerable persons detained under s 136 of the Mental Health Act 1983 must be assessed as soon as possible. An approved social worker and a medical practitioner must be called without delay, in order to examine the person if that assessment is to take place at the police station. That person can no longer be detained under s 136 once this has been done and arrangements have been made for that person's care and treatment. In the meantime, that person should not be released until seen by the approved social worker and medical practitioner.

Earlier in this chapter, the normal procedures in dealing initially with arrested persons were described. Under s 3 of Code C, these procedures must be conducted in the presence of the appropriate adult if already at the police station. If those procedures are not complied with in the appropriate adult's absence, then they must be repeated in that person's presence once he or she arrives. This provision is designed to protect juveniles and mentally disordered or otherwise mentally vulnerable people who may not understand the significance of the rights that are being stated at the time. The appropriate action must be taken immediately if a detained person within that category wishes to have access to legal advice and this should not be delayed, pending the arrival of the appropriate adult. The person detained by the police must be informed by the custody officer that the appropriate adult is there to assist and advise him or her, and that he or she is also entitled to consult privately with the appropriate adult at any time.

Another important aspect of s 3 is directed towards the blind and those who are seriously visually impaired. If such a person suffers from such a disability or is unable to read, the custody officer is under a duty to ensure that a suitable person is available to help in checking any documentation. Such persons may include the solicitor, a relative, the appropriate adult or some other person who is likely to take an interest in the detained person, but who is not involved in the investigation. That person may be asked to sign on the detained person's behalf anything which requires consent or signification. This is because blind or seriously visually impaired people may be unwilling to sign police documents; therefore, the alternative of their representative signing on their behalf is a measure designed to protect the interests of all concerned.

Section 13 of this Code covers the use of interpreters in respect of deaf persons or those who do not understand English, and Annex E provides a summary of provisions relating to the mentally disordered and the otherwise mentally vulnerable, which largely echoes provisions made in different parts of Code C. The remaining aspects of this Code of Practice which affect vulnerable suspects are covered below and also in the following chapter, especially the provisions under Annex E which override some of the above safeguards, but which are subject to several strict prerequisites. It should be noted that, with regard to juveniles, even where delay is authorised under ss 56 and 58 of PACE, the police are under a duty to take all practicable steps in order to ascertain the identity of the person responsible for the welfare of the child or young person and to inform that person of the juvenile's arrest. Also, Note for Guidance 11D states that arresting a juvenile at their place of education is to be avoided if possible. Where this cannot be avoided, the person in charge of that establishment must be informed.

In the section above entitled 'Extensions to normal detention periods', it was mentioned that special provisions now exist regarding juvenile and mentally vulnerable persons who are subject to the normal maximum 24 hour period of detention being extended up to 36 hours by the police. Paragraph 15.2A of Code C, which came into force on 1 August 2004, states the following:

> 15.2A Section 42(1) of PACE as amended extends the maximum period of detention for arrestable offences from 24 hours to 36 hours. Detaining a juvenile or mentally vulnerable person for longer than 24 hours will be dependent on the circumstances of the case and with regard to the person's:
>
>   (a) special vulnerability;
>   (b) the legal obligation to provide an opportunity for representations to be made prior to a decision about extending detention;
>   (c) the need to consult and consider the views of any appropriate adult; and
>   (d) any alternatives to police custody.

Although Home Office Circular 60/2003 states that in the case of juveniles, the police power to extend detention beyond 24 hours should only be used if the matter concerns a serious arrestable offence, the Code does not mention this.[10]

Paragraph 15.3C, which also took effect on 1 August 2004, makes further provisions regarding vulnerable persons as follows:

> 15.3C The decision on whether the review takes place in person or by telephone or by video conferencing (see Note 15G) is a matter for the review officer. In determining the form the review may take, the review officer must always take full account of the needs of the person in custody. The benefits of carrying out a review in person should always be considered, based on the individual circumstances of each case with specific additional consideration if the person is:

---

10 Zander, M, 'Revised PACE Codes of Practice' (2004) 154 NLJ, 23 July.

(a) a juvenile (and the age of the juvenile); or

(b) mentally vulnerable; or

(c) has been subject to medical attention for other than routine minor ailments; or

(d) there are presentational or community issues around the person's detention.

THE CHARGING OF SUSPECTS AND SUBSEQUENT DETENTION

Introduction

Paragraph 16.1 of Code C makes the following provisions regarding the duties of investigating and custody officers, once all that can be achieved from detaining a suspect without charge has been accomplished:

> When the officer in charge of the investigation reasonably believes there is sufficient evidence to provide a realistic prospect of the detainee's conviction, see *paragraph 11.6*, they shall without delay, and subject to the following qualification, inform the custody officer who will be responsible for considering whether the detainee should be charged. See *Notes 11B* and *16A*. When a person is detained in respect of more than one offence, it is permissible to delay informing the custody officer until the above conditions are satisfied in respect of all the offences, but see *paragraph 11.6*.[11] If the detainee is a juvenile, mentally disordered or otherwise mentally vulnerable, any resulting action shall be taken in the presence of the appropriate adult if they are present at the time. *See Notes 16B* and *16C*.

Under new provisions inserted by s 28 of and Sched 2 to the Criminal Justice Act 2003, the Crown Prosecution Service will play a more direct part in deciding what charges should be brought against suspects. Under the amended s 37(7) of PACE, once the custody officer has decided that there is enough evidence to charge a detained suspect, the case should should be referred to the CPS for a decision whether to institute proceedings and what charges should be brought. This will not apply where the suspect may be remanded in custody or if the case is straightforward and minor in nature. Where cases are referred to the CPS under the new procedure, the suspect should be released on bail to which conditions may or may not be attached. In other cases, the suspect may be released without bail or may be charged. Paragraphs 16.1A and 1B of Code C, which took effect on 1 August 2004, make the following provisions regarding the new role of the Crown Prosecution Service in the charging of suspects:

> 161A Where guidance issued by the Director of Public Prosecutions under section 37A is in force the custody officer must comply with that Guidance in deciding how to act in dealing with the detainee. See *Note 16AB*.

> 16.1B Where in compliance with the DPP's Guidance the custody officer decides that the case should be immediately referred to the CPS to make the charging decision,

---

11 Paragraph 11.6 states, *inter alia*, that once police questioning has ceased, this should not prevent certain other investigating officers from inviting suspects to complete a formal questions and answer record after the conclusion of the police interview. These include officers in revenue cases or those acting under the confiscation provisions of the Criminal Justice Act 1988 or the Drug Trafficking Act 1994.

consultation should take place with a Crown Prosecutor as soon as is reasonably practicable. Where the Crown Prosecutor is unable to make the charging decision on the information available at that time, the detainee may be released without charge and on bail (with conditions if necessary) under section 37(7)(a). In such circumstances, the detainee should be informed that they are being released to enable the Director of Public Prosecutions to make a decision under section 37B.

Persons unfit to be charged or released may be kept in police detention until they are fit to be dealt with accordingly (this is commonly due to intoxication). Where a person has been released without being charged and no decision has been taken at that time as to whether that person will be prosecuted, the released suspect must be informed as such. This is to avoid leading the suspect into thinking that the matter is completely finished, when a prosecution may still arise.

It should be noted that instead of charging a person with an offence, the suspect may be issued with a 'written charge' as well as a 'requisition', which states the date and time where that person is to appear before magistrates. This is a new streamlined procedure under ss 29 and 30 of the Criminal Justice Act 2003 which replaces the old method where a person was 'reported' for an offence and then the police had to apply to the court for a summons to be issued ('laying an information'). This means that the police may prosecute a person and proceed by way of a written charge (and a requisition) if the offence proves to be of a minor nature. For instance, a person may be arrested on suspicion of taking a motor vehicle without consent, but further inquiries disclose that the suspect has merely failed in the duty to inform the relevant authority (the DVLA) of a change of the vehicle's ownership. However, some suspects are cautioned rather than charged, depending upon the nature of the offence and the offender's background (this subject is covered in the final part of this chapter). Within the context of the charging of suspects, it should again be mentioned that when a suspect's detention time has expired, that person must either be charged, released unconditionally or on bail (see Appendix 12). When a suspect is charged with an offence, that person must also be cautioned as follows:

> You do not have to say anything. But it may harm your defence if you do not mention now something which you later rely on in court. Anything you do say may be given in evidence.

> [Note the slight difference in wording compared with cautions given under other circumstances.]

This procedure should be followed by the suspect being given a written notice, disclosing the particulars of the offence. Where an appropriate adult has had to be present, the written notice shall be given to that person. Anything said by a detained person when charged shall be recorded.

Release or detention after charge?

Under s 38 of PACE, when a person has been arrested and subsequently charged with an offence (whether or not it is arrestable), provided that person has not been arrested under a warrant endorsed for bail, the custody officer then has to decide on one of four courses of action. The suspect may either be released on bail or without bail, or released on bail, but with conditions attached,[12] or may be detained in police custody until the suspect can be produced in court (see Appendix 12). Section 38 goes on to state that the custody officer may only detain a person in police custody after charge when the following conditions are met:

(a) if the name or address of the person cannot be ascertained or the custody officer has reasonable grounds for doubting whether any name or address given by the suspect is genuine;

(b) where the custody officer has reasonable grounds for believing that the suspect will fail to answer to bail and will not appear in court (in other words, may 'jump bail'). This decision will be influenced by the nature and seriousness of the offence, the relevant background and lifestyle of the suspect, any record of previous bail-jumping and the strength of evidence. These factors must also be applied to the criteria in (c)–(e), below, inclusive;

(c) provided the suspect has been arrested for an offence which is imprisonable, the custody officer may detain that person in police custody after charge where there are reasonable grounds for believing that this is necessary to prevent the suspect from re-offending;

(d) even where a person has been arrested for an offence which is not imprisonable, detention after charge may be authorised by the custody officer where there are reasonable grounds to believe that this is necessary to prevent the suspect from causing physical injury to any other person or causing the loss of or damage to property;

(e) the custody officer may detain the suspect in police custody where there are reasonable grounds to believe that this is necessary to prevent that person from interfering with the administration of justice or with the investigation of any offence;

(f) where there are reasonable grounds for believing that it is necessary for the suspect's own protection, the custody officer may authorise that person to be detained in police custody after being charged;

(g) if the suspect is 14 years or more and the custody officer has reasonable grounds to believe that his or her detention is necessary to take a drug test; this further power of detention is limited to no more than six hours (see Chapter 6 for further details of this power).

---

12 Under the Criminal Justice and Public Order Act 1994, s 27, the police may attach almost any conditions to bail when releasing a charged suspect that a court may impose (except the conditions to reside at a bail hostel and to co-operate in the making of any report). This may only be justified in order to ensure that a charged suspect surrenders to custody at a later date, does not offend whilst on bail, does not interfere with witnesses or generally obstruct the course of justice (these conditions also govern the requirement of a surety or security being imposed). Conditions may also be imposed for the person's welfare or protection. A person given conditional bail may ask the custody officer to vary the conditions. This request may be directed to another custody officer, but at the same police station, although the custody officer has the power to vary the conditions, so as to make them more restrictive. Custody officers granting conditional police bail or varying such conditions must enter their reasons in the custody record and inform the person charged. The Criminal Justice and Public Order Act 1994, Sched 3, para 3 enables persons given conditional police bail to appeal to the magistrates' court, in order to have the conditions varied, although the court also has the power to make the conditions more restrictive and may even withhold bail completely. (See further commentary in Jason-Lloyd, L, *The Criminal Justice and Public Order Act 1994: A Basic Guide for Practitioners* (London: Frank Cass, 1996).)

It should be reiterated that a person detained for a breach of the peace has not committed an offence; therefore there is no power to grant bail except in criminal proceedings (*Williamson v Chief Constable of West Midlands Police* (2004)). Also, in *Addison v Chief Constable of West Midlands Police* (2004), the appellant alleged false imprisonment arising from his arrest and subsequent detention by the police. He had become threatening during a neighbour dispute and was held at a police station and later released. The Court of Appeal held that the appellant was released as quickly as possible once it was decided not to take him before the magistrates' court or to charge him. His detention was therefore lawful.

An additional ground for detaining juveniles

If the person charged is an arrested juvenile, the above grounds may also be applied, although the following additional ground exists, which may justify detention after charge. Section 38(1)(b)(ii) of PACE provides that in the case of juveniles only, the custody officer may order detention after charge where there are reasonable grounds for believing that it is in the interests of that person to be detained. Although detention in the interests of an arrested juvenile may also run very close to detention for his or her own protection, there is a difference, bearing in mind the relative youth and vulnerability of such persons:

> The concept of 'own interests' is intended to be wider than 'own protection', although the distinction will not always be easy to draw. This criterion might apply where the juvenile would otherwise be released to vagrancy, homelessness, prostitution or loneliness.[13]

Juveniles who are not released after being charged must be moved to local authority accommodation, unless it is impracticable to do so or where no secure accommodation is available in the case of arrested 12 to 17 year olds and that other local authority accommodation would be inadequate to protect the public from serious harm from that person. Where any of these conditions are present and such action is taken, this must be certified by the custody officer.

The exception to the above rules

Section 25 of the Criminal Justice and Public Order Act 1994 (as amended by s 56 of the Crime and Disorder Act 1998, and by Sched 6 to the Sexual Offences Act 2003) provides that bail may only be granted to a person charged with an offence from a list of specific crimes, and where that person has a previous conviction for any of those offences, if the police officer (or the court) considering bail is satisfied that there are exceptional circumstances which justify it. Those offences are murder, attempted murder, manslaughter, rape, assault by penetration, causing a person to engage in sexual activity without consent involving penetration, rape of child under 13, assault of child under 13 by penetration, causing/inciting a child under 13 to engage in sexual activity involving penetration, sexual activity with a person with a mental disorder where the touching involved penetration, causing/inciting a person with a mental

---

13 Levenson, H, Fairweather, F and Cape, E, *Police Powers: A Practitioner's Guide* (3rd edn, London: Legal Action Group, 1996).

disorder to engage in sexual activity involving penetration, as well as attempting to commit any of the foregoing eight sexual offences. The original s 25 of the 1994 Act made it a strict rule that bail in the case of those previously convicted of certain offences was automatically refused. The only exception was if any previous manslaughter conviction did not result in a prison sentence or long term detention in the case of a child or young person.

How will a custody officer recognise the 'exceptional circumstances' that would justify granting bail to a person charged with any of the above offences who has a previous conviction for any of them? Some doubt has been cast on the practicality of these new measures, as follows:

> Section 56 removes the absolute ban, but it goes nowhere near reverting to the general presumption in favour of bail under the Bail Act 1976. Instead, it provides that, in the situations with which s 25 is concerned, bail is to be granted only if the court or custody officer is satisfied that there are exceptional circumstances which justify it. Section 56, in effect, introduces a strong rebuttable presumption against the grant of bail in such cases, in place of the absolute ban. This presumption can be rebutted by satisfying the court or, as the case may be, the custody officer considering the grant of bail. *It would seem most unlikely that a custody officer would ever be so satisfied.*[14]

Police bail in general

If a person released on police bail fails to surrender to custody without reasonable cause, that person commits an offence under s 6 of the Bail Act 1976 and may be arrested without warrant. When a person who is released from police detention on bail returns to the police station as required, or is arrested and taken to the police station because of failure to surrender to bail, any unused time from the previous period whilst detained may be used to detain that person further without charge, but not exceeding the maximum period allowed. This is contingent on the custody officer having reasonable grounds for believing that this is necessary to secure or preserve evidence, or to obtain it by questioning the suspect.

Schedule 2 to the Criminal Justice Act 2003 has inserted new ss 37C and 37D into PACE thereby, *inter alia*, enabling the police to impose conditional bail before charge where a case is being considered by the Crown Prosecution Service, and confers a power of arrest on the police where they have reasonable suspicion that such bail conditions have been breached. Under the Bail Act 1976, the police may impose conditions on bail in almost the same way as the courts with just a few exceptions. A custody officer may attach conditions in order to prevent the suspect from: absconding; re-offending whilst on bail; interfering with witnesses or generally obstructing justice, or to protect the suspect, or to ensure a child or young person's welfare or their interests if the suspect is a juvenile (see also footnote 12).

---

14 Card, R and Ward, R, *The Crime and Disorder Act 1998: A Practitioner's Guide* (Bristol: Jordans, 1998) (emphasis added). Note that this refers to the position before the Sexual Offences Act 2003.

Questioning after charge

Once a person has been charged, there are limitations on the extent of any questioning from that point onwards. Under paras 16.4, 16.4A, 16.5 and 16.9 of Code C, these rules are as follows:

16.4 If, after a detainee has been charged with or informed they may be prosecuted for an offence, an officer wants to tell them about any written statement or interview with another relating to such an offence, the detainee shall either be handed a true copy of the written statement or the content of the interview record brought to their attention.[15] Nothing shall be done to invite any reply or comment except to:

(a) caution the detainee, *'You do not have to say anything, but anything you do say may be given in evidence'*; and

(b) remind the detainee about their right to legal advice.

16.4A If the detainee:

- cannot read, the document may be read to them;
- is a juvenile, mentally disordered or otherwise mentally vulnerable, the appropriate adult shall also be given a copy, or the interview record shall be brought to their attention.

16.5 A detainee may not be interviewed about an offence after they have been charged with, or informed they may be prosecuted for it, unless the interview is necessary:

- to prevent or minimise harm or loss to some other person, or the public;
- to clear up an ambiguity in a previous answer or statement;
- in the interests of justice for the detainee to have put to them, and have an opportunity to comment on, information concerning the offence which has come to light since they were charged or informed they might be prosecuted.

Before any such interview, the interviewer shall:

(a) caution the detainee, *'You do not have to say anything, but anything you do say may be given in evidence'*;

(b) remind the detainee about their right to legal advice.

Paragraph 16.9 states that when any questions are put after a suspect has been charged and answers given, these shall be contemporaneously recorded on the forms provided. The record shall then be signed by the suspect. If that person refuses to sign, then this document shall be signed by the interviewing officer and anyone else who is present. The provisions set out in Code E or F will apply where the questions have been tape recorded or visually recorded.

The duty to take a charged person before a court

Section 46 of PACE states that a person charged with an offence who is then kept in police detention, or in local authority accommodation in the case of juveniles, must be brought before a magistrates' court as soon as is practicable and, in any event, not later than the first sitting after being charged. In most cases, both the police station and the relevant magistrates' court will be in the same petty sessions area and the person charged will therefore be produced in court either on the day when charged or the

---

15   This means playing back any tape recording of an interview (*op cit* Clark, fn 7).

following day (this excludes Sundays, Good Friday and Christmas Day). In less straightforward situations, the custody officer must inform the court clerk (justices' chief executive) of the presence of a charged person in custody, in order that a sitting may be arranged in accordance with s 46. There is no requirement for a person charged with an offence who is in hospital to be produced in court if that person is not well enough.

CAUTIONING

Cautioning in this context is different from actually administering cautions to suspects where a warning is given on arrest or prior to formal questions being asked. In many cases, where a suspect may be charged with an offence, the case may be disposed of by means of a caution. As far as children and young persons are concerned (10–17 year olds inclusive), a reprimand and warning scheme was piloted in 1999 and implemented nationwide in April 2000. This scheme is discussed in further detail below. Older offenders are cautioned in accordance with Home Office Circular 18/94, which provides guidance as to the use of this disposal option. This document is entitled 'National Standards for Cautioning (Revised)' and consists of six main sections, which are headed as follows, together with the relevant provisions.

Aims

A caution is not a sentence; therefore, a caution is not contingent upon certain activities being performed, such as reparation or payment of compensation, which only the courts may impose. The aims of cautioning are to deal quickly and simply with less serious offenders, to divert them from unnecessary appearance in the criminal courts and to reduce the prospects of their re-offending.

Decision to caution

Although a caution does not constitute a criminal record, it is still recorded by the police and may be cited in any later court proceedings. Earlier cautions should also be considered by the police if considering whether or not to prosecute. A caution should be administered only where there is a realistic prospect of a conviction and the offender admits to the offence and is capable of understanding the significance of this admission.

Public interest considerations

The police should consider whether giving a caution would be in the public interest and, in this respect, they are referred to the guidance under the Code for Crown Prosecutors. They are also encouraged to be more favourably inclined towards cautioning certain classes of offenders, rather than prosecuting them. These include the elderly and the physically and mentally disabled, although it is stressed that this must not constitute complete immunity in all cases. Much depends upon the offender's attitude to the offence and the degree of wilfulness in which it was committed. Also, where group offending is concerned, each offender's degree of involvement should be considered.

Views of the victim

Prior to any caution being given, the police are advised to contact the victim of the offence, in order to ascertain his or her views, as well as the effect of the crime on that person and whether the offender has made any form of voluntary reparation or compensation. Under no circumstances should the police be involved in arranging or negotiating any such recompense.

Administration of a caution

A caution should be administered by a uniformed police officer and at a police station if practicable. The officer should normally be of the rank of inspector or above, although designated 'cautioning officers' may be appointed where appropriate and this may include using a sergeant instead of an inspector or community or home beat officers.

Recording cautions

Every caution should be recorded as directed by the Home Secretary and their usage should be monitored on a force-wide basis. Cautions should be cited in court where they are relevant to the offence in question, although care must be taken not to confuse cautions with criminal convictions when presenting the offender's antecedents.

CONDITIONAL CAUTIONS

Part 3 of the Criminal Justice Act 2003, headed 'Conditional Cautions', has created a new statutory cautioning scheme that runs alongside the existing non-statutory cautioning arrangements for adults. Section 22 of the 2003 Act states that a police officer, an investigating officer or a person authorised by a prosecutor (an 'authorised person') may give a conditional caution to an offender aged 18 or over, if each of the following five requirements under s 23 of the Criminal Justice Act is satisfied:

(1) The authorised person must have evidence that the offender has committed an offence.

(2) A prosecutor decides that there is sufficient evidence to charge the offender with the offence, and that a conditional caution should be given to that person.

(3) The offender admits having committed the offence to the authorised person.

(4) The authorised person explains the effect of the conditional caution to the offender and warns that person that failure to comply with any of its conditions may result in that person being prosecuted for the offence.

(5) The offender must sign a document which contains details of the offence, his or her admission that they committed it, their consent to being given the conditional caution, and the conditions attached to it.

Section 24 states that the offender may be subject to criminal proceedings for the offence if that person fails, without reasonable excuse, to comply with any of the conditions attached to the conditional caution. It also states that the document mentioned in s 23(5) above is to be admissible in such proceedings. With regard to this procedure, one commentator notes that:

The implications are when someone agrees to a conditional caution they in effect restrict their ability to argue later, when prosecuted, that they were 'not guilty'. Clearly, the intention is to ensure that a guilty plea must automatically follow and in this regard the ground can be seen as moving away from the courtroom and into the hands of police and prosecutors. It remains to be seen what ingenious arguments may emerge at the court stage, and whether the provisions hold good in terms of the European Convention on Human Rights.[16]

Section 22(3) states that the objects of the conditions which may be attached to a conditional caution should be:

(1) the rehabilitation of the offender and/or;

(2) ensuring that the offender makes reparation for the offence.

Section 25 states that the Home Secretary is under a duty to prepare a code of practice in relation to conditional cautions.

The reprimand and warning scheme for juveniles

As mentioned above, a system of reprimands and warnings for juveniles has been in force nationally since April 2000. The reason for the present system is stated in the Home Office publication, entitled *Tackling Youth Crime: Reforming Youth Justice*,[17] as follows:

> While cautioning works well with most first time offenders (about 80% of whom do not re-offend within two years), it becomes progressively less effective once a pattern of offending sets in. If cautioning is used inconsistently or repeated without positive intervention to reverse offending habits, it will not be effective.

The Consultation Paper then points out that approximately one in five offenders do not respond to police cautioning and, subsequently, they become involved in a pattern of offending. There was an obvious need to replace the cautioning system affecting juveniles with something more positive, hence ss 65 and 66 of the Crime and Disorder Act 1998, which make the following provisions.

If the police decide not to prosecute a young offender nor take informal action by giving firm advice to the youngster and his or her parents, they may either issue a reprimand, if the offence is of a minor nature, or they may issue a warning, if the offence is more serious. If the offender re-offends after receiving a reprimand, the police must then issue a warning, assuming they do not prosecute on that occasion. No more than one reprimand may be given and no more than one warning may be issued, unless more than two years have lapsed between the first warning and the latest offence and the latter is not serious enough to require a charge to be brought. Only then may a second warning be given, but under no circumstances will a further warning be issued afterwards.

Final warnings are not intended to be a mere indication that young offenders have reached the final stage before prosecution. Whenever the police issue a juvenile with a final warning, they are under a duty to refer that person to a youth offending team.

---

16 Gibson, B, *Criminal Justice Act 2003: A Guide to the New Procedures and Sentencing* (Winchester: Waterside Press, 2004).

17 Home Office, Consultation Paper (London: HMSO, September 1997).

Where appropriate, it is intended that final warnings should then be accompanied by a programme of intervention to prevent re-offending in conjunction with local youth offending teams, which may also actively involve the offender's parents. The police may also request that the relevant youth offending team makes a prior assessment of the young offender in order to assist in making the decision as to whether a final warning should be given.

If a person is convicted of an offence committed within two years of being given a warning by the police, the courts may not impose a conditional discharge on the offender, unless the court is of the opinion that there are exceptional circumstances relating to the offence or the offender which justify this sentence. Where this applies, the court must state the reasons for its opinion. Any record of a police reprimand, warning or failure to participate in a rehabilitation programme under a warning may be cited in criminal proceedings in the same circumstances as previous convictions.[18]

The drug arrest referral scheme

Before departing from the issue of police powers of detention, it should be mentioned that a relatively new innovation called the 'drug arrest referral scheme' had been piloted up until the year 2000 in a number of police forces, and was implemented nationally by the end of that year. This scheme constitutes an appendage to the detention process regarding suspects arrested for drug-related crimes.

It is now widely known that the funding of drug taking is a major motivation behind certain criminal activities. Research in selected areas has shown that over 80% of all persons arrested for shoplifting, domestic burglaries and car theft tested positive for at least one drug.[19] In an endeavour to try and break the 'revolving door' pattern of offending on the part of drug users, the police have developed an interventionist approach to drug-related crime, rather than adopt purely an enforcement role. The essence of the scheme can be found in three main types of referral: first, the 'information' method, where the arrested person is simply given a leaflet or other document containing the details of a drug agency; secondly, there is the 'proactive' method, involving drug workers actually performing their work in police stations and having direct access to persons detained; and, thirdly, there is the 'incentive' method, where persons who come into contact with the police are motivated to seek help in order to deal with their drug problem. The arrest referral scheme does not alter the suspect's status or treatment whilst being held by the police, such as the granting of bail or decisions regarding detention or charging.[20]

---

18 This commentary on the reprimand and warning scheme has been taken from Jason-Lloyd, L, *The Crime and Disorder Act 1998: A Concise Guide* (2nd edn, Cambridgeshire: Elm, 1999).

19 Bennett, T, *Drugs and Crime: The Results of Research on Drug Testing and Interviewing Arrestees*, Home Office Research Study No 183 (London: HMSO, 1998).

20 See also the relatively new police power to test for drugs in the next chapter.

CHAPTER 6

THE QUESTIONING AND GENERAL TREATMENT OF DETAINED PERSONS

INTRODUCTION

The line of demarcation between Chapter 5 and the present chapter can sometimes be difficult to draw. This is because, among other things, many of the procedures discussed in the previous chapter may be applied to detained persons under a wide variety of circumstances, including the alleged offences involved and the period that they are detained for. The topics that will now be discussed include the general conditions of detention and the treatment of detained persons, the administering of cautions, the conduct of interviews including access to legal advice, the tape and video recording of interviews, confessions, fingerprinting and other identification procedures, including the taking of body samples.

GENERAL CONDITIONS OF DETENTION

The general conditions under which detained persons may be held in police custody are contained in the provisions under s 8 of Code C, as follows. Wherever possible, no more than one person shall occupy a cell. A juvenile must not be placed in a police cell unless no other secure accommodation is available or a cell would be more comfortable than another secure place in the police station. Whenever a juvenile is placed in a cell, this must be recorded and, in any event, a juvenile may not be placed in a cell with a detained adult. Cells must be adequately heated, cleaned, ventilated and lit, although the latter includes such dimming as to allow people to sleep at night time, but without compromising safety and security. Bedding must be of a clean and generally reasonable standard and access to toilet and washing facilities must be available.[1] If practicable, brief outdoor exercise shall be offered daily.

In any 24 hour period, a minimum of two light meals and one main meal shall be offered, together with drinks, and a record must be kept of meals offered. Further drinks should be provided between meals where reasonable. As far as practicable, the meals should be offered at recognised meal times, be of a varied diet and meet any special dietary needs or religious beliefs; whenever necessary, advice shall be sought on medical and dietary matters from the police surgeon. A detained person may have meals supplied by friends or relatives, but not at public expense.

Where it is necessary to remove a detained person's clothes for investigation purposes, for hygiene or health reasons or for cleaning, that person is to be issued with replacement clothing of a reasonable standard and only when adequate clothing has been offered to the suspect may that person be interviewed. Any replacement clothing issued to the suspect must be recorded. Where restraint in a locked cell is absolutely

---

1   In *Hague v Deputy Governor of Parkhurst Prison* (1991), it was held that whilst a claim in negligence could be made where a person was detained in extremely poor conditions, this would not render the detention unlawful.

necessary, only approved equipment may be used and any use of this must be recorded. Particular care must be taken when considering the use of approved restraints in the case of those who are deaf, mentally disordered or otherwise mentally vulnerable.

Under s 9 of Code C, detained persons shall be visited every hour, unless they are drunk, in which case they must be visited at least every 30 minutes and, during the visit, they must be roused and spoken to. Appropriate medical assistance must be sought if there is any concern regarding that person's condition. Whenever possible, juveniles and others at risk should be visited more frequently,[2] although attention is drawn to Chapter 5 regarding the risk assessment required under paras 3.5(c) and 3.6–3.10 of Code C.

Reasonable force may be used if necessary in order to secure compliance with reasonable instructions regarding a person's detention or to prevent escape, injury, damage to property or the destruction of evidence. Although this provision was stated in para 8.9 of the previous edition of Code C before the 2003 Code was published, it is rather strange that it has not been included in the 2003 or 2004 editions of Code C with regard to police officers. Even stranger, the use of force is mentioned in the latest Codes A, B and D and mentions this in connection with police civilians in the latest Code C, but not the police. Fortunately, police officers may rely on their common law powers and s 117 of PACE to use reasonable force in this context (see Professor Zander's comment in *Police and Criminal Evidence Act 1984* (4th edn, London: Sweet & Maxwell, 2003), pp 252–53).

THE TREATMENT OF DETAINED PERSONS

The provisions in respect of the treatment of detained persons are covered under s 9 of Code C, which is concerned with general issues, medical treatment and documentation. First, there is the general provision that where a complaint or concern arises regarding a person's treatment after being arrested, a report must be made, as soon as practicable, to an inspector or above who is not connected with the investigation. Where the matter concerns the possibility of unlawful force being used, an appropriate healthcare professional must be called as soon as practicable. Under the Code of Practice dealing with documentation, it is stated that a record must be made of any such complaint and subsequent arrangements for an examination by a healthcare professional together with any relevant remarks by the custody officer. However, nothing under this section of Code C prevents the police from calling a police surgeon or another healthcare professional to examine a detainee to obtain any evidence relating to any offence that the detainee may be involved in.

Secondly, there are fairly detailed provisions regarding medical matters affecting persons held in police custody. Where a person appears to be suffering from physical or mental illness, is injured, or appears to need medical attention for other reasons, the

---

2   See *Kirkham v Chief Constable of Greater Manchester Police* (1990), where it was held that the police are under a duty of care to prevent a prisoner committing suicide where they are aware that the person has suicidal tendencies.

custody officer must ensure that clinical attention is given as soon as reasonably practicable. In urgent cases, the person must be sent to hospital or the nearest available healthcare professional should be called immediately. The Code of Practice goes on to state that the above action should be taken whether or not the person requests medical attention or has already had treatment elsewhere.

Where a person has been arrested and taken to a police station under s 136 of the Mental Health Act 1983,[3] the above provisions should not delay the transfer of a person to a place of safety in order to be assessed by a medical practitioner. If such an assessment is due to take place at the police station, the custody officer has a discretion not to call a healthcare professional initially, provided that officer believes that the assessment by a suitably qualified medical practitioner can be made without undue delay.

Any detained person may request a medical examination, in which case an appropriate healthcare professional must be called as soon as practicable or be examined by a medical practitioner of his or her own choice, although this will not be at public expense. The provisions under the Code of Practice regarding documentation provide that where this occurs, a record must be kept of any such request, together with the arrangements made for any examination and any medical directions subsequently given to the police. In the Notes for Guidance, it is stated that there is no need to call on clinical attention for minor ailments or injuries which do not need attention, although they must be recorded in the custody record, but, if in doubt, an appropriate healthcare professional must be called. They also go on to remind custody officers that persons who behave in an intoxicated manner may be ill, under the influence of drugs or may have sustained a head or other injury, all of which may not be easily discernible. This also includes withdrawal symptoms experienced by those needing or addicted to drugs. Therefore, when in doubt, the police should always call an ambulance or a healthcare professional with due speed.

Where a person detained in police custody possesses medication relating to a serious condition such as heart disease, diabetes or epilepsy, or claims to need such medication, the advice of a healthcare professional must be sought, even if the person does not appear to need such assistance. If a person has to take or apply any medication which was prescribed before his or her detention, an appropriate healthcare professional should be consulted by the custody officer before it is administered. If this is approved, the custody officer is responsible for ensuring that the medication is available for administration and for its safekeeping in the meantime. However, special provisions apply in the case of medication which is in the form of controlled drugs as defined under the Misuse of Drugs Act 1971.[4] Paragraph 9.10 of

---

3   'Under s 136 of the 1983 Act, if a police officer finds in a place to which the public have access a person who appears to him to be suffering from mental disorder and to be in immediate need of care or control, he may, if he thinks it necessary in the interests of that person or for the protection of other persons, remove the person to a "place of safety" ... this includes (among other places) both a hospital and a police station' (Hoggett, B, *Mental Health Law* (4th edn, London: Sweet & Maxwell, 1996)).

4   For further reading on controlled drugs and their definition, see Jason-Lloyd, L, *Drugs, Addiction and the Law* (9th edn, Cambridgeshire: Elm, 2004). Note that all controlled drugs are listed under the Misuse of Drugs Act 1971 under Classes A, B or C, depending on their degree of social harm when misused.

Code C states that no police officer may administer or supervise the self-administration of controlled drugs listed in Sched 1, 2 or 3 under the Misuse of Drugs Regulations 2001.[5] A detainee may only self-administer such drugs under the personal supervision of the medical practitioner authorising their use. Drugs listed in Sched 4 or 5 under the Misuse of Drugs Regulations 2001[6] may be distributed by the custody officer for self-administration if that officer has consulted the registered medical practitioner authorising their use (this may be done by telephone). However, both the custody officer and the medical practitioner should be satisfied that self-administration will not expose the detainee, police officers or anyone else to the risk of harm or injury. Any such consultation should be noted in the custody record. The provisions governing documentation under this Code of Practice state that the custody officer is under a duty to record all medication in the possession of a person on arrival at the police station and, where applicable, any medication that the detained person claims to need, but does not have at the time; however, this is subject to s 4 of Code C.

Where a detained person appears to be suffering from an infectious disease or condition, or the custody officer is given this information, reasonable steps must be taken by the custody officer to safeguard the health of the detainee and others at the police station. The detainee and his or her property may be isolated until clinical directions have been obtained

The administering of cautions to suspects

Section 10 of Code C is divided into five main Parts. Part (a) deals with when a caution must be given and Part (b) deals with terms of the cautions. Part (c) deals with special warnings under ss 36 and 37 of the Criminal Justice and Public Order Act 1994. Part (d) deals with juveniles and the mentally vulnerable, and Part (e) covers documentation procedures. With regard to Part (a), a caution must be given to a person suspected of an offence before any questions can be put to that person, or where further questions are put arising from answers which have given grounds for suspicion. This rule applies where that person's answers or failure or refusal to answer a question satisfactorily may be given as evidence to a court in a prosecution. Cautions are therefore not necessary when other questions are put, such as establishing the

---

5   In addition to being placed under a class under the Misuse of Drugs Act 1971, each controlled drug is also placed under Scheds 1–5 to the Misuse of Drugs Regulations 2001. Basically, the lower the schedule number, the greater the degree of restrictions on the possession and supply of that drug. Oddly, para 9.10 mentions the self-administration of Sched 1 controlled drugs. These are subject to the greatest restrictions and cannot be prescribed as they have no medicinal value. It is anticipated, however, that this anomaly in the Code may be rectified in the new version due to be drafted around the summer of 2005. Examples of the more well known Sched 1 controlled drugs include cannabis resin, 'ecstasy' and LSD. The situation is different regarding Sched 2 and 3 controlled drugs as they may be prescribed. Schedule 2 controlled drugs include painkillers such as morphine, methadone and codeine. Schedule 3 includes cathine and a number of barbiturates.

6   Schedule 4 controlled drugs include mainly mild sedatives such as diazepam (valium) and nitrazepam (mogadon), and Sched 4 also includes anabolic steroids such as nandrolone and testosterone. Schedule 5 controlled drugs are subject to the least restrictions as they are medicinal compounds that contain very small quantities of controlled drugs, or are prepared in such a way that the extraction of the controlled drugs is extremely difficult.

suspect's identity or in the course of routine searches. Cautions must be administered to suspects prior to questioning, even when they have not been arrested, such as those voluntarily attending police stations. At the same time, that person must be informed that he or she is not under arrest and may leave at will. If that person is subsequently arrested or where a suspect is arrested away from a police station, that person must be cautioned on being arrested, unless it is impracticable to do so because of the suspect's condition or behaviour at the time, or where a caution has been administered prior to being arrested.

With regard to Part (b) under s 10, where there is a break in the course of questioning, the interviewing officer must make the suspect aware that he or she is still under caution and, if there is any doubt, the caution should be given again before the resumption of the interview. The exact wording of the caution is as follows:

> You do not have to say anything. But it may harm your defence if you do not mention when questioned something which you later rely on in court. Anything you do say may be given in evidence.

This is sometimes known as the 'new caution' as it was introduced in April 1995, although in certain circumstances the earlier or 'old' caution may still be administered (see below).

Provided the sense of the caution is unaffected, minor deviations from the exact wording are acceptable. Where a person cannot understand the meaning of the caution, the police officer should explain its meaning in his or her own words.

Under Part (c), if an arrested suspect who is subsequently interviewed does not answer certain questions, or answers them unsatisfactorily, then, after due warning, a court or jury may draw adverse inferences under ss 36 and 37 of the Criminal Justice and Public Order Act 1994. These questions relate to any marks, objects or substances that may be found on or otherwise in the possession of the arrested person, including clothing or footwear or in the place where the arrest took place. The questions may also relate to the suspect's presence in the place where the offence was committed. However, in order for adverse inferences to be drawn, the interviewing officer must first inform the suspect of the following in ordinary language: what offence is being investigated; what the suspect is specifically being asked to account for and that this may be due to the suspect's believed participation in the offence; that a court may draw adverse inferences from failure or refusal to account for that fact; that a record is being made of the interview and may be given in evidence (this procedure is replicated where a suspect's interview is being tape recorded: see below).

There are certain restrictions on drawing adverse inferences from a person's silence where that person is detained in a police station and has requested legal advice, has not been allowed an opportunity to consult any solicitor and has not changed his or her mind about wanting legal advice. In these circumstances, the caution should be:

> You do not have to say anything unless you wish to do so, but what you say may be given in evidence.

This is the 'old' or 'earlier caution', as mentioned above, which also applies when a person is charged with or informed that he or she may be prosecuted for an offence who is shown a statement or content of an interview made by someone else, or is interviewed about that offence, or makes a written statement about that offence.

In some cases, a detained person's failure to co-operate may have consequences regarding his or her immediate treatment even if cautioned. For instance, the suspect may commit an offence under the Road Traffic Act 1988 for failing to provide certain particulars, or may be detained in police custody after being charged with failing to provide a correct name and address. In such circumstances, the suspect should be informed of the relevant consequences and that they are not affected by the caution.

Under Part (d), where a juvenile or a mentally disordered or otherwise mentally vulnerable person is cautioned in the absence of the appropriate adult, the caution must be administered again in the appropriate adult's presence. Under Part (e), any caution given under s 10 shall be recorded either in the police officer's pocket book or in the interview record.

THE GENERAL CONDUCT OF POLICE INTERVIEWS

The overall conduct of police interviews is governed under s 11 of Code C. In summary, these provisions are as follows. First, what is the definition of a police interview? Paragraph 11.1A states: 'An interview is the questioning of a person regarding their involvement or suspected involvement in a criminal offence or offences which ... must be carried out under caution ...' Once it has been decided to arrest a suspect, that person should not be interviewed about the offence in question, except at a police station or other authorised place of detention, although this rule is subject to three exceptions: the first is where the subsequent delay would be likely to lead to evidence or persons being at risk of harm or interference; the second is where delay would lead to alerting accomplices; and the third will apply where delay would hinder the recovery of property obtained in the course of committing an offence. Even so, once the relevant risk no longer exists or the necessary questions have been put in order to avoid that risk, interviewing must cease.

Subject to five main exceptions, which will be explained below, the interviewing officer has a duty to remind the suspect of entitlement to free legal advice and, subject to the exceptions just mentioned, that the interview may be delayed in order that legal advice can be obtained. These reminders should be given immediately before the commencement of any interview or series of interviews, and should be noted in the interview record. An interview may not be delayed for the purposes of obtaining and receiving legal advice under the following circumstances:

(a) where Annex B to Code C applies. This has been discussed above in Chapter 5, namely where a superintendent or above may delay access to legal advice for up to 36 hours in the case of serious arrestable offences, but subject to certain conditions. In such instances the restriction on drawing adverse inferences from silence will apply because the detainee is prevented from obtaining legal advice;

(b) where an officer of the rank of superintendent or above has reasonable grounds for believing that delay will involve a risk of interference or harm to persons or evidence, serious loss or damage to property,[7] alerting accomplices, hinder the recovery of property, or where a solicitor has agreed to attend, but awaiting his or her arrival would cause unreasonable delay in the investigation;

---

7   Code C, para 6.7 provides that questioning must cease until the suspect receives legal advice, once sufficient information to avert the risk has been obtained.

(c) where the solicitor selected by the suspect cannot be contacted, has declined to attend or has previously indicated the wish not to be contacted and the suspect has refused the services of a duty solicitor. In such circumstances, an inspector or above may authorise that the interview takes place without further delay;

(d) where the suspect initially requested legal advice, but has since had a change of mind. In such cases, the interview may be started or continued, but only if the suspect has agreed in writing or on tape to be interviewed without legal advice. Also, an inspector or above must give authority for the interview to proceed in this manner, having first ascertained the suspect's reasons for the change of mind. All these facts, including the name of the authorising officer, must be recorded, either on tape or in the written interview record at the beginning or recommencement of the interview. In the case of (c) and (d), the restriction on drawing adverse inferences from silence will not apply because the detainee is allowed an opportunity to consult a solicitor;

(e) where s 11(d) to Code C applies. This is entitled 'Vulnerable suspects: urgent interviews at police stations' and states that a police superintendent or above may authorise the following action if that officer considers that delay will lead to interference or harm to evidence or interference or physical harm to other persons, alert accomplices or hinder the recovery of property obtained as a result of a criminal offence, or result in serious loss or damage to property:

- the interview of a person heavily under the influence of drink or drugs; or is otherwise unable to appreciate the significance of questions and their answers;

- the interview of a juvenile or mentally disordered or otherwise mentally vulnerable person, without the presence of the appropriate adult; or

- the interview of a person who has difficulty understanding English or has a hearing disability without an interpreter.

However, such interviews may not proceed if they could significantly harm the person's physical or mental state.

Where questioning has been authorised under these circumstances, the interview should be discontinued as soon as information necessary to avert any of the immediate risks mentioned above has been obtained. Also, a record must be made of the grounds for justifying the decision to interview a vulnerable suspect under the above conditions.

At the commencement of an interview at a police station, once the caution has been administered, the suspect should have put to him or her any significant statement or silence which occurred prior to the interview. The suspect should then be asked to confirm or deny any earlier statement or silence and to make any other comments. Paragraph 11.4A states that: 'A significant statement is one which appears capable of being used in evidence against the suspect, in particular, a direct admission of guilt. A significant silence is a failure or refusal to answer a question or answer satisfactorily when under caution, which might, allowing for the restriction on drawing adverse inferences from silence, see *Annex C*, give rise to an inference under the Criminal Justice and Public Order Act 1994, Part III.'

Under para 11.5, no interviewer may try to obtain answers to questions or obtain a statement by the use of oppression. Neither may the police indicate, unless directly asked, what action they will take if the suspect answers or refuses to answer questions or makes a statement or refuses to do either. The exception to this rule has already been mentioned above where, in specific cases, a suspect's failure to co-operate could have an immediate effect on that person's immediate treatment. Where a direct question is asked by the suspect, the police may inform that person of the action the police propose to take in such an event, 'provided that action is itself proper and warranted'.

In the course of a criminal investigation, once the police believe that there is sufficient evidence to justify a prosecution being brought against a detained suspect, that person should be asked if he or she has anything further to say. Any further questioning must then cease once the person indicates that he or she wishes to say nothing more. However, this does not prevent investigating officers pursuing matters under revenue cases or confiscation proceedings from inviting that same person to complete a formal question and answer record, following the conclusion of the interview.

Paragraphs 11.7–11.14 and Note for Guidance 11E contain detailed provisions regarding interview records. The main points arising from these are as follows. An accurate record must be made of each interview which, in turn, must include the location where it took place, the time it began and ended, and any breaks in the interview, together with the names of all those present (except in cases involving terrorism or other cases where police staff reasonably believe they may be in danger, where the officers need to state their warrant or other identification numbers and duty station, but not their names). Written interview records must be both timed and signed by the maker. The record of the interview must be made on the forms provided for this purpose, in the officer's pocket book or on tape, or video recorded in accordance with Codes E and F. The record must be contemporaneous with the interview, unless this is impracticable or would interfere with the conduct of the interview. If either of these exceptions apply, the reasons must be noted in the officer's pocket book and the interview record must be made as soon as practicable after the interview. In any event, it must constitute either a verbatim record of what was stated or an account of the interview which summarises it adequately and accurately.

The suspect should be given the opportunity to read the interview record and sign it, if in agreement with its contents, or indicate any alleged inaccuracies, unless it is impracticable (different arrangements apply where the interview is tape or video recorded). If the suspect cannot read or refuses to read the record or sign it, the senior interviewer present must read it to the suspect and invite that person to sign it (or make their mark) or indicate any alleged inaccuracies. That officer should then certify on the interview record what has occurred. Where an interview has been contemporaneously recorded and signed by the person questioned (or tape or video recorded), a written statement is not normally necessary. Although a suspect may be asked if he or she wishes to make a statement, it is usually only when the suspect expressly wishes to make a statement under caution that one is taken. Note for Guidance 11E states that a suspect, having read and agreed the contents of the interview record, should then be asked to endorse the record with words to the effect, 'I agree that this is a correct record of what was said' and then sign the document. If the suspect disagrees with the record, the interviewer should record details of that disagreement and then ask the suspect to sign accordingly. Any refusal to sign this document or any record of interview must be recorded. This also applies where a suspect refuses to sign a written record of any comment made by him or her which, although outside the context of the interview, may be relevant to the offence (see para 11.13 of Code C).

Paragraphs 11.15–11.17 and Note for Guidance 11D provide additional safeguards regarding juveniles and mentally disordered or otherwise mentally vulnerable persons. Any person falling within these categories must not be interviewed or asked to provide or sign a written statement unless the appropriate adult is present. The exceptions to this rule apply where any delay would be likely to lead to interference or harm to evidence, or interference with or physical harm to other people, or serious loss or damage to property, or to the alerting of accomplices, or where it might hinder the recovery of property obtained in connection with an offence. During the presence of the appropriate adult at an interview, that person shall be informed that he or she is not expected to be a passive observer only. The appropriate adult should then be informed that their role is to advise the person being questioned and to observe whether the interview is being conducted properly and fairly, and also to promote communication with the person being interviewed. Note for Guidance 11C augments these provisions by stating the following:

> Although juveniles or people who are mentally disordered or otherwise mentally vulnerable are often capable of providing reliable evidence, they may, without knowing or wishing to do so, be particularly prone in certain circumstances to provide information that may be unreliable, misleading or self-incriminating. Special care should always be taken when questioning such a person, and the appropriate adult should be involved if there is any doubt about a person's age, mental state or capacity. Because of the risk of unreliable evidence it is also important to obtain corroboration of any facts admitted whenever possible.

Juveniles may be interviewed at their places of education only in exceptional circumstances and with the agreement of the person in charge of that establishment or their nominee.[8] Where the police want to interview a juvenile, every effort should be made to inform the parents or other person responsible for the juvenile's welfare and, if a different person, the appropriate adult. Reasonable time should be allowed for the appropriate adult to be present at the interview. If unreasonable delay would be caused by waiting for the arrival of the appropriate adult, the person in charge of the educational establishment, or their nominee, may act in this capacity, unless the suspected offence was committed against that establishment.

Interviews at police stations

The rules governing the general conduct of interviews in police stations are contained in s 12 of Code C. This begins by stating that the custody officer is responsible for deciding whether to deliver a suspect into the custody of a police officer who wishes to interview or conduct inquiries which require the presence of that detained person. A record must be made, covering the period when the suspect is not in the custody of the custody officer and the reason why and, where applicable, the reason for any refusal to deliver the suspect out of that custody. Bearing in mind the strict rules regarding maximum periods of detention (see Chapter 5), a suspect must be allowed a continuous period of at least eight hours rest in any 24 hour period. This should normally be at night and must be free from questioning, travel or any interruption by

---

8   This is basically the same as the restriction on arresting juveniles in their places of education, as mentioned in Chapter 5.

the police regarding the investigation. This rest period may be interrupted or delayed if there are reasonable grounds for believing that there is risk of harm to persons or of serious damage to or loss of property, or the outcome of the investigation would be prejudiced or that it would delay the suspect's release from custody. Also, the rest period may be interrupted at the request of the detained person, the appropriate adult or the legal representative. Where a person initially attends a police station voluntarily and is later arrested there, the 24 hour period starts from the time of the arrest and not the time of arriving at the police station.

Before any interview commences, each interviewing officer must identify him or herself and any other officers present to the suspect. This will normally be their name and rank, except in cases involving terrorist investigations or other situations where the officers reasonably believe they may be exposed to danger, where their rank and warrant or other identification number, rather than their names, shall be given. Interviews should, as far as practicable, be held in interview rooms, which must be provided with adequate heating, lighting and ventilation. During questioning and the making of statements, suspects must not be required to stand. There must be breaks from interviewing at recognised meal times, lasting at least 45 minutes and, at intervals of approximately two hours, there shall be short refreshment breaks, lasting at least 15 minutes, although this is subject to the discretion of the interviewing officer to delay a break if there are reasonable grounds for believing that this would involve a risk of harm to people or serious loss of or damage to property, unnecessary delay in the suspect's release or otherwise prejudice the investigation. Any prolonged interview should be compensated for by providing a longer break afterwards. Where there is a short interview and it is contemplated that this will be followed by another short period of questioning, the length of the break may be reduced if there are reasonable grounds to believe that to do otherwise would involve the risk of harm to persons or serious loss of or damage to property, unnecessary delay to the suspect's release or otherwise prejudice the investigation. Any decision to delay a break, together with the reasons, must be recorded in the interview record.

With regard to written statements made under caution at police stations, these must be written on the forms provided for this purpose and all such statements must conform to the rules under Annex D, as follows:

(a) **Written by a person under caution**

1 A person shall always be invited to write down what they want to say.

2 A person who has not been charged with, or informed they may be prosecuted for, any offence to which the statement they want to write relates, shall:

   (a) unless the statement is made at a time when the restriction on drawing adverse inferences from silence applies, see Annex C, be asked to write out and sign the following before writing what they want to say:

   I make this statement of my own free will. I understand that I do not have to say anything, but that it may harm my defence if I do not mention when questioned something which I later rely on in court. This statement may be given in evidence.

   (b) if the statement is made at a time when the restriction on drawing adverse inferences from silence applies, be asked to write out and sign the following before writing what they want to say:

   I make this statement of my own free will. I understand that I do not have to say anything. This statement may be given in evidence.

3   When a person, on the occasion of being charged with or informed they may be prosecuted for any offence, asks to make a statement which relates to any such offence and wants to write it they shall:

(a) unless the restriction on drawing adverse inferences from silence, see *Annex C*, applied when they were so charged or informed they may be prosecuted, be asked to write out and sign the following before writing what they want to say:

   I make this statement of my own free will. I understand that I do not have to say anything but that it may harm my defence if I do not mention when questioned something which I later rely on in court. This statement may be given in evidence.

(b) if the restriction on drawing adverse influences from silence applied when they were so charged or informed they may be prosecuted, be asked to write out and sign the following before writing what they want to say:

   I make this statement of my own free will. I understand that I do not have to say anything. This statement may be given in evidence.

4   When a person, who has already been charged with or informed they may be prosecuted for any offence, asks to make a statement which relates to any such offence and wants to write it they shall be asked to write out and sign the following before writing what they want to say:

   I make this statement of my own free will. I understand that I do not have to say anything. This statement may be given in evidence.

5   Any person writing their own statement shall be allowed to do so without any prompting except a police officer or other police staff may indicate to them which matters are material or question any ambiguity in the statement.

(b) Written by a police officer or other police staff

6   If a person says they would like someone to write the statement for them, a police officer or other police staff shall write the statement.

7   If the person has not been charged with, or informed they may be prosecuted for, any offence to which the statement they want to make relates they shall, before starting, be asked to sign, or make their mark, to the following:

(a) unless the statement is made at a time when the restriction on drawing adverse inferences from silence applies, see Annex C:

   I,................wish to make a statement. I want someone to write down what I say. I understand that I do not have to say anything, but that it may harm my defence if I do not mention when questioned something which I later rely on in court. This statement may be given in evidence.

(b) if the statement is made at a time when the restriction on drawing adverse influences from silence applies:

   I,..............wish to make a statement. I want someone to write down what I say. I understand that I do not have to say anything. This statement may be given in evidence.

8   If, on the occasion of being charged with or informed they may be prosecuted for any offence, the person asks to make a statement which relates to any such offence they shall before starting be asked to sign, or make their mark to, the following:

(a) unless the restriction on drawing adverse influences from silence applied, see *Annex C*, when they were so charged or informed they may be prosecuted:

   I,................wish to make a statement. I want someone to write down what I say. I understand that I do not have to say anything but it may harm my defence if I do not mention when questioned something which I later rely on in court. This statement may be given in evidence.

(b) if the restriction on drawing adverse inferences from silence applied when they were so charged or informed they may be prosecuted:

> I,................wish to make a statement. I want someone to write down what I say. I understand that I do not have to say anything. This statement may be given in evidence.

9   If, having already been charged with or informed they may be prosecuted for any offence, a person asks to make a statement which relates to any such offence they shall before starting, be asked to sign, or make their mark to:

> I,................wish to make a statement. I want someone to write down what I say. I understand that I do not have to say anything. This statement may be given in evidence.

10   The person writing the statement must take down the exact words spoken by the person making it and must not edit or paraphrase it. Any questions that are necessary, eg to make it more intelligible, and the answers given must be recorded at the same time on the statement form.

11   When the writing of a statement is finished the person making it shall be asked to read it and to make any corrections, alterations or additions they want. When they have finished reading they shall be asked to write and sign or make their mark on the following certificate at the end of the statement:

> I have read the above statement, and I have been able to correct, alter or add anything I wish. This statement is true. I have made it of my own free will.

12   If the person making the statement cannot read, or refuses to read it, or to write the above mentioned certificate at the end of it or to sign it, the person taking the statement shall read it to them and ask them if they would like to correct, alter or add anything and to put their signature or make their mark at the end. The person taking the statement shall certify on the statement itself what has occurred.

Where a complaint is made by the suspect since their arrest, or where a complaint is made on that person's behalf, the interviewing officer must record it in the interview record and inform an officer of at least the rank of inspector, who is not connected with the investigation and who will be responsible for dealing with the complaint in accordance with s 9 under Code C (see above).

The role of the solicitor during interviews

The rights and restrictions on access to legal advice have been covered earlier under different contexts. The general role and conduct of solicitors during interviews fall under the latter half of s 6 and the Notes for Guidance, which will now be discussed.

A solicitor must be allowed to be present while a suspect is being interviewed if that person is permitted to consult a legal adviser. This is contingent on the solicitor being available. A solicitor may be required to leave an interview only if his or her conduct prevents the interviewing officer from properly putting questions to the suspect.[9] In such cases, the interviewing officer should stop the interview and consult an officer not below the rank of superintendent. If such an officer is not readily available, an officer of at least the rank of inspector may be consulted instead, provided that officer is not connected with the investigation. The officer who has been

---

9   Note for Guidance 6D gives two examples of unacceptable conduct in this context: first, answering questions on the behalf of a suspect and, secondly, providing written answers to questions for the suspect to quote.

consulted should speak to the solicitor and will then decide if the interview should continue with that same solicitor present. If it is decided that it should not, the suspect may consult another solicitor before the interview continues, who will be given the opportunity to be present. A record must be made on the interview record if an interview has been commenced in the absence of a solicitor where one has been requested, or where the solicitor has been required to leave. In view of the serious implications in removing a solicitor from an interview, consideration should be given by the police as to whether the incident should be reported to the Law Society. The superintendent or above who took the decision to remove the solicitor will consider whether such steps should be taken and, if an officer below that rank removed the solicitor, the facts of the incident should be reported to a superintendent or above who, in turn, will consider whether to report the matter to the Law Society. This should also be reported to the Legal Services Commission if it was a duty solicitor who was removed from the interview.

Whether or not a detained person is being interviewed, that person must be informed of a solicitor's arrival at the police station and asked if he or she wishes to see the legal adviser. The exception to this rule is where Annex B applies (see above). Apart from this exception, the detained person has the right to be informed of a solicitor's arrival, even if there was an initial refusal of legal advice or an agreement to be interviewed without it. A note should be made in the custody record regarding the solicitor's attendance and the decision of the detained person. In *R v Franklin* (1994), it was held that failure to inform a suspect that a solicitor has arrived at the police station could result in any subsequent interview being excluded as evidence where the solicitor is absent (see *Rixon and Others v Chief Constable of Kent* (2000), regarding the right of solicitors to see their clients at police stations).

Tape recorded interviews

Section 60 of PACE states the following with regard to the interviewing of suspects:

(1) It shall be the duty of the Secretary of State:

    (a) to issue a Code of Practice in connection with the tape recording of interviews of persons suspected of the commission of criminal offences, which are held by police officers at police stations; and

    (b) to make an order requiring the tape recording of interviews of persons suspected of the commission of criminal offences, or of such descriptions of criminal offences as may be specified in the order, which are so held in accordance with the Code as it has effect for the time being.

(2) An order under sub-s (1) above shall be made by statutory instrument and shall be subject to annulment in pursuance of a resolution of either House of Parliament.

The provisions governing the tape recording of interviews with suspects are to be found in the whole of Code E, which is divided into six sections, each accompanied by its own notes for guidance. A summary of these will now be given in turn.

General

Apart from confirming that the terms 'appropriate adult', 'solicitor' and 'custody officer' mean the same in Code E as they do elsewhere in the Codes of Practice, and the requirement for these Codes to be available for inspection at police stations, this section also states that it does not apply to the following groups of people: persons arrested in Scotland under cross-border arrest powers (see Chapter 3); persons arrested in order to be fingerprinted under s 142(3) of the Immigration and Asylum Act 1999; persons served notice, advising them of their detention under the Immigration Act 1971; convicted or remanded prisoners held in police cells on behalf of the Prison Service; persons detained under Sched 7 and Sched 14, para 6 to the Terrorism Act 2000; and persons detained for searches under Code A.

It then goes on to define the term 'designated person', which refers to a civilian given specified police powers under the Police Reform Act 2002 (see Chapter 7).

Recording and sealing master tapes

The tape recording of interviews should be conducted openly in order to instil confidence in its general integrity. There should always be a master tape, which must be sealed before it leaves the presence of the suspect, and a second or third tape should be used as a working copy. Where a twin or triple deck machine is used, both tapes will record simultaneously, but the use of a single deck machine will necessitate a working copy being made from the master tape in the presence of the suspect. The identities of police officers or civilian support staff conducting the recorded interviews may not be recorded or disclosed in terrorist investigations or if there is reasonable belief that they may be otherwise exposed to danger. The latter is explained in more detail in Note for Guidance 2C with regard to very violent suspects and investigations into serious organised crime. It further advises consultation with an inspector or above in cases of doubt.

Interviews to be tape recorded

Under this section, the following list of circumstances applies under which interviews must be tape recorded; however, this is now the way in which all police interviews are usually conducted, and the police have a discretion to conduct other interviews in this manner (Note for Guidance 3A):

    (a) where a person has been cautioned and detained in respect of an indictable only offence or one which is triable either way;

    (b) in exceptional circumstances, where the police put further questions to a suspect about an offence falling within (a), above, after that person has been charged or informed of a possible prosecution;

    (c) where the police bring to a suspect's attention any written statement or content of an interview with another person where the suspect has already been charged or told he or she may be prosecuted.

Although this Code does not apply to suspects arrested under s 41 or detained under Sched 7 to the Terrorism Act 2000, a separate code of practice is provided for under the 2000 Act regarding the tape recording of interviews.

An interview must be recorded in writing where the custody officer authorises the interviewing officer not to make a tape recording, because of equipment failure or unavailability of a recording room and the interview should not be delayed, or where it becomes obvious that no prosecution will ensue. The reason should be duly noted by the custody officer and in specific terms because, under Note for Guidance 3B, a decision not to tape record an interview may be the subject of comment in court;

therefore, the authorising officer should be prepared to justify the decision. If a person refuses to enter or remain in the interview room, the custody officer may authorise that the interview be conducted in a cell using portable recording equipment or in writing. This should only be done if the custody officer considers on reasonable grounds that the interview should not be delayed; the reasons for this decision must be recorded. This section ends by stating that each interview shall be tape recorded in its entirety, which will include the taking of any statement and the reading back of it to the suspect.

The interview

This section under Code E begins by stating that the overall provisions under Code C regarding cautions and interviews, also apply to this Code, as well as the restrictions on drawing adverse inferences. This section then provides that as soon as the suspect enters the interview room, clean tapes should be unwrapped and then loaded in the machine in full view of that person, and the machine then set to record. The interviewing officer must then tell the suspect that the interview is being tape recorded and the officer must state his or her name and rank, together with the names and ranks of other officers present (there is an exception to this rule with regard to inquiries linked to terrorist investigations, violent suspects or serious organised crime, as mentioned above; in such cases, the officer need only state his or her number). The interviewing officer must then go on to announce the suspect's name and any other person who may be present, such as the solicitor, although it is advised that it will be helpful if each of those present actually identify themselves. The date, time of commencement and location of the interview must also be given and, finally, it should be announced that the suspect will be given a notice describing what will happen to the tapes. This explains how the tape recording will be used and how access to it may be gained, and that if the suspect is charged or prosecuted, a copy will be supplied as soon as practicable. The officer must then administer the appropriate caution in accordance with s 10 of Code C, or put to the suspect any significant statement or silence under para 11.4 of Code C.

The suspect should then be reminded of the right to free and independent legal advice in accordance with the provisions of Code C described earlier (subject to the special rules regarding delaying access to legal advice). If the suspect is deaf or there is any doubt about the suspect's hearing ability, the interview shall be both tape recorded and written contemporaneously.

If a suspect objects to the interview being tape recorded at any stage during the process (including during breaks), it should be explained that there is the requirement for these objections to be recorded on tape. The tape recorder may then be turned off by the officer once the suspect has recorded any objections on tape or has refused to do so, having first explained to the suspect that the tape recorder is being stopped and the reasons for doing so. The exception to this rule is where the officer reasonably considers that questions may continue to be put to the suspect and be tape recorded; otherwise, the interview must be recorded in written form. However, it should be borne in mind that to tape record an interview against the suspect's wishes may be the subject of comment in court.

Where a complaint is received in the course of the tape recording regarding the interview or the suspect's general treatment in custody, the interviewing officer has a duty to record it in the interview record and then inform the custody officer, who must then deal with the matter in accordance with s 9 of Code C (see above). Note for Guidance 4E to Code E states that, wherever possible, the tape recorder should be left running until the custody officer enters the room and speaks to the complainant. The interview may be continued or terminated at the discretion of the interviewing officer whilst awaiting action by the inspector or above, to whom the complaint must be reported (see para 9.2 of Code C). The interviewing officer also has a discretion to continue with the interview if the complaint is not connected with the interview or the suspect's general treatment in custody. Where this occurs, the suspect should be told that the custody officer will be informed as soon as possible about the complaint on completion of the interview, and this must be complied with accordingly.

This section under Code E then goes on to provide details regarding suspects who wish to discuss matters outside the criminal investigation and the procedures concerning the changing of interview tapes. This is followed by provisions in respect of breaks during interviews. If the break is of short duration and the suspect and the officer remain in the room, it should be announced on tape that a break is being taken, together with the reasons and the time. When the break is over, the time of the recommencement of the interview should be recorded. Although the machine may be switched off during the break, there is no need to remove the tapes. Where a break is taken and the suspect is due to vacate the room, this should be recorded, together with the reasons and the time. In such cases, the tape must then be removed from the machine after the suspect has been asked if he or she wishes to clarify or add anything. The interviewing officer is under a duty to ensure that the suspect is aware of the right to legal advice and that he or she is under caution whenever there is a break in questioning. The caution must be given again in full when the interview continues if there is any doubt.

At the conclusion of the tape recorded interview, the suspect must be offered the opportunity to clarify anything already stated or include anything further. Where applicable, the taking and reading back of any written statement will be part of the concluding procedure and, once all this has been completed, the tape recorder should then be switched off. The master tape should be sealed in the prescribed manner and the labelling procedure complied with accordingly.

After the interview

The officer should make a notebook entry that a tape recorded interview has taken place, its date, time and duration, together with the identification number of the master tape. Even where no legal proceedings are taken against the suspect, the interview tapes must still be kept securely, in accordance with the rules under s 6 of Code E, the main provisions of which now follow.

Tape security

The responsibility for making the necessary arrangements for the security of interview tapes falls upon the officer in charge of each police station where interviews with suspects are recorded. This applies not only to their safe storage, but also accounting for their movements on the same basis as other evidence. No police officer may break the seal on a master tape which is required for criminal proceedings. Where this is necessary, the seal must be broken in the presence of a representative of the Crown

Prosecution Service and the defendant, or the defendant's legal adviser shall be given a reasonable opportunity to be present. Either of these two, if present, shall be invited to reseal the master tape and sign it. In the event of refusal or non-attendance, the Crown Prosecution Service representative shall perform this task. It is the responsibility of the chief officer of police to establish arrangements for breaking the seal of a master tape, if necessary, where no criminal proceedings result from the matter which was connected with the tape recorded interview. This also applies where all court proceedings have been concluded.

VIDEO RECORDING OF INTERVIEWS

Section 60A of PACE (inserted by s 76 of the Criminal Justice and Police Act 2001) authorises the Home Secretary to issue a code of practice for the visual recording of interviews at police stations, and to make an order requiring these procedures to be adopted. Code of Practice F applies where an interviewing officer decides to make a visual recording with sound when a suspect is interviewed. The main elements of Code F are reproduced as follows:

2 Recording and sealing of master tapes

2.1 The visual recording of interviews shall be carried out openly to instil confidence in its reliability as an impartial and accurate record of the interview. See *Note 2A*.

2.2 The camera(s) shall be placed in the interview room so as to ensure coverage of as much of the room as is practicably possible whilst the interviews are taking place.

2.3 The certified recording medium will be of high quality, new and previously unused. When the certified recording medium is placed in the recorder and switched on to record, the correct date and time, in hours, minutes and seconds, will be superimposed automatically, second by second, during the whole recording. See *Note 2B*.

2.4 One copy of the certified recording medium, referred to in this code as the master copy, will be sealed before it leaves the presence of the suspect. A second copy will be used as a working copy. See *Notes 2C and 2D*.

2.5 Nothing in this code requires the identity of an officer to be recorded or disclosed if:

  (a) the interview or record relates to a person detained under the Terrorism Act 2000; or

  (b) otherwise where the officer reasonably believes that recording or disclosing their name might put them in danger.

    In these cases, the officer will have their back to the camera and shall use their warrant or other identification number and the name of the police station to which they are attached. Such instances and the reasons for them shall be recorded in the custody record. See *Note 2E*.

Notes for Guidance

2A Interviewing officers will wish to arrange that, as far as possible, visual recording arrangements are unobtrusive. It must be clear to the suspect, however, that there is no opportunity to interfere with the recording equipment or the recording media.

2B   In this context, the certified recording media will be of either a VHS or digital CD format and should be capable of having an image of the date and time superimposed upon them as they record the interview.

2C   The purpose of sealing the master copy before it leaves the presence of the suspect is to establish their confidence that the integrity of the copy is preserved.

2D   The recording of the interview is not to be used for any identification purpose.

2E   The purpose of the paragraph 2.5 is to protect police officers and others involved in the investigation of serious organised crime or the arrest of particularly violent suspects when there is reliable information that those arrested or their associates may threaten or cause harm to the officers, their families or their personal property.

3   Interviews to be visually recorded

3.1 Subject to paragraph 3.2 below, if an interviewing officer decides to make a visual recording these are the areas where it might be appropriate:

   (a) with a suspect in respect of an indictable offence (including an offence triable either way). See *Notes 3A and 3B;*

   (b) which takes place as a result of an interviewer exceptionally putting further questions to a suspect about an offence described in sub-paragraph (a) above after they have been charged with, or informed they may be prosecuted for, that offence. See *Note 3C;*

   (c) in which an interviewer wishes to bring to the notice of a person, after that person has been charged with, or informed they may be prosecuted for an offence described in sub-paragraph (a) above, any written statement made by another person, or the content of an interview with another person. See *Note 3D;*

   (d) with, or in the presence of, a deaf or deaf/blind or speech impaired person who uses sign language to communicate;

   (e) with, or in the presence of anyone who requires an 'appropriate adult'; or

   (f) in any case where the suspect or their representative requests that the interview be recorded visually.

3.2 The Terrorism Act 2000 makes separate provision for a code of practice for the video recording of interviews in a police station of those detained under Schedule 7 or section 41 of the Act. The provisions of this code do not therefore apply to such interviews. See *Note 3E.*

3.3 The custody officer may authorise the interviewing officer not to record the interview visually:

   (a) where it is not reasonably practicable to do so because of failure of the equipment, or the non-availability of a suitable interview room, or recorder, and the authorising officer considers on reasonable grounds that the interview should not be delayed until the failure has been rectified or a suitable room or recorder becomes available. In such cases the custody officer may authorise the interviewing officer to audio record the interview in accordance with the guidance set out in Code E;

   (b) where it is clear from the outset that no prosecution will ensue; or

(c) where it is not practicable to do so because at the time the person resists being taken to a suitable interview room or other location which would enable the interview to be recorded, or otherwise fails or refuses to go into such a room or location, and the authorising officer considers on reasonable grounds that the interview should not be delayed until these conditions cease to apply.

In all cases the custody officer shall make a note in the custody records of the reasons for not taking a visual record. See *Note 3F.*

3.4 When a person who is voluntarily attending the police station is required to be cautioned in accordance with Code C prior to being interviewed, the subsequent interview shall be recorded, unless the custody officer gives authority in accordance with the provisions of paragraph 3.3 above for the interview not to be so recorded.

3.5 The whole of each interview shall be recorded visually, including the taking and reading back of any statement.

3.6 A visible illuminated sign or indicator will light and remain on at all times when the recording equipment is activated or capable of recording or transmitting any signal or information.

The remaining provisions under Code F include procedures during visually recorded interviews, procedures after such interviews and tape security. Many of these broadly reflect the provisions under Code E regarding audio taped interviews. According to Professor Zander:

An audio tape of the interview has to be provided to the defence in the ordinary way, but receipt of the video requires an undertaking by the legal representative not to give the videotape or a copy to the defendant. (This is because in the Scottish pilots it was found that the videotapes were used by criminal elements to try to identify the police officers involved.) A summary of the interview is provided anyway.[10]

CONFESSIONS

Section 82(1) of PACE defines a confession as 'any statement wholly or partly adverse to the person who made it, whether made to a person in authority or not and whether made in words or otherwise'. This can include not only verbal or written communication, but also conduct, such as the re-enactment of an offence recorded on video tape (see *Li Shu-Ling v R* (1989)). Also, an admission need not be confined to the police. Apart from the discretionary power available to the courts under s 78 of PACE to exclude any evidence which, *inter alia*, has been obtained improperly (see *R v Fennelley* (1989) in Chapter 3), s 76(2)(a) and (b) of PACE places a duty on the courts to exclude any confession which has been obtained by oppression or which might have been rendered unreliable 'in consequence of anything said or done'.

What is 'oppression'? In *R v Fulling* (1987), the meaning of this term was considered by the Court of Appeal in a case where the defendant had made a bogus insurance claim and was subsequently convicted of obtaining property by deception.

---

10 Zander, M, *The Police and Criminal Evidence Act 1984* (4th edn, London: Sweet & Maxwell, 2003).

When interviewed by the police, she remained silent until she was told that a woman in the next cell was having an affair with her lover. She then confessed to the charge because, as she stated under cross-examination during the trial, 'I agreed to the statement being taken, it was the only way I was going to be released from the cells' (although not suggesting that bail was offered as an inducement). The defence sought to have the confession excluded at the trial, but the judge ruled that it was admissible, since the word 'oppression' implied some impropriety and he was satisfied that this had not been made out. In dismissing the appeal against conviction, the Court of Appeal held that the word 'oppression' should be given its ordinary dictionary meaning, that is to say: '... the exercise of authority or power in a burdensome, harsh or wrongful manner; unjust or cruel treatment of subjects, inferiors etc; the imposition of unreasonable or unjust burdens.' The court ruled that the trial judge had correctly concluded that the police had not acted oppressively in this case. However, in *R v Paris, Abdullahi and Miller* (1993), one of defendants, Miller, who had a low mental age, was held to have been subjected to hectoring and bullying during questioning which amounted to oppression. The Court of Appeal commented on the extremely hostile and intimidating method used to obtain a confession in this case and severely criticised the solicitor present during the interviews, who did nothing to prevent this treatment. There is a difference between 'proper and robust persistence' and actual hectoring or bullying of a suspect. This case clearly illustrated the dividing line between the two. It should be noted that s 76(8) of PACE provides that, 'In this section, "oppression" includes torture, inhuman or degrading treatment and the use or threat of violence (whether or not amounting to torture)', although this can include a much broader definition of such conduct, as shown in *R v Davison* (1988). In this case, the court regarded a confession as being obtained by oppression where it was obtained in the course of a three hour interview and in the absence of a solicitor, which had started six hours after the suspect had initially been unlawfully detained. In *R v Grieve* (1996), oppressive conduct included, *inter alia*, the unlawful re-interviewing of the co-accused and the subsequent unjustified rearrest of the defendant, and the police should have ensured the presence of a solicitor during the defendant's second interview. The evidence of the latter was therefore excluded.

A confession may be judged 'unreliable' depending on a number of factors surrounding the making of it. In *R v Barry* (1991), it was held that the offer of bail as an inducement to making a confession clearly fell within s 76(2)(b) of PACE and, in *R v Jasper* (1994), this also applies where a suspect is told by the police that he or she will have to remain in custody pending further inquiries unless he or she talks to the police in order that they may conclude the matter. In this case, the defendant was convicted of theft, despite a submission by the defence that during the interview, the police had impliedly said: 'Unless and until you tell us something about this affair, you will remain in custody whilst further inquiries are carried out.' The Court of Appeal held that the evidence obtained in consequence of such comments should have been excluded and subsequently ordered a retrial. However, contrast *R v Weeks* (1995), where an appeal against conviction for drug offences was dismissed where the defendant made a confession shortly after being told that he would remain in custody unless he told the police what they wanted to hear. In this case, the Court of Appeal held that the nature of the admissions was limited and that the defendant was a very astute young man with previous experience of being questioned by the police.

Under s 78 of PACE, mentioned above, the courts have a discretion to exclude any evidence on which the prosecution proposes to rely which, by virtue of the way it has been obtained, *inter alia*, would have such an unfair effect on the fairness of the trial that the court ought not to admit it. This discretionary power can be used to exclude confessions in criminal proceedings in cases which fall short of oppression or unreliability, as in *R v Mason* (1987). In this case, a confession obtained by deceit was excluded under s 78, even though the defendant was legally represented at the time. The confession was made following an interview where the police falsely told both him and his solicitor that his fingerprints had been discovered on a bottle of inflammable liquid near the scene of an arson attack. An interesting interpretation of hostility can be seen in *R v M* (2000),[11] where the Court of Appeal overturned a man's conviction of four counts of rape due to the hostility of his own solicitor who made 'sarcastic interventions' during the police interview. The court held that this may have rendered his confession unreliable. This case serves to illustrate that the hostility need not come from someone in authority.

Special protection for the mentally handicapped

Section 77 of PACE makes provision regarding confessions made by mentally handicapped persons. Oddly, it is only the mentally handicapped who are expressly provided for in this section and not also the mentally disordered, who are both covered under the same safeguards under the Codes of Practice. Where a case against a mentally handicapped person depends wholly or mainly on his or her confession, and that this was not made in the presence of an 'independent person' (a person other than someone in or employed by the police service), the courts must exercise special caution before convicting such a person in reliance on that confession. As far as Crown Court trials are concerned, the judge must give a warning to the jury to this effect and, in summary trials, magistrates must take this into account. In *R v Lamont* (1989), the trial judge failed to give the relevant warning to the jury in a case of attempted murder where little other evidence existed apart from the confession. The Court of Appeal subsequently quashed the conviction and substituted a lesser verdict. The rules under s 77 do not apply where there is other evidence to the extent that the prosecution's case does not depend wholly or mainly on such a confession.

There is some uncertainty as to whom precisely the term 'independent person' applies, especially in view of *R v Bailey* (1995), where a retrial was ordered in a case of murder and arson, on the ground that the trial judge had not given a warning under s 77 where the mentally handicapped defendant confessed to friends and then to the police. A friend was held not to constitute an 'independent person' in this instance, as such a person was not independent of the suspect. Section 77(3) of PACE merely states: '... "independent person" does not include a police officer or a person employed for, or engaged on, police purposes ...' This clearly excludes serving police officers, cadets, special constables and police civilian employees, but it appears that there remains the need for clarification as to whom the term specifically applies; however, in *R v Lewis* (1995), it was held that an 'independent person' would include a solicitor instructed on behalf of the defendant and that the issue of an 'independent person' only arises where a confession was not made in the presence of such a person; therefore, only a small number of cases will involve s 77. However, even where an appropriate adult is not

---

11 Cited in *ibid*.

present when a mentally handicapped person makes an admission, this will not necessarily justify the exclusion of this evidence under s 76(2) of PACE. In *DPP v Cornish* (1997), it was held that, in coming to such a decision, a court should also examine the content of the interview, as well as considering those present, in order to ascertain the effect on the interview of the absence of the appropriate adult.

Section 77(3) also goes on to provide a definition of 'mentally handicapped' as follows: '... "mentally handicapped", in relation to a person, means that he is in a state of arrested or incomplete development of mind, which includes significant impairment of intelligence and social functioning ...' The issue as to whether the defendant is mentally handicapped within this definition is important in view of the decision in *R v Ham* (1995), where it was held that a finding as to whether the defendant was mentally handicapped had to be based on medical evidence and that it was wrong for a judge to place reliance on the evidence of a police officer in this respect. In *R v Everett* (1988) and in *R v Silcott, Braithwaite and Raghip* (1991), it was held that the question of mental handicap is tested objectively; therefore, it is a question of what the defendant's mental condition actually is, rather than the opinion of the police officers.

The term 'mentally handicapped' person as appears in the earlier Codes of Practice, has been replaced by 'otherwise mentally vulnerable' in the more recent Codes when referring to persons with mental conditions other than those classed as suffering from 'mental disorder'.

IDENTIFICATION PROCEDURES

General provisions

The procedures regarding police identification are governed by case law and Code of Practice D as PACE is completely silent on this aspect of the investigation of crime. Section 2 of Code D ('Code of Practice for the identification of persons by police officers') makes a number of general provisions regarding identification by witnesses, identification by fingerprints and photographs, as well as identification by body samples and impressions. Many of these echo similar provisions in Code C; for instance, para 2.1 states that this Code of Practice must be readily available at all police stations, and para 2.6 provides that the terms 'appropriate adult' and 'solicitor' will have the same meaning as defined in Code C. Section 2 also relates many of the safeguards concerning vulnerable persons stated under Code C, to police powers and duties in respect of the identification of persons.

With regard to all suspects, para 3.1 of Code D states that a record must be made of the suspect's description as first given by a potential witness. Unless otherwise specified, this must be done before the witness participates in an identification parade, a group identification, identification using a video film, a confrontation or by the showing of still images. This description must be recorded in a manner which can be accurately reproduced in a visible and legible form, for presentation to the suspect or the suspect's solicitor prior to any of the aforementioned identification procedures being carried out. Under para 3.11, the arrangements and conduct of these identification procedures are the responsibility of the 'identification officer', who must be a police officer of at least the rank of inspector and who is not involved with the investigation. Furthermore, no officer connected with the relevant investigation should actually participate in any of those identification procedures.

Paragraphs 3.17 and 3.18 provide that, before an identification parade or group or video identification, the identification officer must explain 13 relevant points to the suspect, which should be contained in a written notice and then handed to him or her for signature. Some of these main points include the purposes of the identification procedure due to take place, the entitlement to free legal advice, any special arrangements if the suspect is a juvenile or is mentally disordered or otherwise mentally vulnerable, the suspect's right to refuse to consent or co-operate in the identification procedures and the consequences of doing so, as well as the consequences of significantly altering his or her appearance and the right of the suspect or the solicitor to be given details of the first description given by any witness attending the relevant identification procedure. The identification officer should make a record on the forms provided of any identification parade, group or video identification procedure carried out, as well as a person's refusal to co-operate with any of these procedures.

However, under para 3.20, if the identification officer and the officer in charge of the investigation have reasonable grounds to suspect that if the suspect was given the above information and notice, and the suspect would avoid being seen by a witness in any identification procedure, the identification officer may arrange for the suspect's image to be obtained for use in a video film before giving the information and the notice.

It is now quite common for the police to use the media in order to show video films or photographs of incidents to the public, so as to trace and facilitate the recognition of suspects. Any such material released by the police should be preserved and the suspect or the solicitor should be allowed to view it before an identification parade, a group identification, a video identification, examination of still images or a confrontation occurs. This is subject to the proviso that it is practicable to do so and would not unreasonably delay the investigation. Every witness involved in the relevant identification procedure must be asked afterwards whether they have seen any such media coverage and their replies must then be recorded.

Under para 3.4 of Code D, in cases when the suspect is known to the police and that person is available, the following identification procedures may be used:

- video identification;
- identification parade; or
- group identification.

Being 'known' means that there is sufficient information known to the police to justify a particular person's arrest for suspected involvement in the offence. The word 'available' means that the suspect is available either immediately or within a reasonably short time and is also willing to participate in at least one of the above-mentioned identification procedures.

The circumstances in which an identification procedure must be held are stated in para 3.12 as follows:

- whenever a witness states that they have identified a suspect prior to any video identification, identification parade or group identification; or

- whenever there is a witness available who states they are able to identify the suspect; or
- whenever there is a reasonable chance of the witness being able to identify the suspect and they have not been given an opportunity to identify the suspect in any video identification, identification parade or group identification; and
- the suspect disputes being the person the witness claims to have seen.

If the above conditions exist, an identification procedure must be held unless:

- it is not practicable; or
- it would serve no useful purpose in proving or disproving the suspect's involvement in the offence. An example given under para 3.12 is where it is not disputed that the suspect is already well known to the witness who claims to have seen the suspect commit the offence.

Paragraph 3.13 adds that 'Such a procedure may also be held if the officer in charge of the investigation considers it would be useful'.

It is important to note that since the first edition of this book, the order of preference for identification procedures has been changed as a result of amendments to the Codes of Practice. Professor Zander states:

> ... It was felt in some quarters that the mandatory requirement of an identification parade put unreasonable burdens on the police. The view began to be expressed that identification parades were not as useful as the rule suggested and that video libraries could do the job better. The suspect is photographed in front of a neutral background. The photograph is then transferred into the computer system which holds a vast and growing database of digital photos taken in the same way. The suspect and his solicitor are shown a range of photographs similar to the suspect and are asked to agree on eight or nine to be used in the video film. The suspect decides where he wishes to be in the film. A composite video is then made. Each photograph is shown to the witness for the same period of time. The view that video identification is preferable to identity parades has now prevailed.[12]

The criteria for selecting an identification procedure is now to be found in para 3.14, which states that if an identification procedure is to be held because of the circumstances outlined in para 3.12, the suspect must be initially offered a video identification unless the following apply:

- a video identification is not practicable; or
- an identification parade is both practicable and more suitable than a video identification; or
- the officer in charge of the investigation considers that a group identification be initially offered because it is more suitable than a video identification or an identification parade, and the identification officer considers a group identification practicable to arrange.

The identification procedure to be offered will be the result of consultation between the identification officer and the officer in charge of the investigation. Paragraph 3.14 goes on to give examples where an identification parade may not be practicable in relation to witnesses, such as their number, state of health, availability and travel requirements.

---

12 *Ibid.*

Another factor that may make an identification parade impracticable is that a witness may simply be too fearful to take part. A video identification is usually more suitable and may be completed sooner than an identification parade.

Paragraph 3.15 covers the situation where a suspect refuses the identification procedure that is first offered. Where this happens, the suspect must be asked to give their reason (in consultation with their solicitor or appropriate adult if present). They should then be allowed to make representations about why another identification procedure should be used. If appropriate, the identification officer should offer the suspect an alternative which is suitable and practicable. All the relevant points and decisions should be recorded.

Identification parades

The main provisions regarding the general conduct and conditions of an identification parade are contained in Annex B to Code D. These include the following in summary.

Just before the identification parade, the suspect must be reminded of the procedures governing its conduct and must also be given the appropriate caution. No less than eight persons, in addition to the suspect, shall comprise an identification parade and they must, as far as possible, resemble the suspect in overall appearance. Normally, only one suspect should be present in a parade, but two may be paraded together if they broadly resemble each other, although at least 12 other people must also be present on the parade when this occurs. However, no more than two suspects may be included in a parade at the same time and, where separate parades are held, they must be comprised of different persons. No unauthorised persons may be present in a place where a parade is to be conducted (which can be a normal room or one containing a screen, so that witnesses can view members of the parade without themselves being seen). Prior to the parade being held, the suspect must be given a reasonable opportunity to have a solicitor or friend present and either the suspect or the solicitor should be provided with the first description of the suspect. The suspect should be asked to indicate his or her desire to have a solicitor or friend present on a second copy of the notice, containing the 13 points mentioned above.

The suspect must be given the opportunity to raise any objections regarding the general arrangements and the participants in the parade, and these objections should be acceded to where possible. Where this is not practicable, the identification officer should give the reasons to the suspect. Each place in the line must be clearly numbered and the suspect may not only select his or her position in the line, but may also change it if more than one witness is involved. The identification officer must ensure that, prior to attending a parade, witnesses are prevented from communicating with each other about the case or overhearing a witness who has already seen the parade. Witnesses must also be prevented from seeing any member of the parade beforehand or being given any indication or reminder about the suspect's identity, or from seeing the suspect before or after the parade.

Just before a witness inspects the parade, that person should be informed by the identification officer that the suspect may or may not be in the line-up and if the witness cannot positively identify the suspect, then he or she should state this, but not until each person in the parade has been looked at no less than twice by the witness. The identification officer should then go on to inform the witness that he or she should carefully look at each member of the parade at least twice and, once the officer is satisfied that this has been done, the witness shall be asked to state the relevant number if the suspect is on the parade. Identification should be based on the suspect's physical features, instead of clothing. In *R v Hutton* (1998), the Court of Appeal held that it was inappropriate for everyone in an identification parade to wear baseball hats and scarves, masking the lower half of their faces. Although the parade were masked only to a limited extent, this, coupled with the limited opportunity for the witness to have seen the suspect, amounted to insufficient evidence for the case to have continued (see also *D v DPP* (1998) and *Parry v DPP* (1998)). Paragraph 10 to Annex B of Code D makes provision where the suspect has an unusual physical feature, and includes examples such as a facial scar, tattoo or distinctive hairstyle or hair colour. If this cannot be replicated on other persons in the identification parade, that feature may be concealed using, for example, a plaster or a hat, worn by everyone on the parade. This will enable all members of the identification parade to resemble each other. However, this may not be done unless the suspect and his or her solicitor or the appropriate adult agree. In *R v Marrin* (2002), it was held that it would be permissible for other members of an identification parade to wear make up in order to replicate certain features of the suspect. In this case, some of the volunteers used dye to replicate the suspect's facial stubble.

Provision is made whereby a witness may hear any parade member speak or see them move or adopt a specific posture, but not until the witness has been asked if identification can be made on the basis of physical appearance only and, where speech is requested, reminded that the members of the parade have been chosen exclusively on the basis of physical appearance. With regard to voice identification, in *R v Gummerson and Steadman* (1999), it was held that whilst Code D did not create a duty to consider a voice identification parade, if one were held, then, in principle, it would be admissible, although it may be helpful to note the earlier case of *R v Hersey* (1997), where some guidance on this issue was given by the Court of Appeal. In this instance, H was one of two people who robbed a shop whilst wearing balaclava helmets. During the robbery, both of them conversed extensively for a period of about 15 minutes and the shopkeeper was certain that one of them was a customer of long standing. A voice identification parade, consisting of 12 persons, including H, was arranged, during which the shopkeeper identified the voice of H, although two other witnesses failed to pick him out. An expert witness wanted to give evidence that too many voices were used on the parade, that, with one exception, they were of significantly higher pitch and that the only person on the parade who read out the required text in a manner which made sense was H. The trial judge ruled that this expert evidence was not admissible before the jury and allowed in evidence of the voice identification. In upholding this decision, the Court of Appeal held that whilst there may be a danger of the jury placing undue weight on the parade identification, the effect of the shopkeeper's previous association with H on the subsequent identification would be obvious to them. This could be dealt with in the closing speech of defence counsel and also by the trial judge during the summing up. The court stated that the parade provided the witness with the opportunity to test his identification and this, even more importantly, gave the defendant the opportunity to be excluded in the event of an erroneous original identification. In addressing the criticism of the technical aspects of the parade, the court stated that 'the police must do the best they can in such circumstances' and added that 'a judge will undoubtedly rule out the evidence of an identification parade he considers unfair'. However, according to the court, 'There was not a great deal of authority on how a judge should direct a jury in respect of voice identification' (see also *R v Deenik* (1992)).

The conduct of a parade must be fully documented and recorded not only on the relevant forms, but also photographed in colour or video recorded. A copy of the photograph or recording must be supplied on request and in reasonable time to the suspect or the solicitor. These must be destroyed if the person is not charged with a recordable offence, or not informed that he or she may be prosecuted for a recordable offence, or is not prosecuted, cautioned, reprimanded or warned for a recordable offence. However, such a person may give his or her informed consent for the photographs or images to be retained for the purposes of the prevention or detection of crime, the investigation of offences or the conduct of prosecutions.

It has been suggested[13] that although pre-2003 cases regarding the requirement to hold identification parades related to the previous codes of practice, these should still be applied to the current code and to other identification procedures. This applies particularly in the leading case of *R v Forbes* (2001), where the House of Lords held that it was still necessary to hold an identification parade even where a suspect had been positively identified in a street identification, particularly if the suspect disputes the identification. However, this should be viewed in the light of other identification procedures as well as para 3.12 of Code D which, *inter alia*, states: '... an identification procedure shall be held unless it is not practicable or it would serve no useful purpose in proving or disproving whether the suspect was involved in committing the offence. For example, when it is not disputed that the suspect is already well known to the witness who claims to have seen them commit the crime.'

Group identification

This aspect of identification procedure is governed largely by s 3 of Code D, together with Annex C, which concentrates on the conduct of group identification in which a witness views a suspect amongst an informal group of people. This may occur with the suspect's consent and co-operation, although without it, this may take place covertly.

The suspect's consent to a group identification should be sought and the 13 points mentioned above, under paras 3.17 and 3.20 ('Notice to suspect'), should be conveyed to the suspect accordingly. The identification officer has a discretion to proceed with a group identification where consent is refused, using covert methods. The general conduct of this procedure is governed by Annex C, some of the main points of which are summarised as follows.

The location of a group identification should be a place where people congregate informally or generally pass through, so that the suspect can join them and be seen as part of a group. Examples given under Annex C include people leaving an escalator, persons walking through a shopping arcade, people waiting on railway stations and even the foyer of a magistrates' court.[14] In any event, it is up to the identification

13   Hutton, G, Johnston, D and Sampson, F, *Blackstone's Police Investigator's Manual* (Oxford: OUP, 2005).
14   *R v Tiplady* (1994), cited in *op cit*, Zander, fn 10.

officer as to the choice of venue, although account must be taken of any representations made by the suspect, the appropriate adult where applicable or the suspect's solicitor or friend. Police stations should only be used for group identifications where this is necessary by virtue of safety or security reasons, or because it may be impracticable to hold them somewhere else. Where this is the case, the procedure may involve the use of screens or one-way mirrors.[15] If the procedure is to be conducted covertly, then the choice of venue must, of course, include places which the suspect frequents and where sufficient numbers of other people will also be present. This will include regular travel routes used by the suspect.

Many of the safeguards applicable to identification parades are echoed in Annex C. These include details of the first description by witnesses being given to the suspect or the solicitor and reasonable opportunity for the suspect to also have a friend present, as well as the taking of a colour photograph of the procedure whilst in progress, although in the case of group identifications, a video recording may only be made contemporaneously if this is practicable; otherwise, a colour photograph or video recording should be made of the general scene after the event, whether or not the suspect consents. If any photograph or video film includes the suspect, all copies must be destroyed if the suspect is not charged with a recordable offence, or not informed that he or she may be prosecuted for a recordable offence, or is not actually prosecuted for such an offence, or cautioned, reprimanded or warned for it; otherwise, if informed consent is given, the photographs or images may be retained for the purposes of the prevention or detection of crime, the investigation of offences or the conduct of prosecutions. Where the suspect does not consent, covert identifications should, as far as possible, comply with the rules where consent has been given. However, such persons will automatically deny themselves the right to legal advice by virtue of being unaware of the identification procedure at the time.

Any undue impediment of the group identification procedure on the part of the suspect, such as unreasonable delays in joining the group or deliberately concealing him or herself from the view of the witnesses, shall be regarded as a refusal to co-operate. Where a person in the group is singled out by a witness and that person is not a suspect, a police officer should approach that person and request his or her name and address, although that person is under no legal obligation to provide these details.

A distinction is drawn under Annex C between moving and stationary groups. Where moving groups are concerned, one important provision is that the identification officer must tell a witness to point out the suspect and then, if practicable, arrange for that witness to take a closer look at the person indicated and ask if they can make a positive identification. Where this is not possible, the witness should be asked how sure he or she is that the person singled out is the suspect. This same procedure also applies to stationary groups, although a major distinction between this procedure and the one applicable to moving groups is that where the suspect is in a static situation, such as in a queue, the witness should pass along or amongst the group and look at each person at least twice.

---

15 *Op cit*, Zander, fn 10.

Video identification

As mentioned above, para 3.14 of Code D states that a video identification must initially be offered to a suspect unless it is impracticable, or an identification parade or a group identification are both practicable and more suitable. Therefore, a witness may be shown a video of a suspect by the identification officer where the investigating officer considers that this would be the most appropriate course of action. Other factors which may influence such a decision include, *inter alia*, the suspect's refusal to participate in an identification parade or a group identification. The consent of the suspect should be sought although, where this is not given, the identification officer has the discretion to proceed with a video identification using covert means if necessary. Where consent has been obtained, the suspect should be informed of the 13 points mentioned above, under paras 3.17 and 3.20. The general conduct and detailed procedures governing video identification are contained under Annex A and a summary of its main features now follows.

Annex A begins by providing that the overall arrangements for making and subsequently showing a suitable set of images to be used in a video identification are the responsibility of an identification officer who has no direct involvement in the case. The film must include at least eight people plus the suspect and the requirements where more than one suspect is involved also follow the same provisions as those governing 'live' identification parades. Several other provisions in Annex A follow the same pattern as those applicable to identification parades as in Annex B, such as the measures designed to prevent communication between witnesses at the crucial times and avoiding 'leading' witnesses by drawing attention to any person being viewed. The important distinction is that witnesses are seeing a visual recording and not a live identification parade. Witnesses would therefore be unable to request that certain body postures are adopted at the time of the viewing, although para 3 under Annex A provides that all those being filmed shall, as far as possible, be in the same positions or carrying out the same activity. This seems to imply that the video recording might include the participants making certain movements where this was requested in advance. Another consequence of seeing a film, rather than participating in an identification parade, is that the witness does not have to walk along or among the participants and this is particularly beneficial where nervous witnesses are involved. Witnesses should view the set of images at least twice and may request as many other replays as necessary or may ask for a particular picture to be frozen. The Code of Practice emphasises that there is no limit to the number of times that the tape can be viewed in whole or part.

The suspect, a friend, the solicitor or the appropriate adult, where applicable, must be given a reasonable opportunity to see the film prior to it being shown to witnesses. If there is any reasonable objection to it, then all practicable steps should be taken to accommodate these objections. Where this is not possible, the identification officer must explain the reasons and record this on the relevant forms accordingly. The suspect's solicitor shall, where practicable, be given reasonable notice of the time and venue that a video identification is due to occur, so that a representative may attend on the suspect's behalf. If no solicitor is instructed, then the suspect must be informed, but the suspect should not be present at the showing of the video to witnesses. Where the suspect's representative does not attend, the entire viewing procedure must also be recorded on video. The identification officer must, *inter alia*, preserve the overall security of the tapes and ensure that no officer involved in the investigation is allowed to see the contents of the video film before it is shown to witnesses. A video film must be destroyed if the suspect is not charged with a recordable offence, or is not informed that he or she may be prosecuted for a recordable offence or is not actually prosecuted for such an offence, or is not cautioned, reprimanded or warned for a recordable offence, unless informed consent is given for the images to be retained for the purposes of the prevention or detection of crime, the investigation of offences or the conduct of prosecutions.

The overall flexibility and other advantages of using video film in the identification of suspects has increased its usage as time has progressed. The use of video film has replaced other forms of identification to a large extent, as the technology has become more widespread.[16] However, video recorded *interviews* must not be used for identification purposes (see Note for Guidance 2D of Code F). The importance of complying with the correct procedures when conducting video identification was illustrated in *R v Marcus* (2004). In this case, the defendant matched the description of a man allegedly involved in several street robberies, although he said he was innocent. The street robber was described as black, aged between 30 and 40, and had a greying beard as well as greying hair around the temples. A video identification was agreed to by the defence, but no images could be found of anyone who had greying hair in the same places as the defendant. The defence therefore agreed to the use of red masking on all the images. However, the police used a parallel procedure, without informing the defence, where unmasked images were used but only one had the greying beard and temples, and that happened to be the defendant's image. Four out of five witnesses identified the defendant where the unmasked images were used. The defendant's conviction was overturned on the grounds that this evidence should have been excluded at the trial as the identification procedure evaded the protections under Code of Practice D, and was therefore unlawful.

Confrontation

Paragraph 3.23 of Code D provides that a suspect may be confronted by a witness if neither an identification parade, a group identification, a video identification nor a video identification using still images is practicable. A confrontation does not require the consent of the suspect, although in *R v Jones and Nelson* (1999), it was held that it was a breach of the relevant Code of Practice to threaten the use of force in order to effect a confrontation. If a suspect insists on this method of identification in the presence of his or her solicitor, then there is no need to hold any other form of identification procedure.[17] The provisions governing the procedures for a confrontation are to be found under Annex D to Code D, which are summarised as follows.

Most of the procedures stated under Annex D largely echo the provisions applicable to the other methods of identification mentioned above. These include the measures that have to be taken where the police release photographs or video films to

---

16 Levenson, H, Fairweather, F and Cape, E, *Police Powers: A Practitioners' Guide* (3rd edn, London: Legal Action Group, 1996).

17 See *R v Miller* (1991), cited in *ibid*.

the media and the suspect or the solicitor being provided with a first description given by witnesses prior to the identification taking place. However, there is no provision here which requires the suspect to be informed of the 13 points applicable to the other identification procedures covered under paras 3.17 and 3.20, above. The procedure governing the actual confrontation of a suspect by a witness is the responsibility of the identification officer and no officer may take part in the proceedings who is involved in the investigation. In *R v Ryan* (1992),[18] it was held that there had been a major breach of para 2.2 of the earlier edition of Code D where the investigating officer accompanied a witness to a confrontation, although, in this case, the evidence was allowed, because the interests of the defendant had been sufficiently protected by his solicitor.

A confrontation should normally take place in a police station either in an ordinary room or one equipped with a screen in order to prevent witnesses being seen. Where a screen is used, either the suspect's solicitor, friend or appropriate adult must be present or the confrontation must be video recorded. Unless it would cause unreasonable delay, a confrontation must take place in the presence of the suspect's solicitor, interpreter or friend, during which the suspect should be confronted independently by each witness, who shall be asked: 'Is this the person?' It has been asserted that confrontation is the least satisfactory method in identifying suspects.[19]

Fingerprinting

The issue of fingerprinting in its entirety is covered under ss 27, 61, 63A and 64 of PACE, together with s 4 of Code D. Normally, consent is required before a person can be fingerprinted. If this is done at a police station, the consent must be in writing, whereas it can be given orally if performed elsewhere. The latter will include victims of crime, who provide their fingerprints in order that these may be eliminated from others found at the scene of the crime, although these may be destroyed once they are no longer needed. However, if the person consents to their retention, this cannot be withdrawn later. Fingerprints may be taken without consent under the circumstances discussed below and the taking of fingerprints may also include taking a palm print where appropriate.[20] Collectively, this is now regarded as recording the 'skin patterns' of a person's fingers or palms.

Before the police take a person's fingerprints, they have a duty to inform that person of the reasons for taking them, whether or not they are taken with consent. Whether or not consent is given, the person whose fingerprints are to be taken must be informed that those prints may be the subject of a speculative search against other fingerprints. This means that a check may be made against other fingerprints held in records to which the police have access, although this only applies to suspects. Whenever a person has been informed of the possibility of a speculative search, a record shall be made accordingly. All the police duties to inform persons of the

---

18 Cited in *op cit*, Zander, fn 10 and, also, *op cit*, Levenson, Fairweather, and Cape, fn 16.

19 Clark, D, *Bevan and Lidstone's The Investigation of Crime: A Guide to the Law of Criminal Investigation* (3rd edn, London: Butterworths, 2004).

20 Code D, para 4.1. See also *R v Tottenham Justices ex p L (A Minor)* (1985) for a definition of a palm print.

relevant rights and procedures must be given in the presence of the appropriate adult where applicable.

Sections 27 and 61 of PACE provide that fingerprints may be taken without consent from anyone over the age of 10 under the circumstances listed below. Reasonable force may be used if necessary under s 117 of PACE in order to obtain fingerprints and a record must be made of the circumstances under which this occurred, including those present. Where fingerprints are taken without consent, a record must be made as soon as possible, containing the reasons, which must include any of the following:

(a) where a police inspector or above (or a court) authorises such action as a result of having reasonable grounds to believe that the fingerprints will tend to confirm or disprove the suspect's alleged identity. In other words, to ascertain that person's true identity;

(b) where a person is arrested for a recordable offence and detained at a police station, or has either been charged or informed he or she will be reported for a 'recordable offence'.[21] This will apply where that person's fingerprints have not already been taken in connection with that offence and will also apply where a suspect has been cautioned, reprimanded or warned for a recordable offence;

21　'Recordable offences' are those offences which may be held on national police records and include all offences which can attract a term of imprisonment, whether or not this is the sentence actually passed on conviction, as well as a number of other offences which are not imprisonable. These miscellaneous offences are as follows: loitering/soliciting for prostitution; improper use of public telecommunications system; tampering with motor vehicles; sending letters, etc, with intent to cause distress or anxiety; giving intoxicating liquor to child under five; exposing children under 12 to risk of burning; failing to provide for safety of children at entertainments; drunkenness in public; failing to deliver up authority to possess prohibited weapon or ammunition; possession of an assembled shotgun by unsupervised person under 15; possession of an air weapon or ammunition for an air weapon by unsupervised person under 14; possession of an air weapon in public by an unsupervised person under 17; trespassing on land during daytime in search of game; refusal by such a trespasser to provide name and address; five or more persons found armed in daytime in search of game and using violence or refusing to provide name and address; being drunk in the highway or in public; obstructing a constable or local authority officer inspecting premises for use as a registered club; permitting drunkenness on licensed premises; failing to leave licensed premises when requested; allowing prostitutes to assemble on licensed premises; permitting licensed premises to be used as a brothel; allowing a constable to remain on licensed premises when on duty; supplying intoxicants or refreshments to a constable or bribing a constable; making a false statement when applying for a sex establishment licence; falsely claiming a professional qualification; taking or destroying game or rabbits by night; wearing a police uniform with intent to deceive; unlawful possession of a police uniform; causing harassment, alarm or distress; failing to give notice of a public procession; failing to comply with condition imposed on a public procession; taking part in a prohibited public procession; failing to comply with a condition imposed on a public assembly; taking part in a trespassory assembly and failing to comply with directions; failing to provide a roadside specimen of breath; kerb-crawling, persistently soliciting women; in connection with sporting events, allowing alcohol to be carried on public vehicles; being drunk on such a vehicle; allowing alcohol to be carried in some other vehicles; trying to enter a designated sports ground while drunk; unauthorised drinking or supplying alcohol at a designated sports ground; throwing missiles, indecent or racialist chanting, and going on to the playing area; taking/riding a pedal cycle without consent; and purchasing or hiring a crossbow (or part) by a person under 17 and unsupervised possession by a person under 17. (See English, J and Card, R, *Butterworths Police Law* (8th edn, London: Butterworths, 2003).) Note that, as of 1 December 2003, the offence of 'begging' has also been made a recordable offence (see (2003) 167 JP 49, 6 December).

(c) where a person has been convicted of a recordable offence, but has not, as yet, been in police detention for that offence, nor had his or her fingerprints taken. In those circumstances, s 27 of PACE empowers the police to require that person to attend a police station in order to be fingerprinted within one month of conviction. At least seven days' notice must be given and a constable may arrest without warrant any person who fails to comply with this requirement (see Chapter 3);

(d) where a person has either been convicted of, or cautioned, or reprimanded or warned for a recordable offence and that person's fingerprints have been taken but were incomplete or of insufficient quality. In those circumstances, s 27 of PACE also applies.

Increasingly, fingerprints are now taken using electronic means. Where this is used, both the method and the devices employed must be approved by the Home Secretary.

Photographs

The provisions governing the photographing of identifying marks on suspects have been covered earlier in Chapter 5. The photographing of suspects under other conditions is covered under s 64A of PACE and s 5(A) and (B) and Notes for Guidance in Code D. Section 64A of PACE (added by s 92 of the Anti-terrorism, Crime and Security Act 2001) is as follows:

Photographing of suspects etc

64A (1) A person who is detained at a police station may be photographed –

    (a) with the appropriate consent; or

    (b) if the appropriate consent is withheld or it is not practicable to obtain it, without it.

(2) A person proposing to take a photograph of any person under this section –

    (a) may, for the purpose of doing so, require the removal of any item or substance worn on or over the whole or any part of the head or face of the person to be photographed; and

    (b) if the requirement is not complied with, may remove the item or substance himself.

(3) Where a photograph may be taken under this section, the only persons entitled to take the photograph are –

    (a) constables; and

    (b) persons who (without being constables) are designated for the purposes of this section by the chief officer of police for the police area in which the police station in question is situated;

and section 117 (use of force) applies to the exercise by a person falling within paragraph (b) of the powers conferred by the preceding provisions of this section as it applies to the exercise of those powers by a constable.

(4) A photograph taken under this section –

    (a) may be used by, or disclosed to, any person for any purpose related to the prevention or detection of crime, the investigation of an offence or the conduct of a prosecution; and

    (b) after being so used or disclosed, may be retained but may not be used or disclosed except for a purpose so related.

(5) In subsection (4) –

    (a) the reference to crime includes a reference to any conduct which –

        (i) constitutes one or more criminal offences (whether under the law of a part of the UK or of a country or territory outside the UK); or

        (ii) is, or corresponds to, any conduct which, if it all took place in any one part of the UK, would constitute one or more criminal offences; and

    (b) the references to an investigation and to a prosecution include references, respectively, to any investigation outside the UK of any crime or suspected crime and to a prosecution brought in respect of any crime in a country or territory outside the UK.

(6) References in this section to taking a photograph include references to using any process by means of which a visual image may be produced; and references to photographing a person shall be construed accordingly.

Section 5(A)(b) and (B) to Code D makes the following provisions in respect of photographing detainees at police stations. It will be noticed that some of these codes also apply to photographs taken of identifying marks under s 54A of PACE, especially sub-paragraphs (c) and (d), as well as (B) and the notes for guidance that follow. Some annotations have been made in square brackets where appropriate.

5(A)(b) Photographing detainees at police stations

5.12 Under PACE, section 64A, an officer may photograph a detainee at a police station:

    (a) with their consent; or

    (b) without their consent if it is;

        (i) withheld; or

        (ii) not practicable to obtain their consent (see *Note 5E*),

paragraph 5.6 applies to the retention and use of photographs taken under this section as it applies to the retention and use of photographs taken under section 54A, see *Note 5B*.

5.13 The officer proposing to take a detainee's photograph may, for this purpose, require the person to remove any item or substance worn on, or over, all, or any part of, their head or face. If they do not comply with such a requirement, the officer may remove the item or substance. [Note: Reference to any item or substance worn may include head or face coverings such as masks, and may also include face paint.]

5.14 If it is established the detainee is unwilling to co-operate sufficiently to enable a suitable photograph to be taken and it is not reasonably practicable to take the photograph covertly, an officer may use reasonable force:

    (a) to take their photograph without their consent; and

    (b) for the purpose of taking the photograph, remove any item or substance worn on, or over, all, or any part of, the person's head or face which they have failed to remove when asked.

5.15 For the purposes of this Code, a photograph may be obtained without the person's consent by making a copy of an image of them taken at any time on a camera system installed anywhere in the police station.

(c) Information to be given

5.16 When a person is searched, examined or photographed under the provisions as in *paragraph 5.1* and *5.12*, or their photograph obtained as in *paragraph 5.15*, they must be informed of the:

(a) purpose of the search, examination or photograph;

(b) grounds on which the relevant authority, if applicable, has been given; and

(c) purposes for which the photograph may be used, disclosed or retained.

This information must be given before the search or examination commences or the photograph is taken, except if the photograph is:

(i) to be taken covertly;

(ii) obtained as in *paragraph 5.15*, in which case the person must be informed as soon as practicable after the photograph is taken or obtained. [Note: these are alternatives to using force where possible in order to obtain photographs.]

(d) Documentation

5.17 A record must be made when a detainee is searched, examined, or a photograph of the person, or any identifying marks found on them, are taken. The record must include the:

(a) identity, subject to paragraph 2.18, of the officer carrying out the search, examination or taking the photograph;

(b) purpose of the search, examination or photograph and the outcome;

(c) detainee's consent to the search, examination or photograph, or the reason the person was searched, examined or photographed without consent;

(d) giving of any authority as in *paragraph 5.2* and *5.3*, the grounds for giving it and the authorising officer.

5.18 If force is used when searching, examining or taking a photograph in accordance with this section, a record shall be made of the circumstances and those present.

(B) Persons at police stations not detained

5.19 When there are reasonable grounds for suspecting the involvement of a person in a criminal offence, but that person is at a police station *voluntarily* and not detained, the provision of *paragraphs 5.1* to *5.18* should apply, subject to the modifications in the following paragraphs.

5.20 Reference to the 'person being detained' and to the powers mentioned in *paragraph 5.1* which apply only to detainees at police stations shall be omitted.

5.21 Force may not be used to:

(a) search and/or examine the person to:

(i) discover whether they have any marks that would tend to identify them as a person involved in the commission of an offence; or

(ii) establish their identity, see *Note 5A*.

(b) take photographs of any identifying marks, see *paragraph 5.4*; or

(c) take a photograph of the person.

5.22 Subject to *paragraph 5.24*, the photographs or images, of persons not detained, or of their identifying marks, must be destroyed (together with any negatives and copies) unless the person:

(a) is charged with, or informed they may be prosecuted for, a recordable offence;

(b) is prosecuted for a recordable offence;

(c) is cautioned for a recordable offence or given a warning or reprimand in accordance with the Crime and Disorder Act 1998 for a recordable offence; or

(d) gives informed consent, in writing, for the photograph or image to be retained as in *paragraph 5.6.*

5.23 When *paragraph 5.22* requires the destruction of any photograph or image, the person must be given an opportunity to witness the destruction or to have a certificate confirming the destruction provided they so request the certificate within five days of being informed the destruction is required.

5.24 Nothing in *paragraph 5.22* affects any separate requirement under the Criminal Procedure and Investigations Act 1996 to retain material in connection with criminal investigations.

The Notes for Guidance which follow clarify a number of points that are relevant to the above codes. Examples are given regarding what constitutes the prevention of crime, the investigation of offences and the conduct of prosecutions. These include comparing the photograph with others taken previously that are held in records, establishing precisely who is arrested (and when and where this took place), where other suspects are arrested or are likely to be, confirming the real identity of a person, assisting in identification procedures, identifying a person released without charge who may have to be identified later; confirming a person's identity when executing an arrest warrant and, in other circumstances, where a person's photograph is not on record, or where their photograph is on record, but their appearance has changed and they have not yet been released or brought before a court. However, it is stated that there is no power to arrest a person convicted of a recordable offence for the sole purpose of taking their photograph. The power to take any photographs will only apply when the person is in custody following the exercise of another power. An example given is where the person has been arrested for fingerprinting under s 27 of PACE. The Notes for Guidance then go on to give some examples as to when it would not be practicable to obtain a person's consent to being searched, examined or photographed regarding an identifying mark, or being photographed in the general sense. These include instances where the person is intoxicated or otherwise unfit to give consent; or where there are reasonable grounds to suspect that the person would react violently once they knew what was intended and would distort their face or conceal the mark; or if there is insufficient time for the parent or guardian of a juvenile suspect to be contacted. A further example is given, although this applies only to the taking of photographs in a general sense and that is where, in order to obtain a suitable photograph, it is necessary to take it covertly. The Notes for Guidance also make reference to para 2.12 of Code D, which states that:

2.12 If any procedure in this Code requires a person's consent, the consent of a:

• mentally disordered or otherwise mentally vulnerable person is only valid if given in the presence of the appropriate adult;

• juvenile, is only valid if their parent's or guardian's consent is also obtained unless the juvenile is under 14, when their parent's or guardian's consent is sufficient in its own right ... [Note: This part of para 2.12 then goes on to make provisions regarding identification procedures under s 3.]

The actual showing of photographs to witnesses of crime must conform to the procedures under Annex E to Code D, which are summarised as follows. Whilst the actual showing of photographs may be done by a police officer of any rank or even a civilian employee within the police service, a police officer of at least the rank of sergeant must supervise and direct the showing of photographs. The first description of the suspect given by the witness must be recorded and this has to be confirmed before the photographs can be shown. If there is any doubt, the showing must be postponed. Only one witness at a time should be shown the photographs and that person must be given as much privacy as practicable; during this process, each witness shall not be allowed to communicate with any other witnesses in the case. The witness must be told that the person seen may or may not be among the photographs shown and he or she should be left to make any selection without any help; therefore, there must be no prompting or guidance. If no positive identification can be made, the witness should say so; and if a witness selects a photograph but is unable to confirm the identification, that person should be asked how sure they are. No less than 12 photographs at a time may be shown, which should all be of a similar type as far as possible, and a record of the showing must be kept, including comments made by the witness, whether or not an identification is made.

If a witness makes a positive identification from photographs (or a photofit, identikit or similar picture), then, unless the person identified has been cleared of suspicion by the police, any other witnesses involved shall not be shown the photograph or other picture. Where this occurs, all witnesses, including the one who identified the alleged suspect, should be asked to attend an identification parade or take part in group or video identification if possible, unless there is no dispute about the suspect's identification. The suspect and that person's solicitor must be informed prior to an identification parade if a witness has already been shown any pictures beforehand. Any photographs used must not be destroyed, regardless of whether or not an identification has been made, as they may be required by the court.

When photographs taken by the police are circulated to persons outside the police service, provided those photographs are used reasonably for the prevention and detection of crime, such action is not unlawful. In *Hellewell v Chief Constable of Derbyshire* (1995), the court ruled that the police had a public interest defence to an action brought against them for breach of confidence. In this case, the claimant had numerous previous convictions, and most of them were for theft. The police circulated the claimant's photograph to local traders, although not for public display, but to enable staff to identify troublemakers.

TAKING FORENSIC SAMPLES FROM SUSPECTS

Introduction

The taking of forensic samples from suspects is an important aspect of police duties in the detection of crime. One of the most well known is the police power under the Road Traffic Act 1988 to require a person to provide a specimen of breath, urine or blood in cases of suspected drink-driving. The power to take samples from suspects under the common law was significantly extended by PACE; as a result of amendments under the Criminal Justice and Public Order Act 1994, arising from the development of DNA profiling in particular, the legal rules regarding the taking and retention of samples are contained under the amended provisions of ss 62, 63, 63A, 64 and 65 of PACE, augmented by s 6 of Code D (ss 63B and 63C of PACE will be discussed below under the heading 'New powers to take samples'). Forensic samples are either classed as intimate or non-intimate. Those which are non-intimate may be taken by force if necessary, whereas intimate samples cannot, although any refusal to provide the latter may result in the court drawing inferences which may corroborate any evidence against that person.[22]

Intimate samples

The definition of an intimate sample means blood, semen or any other tissue fluid, urine, pubic hair, a dental impression and a swab taken from a person's body orifice except the mouth.[23] An intimate sample may be taken from a suspect where a police inspector or above has authorised it and has reasonable grounds for suspecting that the person has been involved in a recordable offence, has reasonable grounds for believing that the sample will either confirm or disprove the suspect's involvement in that offence and that person has given the appropriate written consent.[24] The authorisation may be given orally initially, but this must be put into writing as soon as possible. Where the required consent is given, the suspect must be informed that the authorisation to take the sample has been made, together with the grounds and the nature of the offence, which must be duly confirmed in the custody record. The authorisation, the grounds and confirmation of the consent must be recorded as soon as practicable in the custody record after the sample has been taken. A suspect who is mentally disordered or otherwise mentally vulnerable, or a juvenile, may request the presence of an appropriate adult of the opposite sex. Where a juvenile is concerned, unless he or she objects, an appropriate adult must be present if any clothing is removed and the appropriate adult must agree to being absent if this is requested.

Under the original s 62 of PACE, the taking of intimate samples applied only to serious arrestable offences. The downgrading to recordable offences (see fn 21) significantly increases the size and scope of the use of this power:

> This means that offences such as assault and most burglaries, which had previously been excluded from the power, will now be subject to it and the range of offences in which samples can be taken is equivalent to that for taking fingerprints, the difference being, at least in respect of intimate samples, that written consent must be obtained. Indeed, the objective is to create a data bank of DNA profiles of all those convicted of recordable offences, similar to that which exists for fingerprints.[25]

---

22 *Op cit*, Clark, fn 19.

23 The exclusion of swabs and saliva samples, etc, taken from the mouths of suspects from the ambit of intimate samples was effected through the Criminal Justice and Public Order Act 1994, ss 58(2) and 59.

24 'Appropriate written consent' is defined under PACE, s 65, as:
    (a) in relation to a person who has attained the age of 17 years, the consent of that person;
    (b) in relation to a person who has not attained that age, but has attained the age of 14 years, the consent of that person and his parent or guardian;
    (c) in relation to a person who has not attained the age of 14 years, the consent of his parent or guardian.

25 *Op cit*, Clark, fn 19.

An intimate sample, with the appropriate authority and consent, may be taken from a person who is not in police custody, but from whom at least two non-intimate samples have been taken, but have proved insufficient. This power may be used on persons on remand, in prison or on bail, and this removes the need for the police to request an intimate sample where a non-intimate sample will be sufficient. Since they will be able to request intimate samples when the person is no longer in police detention, there is no need to request them unnecessarily as a safe measure whilst detained by the police.[26] Note for Guidance 6C under Code D states that these provisions do not prevent the taking of intimate samples in order to enable persons to be eliminated from suspicion of having committed certain crimes. Where a person attends a police station voluntarily in order for this to be done, that person should be advised of the entitlement to free legal advice and the safeguards regarding the role of the appropriate adult should be observed where applicable. All samples taken from persons not suspected of a crime must usually be destroyed at the conclusion of the proceedings, unless they were used to investigate an offence where someone has been convicted and samples were also taken from that convicted person. This is to assist in a later investigation should there be an alleged miscarriage of justice.

Prior to the police requesting an intimate sample, the suspect must be warned that refusal without good cause[27] may harm that person's defence. Note for Guidance 6D provides that the following form of words may be used:

> You do not have to provide this sample/allow this swab or impression to be taken, but I must warn you that if you refuse without good cause, your refusal may harm your case if it comes to trial.

A record of the above warning must be made after it is administered. If the suspect is in police detention and not legally represented, that person must be reminded of the entitlement to free legal advice, which should, in turn, be entered in the custody record. The suspect should also be told that any sample taken may be the subject of a speculative search and this fact must be duly recorded as soon as practicable in the custody record. Only urine samples may be obtained by the police. Dental impressions may only be obtained by dental practitioners and all other samples must be taken by medical practitioners, nurses or registered healthcare professionals such as paramedics.

Non-intimate samples

The definition of non-intimate samples includes non-pubic hair, a sample taken from a nail or under it, a swab taken from any part of the body including the mouth (but excluding any other body orifice), saliva, a skin impression such as a footprint or any similar impression of part of a person's body, except part of the hand (because this will usually be a finger or palm print). It should be noted that dental impressions, whilst technically falling under an impression of part of a person's body, are expressly classed as intimate samples.

---

26 Wasik, M and Taylor, R, *Blackstone's Guide to the Criminal Justice and Public Order Act 1994* (London: Blackstone, 1995).

27 According to Clark (*op cit*, fn 19), the term 'good cause' may include religious objections, a parent's belligerence at the prospect of having one's child treated in this manner, drunkenness or general indignation. Ultimately, it is for the jury to decide.

Non-intimate samples can be taken with or without the appropriate written consent (see fn 24 for what constitutes 'appropriate written consent'). Whether or not consent is given, the police should tell the suspect that the sample may be the subject of a speculative search, which must then be written in the custody record after the sample has been taken. If the appropriate consent is not given, a non-intimate sample may be taken using reasonable force if necessary.[28] This will apply where the suspect is being held in police custody on the authority of a court, and where an officer of the rank of inspector or above authorises the taking of a sample without the suspect's consent. This will occur where that officer has reasonable grounds for suspecting the suspect's involvement in a recordable offence and has reasonable grounds to believe that the sample will tend to confirm or disprove his or her involvement in the offence. The authorisation may be given orally initially, but must be confirmed in writing. However, a non-intimate sample may not be taken without consent if it is a skin impression already taken from the same part of the body and it has not proved insufficient.

A non-intimate sample may also be taken without consent, whether or not the person is in police detention or held in police custody on the authority of a court, if that person has been charged or reported for a recordable offence and either a non-intimate sample has not been taken during the investigation or one has been taken, but is unsuitable or insufficient. A non-intimate sample may also be taken without consent where a person has been convicted of a recordable offence. Section 10 of the Criminal Justice Act 2003 has amended s 63 of PACE and included two further grounds for taking non-intimate samples without consent, namely:

The first is that the person is in police detention in consequence of his arrest for a recordable offence. The second is that –

(a) he has not had a non-intimate sample of the same type and from the same part of the body taken in the course of the investigation of the offence by the police, or

(b) he has had such a sample taken but it proved insufficient.

Where applicable, depending on whether or not such action was taken during police detention or custody, the suspect must be informed of the authorisation and the grounds or reasons for it which, in turn, should be recorded in the custody record as soon as practicable.

Any non-pubic hair required as non-intimate samples may be plucked or cut. Where it is necessary to pluck hair for DNA purposes, the suspect should be given a choice as to which part of the body it should be taken from and, normally, hairs should be removed individually, unless the suspect expresses a contrary wish. In any event, no more should be taken than the police consider to be reasonably necessary.

Any constable may require a person not in police detention or custody to attend a police station to have a non-intimate sample taken where that person has been charged or reported for a recordable offence and where either no sample was taken during the investigation or one was taken, but has proved to be unsuitable or insufficient. The same provision also applies where a person has been convicted of a recordable offence and either no sample has been taken or one was taken, but is insufficient or unsuitable.

---

28 PACE, s 117. Where force is used to obtain a non-intimate sample, a record must be made of the circumstances which must also include a record of all those present.

This requirement must be exercised within one month, where applicable, from either the date that the suspect was charged or reported, or from the date of the appropriate officer[29] being informed of the unsuitability or insufficiency of the sample for analysis or from the date of conviction. The actual period of notice under which the person may be required to attend a police station for this purpose is at least seven days and anyone who fails to meet this requirement may be arrested without warrant.

It has been submitted that the above power to require the attendance of a suspect also applies to the taking of intimate samples:

> Although the procedure seems primarily to be directed at the new powers to take non-intimate samples without consent, there is nothing in the sub-section to limit it to non-intimate samples, so it would seem also that a person can be required to attend for the purposes of an intimate sample being taken under the new s 62(1A) of PACE (where two or more non-intimate samples have proved insufficient). However, this power is exercisable only if the suspect gives consent and this cannot be overridden by s 63A, but the power to require attendance may still be useful to the police, since the suspect may, in fact, consent, either because he hopes the sample will clear him or because his refusal permits inferences to be drawn against him under s 62(10).[30]

The destruction of intimate and non-intimate samples

Samples need not be destroyed if they were taken for the purpose of a criminal investigation for which someone has been convicted and from whom a sample was taken. The retention of samples under this provision is designed to allow all samples in a case to be available for any later miscarriage of justice investigation. Samples and any information derived from them may not be used against any person who would otherwise be entitled to have his or her sample destroyed. In addition, samples (including fingerprints) may be retained, but only after they have fulfilled their purpose and must not be used except in the prevention or detection of crime, the investigation of an offence or the conduct of a prosecution (s 64(1A) of PACE). In *R (on the Application of S) v Chief Constable of South Yorkshire* and *R (on the Application of Marper) v Chief Constable of South Yorkshire* (2004), the House of Lords held that the retention of fingerprints and DNA samples under s 64(1A) of PACE did not interfere with Art 8(1) or 14 of the European Convention on Human Rights. Lord Steyn stated that the policy of chief constables in retaining fingerprints and samples, except in exceptional circumstances, was therefore lawful.

---

29   The 'appropriate officer' can have one of two meanings, depending upon which provisions apply in each case. Where a person has been either charged or reported for a recordable offence and has not had a sample taken in the course of the investigation or did have one taken, but it was insufficient or unsuitable for analysis, the appropriate officer will be the investigating officer in the case. Where a person has been convicted of a recordable offence and either a sample has not been taken since the conviction or he has had one taken before or after conviction, but the sample has proved to be unsuitable or insufficient for analysis, the appropriate officer will be the police officer in charge of the police station where the criminal investigation was conducted.

30   *Op cit*, Wasik and Taylor, fn 26.

New power to take samples

Section 57 of the Criminal Justice and Court Services Act 2000 inserted a new s 63B and s 63C into PACE. The police now have the power to test persons in police detention for the presence of certain drugs. The main purposes behind this power are to assist in the monitoring of drug misuse and to provide assistance to the courts when making bail decisions. This power, so far, applies only to heroin, cocaine and 'crack' cocaine ('specified' Class A drugs), although there is provision for the Home Secretary to include other controlled drugs if necessary at a later date.

A sample of urine or a non-intimate sample such as a saliva swab may be taken from a person in police detention in order to ascertain whether that person has any of these 'specified' Class A controlled drugs in his or her body. However, there are several conditions that must be fulfilled. The detained person must be *charged* with any of the following offences under the Theft Act 1968: theft; robbery; burglary; aggravated burglary; taking a conveyance without consent; aggravated vehicle taking; obtaining property by deception; and going equipped for stealing, or any of the following offences under the Misuse of Drugs Act 1971: the production or supply of controlled drugs; simple possession; or possession with intent to supply. Alternatively, the detained person may be charged with another offence, but may still fall within the scope of this power. This will apply if an inspector or above has reasonable grounds for suspecting that the misuse of any of the specified Class A drugs caused or contributed to the offence, and subsequently authorises the drug test accordingly. The detained person must be at least 14 years old[31] and will only be obliged to provide a body sample where this is requested by the police, including where an authorisation has been made by an inspector or above. A warning must then be given that a failure to provide a sample without good cause is an offence punishable on summary conviction, to a maximum of three months' imprisonment[32] and/or a level 4 fine on the standard scale (currently £2,500). Force may not be used to obtain a sample. Where the detainee is under 17 years old, an appropriate adult must be present.

Section 57 of the Criminal Justice and Court Services Act also amended s 38 of PACE ('duties of custody officer after charge'). As discussed in Chapter 5, the custody officer is under a duty to release a suspect once charged, unless certain conditions are present. Section 57 inserted an additional ground for detaining suspects after charge where a drug test is required, although this is restricted to a time limit of no more than six hours from the time that the charge was made.

This power is currently being exercised by a selected number of police stations within a limited range of police areas for the main age groups. The Home Secretary will be empowered to change a number of these provisions where appropriate. These include extending, where necessary, the range of specified Class A drugs as mentioned above, and he may extend the drug testing provisions to persons arrested, but not charged, with a relevant offence. The Home Secretary will also be under a duty to make regulations regarding the taking of samples from detained persons, including provisions as to who may perform this procedure. The procedures under ss 63B and

---

31 This was reduced from 18 to 14 years by s 5 of the Criminal Justice Act 2003, although currently some police areas are still piloting this drug testing power, based on the original minimum age criteria of 18.

32 Due to be increased to 51 weeks by the Criminal Justice Act 2003.

63C of PACE are covered in Code C under paras 17.1–17.14, as well as Notes for Guidance 17A–G. In addition, Annexes I and J to Code C list the police areas currently participating in this scheme. Annex I lists 19 police forces where the power to test persons for specified Class A drugs has been brought into force, but only for 18 year olds and above. Annex J lists seven of these police forces which are also using this power for 14 year olds and over.

INDEPENDENT CUSTODY VISITORS

This chapter would not be complete without mentioning an important safeguard regarding the general treatment of persons who are detained by the police. Section 51 of the Police Reform Act 2002 has placed the inspection of custody facilities at police stations on a statutory footing. For many years, volunteers who are not part of the police service or any other aspect of the criminal justice system have been visiting custody suites in order to inspect the conditions under which detainees are held, as well as report on their treatment. Previously, this was done on an optional basis by police authorities, but it is now a mandatory requirement which will be supported by a code of practice in order to ensure greater uniformity. This code of practice must be issued by the Home Secretary, and may be revised where necessary. Before issuing or revising this code, the Home Secretary is under a duty to consult with representatives of police authorities, chief officers of police, and any other persons as he thinks fit.

Police authorities are under a duty to make arrangements for detainees to be visited by independent custody visitors, and to keep these arrangements under review. They must be independent of the relevant police authority and the chief officer of police for that area. Police authorities may confer independent custody visitors with such powers as are considered necessary in the exercise of their functions, which in particular may include the following:

- To require access to be given to each police station.
- To examine records relating to the detention of persons.
- To meet detainees for the purposes of a discussion about their treatment and conditions while detained.
- To inspect the facilities in custody suites including, in particular, cell accommodation, washing and toilet facilities, and the facilities for the provision of food.

Provision may be made regarding the denial of access by an independent custody visitor to a detainee on the authority of an inspector or above in specific circumstances. However, the grounds for such action must be in accordance with the code of practice.

CHAPTER 7

POLICING BY CIVILIANS

INTRODUCTION

The use of civilian employees in assisting the police has been an ongoing process for many years. One of the most common and long-standing examples of this trend is the performance of administrative and general office duties by civilian staff. As time has progressed, they have become involved in more specialised and direct support roles within the police service, such as Scenes of Crime Officers (SOCOs). However, the Police Reform Act 2002 has made very significant changes to the police service as a whole, some of which have already been discussed earlier in this book. The part of the 2002 Act that will be the focus of this chapter is Pt 4, Chapter 1 and Scheds 4 and 5, for it is these parts of the Act that created the concept of the 'extended police family'.

Among many other things, the Government White Paper entitled *Policing a New Century: A Blueprint for Reform*[1] proposed a new dimension in the civilianisation of certain aspects of police work. It is important at this stage to distinguish this concept from the special constabulary, mentioned in Chapter 1. As discussed in that chapter, the special constabulary is the voluntary, unpaid section of the police service, where suitable men and women are sworn in or attested as constables in the same way as regular police officers. Although their training and overall scope is subject to certain limitations compared to their full time counterparts, special constables often fulfil an important role in many front-line police duties, and this was acknowledged in the Government White Paper. Its main emphasis on 'specials', however, was centred around their recruitment and retention, as increased numbers of unpaid volunteers within a high cost public service is always an attractive proposition. Concern was expressed regarding the diminishing number of specials overall, and proposals were put forward that were designed to enhance recruitment and retention rates; these included more effective management of specials and a greater use of their time and skills. With very minor exceptions, specials wear the same uniform and carry the same basic equipment as regular police officers; they also have full police powers both on and off duty. The only slight difference is that specials may only exercise these powers within their own police area and also within immediately adjoining police areas. This is in contrast to regular police officers, who have nationwide jurisdiction, although if specials are deployed outside their normal police area on mutual aid, they have full police powers within that area. The special constabulary was instituted as far back as 1831 – just two years after the Metropolitan Police in London were created. Since then, the specials have played an important role in the policing of this country, especially at crucial times in our history.[2] The special constabulary could therefore be described as part of the police family but not an 'extended' part of it, unlike the civilians described in the Police Reform Act 2002.

---

1   Cm 5326, Home Office, 2001.
2   These include the Chartist march on London in 1848, the Trafalgar Square riots of 1887, the Railway Strike of 1911, the General Strike in 1926, and both World Wars, to name but a few.

The introductory pages of the Government White Paper contained a broad statement of the intention to create the extended police family by saying:

> Front line policing can be strengthened by enhancing the role of police support staff, and by giving them new powers which will allow them to take over tasks currently carried out by police officers for example in custody suites. Other support staff ('Community Support Officers') will be empowered to carry out basic patrol functions. They will provide a visible presence in the community with powers sufficient to deal with anti-social behaviour and minor disorder. Staff from outside the police service may also be given limited powers subject to the necessary training and police accreditation.[3]

A further indication as to the formation of the extended police family was given later in the White Paper regarding 'specialist civilian investigators', where it stated:

> Money laundering, fraud, intellectual property theft, and other crimes are becoming increasingly sophisticated. Information technology and communications systems are both the means of crime and its object – and at the same time vital investigative tools in the fight against criminals. Too few officers currently have the necessary skills to deal with the most complex IT based crime. Even with more specialist detectives we will not be able to guarantee an adequate capacity in the most specialised fields. We must be able to attract career specialists in these areas to work as part of police investigative teams. Chief officers can already appoint civilians from these backgrounds, but they are unable themselves to exercise police powers necessary to pursue an investigation; and they have limited career opportunities open to them. Civilian investigators must be able to function as a full member of a police investigating team. They should have the capacity to supervise and direct police officers in relevant parts of an investigation, acting under the Senior Investigating Officer. Given the right skills, such staff should also be able to take on the role of Senior Investigating Officer themselves in time. To be fully effective, they would need to be given certain police powers. These would include, for example, authority to search and seize evidence, to interview suspects and witnesses, to execute warrants and to present evidential summaries as expert witnesses.[4]

In connection with the above, particular reference was later made regarding scenes of crime officers:

> More than three-quarters of Scenes of Crime Officers are now support staff rather than police officers. Since most of their work is carried out on the basis of consent, they are normally able to conduct their business effectively without the need for formal powers. It would be sensible, however, to provide for the occasions when this is not the case, to ensure that they have the necessary powers of entry, search and seizure to enable them to preserve evidence which might otherwise be lost.[5]

On 24 July 2002, the Police Reform Act received the Royal Assent, and part of its long title is thus: '... to provide for the exercise of police powers by persons who are not police officers ...' This part of the Act put into effect the concept of the extended police family, which came into force on 2 December 2002. Its provisions will now be discussed.

---

3 *Op cit*, fn 1, 3.
4 *Op cit*, fn 1, 44.
5 *Op cit*, fn 1, 81.

CIVILIANS GIVEN POLICE POWERS

Part 4, Chapter 1 and Scheds 4 and 5 to the Police Reform Act 2002 have created five main classes of designated civilians who have been given a range of police powers, and these comprise the extended police family.[6] These are as follows:

- community support officers;
- investigating officers;
- detention officers;
- escort officers;
- accredited civilians.

(See the diagram in Appendix 13.)

Section 38(1) of the 2002 Act empowers chief officers of police in England and Wales to designate any person employed by his or her police authority to perform one or more duties of any of the first four listed above. In other words, with the exception of accredited civilians, a person may be appointed to perform more than one set of duties. For instance, a person may be designated as an escort officer as well as a detention officer, although some designated civilians may only perform one function. It is very important to note that all designated and accredited civilians are subject to the provisions of the PACE Codes of Practice.

Community support officers

Community support officers (CSOs) are the most visible of all the designated civilians working as part of the extended police family, and possibly the most controversial. Currently, most police forces in England and Wales employ CSOs, and their numbers are destined to increase significantly over the next few years and possibly beyond. It is important to note that CSOs are not the same as community or neighbourhood wardens, or similar classes of persons who are engaged in community safety duties, for instance. The latter could be included as part of a community safety accreditation scheme and become accredited civilians, although others may not. This will be covered later in this chapter.

All CSOs are employees of the police authorities within the police areas where they perform their duties, and are under the direction and control of the relevant chief officer of police for that area. Section 38(4) of the 2002 Act states that no one may be designated to perform any of these duties unless the chief officer of police is satisfied that they are suitable candidates who are capable of effectively performing these duties, and have received the appropriate training. The 2002 Act contains a range of police powers that may be conferred on CSOs at the discretion of their chief police officers. This means that all or some of them may be conferred on CSOs depending on local needs. This provision was questioned in Parliament when the Police Reform Bill

---

6   A substantial increase in the powers of CSOs was effected by the Anti-social Behaviour Act 2003 which, in turn, amended the Police Reform Act 2002. These changes have been incorporated in the list of their powers accordingly. See Jason-Lloyd, L, 'Community support officers: more powers in the pipeline' (2003) 167 JP 34, 23 August. See also Jason-Lloyd, L, 'A new dimension in policing' (2002) 166 JP 45, 9 November.

was being debated. It was argued that this could cause confusion in different areas if CSOs had varying powers. Some asserted that a more consistent approach was desirable where all CSOs had the same powers, regardless as to where they worked. Section 38(7) states that CSOs (or other designated civilians) must not engage in conduct that is outside the scope of their employment and that they shall be subject to any restrictions and conditions regarding their designation. This prohibits them from exceeding their powers, and includes not placing themselves on duty when not working, as police officers do in appropriate circumstances. Section 38(8) covers the use of reasonable force and states that when a CSO (or other designated civilian) exercises any power which is also a police power, and the use of reasonable force is part of it, that CSO may also use reasonable force where necessary. Section 38(9) also addresses the use of force and provides that where a power to enter premises is part of a CSOs duties (or other designated civilians), this must only be exercised in the company and under the supervision of a police officer. The exception to this rule is where it is necessary for the CSO (or other designated civilian) to force entry in order to save life or limb or prevent serious damage to property. In any of these circumstances, it is not necessary to be accompanied by a police officer.

Although s 38 is addressed to all designated civilians, Sched 4, Pt 1 of the 2002 Act specifically addresses the powers and duties of CSOs. Before listing these, it is important to mention that not all these powers may necessarily be conferred upon any designated civilian, including CSOs. The powers listed under this part of the 2002 Act may be given in whole or part at the discretion of each chief officer of police. Furthermore, they may also impose restrictions and conditions on any of these powers, such as where and when they may be used.

Schedule 4, Pt 1, para 1: powers to issue fixed penalty notices

Under para 1(2) of Sched 4, Pt 1 of the 2002 Act, the offences to which CSOs have the power to issue fixed penalty notices are as follows where there is reason to believe that the offender is aged at least 10 years:[7]

(a) The powers of a constable in uniform, or an authorised constable, to give a penalty notice under Chapter 1 of Part 1 of the Criminal Justice and Police Act 2001 (fixed penalty notices in respect of offences of disorder).[8]

(aa) The power of a constable to give a penalty notice in respect of failure to secure a pupil's regular attendance at school.

(b) The power of a constable in uniform to give a person a fixed penalty notice for riding a bicycle on a footway.

(c) The power to give a fixed penalty notice in respect of dog fouling.

(ca) The power of an authorised officer of a local authority to give a notice under s 43(1) of the Anti-social Behaviour Act 2003 (penalty notices in respect of graffiti or fly-posting).

(d) The power to give a fixed penalty notice in respect of litter.

---

7   This was reduced from 18 to 16 years by s 87(2) of the Anti-social Behaviour Act 2003, then reduced to 10 years by the Penalties for Disorderly Behaviour (Amendment of Minimum Age) Order 2004 (SI 2004/3166).

8   These offences are listed under paragraphs (a)–(r) at the end of Chapter 3 (police powers of arrest).

The issuing of a fixed penalty notice regarding any of the above offences is, of course, contingent on the person providing his or her correct name and address. In the event of a failure to do so, there are measures designed to deal with those who either refuse to provide these particulars or give false details. These measures are covered below.

Designated CSOs may be given further powers to require a suspect's name and address, and the offences to which they relate are to be found under para 2(6)(b)(i) and (ii) as follows:

    (e) an offence which appears to have caused injury, alarm or distress to any other person, or which involves any other person's property being lost or damaged;

    (f) an offence under s 32(2) of the Anti-social Behaviour Act 2003.

The broad description of offences under (e) can include a very wide range of crimes such as criminal damage, non-fatal harms against the person, public order offences, and even homicides! The offence under (f) is related to s 30(4) of the Anti-social Behaviour Act 2003 which empowers designated CSOs (and police officers in uniform), *inter alia*, to disperse groups of persons acting in an anti-social manner. Under s 32(2) of the 2003 Act, it is an offence to contravene a direction by a CSO (or the police) to disperse (see further below). It should be noted that under para 2(6), all the offences (a) to (f) are regarded as 'relevant offences'.

Paragraph 2: power to detain, etc

As mentioned above, a designated CSO may require a person to give his or her name and address if any of the relevant offences have been committed. If the person refuses to give those particulars, or the CSO has reasonable grounds to suspect that those details are false, the CSO may require that person to wait with him or her for up to 30 minutes for a police officer to arrive (sub-para (3)). Alternatively, sub-para (4) provides that a person liable to be detained under that power may be given the option to accompany the CSO to a police station. Anyone who fails to provide a name and address or gives false particulars, or makes off when subject to the 30 minute detention power or makes off when accompanying a CSO to a police station, commits an offence; this is punishable by a maximum level 3 fine (£1,000). Up until recently, six police forces have been piloting the use of the CSOs detention power under a two-year evaluation scheme. The Police Reform Act 2002 (Commencement No 10) Order 2004, now enables designated CSOs in all police areas to exercise the detention power, as well as use the accompaniment to the police station option.

Paragraph 3: power to require name and address of persons acting in an anti-social manner

Designated CSOs have the power of a police officer in uniform to exercise the power under s 50 of the Police Reform Act 2002. Paragraph 3(1) of Sched 4 enables a CSO who has reason to believe that a person has been or is acting in an anti-social manner to require that person to provide their name and address. Under s 50(2) of the Police Reform Act, failure to provide these details or the giving of false particulars is an offence punishable by a maximum level 3 fine. A person who refuses to give their name and address or gives false particulars may also be subject to the 30 minute detention power, or the option to accompany a designated CSO to a police station. A further offence will be committed if that person makes off either when being detained or when accompanying the CSO to a police station.

Paragraph 4: power to use reasonable force to detain a person

A designated CSO may use reasonable force to prevent a person making off who is either being detained under the 30 minute detention power or is accompanying the CSO to a police station.

Paragraphs 4A and 4B: power to disperse groups and remove young persons to places of residence

Designated CSOs (as mentioned above) have the powers of a uniformed constable under s 30 of the Anti-social Behaviour Act 2003 to disperse groups and remove persons under 16 years old to their places of residence. Paragraph 4B gives designated CSOs the power of a constable to remove children to their place of residence who are in contravention of a local child curfew. Both 4A and 4B are also mentioned in Chapter 3 (police powers of arrest).

Paragraph 5: alcohol consumption in designated public places

Section 12 of the Criminal Justice and Police Act 2001 states that where a police officer reasonably believes that a person is, or has been, consuming intoxicating liquor in a designated public place, or intends to do so, that police officer may require a person not to consume the drink in that place, to surrender it, and the officer may then dispose of it. Failure to comply with any of these requirements is an offence punishable by a maximum level 2 fine (£500), although there must be prior warning that failure to comply with any requirement is an offence. Paragraph 5 of Sched 4 enables designated CSOs to impose the same requirements as the police as well as dispose of the alcoholic drink. However, there is one fundamental difference: any failure by a person to comply when directed by a police officer constitutes an arrestable offence, whereas this is excluded from the specific provisions of para 5 of Sched 4. This anomaly, and many others, will be discussed towards the end of this chapter.

Paragraph 6: confiscation of alcohol

This power was originally given to the police under s 1 of the Confiscation of Alcohol (Young Persons) Act 1997.[9] This power is similar to that contained in s 12 of the Criminal Justice and Police Act 2001, except that it applies to the confiscation and disposal of alcoholic drink from persons under 18 years old and persons who are nearby (this is up to the judge to decide) and over 18. There is the additional

---

9   See Jason-Lloyd, L, 'The Confiscation of Alcohol (Young Persons) Act 1997: an overview' (1997) 161 JP 37, 13 September and 'The Confiscation of Alcohol (Young Persons) Act 1997: implications for the police service' (1997) LXX The Police Journal 4, October–December.

requirement that the person provides their name and address, and it is an offence if the person fails to do this or surrender the alcohol. The maximum penalty for this offence is a fine not exceeding level 2. Although the police have a power of arrest for this offence, this has been expressly removed by para 6 and thus it is not available to CSOs.

Paragraph 7: confiscation of tobacco, etc

Section 7(3) of the Children and Young Persons Act 1933 enables police officers in uniform to confiscate and dispose of tobacco and cigarette papers from persons under 16 years old in public places; this power is extended to designated CSOs.

Paragraph 8: entry to save life or limb or prevent serious damage to property

The high visibility of CSOs on the streets will inevitably lead to them being called upon to deal with many matters concerning public safety that do not necessarily involve law enforcement. The provision under para 8 mirrors s 17 of PACE, which enables the police to enter and search any premises in order to save life or limb, or to prevent serious damage to property. Designated CSOs have also been given the same powers, including the power to use reasonable force in the execution of this duty and, furthermore, they do not have to be accompanied by a police officer at the time.

Paragraph 9: seizure of vehicles used to cause alarm, etc

In response to increasing concerns regarding persons who engage in anti-social and dangerous behaviour, s 59 of the Police Reform Act 2002 has given a power to the police in order to deal with motor vehicles that are driven carelessly and inconsiderately, or driven off the road, and which cause, or are likely to cause, alarm, distress or annoyance to the public. Under this power, where a police officer in uniform reasonably believes that a motor vehicle is being used in this manner, he or she may stop the vehicle if it is moving, and seize and remove it. The latter may be effected by entering premises, unless this is a private dwelling house, and reasonable force may be used if necessary in effecting any of these powers. Under sub-s (4), a warning must usually be given before a motor vehicle may be seized, although there are exceptions to this rule as stated in sub-s (5). These powers are subject to regulations made by the Home Secretary under s 60 of the Police Reform Act 2002. Anyone who fails to stop when directed to do so by a police officer in uniform commits an offence punishable by a maximum level 3 fine (£1,000).

Paragraph 9 of Sched 4 empowers designated CSOs to exercise nearly all of the above powers of a police officer. The exception is that when exercising the power to enter premises, a CSO may only do this when in the presence of a police officer.

Paragraph 10: abandoned vehicles

Paragraph 10 of Sched 4 enables designated CSOs to exercise the power of a constable to remove, or arrange the removal of, abandoned vehicles. This power exists under various regulations made under s 99 of the Road Traffic Regulation Act 1984.

Paragraph 11: power to stop vehicle for testing

Paragraph 11 of Sched 4 gives designated CSOs the power of a constable in uniform to stop a vehicle in order to test it. This power originates from s 67(3) of the Road Traffic Act 1988.

Paragraph 11A: power to stop cycles

Under para 1(b), mentioned above, a designated CSO may issue a fixed penalty notice in respect of persons riding on the footway. Shortly after this provision was put into force, it was discovered that they had no power to actually stop cycles being ridden in order to issue such a notice. Subsequently, this new para 11A was inserted empowering CSOs initially to stop cyclists riding on the footway in order to use their powers under para 1(b).

Paragraph 12: power to control traffic for the purposes of escorting a load of exceptional dimensions

Designated CSOs are empowered to regulate road traffic and pedestrians when in the process of escorting vehicles or trailers that are carrying abnormal loads. This includes powers to direct vehicles and pedestrians to stop, or direct vehicles to proceed in or keep to a particular line of traffic. Under ss 35 and 37 of the Road Traffic Act 1988, failure to comply with such directions by the police is an offence punishable by a maximum level 3 fine. This will also apply where the directions are made by a CSO. Designated CSOs performing their duties under para 12 of Sched 4 are the exception to the rule that CSOs may only perform duties within their own police area. As their traffic escort duties may take them outside their particular areas, sub-para (3) states that: 'The powers conferred by virtue of this paragraph may be exercised in any police area in England and Wales.'

Paragraph 13: carrying out road checks

In Chapter 2 (police powers of stop and search), coverage was made regarding s 4 of PACE in respect of road checks (or road blocks) by the police. Paragraph 13 of Sched 4 confers the same powers to designated CSOs, including the general power to stop vehicles under s 163 of the Road Traffic Act 1988. However, it should be noted that the powers under s 4 of PACE do not extend to searching the vehicle or its occupants. The police may only do this under specific powers that have not been conferred upon CSOs.

Paragraph 14: cordoned areas

CSOs may be used in a number of situations in order to assist the police in dealing with terrorism. Those CSOs designated for this purpose are authorised under para 14 of Sched 4 to exercise all the powers of uniformed constables to give orders, make arrangements or impose prohibitions or restrictions, within areas cordoned-off under s 36 of the Terrorism Act 2000. The complete range of powers to impose cordons were covered under Chapter 2 (police powers of stop and search), although note that the powers under para 3 of Sched 5 to the 2000 Act (entry, search and seizure within premises) do not apply to CSOs.

Paragraph 15: power to stop and search vehicles, etc, in authorised areas

Further anti-terrorism duties may be designated to CSOs by para 15 of Sched 4 of the Police Reform Act 2002. This confers upon them the powers of uniformed police officers of stop, search and seizure under ss 44(1)(a), (d), (2)(b) and 45(2) of the Terrorism Act 2000. The full scope of police powers under ss 44–47 of the 2000 Act was given in Chapter 2, although there are some important restrictions on the use of these powers by CSOs compared with police officers. First, CSOs must confine their searches to property carried in or on vehicles, or carried by persons either in vehicles or on foot; in other words, they must not search persons, but only items such as bags and cases. Secondly, CSOs must be under the supervision of a police officer when exercising their powers of stop, search and seizure.

Investigating officers

Schedule 4, Pt 2

In the introduction to this chapter, the intended role for civilian investigating officers (IOs) was briefly discussed. These are now part of the extended police family, and the powers and duties of this class of designated civilians under the Police Reform Act 2002 are specified under Pt 2 of Sched 4 below. It is important to note that these powers may only be exercised within the IO's police area.

Paragraph 16: search warrants

Designated IOs have the power of a police officer to apply to a justice of the peace for a warrant to enter and search premises in accordance with s 8 of PACE. Any warrant issued must include the IO who applied for it and the premises in question must be within the police area where the IO is based. The power under s 8(2) of PACE to seize and retain anything relating to the search also applies to a designated IO as it does to a police officer. IOs are also subject to the following provisions under PACE, as are the police, regarding safeguards and procedures in the exercise of their powers: s 15 (safeguards); s 16 (execution of warrants); s 19(6) (protection for legally privileged material from seizure); s 20 (extension of powers of seizure to computerised information); s 21(1) and (2) (provision of record of seizure); ss 21(3) to (8) and 22 (access, copying and retention).

Paragraph 17: access to excluded and special procedure material

Designated IOs have the same powers as police officers in relation to access to excluded material or special procedure material under s 9(1) of and Sched 1 to PACE. IOs are also subject to the following duties and safeguards under PACE: s 15, s 16, s 19(6), s 20, s 21(1) and (2), s 21(3)–(8) and s 22.

Paragraph 18: entry and search after arrest

The powers and duties of police officers to enter and search premises without warrant under s 18 of PACE are also conferred on designated IOs (see Chapter 4). They are also subject to the following controls and obligations under PACE: s 19(6), s 20, s 21(1) and (2), s 21(3)–(8) and s 22.

Paragraph 19: general power of seizure

When lawfully on premises, designated IOs will have the same powers of seizure as a police officer under s 19 of PACE, and will also have the power to require any computerised information to be produced in a form where it can be removed and is visible and legible. In the exercise of these powers, IOs are under a duty to comply with the following provisions of PACE: s 19(6) (protection of legally privileged material), s 21 and s 22.

Paragraph 20: access and copying in the case of things seized by constables

Designated IOs are under the same duties as a police officer with regard to the following provisions under PACE: s 21(3), (4) and (5).

Paragraph 21: arrest at a police station for another offence

Section 31 of PACE enables a constable to arrest a person for a further offence where that person is already detained at a police station having been arrested for an offence. This power may be exercised by designated IOs to whom the provisions of s 36 of the Criminal Justice and Public Order Act 1994 may apply (consequences of failure by arrested person to account for objects, substances or marks).

Paragraph 22: power to transfer persons into custody of investigating officers

This provision enables a custody officer to transfer a suspect in police detention to an IO who is investigating the offence. The suspect will then be in the designated IO's lawful custody and the IO will be under a duty to prevent the suspect's escape, in which reasonable force may be used if necessary. In addition to these powers and duties, an IO also will be subject to the same responsibilities in relation to the detained person as a police officer under s 39(2) and (3) of PACE.

Paragraph 23: power to require arrested person to account for certain matters

A designated IO has the power of a constable, under ss 36(1)(c) and 37(1)(c) of the Criminal Justice and Public Order Act 1994, to request a suspect to account for the presence of an object, substance or mark, or for his or her presence at a particular place (see also para 21 above).

Paragraph 24: extended powers of seizure

In Chapter 4, the relatively new extended powers of seizure were discussed. This is the power to 'seize and sift' under Pt 2 of the Criminal Justice and Police Act 2001. Designated IOs may also exercise this power as well as police officers where appropriate. This also applies to s 56 of the 2001 Act (retention of property seized by a constable).

Paragraph 24A: persons accompanying investigating officers

Paragraph 19 of Sched 1 to the Criminal Justice Act 2003 inserted this new para 24A into Sched 4, Pt 2 to the Police Reform Act 2002. This was necessary in view of the enhanced role of certain civilians, as well as IOs, in the execution of search warrants and the seizure of property. The text of para 24A is as follows:

(1) This paragraph applies where a person ('an authorised person') is authorised by virtue of section 16(2) of the 1984 Act to accompany an investigating officer designated for the purposes of paragraph 16 (or 17) in the execution of a warrant.

(2) The reference in paragraph 16(h) (or 17(e)) to the seizure of anything by a designated person in exercise of a particular power includes a reference to the seizure of anything by the authorised person in exercise of that power by virtue of section 16(2A) of the 1984 Act.

(3) In relation to any such seizure, paragraph 16(h) (or 17(e)) is to be read as if it provided for the references to a constable and to an officer in section 21(1) and (2) of the 1984 Act to include references to the authorised person.

(4) The reference in paragraph 16(i) (or 17(f)) to anything seized by a designated person in exercise of a particular power includes a reference to anything seized by the authorised person in exercise of that power by virtue of section 16(2A) of the 1984 Act.

(5) In relation to anything so seized, paragraph 16(i)(ii) (or 17(f)(ii)) is to be read as if it provided for –

  (a) the references to the supervision of a constable in subsections (3) and (4) of section 21 of the 1984 Act to include references to the supervision of a person designated for the purposes of paragraph 16 (or paragraph 17), and

  (b) the reference to a constable in subsection (5) of that section to include a reference to such a person or an authorised person accompanying him.

(6) Where an authorised person accompanies an investigating officer who is also designated for the purposes of paragraph 24, the references in sub-paragraphs (a) and (b) of that paragraph to the designated person include references to the authorised person.

Investigating officers are not solely confined to the police service. Section 38(3) of the Police Reform Act enables the Director General of the National Criminal Intelligence Service or the Director General of the National Crime Squad to designate persons as investigating officers as employees of their Service Authority.

Detention officers

Schedule 4, Pt 3

The next two classes of designated civilians to be covered in this commentary are detention officers and escort officers. Although s 38 of the Police Reform Act provides that both may be employed by police authorities, s 39 enables police authorities to enter into a contract with companies who may supply the services of detention officers and escort officers (see Appendix 13). Where designated accordingly by the relevant chief officer of police, these civilians may have the same powers and duties as those who are directly employed by the police authorities. Section 38(1) states that a civilian may be designated to perform one or more functions listed in sub-para (2), namely that of a community support officer, investigating officer, detention officer or escort officer. It has been stated that in the case of the last two, a designated civilian may perform the duties of both.[10] First, the role of detention officers (DOs) will now be examined under Sched 4, Pt 3 to the Police Reform Act 2002.

Paragraph 25: attendance at police station for fingerprinting

Designated DOs have the power of a police officer to require the attendance of suspects at a police station within the relevant police area, in order to have their fingerprints taken in accordance with s 27(1) of PACE.

Paragraph 26: non-intimate searches of detained persons

Designated DOs have the power of police officers to carry out non-intimate searches of detained persons under s 54 of PACE, including the seizure and retention of anything discovered in the course of the search. However, the provisions under s 54(6C) and (9) of PACE apply to DOs as well as to police officers regarding certain safeguards in the exercise of these searches. Reasonable force may be used where necessary when conducting these powers.

Paragraph 27: searches and examinations to ascertain identity

As seen in that part of Chapter 5 which dealt with the searching of detained persons, s 54A of PACE empowers the police to examine and/or search detainees for identifying marks. This power may be exercised with or without the detainee's consent and reasonable force may be used where necessary. Under para 27 of Sched 4, this power is also conferred upon designated DOs.

---

10   See Jason-Lloyd, L, *Quasi-Policing* (London: Cavendish Publishing, 2003), p 64.

Paragraph 28: intimate searches of detained persons

Chapter 5 also dealt with the police power to carry out intimate searches of detained suspects under s 55 of PACE (except instances where only medical personnel may conduct the search). Designated DOs have been given this power, which includes all the relevant safeguards under PACE, including the power to use reasonable force where necessary.

Paragraph 29: fingerprinting without consent

Designated DOs have the power of a constable, under s 61 of PACE, to take fingerprints without consent using reasonable force if necessary. They are also authorised to exercise the requirement under s 61(7A)(a) of PACE to inform a suspect, prior to taking his or her fingerprints, that he or she may be the subject of a speculative search.

Paragraph 30: warnings about intimate samples

Designated DOs have the power of a constable to give the following information to detained suspects prior to the taking of intimate samples under s 62(7A)(a) of PACE:

(7A) If an intimate sample is taken from a person at a police station –

    (a) before the sample is taken, an officer shall inform him that it may be the subject of a speculative search.

Paragraph 31: non-intimate samples

Police powers and duties under s 63 of PACE regarding the taking of non-intimate samples, is also given to designated DOs. This includes, *inter alia*, using reasonable force if necessary where consent is not given, as well as informing suspects that the non-intimate sample may be the subject of a speculative search.

Paragraph 32: attendance at police station for the taking of a sample

Police powers under s 63A(4) of PACE may be given to designated DOs. As seen in Chapter 6, this is the power to require a person who is not in police detention to attend a police station in order to have a sample taken.

Paragraph 33: photographing persons in police detention

Section 64A of PACE makes provision for a person detained at a police station to be photographed, with or without their consent. Those persons may also be required to remove anything that is worn which conceals all or part of the face or head. In the event of a refusal to comply with this requirement, the person proposing to take the photograph may remove the item or substance. If necessary, reasonable force may be used in the exercise of these powers. Paragraph 33 of Sched 4, Pt 3 to the Police Reform Act confers police powers on designated DOs in order that they may perform these duties under s 64A of PACE.

Escort officers

Schedule 4, Pt 4

As mentioned above, escort officers as well as detention officers may either be directly employed by police authorities or their services may be contracted-out by private sector organisations. Whichever applies, they have the same powers and responsibilities, and must be suitable persons to perform these tasks, including being properly trained for this purpose. The powers and duties that may be conferred upon designated escort officers (EOs) under Sched 4, Pt 4 are as follows.

Paragraph 34: power to take arrested person to a police station

A designated EO has the power to take a person to a police station who has been arrested elsewhere. This may not have to be done immediately if, for instance, the arrested person is needed somewhere else for investigative purposes before being taken to a police station. In the exercise of this power, designated EOs are treated as having arrested persons in their lawful custody and are under a duty to prevent their escape. EOs also have the power to conduct non-intimate searches of arrested persons and seize and retain anything found. Reasonable force may be used where necessary in the exercise of these powers. Designated EOs are, however, subject to the same safeguards and restrictions under PACE that apply to the police in respect of the searching of suspects.

Paragraph 35: escort of persons in police detention

Custody officers at police stations may authorise a detainee's transfer to other police stations or elsewhere. The detainee may then be placed into the lawful custody of designated EOs, who will be subject to the same powers and duties as mentioned above under para 34 regarding searches and preventing the escape of detainees, including the use of reasonable force, as well as ensuring their proper treatment. EOs conducting these transfers are not confined to destinations within their police area.

Accredited civilians

Community Safety Accreditation Schemes

Section 40 of the Police Reform Act 2002 introduces this new scheme, which is designed to extend limited police powers to persons already engaged in community safety duties. These include local authority street and neighbourhood wardens, as well as football stewards and security guards within the private security industry, to name but a few. Even persons already exercising official powers, such as environmental health officers, may be included.[11]

---

11 This is according to Cm 5326, *Policing a New Century: A Blueprint for Reform* (London: The Stationery Office, 2001).

Where it is considered appropriate, in order to contribute to community safety and security, as well as combating crime and disorder, public nuisance and other forms of anti-social behaviour, a chief officer of police may establish a community safety accreditation scheme (this provision became effective from 2 December 2002). Prior to starting such a scheme, the chief police officer must consult with his or her police authority and every local authority within the relevant police area. The exception to this rule is the Commissioner of Police of the Metropolis, who must consult with the Metropolitan Police Authority, the Mayor of London and every local authority within the metropolitan police district.

Details regarding any accreditation scheme which is either operating or proposed within a police area must be included within every police plan submitted by each police authority. The submission of an annual police plan to the Home Secretary is incumbent upon police authorities under s 8 of the Police Act 1996. Initially, this is drafted by its chief officer of police and any changes are made in consultation with him or her. Section 40(7) of the Police Reform Act states that every police plan must set out whether a community safety accreditation scheme is maintained within the police area in question and whether any changes to that scheme are proposed. If no accreditation scheme exists, there is the requirement to provide details of any proposed scheme. The police plan must also include the extent of any police powers conferred upon designated persons who are employed by that police authority, and the extent to which any existing or proposed accreditation scheme will supplement those arrangements.

The employers of civilians who are part of a community safety accreditation scheme will be expected to supervise them; therefore, sub-s (8) provides that these employers must carry on business related to or within the relevant police area. However, somewhat controversially, the employers of civilians operating within an accreditation scheme will also be expected to handle complaints regarding their alleged misconduct. Considerable concern was expressed regarding this latter provision as the Bill was proceeding through Parliament. It was strongly asserted that accredited civilians should be brought within the remit of the Independent Police Complaints Commission, as are those directly employed by police authorities, as well as contracted out escort and detention officers.

Section 41 of the Police Reform Act 2002 states the procedures regarding accreditation under community safety accreditation schemes, once a chief police officer has entered into such arrangements with an employer. Accreditation shall not be granted to anyone unless the chief officer of police is satisfied that the employer of that individual is a fit and proper person to supervise him in the carrying out of his accredited functions. It is also a requirement that the individual is a suitable person to be accredited, and is capable of exercising any powers conferred on himself; that person must therefore be adequately trained for this purpose. It is submitted that these provisions generally fall in line with the licensing requirements for certain private security operatives under the Private Security Industry Act 2001. This is one of several examples where the Police Reform Act 2002 and the Private Security Industry Act 2001 are closely linked.

Chief police officers may charge appropriate fees for granting accreditations and/or for considering applications for accreditation or any renewals of existing arrangements. Individual operatives must not engage in conduct outside their employment under an accreditation scheme, and an accreditation shall cease if the operative leaves their employment, or accreditation arrangements are terminated or expire.

The powers, in whole or part, that *may* be conferred on accredited civilians are provided under Sched 5 to the Police Reform Act 2002 (see below). As is the case of designated civilians who are directly employed by police authorities, the conferring of powers from the following menu is at the discretion of the relevant chief officer of police, who may also attach restrictions and conditions regarding the exercise of these powers accordingly. It will be apparent that where accredited civilians are given special powers, these are significantly limited compared to those of community support officers. One of the distinctions between the two is the omission of the power for accredited civilians to use reasonable force when exercising powers attributable to those of a police officer. Neither are they given the limited detention and other powers held by CSOs, when requests for names and addresses are not complied with. The powers that may be given to accredited persons under Sched 5 follow below.[12] As the offences to which they relate echo those applicable to the powers of CSOs stated above, full references have not been given.

Schedule 5, paragraph 1: power to issue fixed penalty notices

An accredited civilian shall have the power to issue the following fixed penalty notices, within the relevant police area, where that civilian has reason to believe that a person has committed or is committing any of the following offences:

(a) The power of a police officer in uniform to give a person a fixed penalty notice for riding on the footway.

(aa) The powers of a police officer to give a penalty notice under Chapter 1 of Part 1 of the Criminal Justice and Police Act 2001 in respect of disorder, *except* the offences of being drunk, or drunk and disorderly in a public place [see the list of these offences in (a)–(r) at the end of Chapter 3 of this book].

(ab) The power of a police officer to give a penalty notice for a person's failure to secure regular attendance of a pupil at school.

(b) The power of an authorised local authority officer to issue a fixed penalty notice in respect of dog fouling.

(c) The power of an authorised officer to give a fixed penalty notice regarding litter.

(ca) The power of an authorised local authority officer to give a penalty notice in respect of graffiti or fly-posting.

Paragraph 2: power to require giving of name and address

Where an accredited civilian has reason to believe that a person has committed any of the fixed penalty offences mentioned in para 1 above, or that person has committed an offence which has caused injury, alarm or distress to any other person, or the loss of, or any damage to, any other person's property, the accredited civilian may require that person to give their name and address. However, certain conditions may be attached

---

12 This commentary has been reproduced from pp 67–68 of Jason-Lloyd, L, *Quasi-Policing* (London: Cavendish Publishing, 2003).

to the accreditation regarding some of these offences. Failure to provide a name and address is an offence punishable by a fine not exceeding level 3 on the standard scale (£1,000).

Paragraph 3: power to require name and address of a person acting in an anti-social manner

A police officer in uniform has powers under s 50 of the Police Reform Act to require the name and address of a person reasonably believed to have been acting, or who is acting, in an anti-social manner. This power may be given to accredited civilians, and failure to provide a name and address also attracts a maximum penalty of a level 3 fine.

Paragraph 4: alcohol consumption in designated public places

Accredited civilians have the powers of a constable under s 12 of the Criminal Justice and Police Act 2001 to direct persons in designated public places not to consume anything reasonably believed to be intoxicating liquor, and to confiscate the drink and dispose of the alcohol accordingly. Failure to comply without reasonable excuse is an offence, which must be communicated to the person, and if committed is punishable by a fine not exceeding level 2 on the standard scale (£500).

Paragraph 5: confiscation of alcohol

Accredited civilians have the powers of police officers under s 1 of the Confiscation of Alcohol (Young Persons) Act 1997. This reflects the same powers conferred upon designated CSOs in para 6 of Sched 4, Pt 1. It also echoes the absence of an arrest power in the event of non-compliance, unlike the police where they may arrest without warrant.

Paragraph 6: confiscation of tobacco, etc

This paragraph reflects the same powers conferred on designated CSOs under para 7 of Sched 4, Pt 1. This is the power under s 7(3) of the Children and Young Persons Act 1933, enabling a constable in uniform to confiscate and dispose of tobacco and cigarette papers from persons under 16 years old in public places.

Paragraph 7: abandoned vehicles

The provisions under this paragraph are almost identical to those relating to designated CSOs under para 10 of Sched 4, Pt 1. In this instance, accredited civilians have the power to remove abandoned vehicles or arrange their removal under s 99 of the Road Traffic Regulation Act 1984.

Paragraph 8: power to stop vehicle for testing

Accredited civilians have the power of a constable in uniform to stop a vehicle under s 67(3) of the Road Traffic Act 1988 in order for the vehicle to be tested. These provisions also reflect those applicable to designated CSOs under para 11 of Sched 4, Pt 1.

Paragraph 8A: power to stop cycles

Accredited civilians have identical powers under this paragraph to those held by designated CSOs under para 11A of Sched 4, Pt 1. This is the power of a police officer in uniform to stop a cycle under s 163(2) of the Road Traffic Act 1988 in respect of the offence of riding on a footway (s 72 of the Highway Act 1835).

Paragraph 9: power to control traffic for purposes of escorting a load of exceptional dimensions

This power is the same as that conferred upon designated CSOs under para 12 of Sched 4, Pt 1. It may also be applied anywhere in England and Wales provided the load is being escorted to or from the police area where the accredited civilians are based.

Offences against (and by) designated and accredited civilians

Section 46(1) of the Police Reform Act states that it is an offence to assault a designated or accredited civilian in the execution of his or her duty; this also applies to anyone who is assisting an officer. This offence is punishable by a maximum of six months' imprisonment,[13] or a fine not exceeding level 5 on the standard scale (£5,000), or both. Resisting or wilfully obstructing any of the above is an offence under s 46(2), and this is punishable by a term of imprisonment not exceeding one month,[14] or a fine not exceeding level 3 (£1,000), or both. Although no *specific* power of arrest has been given to any of the above if they are assaulted, it may be possible to use the powers under para 2(6)(b)(i) and (ii) of Sched 4 and para 2(3)(b)(i) and (ii) of Sched 5. In addition, they may be able to make a citizens' arrest for a common assault which is made an arrestable offence under s 10 of the Domestic Violence, Crime and Victims Act 2004 as mentioned below under the section headed 'Some operational concerns'.

Section 46(3) makes it an offence for anyone to impersonate a designated or accredited person, or suggest that they are such an officer, with intent to deceive. Furthermore, an offence may be committed *by* a designated or accredited civilian if that person, with intent to deceive, makes any statement or does any act that suggests he or she has powers that they do not possess. All the offences under s 46(3) are subject to a maximum sentence of six months' imprisonment[15] or a fine not exceeding level 5 on the standard scale, or both.

---

13 Due to be increased to 51 weeks by the Criminal Justice Act 2003.
14 The Criminal Justice Act 2003 is due to increase this to 51 weeks.
15 Due also to be increased to 51 weeks by the Criminal Justice Act 2003.

Some operational concerns[16]

Having read the previous chapters of this book, the discerning reader will have realised that there are a number of anomalies in the powers of those who are part of the extended police family. This is especially the case with CSOs and accredited civilians. Some of these anomalies will now be discussed.

Paragraph 2(6)(b)(i) and (ii) of Sched 4 and para 2(3)(b)(i) and (ii) of Sched 5 to the Police Reform Act state a very broad criteria under which designated CSOs and accredited civilians may require a person's name and address. This is in respect of an offence which appears to have caused injury, alarm or distress to any other person, or which involves any other person's property being lost or damaged. No precise list of these offences has been given under the Act, although potentially this could include quite a large number. As mentioned above, these include a range of offences in respect of non-fatal harms against the person, criminal damage, public order offences, and even fatal harms against the person, to name but a few. Many offences that come under this broad category fall under the heading of arrestable offences as detailed in Chapter 3. This includes common assault, which was recently made an arrestable offence by s 10 of the Domestic Violence, Crime and Victims Act 2004. As already discussed in that chapter, the power to make arrests for these offences, subject to certain operational constraints, also applies to ordinary citizens, hence the term 'citizens' arrest'. Although CSOs and accredited civilians have the power to demand a person's name and address when such crimes have been committed, it would be somewhat ridiculous to take such action if a particularly serious offence was committed. A more appropriate course of action would be to call for police assistance, but that is not always immediately forthcoming. So what can CSOs or accredited civilians do if immediate action is required, especially if it will be some time before the police arrive? An obvious answer would be to use their citizen's power of arrest if the offence was arrestable. However, it appears that situations such as this are not catered for as part of their training. According to the Home Office, this is because designated civilians are not intended to become involved in situations with members of the public which are overly confrontational. It is respectfully submitted that this approach is more idealistic than realistic. Members of the public would expect CSOs and accredited civilians to take positive action in the event of a serious crime being committed, and it would therefore be logical for them to resort to their powers as citizens to take the necessary steps to apprehend the suspect. However, would this mean that they will commit an offence under s 46(3)(c) of the Police Reform Act 2002, namely exceeding their powers as CSOs or accredited civilians? It would appear that their instincts, as well as their overriding duty in such circumstances, would be to use their citizen's powers under s 24 of and Sched 1A to PACE and s 3(1) of the Criminal Law Act 1967, as would many other citizens. This would certainly fall in line with public expectations, therefore why not give them appropriate awareness of the use of citizen's powers as part of their training?[16] Even if they were instructed to use these powers only in exceptional circumstances, this would fill a significant gap in their ability to protect the public.

---

16 See Jason-Lloyd, L, 'Community support officers: their powers and limitations' (2002) 166 JP 49, 7 December.

Paragraph 2(6)(b)(i) and (ii) of Sched 4 and para 2(3)(b)(i) and (ii) to the Police Reform Act 2002 are also rather anomalous by virtue of their wording. They refer to offences causing injury, alarm or distress to any *other* person, or loss or damage to any *other* person's property. Why should this apply only to third parties who are subjected to these offences and not to CSOs and accredited civilians as well? The restriction imposed by the words 'other person' means that the officers cannot act on their own accord if they are victims of such crimes (unless using their citizen's powers). Fortunately, this restriction may not preclude the intervention of another CSO or accredited civilian who is in close proximity at the time of the incident. In addition, if a member of the public is nearby and is affected by the conduct in question, that person may constitute the required third party and thus enable the CSO or accredited civilian to use his or her powers. It is, however, rather unfortunate that such an indirect route may have to be followed in order to enable such officers to act on their own accord when they are the victims of an assault or damage to their uniform, etc. There is also the common law power available to citizens to deal with or prevent a breach of the peace. As stated in Chapter 3, the exercise of this power can take more than one form in order to deal with or prevent violence or damage to property. This also does not appear to be on the training agenda for CSOs. If ordinary citizens may use this, and other powers, then why not those persons who are specifically employed to perform community protection duties?

With regard to para 2 of Sched 4, the power of designated CSOs to detain appears to be straightforward until one analyses the wider aspects of this procedure. Failure by a person to give a designated CSO a correct name and address, whether by itself or as part of the process in issuing a fixed penalty notice, constitutes an offence punishable by a maximum level 3 fine (£1,000). It also enables designated CSOs to detain that person for up to 30 minutes in order for the police to arrive. At the time of writing this book, six police forces have recently completed a two year pilot scheme regarding the limited detention power among their CSOs. This power is now available to designated CSOs in all the police areas where they have been deployed. However, the limitation of this power to 30 minutes has been criticised. Although para 4 states that reasonable force may be used to compel the detained person to remain with the CSO, what happens if the time expires before the police arrive? It appears that the CSO will have to let that person free, although there have been suggestions that he or she may be asked again for their correct name and address, and detained for up to a further 30 minutes if that requirement is not met. This is one of many points that requires clarification in the future. Further grey areas are disclosed when considering whether this detention power is actually an arrest. This was the subject of extensive debate in Parliament, although the matter remains unclear.[17] There is no mention of the need for a caution to be given to the detained person, nor is a designated CSO allowed to search that person. The absence of a power to do the latter is potentially dangerous to CSOs as detained persons may be carrying weapons.[18] Anyone who makes off whilst being detained commits an offence punishable by a maximum level 3 fine.

---

17   See for instance, *Hansard*, House of Commons, Standing Committee A, 20 June 2002, col 253 and *Hansard*, House of Lords, 7 March 2002, col 445.

18   Consideration is now being given to allow CSOs to search those whom they detain in the Serious Organised Crime and Police Bill (see also the Government White Paper *Policing: Modernising Police Powers to Meet Community Needs* (Home Office, 2004)).

Curiously, if a CSO exercised his or her citizen's power of arrest in appropriate cases, the 30 minute time constraint would not apply. The only duty in this context would be to deliver the arrested person into the custody of a police officer as soon as possible. It is interesting to note that a power of detention rather than a power of arrest is not unique to designated CSOs. For instance, the police have a power to detain persons for up to four hours (extendable to six hours) under s 21A of the Football Spectators Act 1989 in order to ascertain whether that person is subject to a football banning order; and under paras 2–6 of Sched 7 to the Terrorism Act 2000, an examining officer (namely a police, immigration or customs officer) may detain and question a person for up to nine hours, to determine if he or she is a terrorist.

As an alternative to detaining a person, a CSO may give the recalcitrant individual the option to accompany the officer to a police station. Under para 4, reasonable force may be used to ensure that the person remains with the CSO when going to a police station and it is an offence to make off before reaching that destination.[19] However, under the current rules, CSOs do not have the power to arrest a person who makes off, irrespective of whether he or she was being detained or accompanying the officer to a police station. Therefore, how can this law be enforced? Escape from lawful custody is a common law offence for which the maximum penalty is open-ended; therefore, this is an arrestable offence. However, whilst this gives ordinary citizens a power of arrest, are CSOs made aware of this during their training? This would seem doubtful. In any event, the practice of accompanying an officer to a police station by simply walking there is one that many believe had ceased a long time ago. As time has progressed, arrested suspects have generally proved to be less co-operative when being detained, and vehicular assistance is the norm. This is not only necessary for safety reasons, but one also has to consider such things as weather conditions and the distance to the nearest police station. There may even be human rights implications where a person under legal restraint in this respect may be virtually marched in full view of the public when being taken to a police station by a CSO.

With regard to accredited civilians, they have no powers of detention; nor may they use reasonable force in the exercise of any of their powers and duties. This places them in an even greyer area than CSOs. Despite their powers to require names and addresses and to issue penalty notices to persons, these powers are likely to have little impact if those persons do not co-operate. Where accredited civilians and CSOs are assaulted, resisted or wilfully obstructed, despite the criminal sanctions attached to these offences under s 46(1) of the Police Reform Act 2002, no powers of arrest have been given to them in order to bring the culprits before the courts. In terms of physical protection, CSOs have the option to wear protective vests, but are not issued with batons, handcuffs or incapacitant sprays such as CS gas.

With regard to the other designated civilians, namely investigating officers, detention officers and escort officers, these too may possibly encounter grey areas and gaps in their powers. However, they are not generally as visible as CSOs in terms of their public profile, and in many cases police assistance will often be at hand. Other grey areas are identifiable regarding the powers held by those within the extended police family, but hopefully this discussion will suffice in giving an insight into some potential legal and operational problems. The extent to which these anomalies are

19   Punishable by a maximum level 3 fine.

likely to impede the functions of all classes of civilians within the extended police family remains to be seen. Whatever the outcome, it seems unlikely that policing will ever revert to being the sole dominion of those who hold the office of constable. As one commentator has stated:

> A further feature of the Police Reform Act 2002 lies in what has been called the 'extended police family'. Given the nature of the roles that the legislation creates, it is perhaps more accurate to refer ... to an extended *policing* family as some of the people endowed with powers of enforcement and regulation under the Act will not be employed by the police at all, though they will have policing responsibilities.[20]

However, it is to be hoped that the structure of policing in this country will not be any more complex and fragmented than it already is, although an alternative has been suggested.[21] As far as police powers are concerned, the Government has proposed certain changes that it states are intended to clarify, simplify and modernise police powers. These will be briefly discussed in Chapter 9.

---

20 Sampson, F, *Blackstone's Police Manual Vol 4: General Police Duties* (Oxford: OUP, 2005).
21 See Jason-Lloyd, L, 'Police reform – a better way?' (2003) 167 JP 43, 25 October.

CHAPTER 8

POLICING AND THE HUMAN RIGHTS ACT 1998

INTRODUCTION

On 2 October 2000, the Human Rights Act 1998 came into force. In effect, this Act incorporates the European Convention on Human Rights[1] into our own domestic law and, for the first time, enables those rights to be directly enforceable in the courts of the UK. It is not the purpose of this chapter to provide a complete coverage of the entire issue of the Convention or every aspect of the 1998 Act. Instead, the ongoing effects of the Human Rights Act on some of the key policing issues covered in this book will be focused on. Comprehensive reading is already available on the broader aspects of the Convention and the 1998 Act, and some of these are referred to in the relevant footnotes where appropriate. Some of the contents of this chapter are speculative as only time will disclose the exact path that the 1998 Act will eventually take policing and, indeed, other criminal justice institutions into the future. In this context, it was rightly stated prior to the implementation of the Human Rights Act that: '... the effect of the Convention in domestic law after the Human Rights Act 1998 will depend on the inventiveness of lawyers and the attitude of the judiciary.'[2] A number of cases concerning the effects of the 1998 Act have already been explained in previous chapters where appropriate. The purpose of this chapter is to provide a wider perspective on this increasingly important aspect of the law, and the way it has affected policing in this country, as well as how it may determine its future direction.

THE HUMAN RIGHTS ACT 1998

This statute was enacted on 9 November 1998 and its long title states that it is:

> An Act to give further effect to rights and freedoms guaranteed under the European Convention on Human Rights; to make provision with respect to holders of certain judicial offices who become judges of the European Court of Human Rights and for connected purposes.

The main effects of the 1998 Act are threefold. First, when deciding cases before them, all courts and tribunals are now required to take into account the Convention, as well as the decisions made by its institutions. These include the European Court of Human Rights, the Council of Europe and, when it existed, the European Commission of Human Rights. Secondly, our national courts should read, if at all possible, both primary and secondary legislation in a manner which is compatible with the Convention. This may enable our national courts in certain instances to even override secondary legislation or binding decisions of higher courts for the purposes of protecting human rights under the Convention (although the High Court and above

---

1   The full title is 'The European Convention on Human Rights and Fundamental Freedoms' but, for the sake of brevity, it will be referred to as 'the Convention'.

2   Wadham, J and Mountfield, H, *Blackstone's Guide to the Human Rights Act 1998* (London: Blackstone, 1999).

cannot override primary legislation but, under the 1998 Act, may notify the Government of any incompatibility with the view to the relevant statute being amended). Thirdly, public authorities are under a duty to act in accordance with the Convention and failure to do so could lead to civil action being taken against them. The mechanisms within the 1998 Act, however, fall short of creating a special constitutional court or human rights commission, although it has been stated that none of these possibilities have been completely ruled out.[3]

HUMAN RIGHTS UNDER THE CONVENTION

The Convention itself is a document formulated by the Council of Europe in the wake of the devastation caused by the Second World War and the atrocities arising from years of fascist tyranny in Europe. Its purpose then, as now, was to proclaim a series of universal human rights which militate against a repetition of those events which had caused such immeasurable suffering. Although the UK ratified the Convention in 1951, it was not until 1966 that this country allowed its own citizens to take action in appropriate cases. Originally, petitions were confined to challenges by States against other States regarding alleged violations under the Convention.

The statements of individual human rights under the Convention are contained within its 'Articles', augmented by a number of 'Protocols', which have been added since its formulation. Towards the end of 1998, no fewer than 40 States had signed the Convention and this necessitated substantial reforms of its institutions, including the European Court of Human Rights in Strasbourg, which now deals with all cases alleging violations of the Convention. Previously, an institution known as the European *Commission* of Human Rights played a major part in dealing with petitions originally made but, since November 1998, this body no longer exists for the purposes of considering the admissibility of applications made after that date. Under the new Protocol 11, this function is now being performed by sections of the European Court of Human Rights.

Schedule 1 to the 1998 Act contains the Articles and Protocols which have been adopted within UK law. Those relevant to the main policing issues covered in this book will now be discussed.

Article 2 of the European Convention on Human Rights covers the right to life and reads as follows:

1   Everyone's right to life shall be protected by law. No one shall be deprived of his life, save in the execution of a sentence of a court following his conviction of a crime for which the penalty is provided by law.

2   Deprivation of life shall not be regarded as inflicted in contravention of this article when it results from the use of force which is no more than absolutely necessary:

   (a) in defence of any person from unlawful violence;

   (b) in order to effect a lawful arrest or to prevent the escape of a person lawfully detained;

   (c) in action lawfully taken for the purpose of quelling a riot or insurrection.

---

3   Ashcroft, P, Barrie, F, Bazell, C, Damazer, A, Powell, R, Tranter, G and Gibson, B, *Human Rights and the Courts: Bringing Justice Home* (Winchester: Waterside, 1999).

For general purposes, Article 2 should be read in conjunction with the Sixth Protocol, which is one of those Protocols adopted by the UK under the 1998 Act and which reads as follows:

Abolition of the death penalty

The death penalty shall be abolished. No one shall be condemned to such penalty or executed.

Death penalty in time of war

A State may make provision in its law for the death penalty in respect of acts committed in time of war or of imminent threat of war; such penalty shall be applied only in the instances laid down in the law and in accordance with its provisions. The State shall communicate to the Secretary General of the Council of Europe the relevant provisions of that law.

On 30 September 1998, s 36 of the Crime and Disorder Act 1998 abolished the sentence of death for the two last remaining civilian offences which, technically at least, attracted the death penalty. These are treason and piracy with violence. However, certain offences committed under military law in times of war, such as mutiny and assisting the enemy, still attract capital punishment. The passing of these provisions under our domestic law has, *inter alia*, enabled the UK to ratify the Sixth Protocol to the Convention.

Whilst the Sixth Protocol has no direct relevance to the exercise of police powers, Art 2 of the Convention does have implications where the use of force falls into the realms of lethal force. Where, particularly, the deliberate use of lethal force is used, the European Court of Human Rights,[4] in *McCann v UK* (1995),[5] has stated that it will subject such actions to the 'most careful scrutiny'. It stated earlier that the use of such force must be 'strictly proportionate' when defending any person from unlawful violence or in order to effect a lawful arrest or to prevent a lawfully detained person from escaping, or to quell a riot or insurrection (Art 2(2)(a), (b) and (c)).[6] The Court went on to say that it will consider 'not only the actions of the organs of the State who actually administer the force, but also the surrounding circumstances, including such matters as the planning and control of the actions under examination'.[7] However, in *Andronicou and Constantinou v Cyprus* (1997), it was held that there was no violation of Art 2(2) where the police had shot dead a gunman and his hostage, believing that the former was more heavily armed than he was. The Court paid particular attention to the issue of 'planning and control', which featured prominently in *McCann v UK*, and concluded that the force used by the police was 'strictly proportionate' in relation to the situation, since they had employed actions which minimised the risk to both

---

4   Henceforward, this will be referred to simply as 'the Court'.

5   This case was featured in a well known investigatory TV programme entitled 'Death on the Rock', which was so named because its subject was the fatal shooting of three members of the Provisional IRA by soldiers from the Special Air Service in Gibraltar. By a majority of 10 to nine, the Court held that there had been a violation of Art 2.

6   Article 2(2)(a) does not apply to the defence of property (see Baker, C, *Human Rights Act 1998: A Practitioner's Guide* (London: Sweet & Maxwell, 1998)).

7   When commenting on the possible effects of the Human Rights Act, Lord Lester stated: 'I have no doubt that if the *McCann* case could have been dealt with by our own courts, using the criteria of the Convention, it might well have led to a different outcome in Strasbourg' (cited in Cheney, D, Dickson, L, Skilbeck, R, Uglow, S and Fitzpatrick, J, *Criminal Justice and the Human Rights Act 1998* (2nd edn, Bristol: Jordans, 2001)).

parties. The Court stated that the police had good reason to believe that the gunman was heavily armed, notwithstanding that they were mistaken, although some concern was expressed regarding the deployment of machine guns in a confined area. Despite regrets expressed by the Court regarding the extent of the fire power used, the decision that there was no breach was carried by five votes to four. The term 'absolutely necessary', used in Art 2(2) in relation to the use of lethal force, is extremely important in testing whether or not such action falls under the three main exceptions mentioned above, which fall under the general description of: '... curbing violence or the control of prisoners or criminals – generally, maintaining law and order.'[8] In *Stewart v UK* (1984), a teenager was accidentally killed by a plastic baton round fired into a crowd of rioters by security forces. The Commission stated that the force used was 'strictly proportionate to the achievement of the permitted purpose' and therefore was 'absolutely necessary'; as such, Art 2 had not been violated. The Commission went on to state, *inter alia*, that due regard must be paid to all the relevant circumstances, which includes the risk to life and limb and the aim which is being pursued. The further point was made that these provisions also apply to lethal force where the actual killing was not intended.

In view of the increasing level of violence faced by the police in this country, and especially where firearms are used in the commission of crime, the police service has re-examined its procedures regarding the use of firearms in particular, in order to be doubly sure that the 'planning and control' element, as stated in *McCann v UK*, is complied with, since it was this element that made the UK liable. At present, s 3 of the Criminal Law Act 1967 is relied upon, which allows the use of lethal force based on the honestly held belief of the person using it; in other words, the 'reasonableness' of such action is tested subjectively:

> The test in Article 2 is different and imposes a higher standard. The standard in the Convention is whether the use of the force was 'absolutely necessary'. On the basis of that test, the determination of whether the force used was reasonable must be objectively assessed by deciding whether the force used was disproportionate to the apparent threat that it was intended to prevent.[9]

According to one commentator, it has been suggested that: '... the application of Art 2 in *Andronicou* suggests that even in respect of trained law enforcement officers, some indulgence should be granted to "heat of the moment" reactions, along the lines of *Palmer v R* (1971).'[10] Reference to the latter case is particularly important in view of the speech made by Lord Morris of Borth-Y-Gest, in which he said:

> If there has been an attack so that defence is reasonably necessary, it will be recognised that a person defending himself cannot weigh to a nicety the exact measure of his necessary defensive action. If a jury thought that, in a moment of unexpected anguish, a person attacked had only done what he honestly and instinctively thought was necessary, that would be most potent evidence that only reasonable defensive action had been taken.

---

8   *Op cit*, Wadham and Mountfield, fn 2.
9   *Op cit*, Wadham and Mountfield, fn 2.
10 [1998] Crim LR 825.

Article 3 of the Convention may also be relevant regarding any future challenges to the legitimacy of certain police powers. Under the heading of 'Prohibition of torture', it goes on to provide: 'No one shall be subjected to torture or to inhuman or degrading treatment or punishment.' Although torture can be clearly disregarded from the ambit of police activities in this country,[11] inhuman and degrading treatment are matters closely linked with other relevant Articles under the Convention, particularly Art 5 (see below) and cover, *inter alia*, generally oppressive conduct. As discussed earlier in this book, there are many safeguards designed to prevent oppressive conduct and also to alleviate unnecessary embarrassment on the part of suspects and others whose liberty has been interfered with in the exercise of police powers and duties. The Codes of Practice, in their entirety, contain provisions which are designed to minimise these intrusions on the liberty of citizens, whether in the course of temporary detention (stop and search), making arrests or the detention of persons in police custody. In short, the Codes endeavour, as much as possible, to preserve the dignity of those whose personal liberties have been lawfully impeded for any of these purposes. Indeed, as time has progressed, the Codes appear to have been increasingly mindful of these necessities.

In *McFeeley v UK* (1980), it was held that intimate searches were not sufficiently humiliating so as to constitute a violation of Art 3 (neither was the wearing of a prison uniform) and, with reference to the searching of suspects in general, it has been stated that:

> The right to bodily integrity and, generally, the freedom against compulsory physical interference is protected by the right to privacy in Article 8, as well as the guarantees against degrading and inhuman treatment under Article 3 ... There is a need for a balance to be drawn between physical interference with the person by State agents for legitimate purposes, such as the gathering of evidence or prevention of crime, and the individual's interest in preserving bodily integrity. *In England, that balance is present in the legislation and probably conforms to Convention requirements.*[12]

With regard to the exercise of police stop and search powers, para 3.1 of Code of Practice A makes the point that: 'Every reasonable effort must be made to minimise the embarrassment that a person being searched may experience.' There then follows a series of provisions, already discussed in previous chapters, which are designed to achieve this end and to avoid unnecessary inconvenience and antagonism. The latter is reinforced under Notes for Guidance 10–14 to Code A, regarding the authorisations applicable to stop and search in order to prevent serious violence and acts of terrorism. In both instances, authorising officers are urged to set the minimum time and geographical parameters in order to avoid the mistrust of the police by the community as a whole (Notes for Guidance 12 and 13). PACE itself makes its own contribution to preventing treatment that may be construed as degrading by placing restrictions on the extent of removal of any clothing in public. Section 2 confines this to no more than the removal of an outer coat, jacket or gloves. The avoidance of degrading treatment is also implicit in s 30(1)(b) of PACE, which provides that an arrested person should be taken to a police station as soon as practicable after an arrest (subject to 'street bail'),

---

11   See *Selmouni v France* (2000), where severe beatings in a police cell were held to amount to torture.

12   *Op cit*, Cheney *et al*, fn 7 (emphasis added).

although appearing in handcuffs in public would not constitute degrading treatment.[13] Code B also contains safeguards which, it is submitted, should fall within the minimum requirements laid down by the Convention. Paragraph 6.10, for instance, requires that any police search operation should cause no more disturbance than necessary.

Code C contains an abundance of safeguards against inhuman and degrading treatment, some of which overlap with the provisions under Art 5 of the Convention, for instance, the requirement under para 1.1, which states that all persons held in police custody must be dealt with and released without delay. Code C also provides that detained persons are entitled to adequate food and drink, toilet and washing facilities, clothing and, where necessary, medical attention, as well as exercise where possible. Police cells must meet certain minimum standards of physical comfort and this includes the provision of bedding, which must also be of a reasonable standard. There is also the right not to be held incommunicado, unless the criminal investigation or persons involved could be endangered were contact to be made with persons outside the police station. In any event, this only applies to serious arrestable offences.

The many provisions under Codes C and D designed to protect special groups have also been discussed in previous chapters. The avoidance of inhuman or degrading treatment being inflicted on particularly vulnerable persons, such as those who are mentally disordered or otherwise mentally vulnerable, is made very positively under the relevant Codes of Practice. This includes provision for the appropriate adult in cases where such persons are detained by the police, which also extends to other vulnerable suspects, including juveniles.

Article 5 of the Convention, headed 'Right to liberty and security', reads as follows:

1   Everyone has the right to liberty and security of person. No one shall be deprived of his liberty, save in the following cases and in accordance with a procedure prescribed by law:

    (a) the lawful detention of a person after conviction by a competent court;

    (b) the lawful arrest or detention of a person for non-compliance with the lawful order of a court or in order to secure the fulfilment of any obligation prescribed by law;

    (c) the lawful arrest or detention of a person effected for the purpose of bringing him before the competent legal authority on reasonable suspicion of having committed an offence or when it is reasonably considered necessary to prevent his committing an offence or fleeing after having done so;

    (d) the detention of a minor by lawful order for the purpose of educational supervision or his lawful detention for the purpose of bringing him before the competent legal authority;

    (e) the lawful detention of persons for the prevention of the spreading of infectious diseases, of persons of unsound mind, alcoholics or drug addicts or vagrants;

    (f) the lawful arrest or detention of a person to prevent his effecting an unauthorised entry into the country or of a person against whom action is being taken with a view to deportation or extradition.

2   Everyone who is arrested shall be informed promptly, in a language which he understands, of the reasons for his arrest and of any charge against him.

---

13 *Op cit*, Cheney *et al*, fn 7.

3   Everyone arrested or detained in accordance with the provisions of paragraph 1(c) of this Article shall be brought promptly before a judge or other officer authorised by law to exercise judicial power and shall be entitled to trial within reasonable time or to release pending trial. Release may be conditioned by guarantees to appear for trial.

4   Everyone who is deprived of his liberty by arrest or detention shall be entitled to take proceedings by which the lawfulness of his detention shall be decided speedily by a court and his release ordered if the detention is not lawful.

5   Everyone who has been the victim of arrest or detention in contravention of the provisions of this Article shall have an enforceable right to compensation.

Arrest procedures under PACE and other statutes appear to comply with Art 5, since they usually require reasonable suspicion, but the position is less certain in respect of the common law power to arrest for a breach of the peace. In *Steel v UK* (1998), it was held that whilst the definition of a breach of the peace did not contravene Art 5, an arrest for this purpose may violate it if the arrest is disproportionate to the anticipated risk and affects an individual's right to freedom of expression under Art 10 (see also *McLeod v UK* (1999), below).

Some concern has been expressed regarding the issue of police stop and search powers which involve the temporary detention of suspects. It has been suggested that this form of temporary detention may fall within the ambit of Art 5(1)(b), where detention is permitted: '... in order to secure the fulfilment of any obligation prescribed by law.'[14] However, further concern has been expressed as to whether s 60 of the Criminal Justice and Public Order Act 1994 (see Chapter 2) complies with Art 5, although this argument is based on the interpretation of Art 5(1)(c), which makes the essential requirement for reasonable suspicion.[15] The relevance of Art 3 to police powers of stop and search with regard to the conduct of such procedures has already been noted above.

With regard to Art 6, its relevance to the exercise of police powers (the right to a fair trial) is largely confined to Art 6(3)(b) and (c), which provides that everyone charged with a criminal offence has the right 'to have adequate time and facilities for the preparation of his defence' and 'to defend himself in person or through legal assistance of his own choosing or, if he has not sufficient means to pay for legal assistance, to be given it free when the interests of justice so require'. As discussed earlier in this book, there are many safeguards which are designed to ensure adequate provision for legal representation at police stations. A potential difficulty may lie in justifying the grounds under which this can be delayed against the decision in *Bonzi v Switzerland* (1978), where it was stated that access to legal advice is an essential part of a person's defence.

Article 8 covers the right to respect for private and family life and states that:

1   Everyone has the right to respect for his private and family life, his home and his correspondence.

---

14   *Op cit*, Cheney *et al*, fn 7.
15   *Op cit*, Ashcroft *et al*, fn 3.

2   There shall be no interference by a public authority with the exercise of this right, except such as is in accordance with the law and is necessary in a democratic society in the interests of national security, public safety or the economic well being of the country, for the prevention of disorder or crime, for the protection of health or morals or for the protection of the rights and freedoms of others.

Whilst it has been stated that 'in England, the power to search premises under Pt II of PACE 1984 probably conforms to Convention requirements',[16] further opinion offers the following caveat in relation to search warrants:

... an obvious case where this Article may affect the work of magistrates is in relation to applications for search warrants. The relevant UK law (principally contained in the PACE 1984) contains safeguards that should comply with Article 8. However, magistrates will need to continue to be meticulous when dealing with such applications. If valid reasons do not exist or are not properly recorded, challenges under the Convention might be hard to defend.[17]

In *McLeod v UK*, which was discussed in Chapter 3, the Court held that Art 8 had been violated where police officers entered the applicant's home without reasonable grounds to apprehend a breach of the peace.

Other police activities may also be subject to challenge under Art 8. For instance, Pt III of the Police Act 1997 governs the procedures to be adopted regarding covert surveillance operations. Such activities could be challenged on the grounds that judicial scrutiny does not always occur prior to such action. In *R v Khan* (1995), police officers placed a listening device in premises occupied by the defendant, who was suspected of importing heroin. During his trial for this offence, it was submitted that the incriminating conversation recorded on tape as a result of police 'bugging' the premises should be ruled inadmissible, since this had been obtained as a result of trespass and criminal damage. Whilst admitting the lack of statutory guidance governing police action in this respect, the trial judge proceeded to admit this evidence. The Court of Appeal upheld this decision, but also commented on the lack of statutory regulation regarding this form of covert surveillance by the police. This view was later upheld by the House of Lords. This case then reached the European Court of Human Rights (*Khan v UK* (2000)), where it was alleged that there had been infringements of Art 6 (the right to a fair trial), Art 8 (right to respect for private and family life) and Art 13 (the right to an effective remedy). The Court ruled that there had been no violation of Art 6 due to the applicant having had ample opportunity to challenge the use of the evidence in all the domestic courts, and he had already done so. On the issue of Art 8, there was a violation as the covert surveillance was unlawful due to the absence of statutory authority to conduct it. In addition, there had been a violation of Art 13 due to a lack of sufficient independence in the police complaints system (as mentioned in Chapter 1).

On the issue of telephone tapping, in *Huvig v France* (1990) and *Kruslin v France* (1990), violations against Art 8 were held to have occurred due to a number of procedural deficiencies which constituted insufficient safeguards against possible abuse. These included failure to set a time limit on the tapping operation or to specify the offence likely to justify such action, or to specify any measures regarding the

---

16   *Op cit*, Cheney *et al*, fn 7.
17   *Op cit*, Ashcroft *et al*, fn 3.

destruction of the recordings. The scope of the interception of communications by law enforcement bodies in this country has been expanded by the Regulation of Investigatory Powers Act 2000. Among other caveats, one commentator had this to say regarding this statute in relation to the Human Rights Act 1998:

> Since the definition of intrusive surveillance confines it to covert surveillance of residential premises or private vehicles, the Bill is likely to fall foul of Article 8, since the ECHR has, in a number of cases, extended the notion of private life beyond the home. Furthermore, wiring up an informant or undercover officer to obtain information from a suspect in their own home is treated as directed surveillance, requiring only internal authorisation, which, again, may well not satisfy Convention requirements.[18]

Conclusion

The Human Rights Act 1998 has created much challenge and subsequent controversy throughout the entire panoply of the criminal justice system, and it is hoped that the continuing reforms occurring in the wake of its implementation will significantly improve our quality of justice. As far as the police are concerned, continuing changes in their powers, duties and procedures must be commensurate with this aim, and it is hoped that future reforms will assist in maintaining their credibility in order to preserve the cherished concept of policing by consent. Whatever future changes are in store for them, it is very important that these amount to positive and constructive measures, without constituting unnecessary obstacles in their increasingly difficult and important tasks in society. But, as always, much depends not only on new rules in dealing with suspects or other persons dealt with by the police, but, equally, on the manner in which individual police officers exercise their powers and duties in the future. The tasks ahead of them will continue to be challenging indeed.

18 Cape, E, 'Regulating police surveillance' (2000) 150 NLJ 452.

CHAPTER 9

POLICE POWERS IN THE FUTURE?

Predicting the future direction of police powers is a daunting task to say the least. Much depends upon the continuing effects of the Human Rights Act 1998, the general political climate, and the views of the judges in specific cases brought before them. Other influences also account for changes in police powers such as those exerted by various pressure and interest groups, and the work of prominent academics, to name but a few. As this book is being compiled, major changes are being considered regarding the overall structure of policing and police powers. With regard to the latter, the Consultation Document *Policing: Modernising Police Powers to Meet Community Needs*[1] proposes many significant changes in the way in which police powers are effected. Many of these are very controversial and this has already attracted extensive comment.[2] On the other hand, certain aspects of police powers are in need of streamlining and rationalisation, as many readers of this book may readily testify! The Consultation Paper asserts that the police must have the powers needed to deal effectively and proportionately with crime and disorder whilst maintaining 'the crucial balance between the powers of the police and the rights of the individual'. According to the Paper, there are a number of specific police powers which may need to be extended as well as those requiring 'clarification, simplification and modernisation'. A full summary of these powers is provided under s 8 of this Paper, which is reproduced as follows:

Section 8   Summary

Section 2   Arrest – concept of seriousness

- Redefine the framework of arrest powers so that a police officer can arrest for any offence subject to the necessity test as set out at paragraph 2.6 above.

- Revise the seriousness criterion and the concepts of the 'arrestable' and 'serious arrestable offence'.

- Introduce a new requirement for an offence to be triable either way or on indictment before the 'trigger' powers following arrest can be applied.

- Set clear criteria for the exercise of a citizen's power of arrest.

- Abolish the capacity to arrest in relation to a breach of the peace.

Section 3   Search warrants – raising capacity

- Search warrants authorising any premises occupied or controlled or accessible by a named individual.

- Warrant focusing on the person and his or her whereabouts rather than on a specific single address.

- The officer applying to the court would have to satisfy the court that a 'multi-premises' warrant was necessary.

---

1   Home Office, August 2004.
2   See, for example, Jason-Lloyd, L, 'Modernising police powers – a response' (2004) 168 JP 42, 16 October.

- The lifetime of the warrant would be a matter for the court based on the application setting out the period considered necessary and relevant.
- The court would be required to sanction multiple use of the warrant within the agreed timeframe.
- Accessing telephone and electronic communication in application for and granting of warrants.

Section 4   Workforce modernisation

- Powers to direct traffic – in response to specified situations rather than routinely.
- Custody area – extending key involvement around custody and identification roles.
- Begging – providing CSOs and accredited persons with new powers to issue a warning.
- Enforcing byelaws – subject to central or local determination.
- Searching the person for weapons and dangerous articles – a new power subject to suitable training and procedures.
- Remove the absolute requirement for civilian staff to wear a uniform.
- Raising CSOs' enforcement powers for certain licensing offences.
- Working with stakeholders on police charging for services.
- Designate chief officers as a 'corporation sole' for the purposes of health and safety legislation.

Section 5   Increasing prevention and detection powers

Drug-related crime

- Testing people on arrest (rather than charge) for certain 'trigger' offences.
- Enhancing the ability to encourage drug-misusing offenders leaving custody to undergo appropriate drug treatment.
- Court to draw inferences from refusal to submit to a search.
- Power to apply to the courts for extended detention after charge.

Road/driver offences

- Create a new offence of using or keeping an incorrectly registered vehicle.
- Confer on the Secretary of State a power to fund ANPR through fixed penalty generated revenue.
- provide civilian staff access to PNC data for supporting roadside enquiries.

Misuse of fireworks

- Create a power of stop, search, seizure and confiscation in relation to:
  — Possession of fireworks by a person under 18 in a public place;
  — Category IV fireworks unless authorised.

Protests outside homes

- Create a new offence of harassment, causing alarm or distress to complement existing powers under the Criminal Justice and Police Act 2001.
- Extend the period to three months for a person subject to a direction on returning to premises.

- Extend the Protection from Harassment Act 1997 to cover harassment of two or more people who are connected, such as employees of the same company, even if each individual is harassed on only one occasion.

Dealing with protests outside Parliament

- Ensure that legislation to deal with demonstrations outside Parliament is effective and introduce new legislation if necessary.

Section 6   Identification

- Power to take fingerprints of a suspect elsewhere other than a police station for the purpose of confirming the identity of a suspect.
- Taking of footwear impressions with or without the suspect's consent.
- Power to take a visual image of an arrested person elsewhere other than a police station.
- Power of retention of moving images.
- Clarify the ability to take a penile swab with consent.
- Establish a missing persons database for the purposes of identification only.
- Power to use fingerprints/DNA taken covertly for speculative searches to confirm or disprove a person's involvement in an offence.

Section 7   Forfeiture of electronic devices used to store or handle indecent photographs of children

- Removing indecent photographs of children from circulation.
- Need for increased powers on forfeiture.
- Maintaining co-operation from people and organisations.

Many of the above proposals have now been included in the Serious Organised Crime and Police Bill. The following example regarding powers of arrest will perhaps give a general 'flavour' of what is to come:

Serious Organised Crime and Police Bill

Part 3

POLICE POWERS ETC

Powers of arrest

101 Powers of arrest

(1) For section 24 of PACE (arrest without warrant for arrestable offences) substitute–

'24 Arrest without warrant: constables

(1) A constable may arrest without a warrant–

    (a) anyone who is about to commit an offence;

    (b) anyone who is in the act of committing an offence;

    (c) anyone whom he has reasonable grounds for suspecting to be about to commit an offence;

    (d) anyone whom he has reasonable grounds for suspecting to be committing an offence.

(2) If a constable has reasonable grounds for suspecting that an offence has been committed, he may arrest without a warrant anyone whom he has reasonable grounds to suspect of being guilty of it.

(3) If an offence has been committed, a constable may arrest without a warrant–

    (a) anyone who is guilty of the offence;

    (b) anyone whom he has reasonable grounds for suspecting to be guilty of it.

(4) But the power of summary arrest conferred by subsection (1), (2), or (3) is exercisable only if the constable has reasonable grounds for believing that for any of the reasons mentioned in subsection (5) it is necessary to arrest the person in question.

(5) The reasons are–

    (a) to enable the name of the person in question to be ascertained (in the case where the constable does not know, and cannot readily ascertain, the person's name, or has reasonable grounds for doubting whether a name given by the person as his name is his real name);

    (b) correspondingly as regards the person's address;

    (c) to prevent the person in question–

        (i) causing physical injury to himself or any other person;

        (ii) suffering physical injury;

        (iii) causing loss of or damage to property;

        (iv) committing an offence against public decency (subject to subsection (6)); or

        (v) causing an unlawful obstruction of the highway;

    (d) to protect a child or other vulnerable person from the person in question;

    (e) to allow the prompt and effective investigation of the offence or of the conduct of the person in question;

    (f) to prevent any prosecution for the offence from being hindered by the disappearance of the person in question.

(6) Subsection (5)(c)(iv) applies only where members of the public going about their normal business cannot reasonably be expected to avoid the person in question.

24A Arrest without warrant; other persons

(1) A person other than a constable may arrest without a warrant–

    (a) anyone who is in the act of committing an offence;

    (b) anyone whom he has reasonable grounds for suspecting to be committing an offence.

(2) Where an offence has been committed, a person other than a constable may arrest without a warrant–

    (a) anyone who is guilty of the offence;

    (b) anyone whom he has reasonable grounds for suspecting to be guilty of it.

(3) But the power of arrest conferred by subsection (1) or (2) is exercisable only if–

    (a) the person making the arrest has reasonable grounds for believing that for any of the reasons mentioned in subsection (4) it is necessary to arrest the person; and

    (b) it appears to the person making the arrest that it is not reasonably practicable for a constable to make it instead.

(4) The reasons are to prevent the person in question–

    (a) causing physical injury to himself or any other person;

    (b) suffering physical injury;

    (c) causing loss of or damage to property; or

    (d) making off before a constable can assume responsibility for him.'

(2) Section 25 of PACE (general arrest conditions) shall cease to have effect.

(3) In section 66 of PACE (codes of practice), in subsection (1)(a) –

    (i) omit 'or' at the end of sub-paragraph (i),

    (ii) at the end of sub-paragraph (ii) insert 'or (iii) to arrest a person'.

(4) Any rule of common law conferring power to arrest a person without a warrant is abolished.

(5) The sections 24 and 24A of PACE substituted by subsection (1) are to have effect in relation to any offence whenever committed.

The above extract from the Serious Organised Crime and Police Bill contains a number of significant changes to police arrest powers. It also enhances the concept of a citizen's arrest power, notwithstanding the abolition of the common law power to arrest for a breach of the peace. Interestingly, it is intended that there will be a PACE code of practice regarding arrests. Whilst other police powers have been covered under the codes, the making of arrests has always been excluded. Now it seems that this omission will be remedied in the not too distant future. As mentioned above, Pt 3 is just one aspect of the Bill that is intended to streamline police powers as well as create the Serious Organised Crime Agency.

Other sources of police powers under PACE that are earmarked for change include: s 1 (powers of constables to stop and search); s 8 (power to authorise entry and search of premises); s 15 (search warrants-safeguards); s 16 (execution of warrants); s 36 (custody officers at police stations); s 39 (responsibilities in relation to persons detained); s 61 (fingerprinting); s 63A (fingerprints and samples: supplementary provisions); s 64 (destruction of fingerprints and samples); s 64A (photographing of suspects, etc); s 65 (fingerprints and samples – supplementary); Sched 1 (special procedure), as well as important changes under the Police Reform Act 2002 regarding the use of civilians.

In addition to the above changes, the Drugs Bill was introduced in Parliament just before Christmas 2004. A large proportion of this Bill will directly affect police powers that include the following examples: an amendment to s 55 of PACE (intimate searches) requiring a suspect's consent before a drugs only intimate search is carried out; the insertion of a new s 55A into PACE enabling the police to authorise an X-ray and/or ultrasound scan of persons suspected of swallowing Class A controlled drugs; an amendment to s 152 of the Criminal Justice Act 1988 enabling the extension of police detention powers of suspected drug offenders; the amendment of s 63B of PACE permitting 18 year olds and over to be tested on arrest for specified Class A drugs, and the introduction of a discretionary power to require persons tested positive for specified Class A drugs to attend assessments of their drug misuse. It appears that some of these provisions will be piloted or introduced piecemeal before national implementation.

At the time of writing, the Serious Organised Crime and Police Bill and the Drugs Bill are still in their early parliamentary stages. If they are enacted, the Royal Assent may not occur until about mid- to late 2005 and, of course, parts of them may be subject to change beforehand. Many of the proposed changes are unlikely to come into force immediately and some may not be fully implemented for several months, or even longer. It is therefore not expected that this book will become significantly out of date too soon after publication!

APPENDICES

Appendix 1: the Metropolitan Police Service

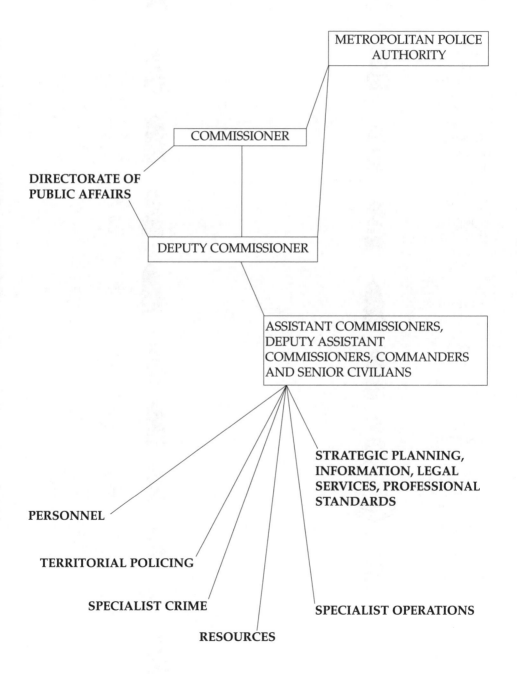

METROPOLITAN POLICE AUTHORITY

COMMISSIONER

DIRECTORATE OF PUBLIC AFFAIRS

DEPUTY COMMISSIONER

ASSISTANT COMMISSIONERS, DEPUTY ASSISTANT COMMISSIONERS, COMMANDERS AND SENIOR CIVILIANS

STRATEGIC PLANNING, INFORMATION, LEGAL SERVICES, PROFESSIONAL STANDARDS

PERSONNEL

TERRITORIAL POLICING

SPECIALIST CRIME

RESOURCES

SPECIALIST OPERATIONS

Appendix 2: the police rank structure

Outside London		Within London

Outside London

CHIEF
CONSTABLE

DEPUTY
CHIEF
CONSTABLE

ASSISTANT
CHIEF
CONSTABLE

CHIEF
SUPERINTENDENT

SUPERINTENDENT

CHIEF
INSPECTOR

INSPECTOR

SERGEANT

CONSTABLE

Within London

 COMMISSIONER

 DEPUTY
COMMISSIONER

 ASSISTANT
COMMISSIONER

 DEPUTY
ASSISTANT
COMMISSIONER

 COMMANDER

 CHIEF
SUPERINTENDENT

 SUPERINTENDENT

 CHIEF
INSPECTOR

 INSPECTOR

 SERGEANT

 CONSTABLE

Appendix 3: the headquarters command structure of a police force

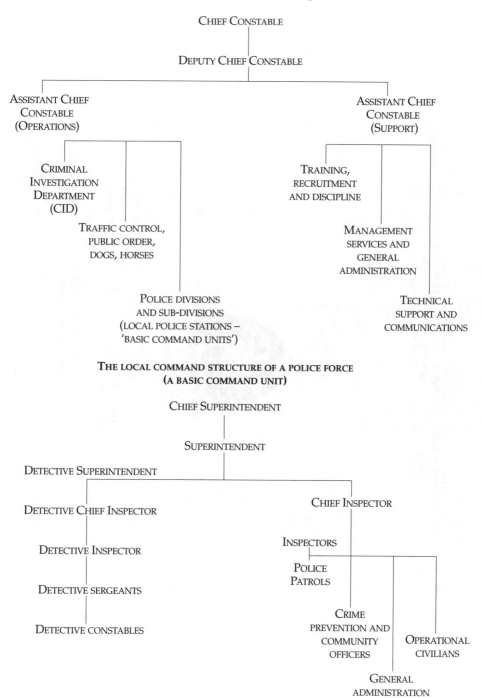

CHIEF CONSTABLE

DEPUTY CHIEF CONSTABLE

ASSISTANT CHIEF CONSTABLE (OPERATIONS)

ASSISTANT CHIEF CONSTABLE (SUPPORT)

CRIMINAL INVESTIGATION DEPARTMENT (CID)

TRAINING, RECRUITMENT AND DISCIPLINE

TRAFFIC CONTROL, PUBLIC ORDER, DOGS, HORSES

MANAGEMENT SERVICES AND GENERAL ADMINISTRATION

POLICE DIVISIONS AND SUB-DIVISIONS (LOCAL POLICE STATIONS – 'BASIC COMMAND UNITS')

TECHNICAL SUPPORT AND COMMUNICATIONS

THE LOCAL COMMAND STRUCTURE OF A POLICE FORCE (A BASIC COMMAND UNIT)

CHIEF SUPERINTENDENT

SUPERINTENDENT

DETECTIVE SUPERINTENDENT

DETECTIVE CHIEF INSPECTOR

CHIEF INSPECTOR

DETECTIVE INSPECTOR

INSPECTORS

POLICE PATROLS

DETECTIVE SERGEANTS

DETECTIVE CONSTABLES

CRIME PREVENTION AND COMMUNITY OFFICERS

OPERATIONAL CIVILIANS

GENERAL ADMINISTRATION

Appendix 4: some sources of police powers

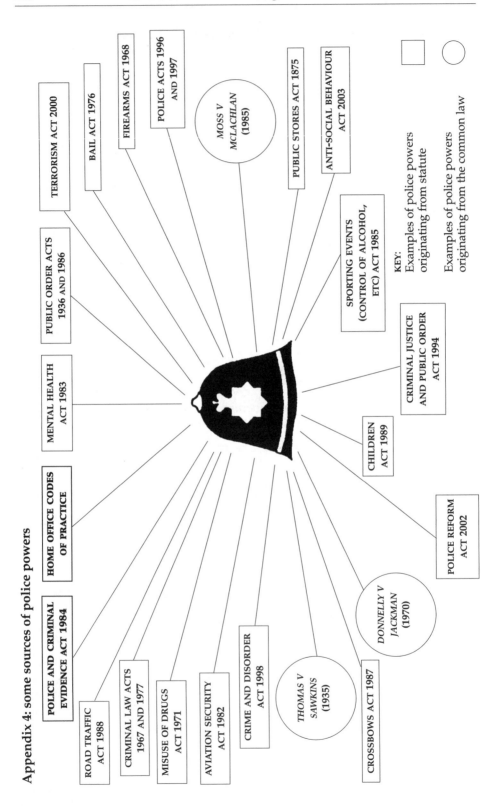

TERRORISM ACT 2000

BAIL ACT 1976

FIREARMS ACT 1968

POLICE ACTS 1996 AND 1997

MOSS V MCLACHLAN (1985)

PUBLIC STORES ACT 1875

ANTI-SOCIAL BEHAVIOUR ACT 2003

PUBLIC ORDER ACTS 1936 AND 1986

SPORTING EVENTS (CONTROL OF ALCOHOL, ETC) ACT 1985

KEY:
Examples of police powers originating from statute

Examples of police powers originating from the common law

MENTAL HEALTH ACT 1983

CRIMINAL JUSTICE AND PUBLIC ORDER ACT 1994

HOME OFFICE CODES OF PRACTICE

CHILDREN ACT 1989

POLICE AND CRIMINAL EVIDENCE ACT 1984

POLICE REFORM ACT 2002

ROAD TRAFFIC ACT 1988

CRIMINAL LAW ACTS 1967 AND 1977

MISUSE OF DRUGS ACT 1971

AVIATION SECURITY ACT 1982

CRIME AND DISORDER ACT 1998

DONNELLY V JACKMAN (1970)

THOMAS V SAWKINS (1935)

CROSSBOWS ACT 1987

Appendix 5: police powers to stop, detain and search under PACE

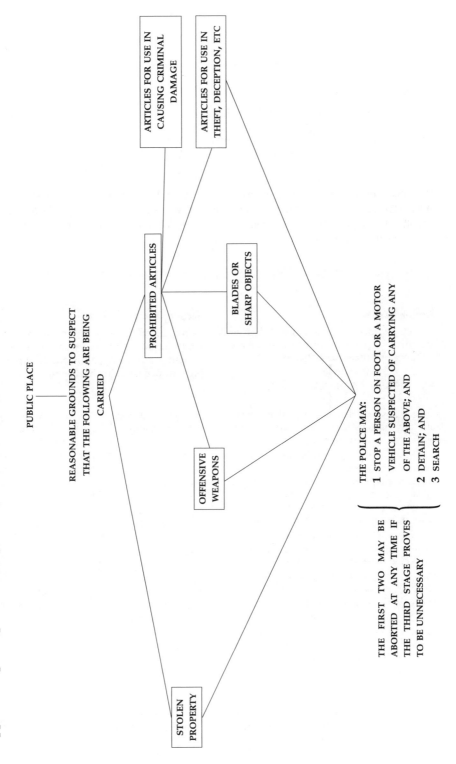

PUBLIC PLACE

REASONABLE GROUNDS TO SUSPECT
THAT THE FOLLOWING ARE BEING
CARRIED

PROHIBITED ARTICLES

ARTICLES FOR USE IN
CAUSING CRIMINAL
DAMAGE

ARTICLES FOR USE IN
THEFT, DECEPTION, ETC

BLADES OR
SHARP OBJECTS

OFFENSIVE
WEAPONS

STOLEN
PROPERTY

THE POLICE MAY:
1 STOP A PERSON ON FOOT OR A MOTOR
VEHICLE SUSPECTED OF CARRYING ANY
OF THE ABOVE; AND
2 DETAIN; AND
3 SEARCH

THE FIRST TWO MAY BE
ABORTED AT ANY TIME IF
THE THIRD STAGE PROVES
TO BE UNNECESSARY

Appendix 6: ss 60 and 60AA of the Criminal Justice and Public Order Act 1994

Section 60

Inspector or above reasonably believes that:

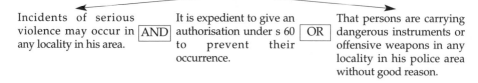

| Incidents of serious violence may occur in any locality in his area. | AND | It is expedient to give an authorisation under s 60 to prevent their occurrence. | OR | That persons are carrying dangerous instruments or offensive weapons in any locality in his police area without good reason. |

That officer may give written authorisation (specifying the grounds) for uniformed police officers to stop/search vehicles or persons within that specified locality for up to 24 hours. (If authorisation given by an inspector, a superintendent or above must be informed as soon as it is practicable to do so.)

↓

An authorisation under s 60 and/or s 60AA empowers any uniformed police officer:

Section 60 only

To stop any pedestrian and search him or anything carried by him for offensive weapons or dangerous instruments ...

AND/OR

↓

To stop any vehicle and search it, its driver and any passenger for offensive weapons or dangerous instruments.

A uniformed police officer may, in the exercise of these powers, stop any person or vehicle and make any search he thinks fit, whether or not he has any grounds for suspecting that the person or vehicle is carrying weapons or articles of that kind.

A uniformed police officer may seize any dangerous instrument or article reasonably suspected to be an offensive weapon.

The driver of a vehicle stopped under s 60 shall be entitled to a written statement that the vehicle was stopped if applied for within 12 months, or immediately.

A person searched under s 60 shall be entitled to a written statement that he was searched if applied for within 12 months, or immediately.

Section 60 and/or s 60AA

To require any person to remove any item which the police officer reasonably believes is being worn wholly or partly for the purpose of concealing his identity.

↓

A uniformed police officer may seize any item reasonably believed to be intended to be worn wholly or mainly for the above purpose (although no special search power is available for the purpose of finding masks, etc).

↓

Failure to remove an item as above when required by a uniformed police officer is an arrestable offence under s 24(2) of PACE.

The above power to require the removal of disguises can be authorised under s 60AA alone if an inspector or above reasonably believes the commission of offences may take place and it is expedient to give an authorisation to prevent or control such activities in his or her police area.

An authorisation under s 60 and/or 60AA may be extended for a further 24 hours, but only by a superintendent or above.

Appendix 7: police powers to stop/search under ss 44–47 of the Terrorism Act 2000

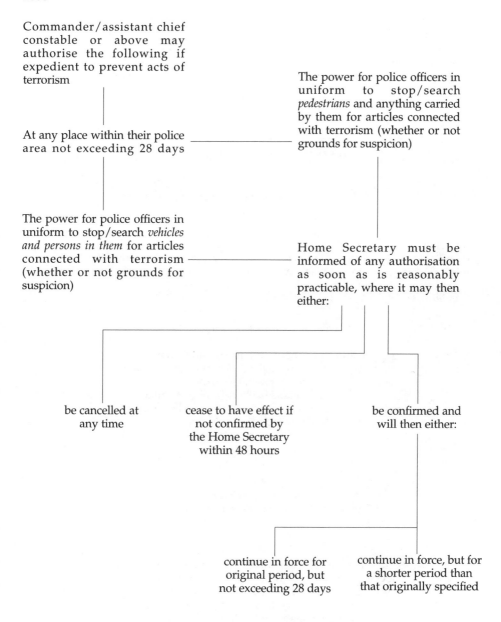

Commander/assistant chief constable or above may authorise the following if expedient to prevent acts of terrorism

The power for police officers in uniform to stop/search *pedestrians* and anything carried by them for articles connected with terrorism (whether or not grounds for suspicion)

At any place within their police area not exceeding 28 days

The power for police officers in uniform to stop/search *vehicles and persons in them* for articles connected with terrorism (whether or not grounds for suspicion)

Home Secretary must be informed of any authorisation as soon as is reasonably practicable, where it may then either:

be cancelled at any time

cease to have effect if not confirmed by the Home Secretary within 48 hours

be confirmed and will then either:

continue in force for original period, but not exceeding 28 days

continue in force, but for a shorter period than that originally specified

Appendix 8: police cordons (ss 33–36 of the Terrorism Act 2000)

Superintendent or above may authorise a cordon to be imposed within a specified area if expedient to do so in connection with an investigation into terrorism ← Police officers below the rank of superintendent may authorise a cordon if the matter is of great urgency, but must inform a superintendent or above as soon as is reasonably practicable, who may either confirm or cancel it

↓

Initial authorisation must not exceed 14 days (renewable for overall period not exceeding 28 days)

↓

Police officers at the scene have powers to:

order persons to leave the cordoned area, including persons in buildings

order persons in charge of vehicles to remove them

reposition any vehicle

prohibit or restrict any vehicular or pedestrian access

Sched 5, para 3 to the Terrorism Act 2000

Superintendent or above (or officer of lower rank in an emergency) may authorise police officers within the area of a cordon to do the following if reasonable grounds for believing material likely to be of substantial value to a terrorist investigation is likely to be found on premises within the cordoned area (excluding items subject to legal privilege, excluded or special procedure material)

↓

Search premises specified in the authorisation and any person found there

↓

Seize and retain anything found if reasonable grounds for believing it is likely to be of substantial value to the terrorist investigation and it is necessary to prevent it from being concealed, lost, damaged, altered or destroyed (except items subject to legal privilege)

Appendix 9: powers of arrest under ss 24, 116 and Scheds 1A and 5 of the Police and Criminal Evidence Act 1984

	ALL CITIZENS	POLICE ONLY
	MAY ARREST ANYONE:	
Suspect caught *in* the act	Actually committing an arrestable offence or there are reasonable grounds for suspecting to be committing an arrestable offence.	→ These conditions apply also to the police.
	OR	
Suspect caught *after* the act	Anyone who is guilty of having committed an arrestable offence or there are reasonable grounds for suspecting this.	These conditions apply also to the police → Or only reasonable grounds to suspect that an arrestable offence has been committed in the first place.
Suspect caught *before* the act	No power for an ordinary citizen to arrest under PACE although s 3 of the Criminal Law Act 1967 gives both citizens and the police power to use reasonable force to prevent crime, etc.	May arrest anyone about to commit an arrestable offence or has reasonable grounds for suspecting they are about to do so.

Appendix 10

ARRESTABLE OFFENCES
(s 24 and Sched 1A of PACE)

Offences where sentence fixed by law; offences where a person 21 years or over (due to be reduced to 18) may be given a five year term of imprisonment on a first conviction; also offences under: the Customs and Excise Acts; the Official Secrets Acts of 1920 and 1989; s 36 of the Criminal Justice Act 1925 (untrue statement for procuring a passport); s 14(1) of the Wireless Telegraphy Act 1949 (triable either way offences under that Act); s 1(1) of the Prevention of Crime Act 1953 (carrying offensive weapons); s 2 of the Obscene Publications Act 1959 (publication of obscene matter); s 12(1) or 25(1) of the Theft Act 1968 (taking motor vehicle without consent and going equipped for stealing); s 19 of the Firearms Act 1968 (carrying firearm/imitation firearm in public place); s 5(2) of the Misuse of Drugs Act 1971 (possession of cannabis or cannabis resin); s 3 of the Theft Act 1978 (making off without payment); s 1 of the Protection of Children Act 1978 (indecent photographs/pseudo-photographs of children); s 1(1) or (2) or 6, 1(5), 9 or 13(1)(a) or (2) or 14 of the Wildlife and Countryside Act 1981 (various offences regarding wild birds, wild animals and plants); s 39(1) of the Civil Aviation Act 1982 (trespass on aerodrome), Order in Council under s 60 of the Civil Aviation Act 1982 (prohibited behaviour in an aircraft towards or in relation to a crew member, or passengers being drunk on an aircraft); s 21C(1) or 21D(1) of the Aviation Security Act 1982 (unauthorised presence in a restricted zone or aircraft); s 1 of the Sexual Offences Act 1985 (kerb-crawling); s 19 of the Public Order Act 1986 (publishing, etc, material likely to stir up racial or religious hatred); s 39, 139(1), 139A(1) or (2) of the Criminal Justice Act 1988 (common assault, and offensive weapons/ knives, etc, in schools); s 103(1)(b), 170(4) or 174 of the Road Traffic Act 1988 (driving whilst disqualified, failing to stop/report a personal injury road traffic accident or false statements and withholding material information); s 14J or 21C of the Football Spectators Act 1989 (contravention of banning order or notice); the Football (Offences) Act 1991 (pitch-invasion, indecent or racialist chanting, throwing missiles); s 60AA(7), 166 or 167 of the Criminal Justice and Public Order Act 1994 (failure to remove disguise, ticket or taxi touting); s 89(1) of the Police Act 1996 (assault on police); s 2 of the Protection from Harassment Act 1997 (harassment); s 32(1)(a) of the Crime and Disorder Act 1998 (racially or religiously aggravated harassment); s 12(4) or 46 of the Criminal Justice and Police Act 2001 (failure to surrender alcohol and placing advertisements for prostitution); s 143(1) of the Licensing Act 2003 (failure to leave licensed premises, etc); and ss 66, 67, 69, 70 and 71 of the Sexual Offences Act 2003 (exposure, voyeurism, intercourse with an animal, sexual penetration of a corpse, or sexual activity in public lavatory). Also, conspiring, inciting, aiding, abetting, counselling or procuring any of the above, including attempting except those offences that are triable summarily only.

CRIMES WHICH ARE ALWAYS
SERIOUS ARRESTABLE OFFENCES
(s 116 and Sched 5)

Can be transformed into serious arrestable offences under s 116 of PACE if: serious harm to State security or public order; death or serious injury to any person; serious interference with the administration of justice; or substantial financial gain or loss; or the making of threats which if carried out would be likely to lead to any of the above consequences.

Treason, murder, manslaughter, kidnapping, s 170 of the Customs and Excise Management Act 1979 (importing indecent or obscene articles), s 2 of the Explosive Substances Act 1883 (causing explosion likely to endanger life or property), s 16, 17(1) or 18 of the Firearms Act 1968 (possession of firearms with intent to injure, use of firearms/imitation firearms to resist arrest, and carrying firearms with criminal intent), s 1 of the Taking of Hostages Act 1982 (hostage-taking), s 1 of the Aviation Security Act 1982 (hijacking), s 134 of the Criminal Justice Act 1988 (torture), s 1 or 3A of the Road Traffic Act 1988 (causing death by dangerous driving or causing death by careless driving when under the influence of drink or drugs), s 1, 9 or 10 of the Aviation and Maritime Security Act 1990 (endangering safety at aerodromes, hijacking ships, or seizing or exercising control of fixed platforms), Arts 4 and 5 of the Channel Tunnel (Security) Order 1994 (hijacking Channel Tunnel trains, or seizing or exercising control of the tunnel system), s 1 of the Protection of Children Act 1978 (indecent photographs/pseudo-photographs of children), s 2 of the Obscene Publications Act 1959 (publication of obscene matter), ss 327–29 and para 1 of Sched 2 to the Proceeds of Crime Act 2002 (drug trafficking offences and certain money laundering offences), ss 1, 2, 4, 5, 6, 8, 30 and 31 of the Sexual Offences Act 2003 (rape, assault by penetration, causing a person to engage in sexual activity without consent involving penetration, rape of child under 13, assault of a child under 13 by penetration, causing or inciting a child under 13 to engage in sexual activity involving penetration, sexual activity with a person with a mental disorder where the touching involved penetration, causing or inciting a person with a mental disorder to engage in sexual activity involving penetration) and s 5 of the Domestic Violence, Crime and Victims Act 2004 (causing or allowing the death of a child or vulnerable adult).

Appendix 11: examples of 'any person' arrest powers

Section 3(4) of the Theft Act 1978[1]

Making off without payment.

Section 25(1) of the Theft Act 1968[2]

Going equipped for stealing, etc.

Section 91 of the Criminal Justice Act 1967

Arrest of a person who is drunk and disorderly in a public place.

Section 6 of the Vagrancy Act 1824

> It shall be lawful for any person whatsoever to apprehend any person who shall be found offending against this Act, and forthwith to take and convey him or her before some justice of the peace, to be dealt with in such manner as is herein-before directed, or to deliver him or her to any constable or other peace officer of the place where he or she should have been apprehended, to be so taken and conveyed as aforesaid …

Other examples of 'any person' arrest powers can be found under s 1 of the Licensing Act 1902 and s 11 of the Prevention of Offences Act 1851.

---

1   This offence was made an arrestable offence under Sched 1A to PACE by virtue of s 48 of the Police Reform Act 2002.

2   This offence is also an arrestable offence under Sched 1A to PACE.

Appendix 12: police detention – the basic rules

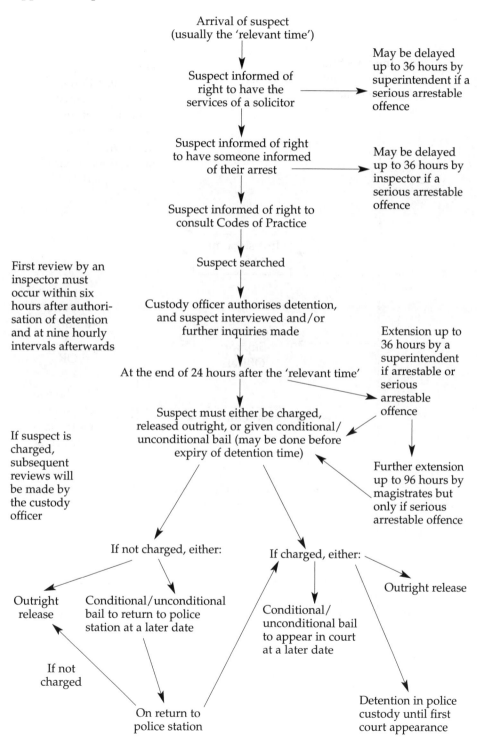

Arrival of suspect (usually the 'relevant time')

Suspect informed of right to have the services of a solicitor → May be delayed up to 36 hours by superintendent if a serious arrestable offence

Suspect informed of right to have someone informed of their arrest → May be delayed up to 36 hours by inspector if a serious arrestable offence

Suspect informed of right to consult Codes of Practice

Suspect searched

First review by an inspector must occur within six hours after authorisation of detention and at nine hourly intervals afterwards

Custody officer authorises detention, and suspect interviewed and/or further inquiries made

At the end of 24 hours after the 'relevant time'

Extension up to 36 hours by a superintendent if arrestable or serious arrestable offence

If suspect is charged, subsequent reviews will be made by the custody officer

Suspect must either be charged, released outright, or given conditional/unconditional bail (may be done before expiry of detention time)

Further extension up to 96 hours by magistrates but only if serious arrestable offence

If not charged, either:

If charged, either:

Outright release

Outright release

Conditional/unconditional bail to return to police station at a later date

Conditional/unconditional bail to appear in court at a later date

If not charged

On return to police station

Detention in police custody until first court appearance

Appendix 13: the basic structure of the extended police family

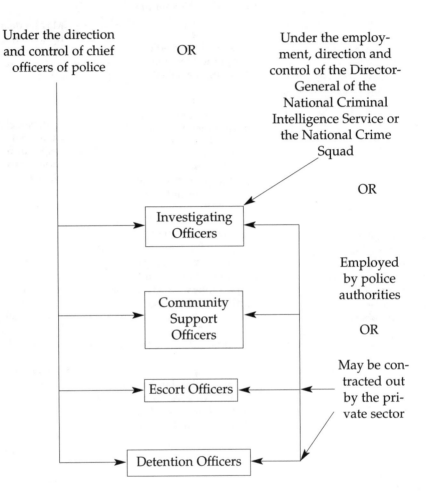

Under the direction and control of chief officers of police

OR

Under the employ-ment, direction and control of the Director-General of the National Criminal Intelligence Service or the National Crime Squad

OR

Investigating Officers

Employed by police authorities

OR

Community Support Officers

Escort Officers

May be con-tracted out by the pri-vate sector

Detention Officers

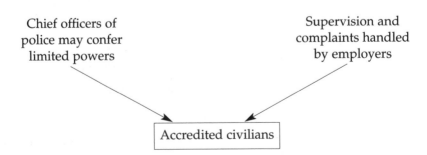

Chief officers of police may confer limited powers

Supervision and complaints handled by employers

Accredited civilians

INDEX